POPE INNOCENT III (1160/61–1216)

POPE INNOCENT III

(1160/61–1216)

To Root Up and to Plant

JOHN C. MOORE

University of Notre Dame Press

Notre Dame, Indiana

Published in 2009 by University of Notre Dame Press
Notre Dame, Indiana 46556
www.undpress.nd.edu

Cloth edition published in 2003 by Brill

Library of Congress Cataloging-in-Publication Data

Moore, John C. (John Clare), 1933–
    Pope Innocent III (1160/61/1216) : to root up and to plant / John C. Moore.
        p.   cm.
    Originally published: Leiden ; Boston : Brill, 2003, in series: The medieval
Mediterranean.
    Includes bibliographical references and index.
    ISBN-13: 978-0-268-03514-3 (pbk. : alk. paper)
    ISBN-10: 0-268-03514-8 (pbk. : alk. paper)
    1. Innocent III, Pope, 1160 or 61–1216.   2. Popes—Biography.   I. Title.
    BX1236.M66 2008
    282.092—dc22
    [B]
                                2008043598

See, I have set you this day over nations and over kingdoms, to root up and to pull down, to destroy and to overthrow, to build and to plant.

Jeremiah 1:10

To the Greeks and to the barbarians, to the wise and to the unwise, I am a debtor.

Romans 1:14

Show me a sign of thy favor, that those who hate me may see and be put to shame because thou, Lord, hast helped me and comforted me.

Psalm 86 (85):17

CONTENTS

List of Illustrations xi

Preface xiii

Abbreviations and Notes on Sources xvii

Map: Europe and the Mediterranean Lands about 1200 xix

Map: Western Central Italy xx

CHAPTER ONE Lotario dei Conti of Segni 1

CHAPTER TWO The Beginning 25

CHAPTER THREE The Great Princes (1198–1200) 50

CHAPTER FOUR Curia and City (1200–1203) 77

CHAPTER FIVE The Fourth Crusade (1203–1204) 102

CHAPTER SIX Jews and Heretics (1205–1207) 135

CHAPTER SEVEN Defense of the Church (1207–1212) 169

CHAPTER EIGHT Renewal (1212–1214) 203

CHAPTER NINE Council and Crusade (1215) 228

CHAPTER TEN The End (1215–1216) 253

Bibliography 293

Index 303

LIST OF ILLUSTRATIONS

Frontispiece
This marble relief sculpture by Joseph Kiselewski, twenty-eight inches in diameter, was created in 1950. It is one of twenty-three portraits of famous "lawgivers" located in the House of Representatives Chamber in the U.S. Capitol. Further information can be found at www.aoc.gov/cc/art/lawgivers/lawgivers.htm.

Photograph reproduced here by permission of the Architect of the Capitol.

(between pages 36 and 37)
Reg. Vat. 5, f. 72r (about 32 × 23 cm.) This is the first page of Innocent's register for his sixth year. The image in the margin forms the initial "I" of the word "Inter", the first word of Reg. Inn. 6:1 (24 February 1203), addressed to the monks at Subiaco. Innocent is portrayed as the central figure, with a Cardinal John and two clerks in subordinate positions. The banner in the pope's hands reads, "Children, may our blessing so profit you in bearing fruit in this life that it may be a source of help to you [in the next]." The banners held by the clerks read, "Holy and just father, we beseech you to help your [people]"; "And on me, a flea, kind father, bestow your blessing." (Was "the flea" the artist?) The illuminated initial was added probably a year or two after the text of the letter was entered, in the space left by the scribe. (See Reg. 6:1, p. 3, n. 1.)

Photograph reproduced here by permission of the Prefect, Archivio Segreto Vaticano.

(between pages 88 and 89)
This fresco is located in the Benedictine monastery of Sacro Speco in Subiaco. It portrays Innocent III, St. Benedict (on the left) and Abbot Romano. The text beneath the image of Innocent is a copy of the same letter shown in Illustration 2 (Reg. Inn. 6:1). It is addressed to Prior John and the brothers, granting to them in perpetuity an annual subsidy of six pounds of silver, to be paid from papal revenues. The letter was dated 24 February 1203, and the

fresco was probably executed about thirteen years later. Further information can be found at www.benedetti-subiaco.it.

Brill Academic Publishers and the author did their best to establish rights to the use of the materials printed here. Should any other party feel that its rights have been infringed we would be glad to take up contact with them.

PREFACE

In the 1830s, Friedrich Hurter published a laudatory and lengthy biography of Pope Innocent III organized on strictly chronological lines. Although true to the way Innocent experienced his life, the result was, in its abundant detail, somewhat difficult to follow. Later biographers, perhaps learning from Hurter's experience, have all organized their studies of Innocent's life topically. In his six volume biography of Innocent, Achille Luchaire devoted each volume to a separate aspect of the pope's life: *Les Royautés Vassales, La Question d'Orient*, and so forth. This approach by Luchaire and later students of Innocent, including the distinguished scholars Jane Sayers[1] and Colin Morris,[2] has revealed a great deal about Innocent and his pontificate, but at a cost. Readers can rarely learn from these studies how Innocent experienced his pontificate from day to day and how the events in one area of his experience may have influenced his reaction to events in others. A "sign of God's favor" in Spain, for example, could play a role in his deciding to try again to organize a great crusade to the Holy Land.

Another common tendency among students of Innocent has been to stress certain of his decretals that were influential in the development of canon law after his death. This approach too has produced a body of very valuable historical literature, but it has also somewhat distorted our understanding of Innocent. A phrase used once or twice by Innocent may be very important to later history without being especially important for understanding Innocent's mind. He claimed the right to intervene in the conflict between John of England and Philip of France *occasione peccati* or *ratione peccati*, by reason of sin, a phrase to assume considerable importance because of its inclusion in canon law. But Innocent used it only on this one occasion and it is not the best entry into his understanding of his office. The same can be said of several of his other decretals.

---

[1] *Innocent III: Leader of Europe 1198-1216* (London, 1994).
[2] *The Papal Monarchy: The Western Church from 1050 to 1250* (Oxford, 1989), pp. 417–451.

A similar tendency of scholars has been to quote a rarely used but striking phrase from Innocent's records as though it characterized his entire papacy. Innocent's attitudes, or at least his moods, varied over his eighteen-year pontificate. He was not always the "cool and calculating pope" presented by Walter Ullmann.[3] He was sometimes over-confident, sometimes discouraged, sometimes elated, frequently ineffectual, and in his uncertainties he searched the developments of his day for signs of divine approval or disapproval.

This book, while not completely abandoning topical emphases, returns to a chronological approach in order to recapture events as Innocent experienced them and to look for their impact on him personally and on the decisions he made. It also looks to phrases, such as those in the front pages of this book, that tell more about Innocent's fundamental views than do some expressions that were later enshrined in decretal collections. The book is not intended to revisit the many controversies surrounding Innocent and his pontificate but to give as clear and full a picture as possible of Innocent the man and of his life as he experienced it. At the same time, it is intended to be solidly based on evidence. I hope that even well-informed scholars, while testing my assertions against the evidence cited, can learn something from this approach and that general readers will find here a comprehensible and reliable introduction to Pope Innocent III.

In pursuit of this purpose, I have quoted generously from Innocent's sermons and letters, all the while knowing that there is at present no way of knowing how much of that material was actually written by him, how much was written by others on his behalf. Consequently, we cannot always be sure that a perceptive observation or a neat turn of phrase originated with him. But just as we attribute to modern heads of states opinions presented in speeches that were nearly always drafted by others, I do not hesitate to attribute to Innocent ideas and attitudes that appear frequently in his writing, even though the text may have been first drafted by advisers or curial clerks. Few historians would doubt that Innocent was a strong personality, and few would find it likely that the prevailing themes and attitudes of his papacy were created and maintained by anyone but him.

The annotation of this book clearly shows my dependence on the work of many other scholars, but it does not convey my debt espe-

---

[3] "Innocent III, Pope," *New Catholic Encyclopedia* (New York, 1967), 7:521.

cially to a few scholars of an earlier generation. The thorough and scrupulous scholarship of C. R. Cheney, Raymonde Foreville, Michele Maccarrone, and Helene Tillmann made this book possible.

I am also especially grateful to Professors Alfred Andrea and James Powell, and to my long-time friend and colleague Professor Linton S. Thorn. Each of them read the entire manuscript of this book and offered many helpful suggestions.

John C. Moore
Bloomington, Indiana
November, 2002

ABBREVIATIONS AND NOTES ON SOURCES

Note: Biblical translations are generally based on the Revised Standard Version, but I have frequently modified the translation, considering both the Latin Innocent used and the Douay Rheims translation of the Vulgate. Other translations are mine unless otherwise indicated, but I have consulted other translations in making my own, especially those in Andrea, *Contemporary Sources*.

Andrea, *Contemporary Sources*. Alfred J. Andrea, *Contemporary Sources for the Fourth Crusade* (Leiden, 2000). This work provides translations and commentary for many letters of Innocent III, as well as for other sources.

Biographer. A title used in this book to refer to the anonymous author of the *Gesta* (see below). James M. Powell has argued persuasively that this author was Cardinal Petrus Beneventanus. See Powell, "Innocent III and Petrus Beneventanus: Reconstructing a Career at the Papal Curia," in *Pope Innocent III and His World*, ed. John C. Moore (Aldershot, 1999), pp. 51–62.

Cheney and Semple. C. R. Cheney and W. H. Semple, *Selected Letters of Pope Innocent III concerning England (1198–1216)* (London, 1953). This work provides Latin texts and English translations, together with Cheney's excellent introduction to the papal materials.

Gesta.	*Gesta Innocentii III*. This is an account of Innocent's life up to 1208, written by a contemporary. It is available in an old and unreliable edition in PL 214 and in a modern edition as the doctoral dissertation of David Gress-Wright, "The 'Gesta Innocent III': Text, introduction and commentary" (Bryn Mawr College dissertation, 1981). It is cited in this book by chapter number, with corresponding page references to Gress-Wright's edition. Regarding its author, see "Biographer" above. James M. Powell's translation of the *Gesta* is forthcoming.
Gress-Wright.	See *Gesta*.
MHC.	*De miseria humanae conditionis*. A treatise by Innocent III. An old edition of the Latin text is in PL 217:701–746. For a modern edition see Michele Maccarrone (ed.), Lotharii Cardinalis (Innocentii III), *De miseria humanae conditionis* (Lugano, 1955). English versions are: Donald Howard (ed.), Lothario dei Segni (Pope Innocent III), *On the Misery of the Human Condition*, trans. Margaret Mary Dietz (Indianapolis and New York, 1969) and Robert E. Lewis (ed. and trans.), Lotario dei Segni (Pope Innocent III), *De miseria Condicionis Humane* (Athens, Georgia, 1978). This treatise is cited herein by book and chapter.
MGH.	*Mounumenta Germaniae Historica*. Begun in the early nineteenth century, this is a multi-volume set containing a vast collection of primary sources from the middle ages, especially those related to Germany and the medieval Roman empire.
PL.	*Patrologia latina*, or *Patrologiae cursus completus . . . series Latina*, ed. J. P. Migne (Paris, 1844–1864). Volumes 214–217 of this 221-volume set are devoted entirely to sources related to Innocent III and his pontificate. Usually cited herein by volume and column number.

Pott. Augustus Potthast, *Regesta Pontificum Romanorum inde ab a. post Christum natum MCXCVIII ad a. MCCCIV*, vol. 1 (Berlin, 1874). Calendar of papal letters with brief summaries. Normally cited by item number rather than by page.

QSN. *De quadripartita specie nuptiarum* = *The Four Kinds of Marriage*. A treatise by Innocent III. Latin text in PL 217:921–968.

Reg. This indicates a register of Innocent III. Together with other materials related to Innocent's pontificate, his registers are available in PL, vols. 214–217. A new, more informative and more reliable edition of the registers is in progress, being published by the Austrian Academy of Sciences as *Die Register Innocenz' III*, ed. Othmar Hageneder et al. (Vienna, 1964–), with each volume corresponding to an extant register. The registers are cited in this book according to the year and the number of the letter, so that Reg. 5:1 means the first letter of the fifth year of Innocent's pontificate. Each papal year begins February 22, the anniversary of his consecration as pope. A citation like this, Reg. 2:104 (113), means that the letter is numbered 104 in the Austrian edition but 113 in PL. For the registers that have not yet appeared in the Austrian edition, the place of the letter in the PL edition is given by volume and column number.

RNI. *Regestum Innocentii III papae super negotio Romani imperii* (ed. Friedrich Kempf, S.J. (Rome, 1947). This work is also available in a less reliable edition in PL 216:995–1172. It is a separate register that was maintained by the curia, containing materials having to do with the disputed succession to the office of emperor of the Romans. It is cited by item number.

SAM. *De sacro altaris mysterio* = *The Sacred Mystery of the Altar*. A treatise by Innocent III. Latin text in PL 217:773–916.

Tanner. *Decrees of the Ecumenical Councils*, 2 vols., ed. Norman P. Tanner, S.J. (London, 1990). Contains all the decrees of the councils in the original language, with English translations on facing pages.

X. *Liber Extra* (The Decretals of Pope Gregory IX). In vol. 2 of *Corpus iuris canonici*, 2nd ed. Emil Friedberg (Leipzig, 1879, repr. Graz, 1959).

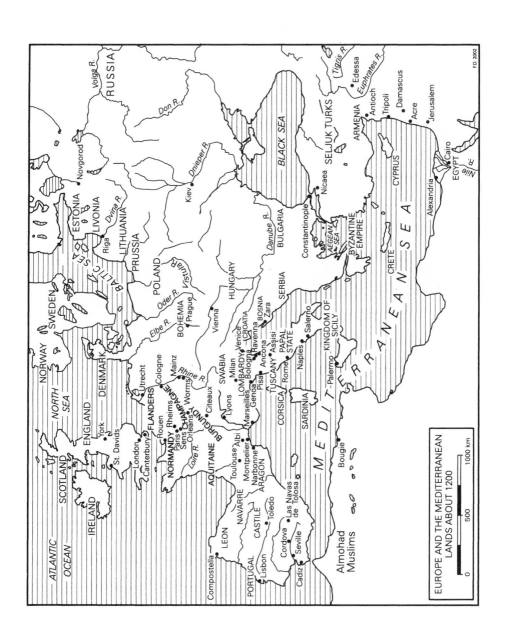

EUROPE AND THE MEDITERRANEAN
LANDS ABOUT 1200

FD 2002

ATLANTIC OCEAN

RUSSIA

Volga R.

Don R.

Novgorod

NORTH SEA

BALTIC SEA

NORWAY

SWEDEN

DENMARK

ENGLAND

SCOTLAND

IRELAND

ESTONIA

LIVONIA

LITHUANIA

PRUSSIA

POLAND

Riga

Dvina R.

Dnieper R.

Kiev

Vistula R.

Oder R.

Elbe R.

Prague

BOHEMIA

Vienna

HUNGARY

Danube R.

BULGARIA

BLACK SEA

SELJUK TURKS

Tigris R.

Euphrates R.

Edessa

Antioch

ARMENIA

Tripoli

Damascus

Acre

Jerusalem

Cairo

EGYPT

Nile R.

Alexandria

CRETE

CYPRUS

BYZANTINE EMPIRE

Nicaea

AEGEAN SEA

Constantinople

SERBIA

BOSNIA

CROATIA

Zara

Venice

Ravenna

Ancona

LOMBARDY

Milan

Bologna

Pisa

Genoa

TUSCANY

Assisi

PAPAL STATE

Rome

Salerno

Naples

KINGDOM OF SICILY

Palermo

CORSICA

SARDINIA

M E D I T E R R A N E A N   S E A

Bougie

Almohad Muslims

SWABIA

Cologne

Mainz

Worms

Rhine R.

Utrecht

FLANDERS

Rouen

NORMANDY

Paris

CHAMPAGNE

Rheims

Sens

Orleans

Loire R.

BURGUNDY

Citeaux

Lyons

Marseilles

Montpelier

Narbonne

Albi

Toulouse

AQUITAINE

NAVARRE

ARAGON

Las Navas de Tolosa

Toledo

CASTILE

Cordova

Seville

Cadiz

LEON

PORTUGAL

Lisbon

Compostella

St. Davids

York

London

Canterbury

0   500   1000 km

F.D. 2002

WESTERN CENTRAL ITALY

0   50 km

Tiber R.

Perugia
Assisi
Foligno
Todi
Orvieto
Spoleto
Amelia
Terni
Montefiascone
Rieti
Viterbo
Civita
Castellana
Tiber R.
Subiaco
Rome
Via Casilina
Albano
Anagni
Alatri
Sora
Segni
Velletri
Ferentino
Ceccano
Ceprano
Via Casilina
Monte
Cassino
San
Germano

CHAPTER ONE

LOTARIO DEI CONTI OF SEGNI

The old man finally died on 8 January 1198. Anticipating trouble, some of the cardinals retired immediately to the fortified Septizonium monastery on the Palatine hill to prepare for the election. Others, including the young cardinal-deacon Lotario dei Conti of Segni went first to the funeral in the Basilica Nova in the forum, then proceeded to the Septizonium. Once gathered, the twenty or so cardinals celebrated a mass of the Holy Spirit, bowing to one another in ritualized humility and exchanging the kiss of peace. They elected examiners to tally the votes and then submitted their secret ballots. The examiners reported the results: four names had been listed, but Lotario had received more votes than any other. Lotario moved his chair away from the other cardinals to let them speak more freely. No one challenged his character or his learning, at least not openly, but he was, after all, only thirty-seven. As they spoke, three doves penetrated the hall, and one came to rest near Lotario's chair. The cardinals were not credulous men, nor were they inclined to surrender their right of election to a supposed divine intervention. Still, the descent of the dove, the whitest of the three, made its impression and perhaps gave them the courage to place youth and vigor on the chair of Peter. The election was done. For reasons we do not know, they called him Innocent.

The cheering crowd of clergy and laity who waited outside joined Lotario and the cardinals in a ragged procession back down to the Basilica Nova and then up the long hill to the basilica of St. John Lateran, now to become Lotario's episcopal church. There, a red cloak was placed on his shoulders and at the entrance of the church, he sat for a moment in the "seat of dung," to enact the words of Psalm 113, "raising up the needy from the earth and lifting up the poor out of the dunghill, that he may make him sit with princes . . ." Here, Innocent threw handfuls of coins to the assembled crowd as a symbol of the fact that the wealth controlled by the papacy was to be used for the service of others. As the schola chanted the *Te Deum*, he entered the church and sat on the patriarchal throne. The cardinals led a procession of upper clergy to prostrate themselves at his feet and receive the embrace of peace. He was then led to the chapel of St. Silvester to sit on two marble chairs on either side of the entrance. Again, coins were thrown to the crowd, and he received the keys to the Lateran and other symbols of authority. Lotario dei Conti of Segni, who was not yet a priest, was now Pope Innocent III.[1]

*   *   *

The ancient Via Casilina runs east and a little south from Rome, following a fertile plain that stretches between two lines of hills, in the area known as the Campagna. As one leaves Rome, the Alban hills rise on the right, revealing some, but concealing many more, of their hill-top towns and fortresses: Frascati, Monte Porzio, Rocca Priora, Tusculum. Many of the fortifications rest on huge irregular stones first dragged into place long before there was a Rome. On the left of the Via Casilina, about twenty-five km. from Rome, Palestrina rises in terraces, its Christian monuments dwarfed by the remnants of the ancient shrine of Fortune. Another twenty-five km. further, still on the left, Anagni stands high on its own hill, providing a good view of the next hill-top town in the series, Ferentino, about ten km. further on. On the other side of the plain, across from Anagni and about two hundred meters higher, stands the little town of Segni.

The city of Rome, this plain of the Via Casilina, and the hill-top towns of Segni on the right and Palestrina, Anagni, and Ferentino on the left made up the environment where Lotario of Segni began his life and lived most of it.[2] Born in 1160 or early 1161 in the cas-

---

[1] *Gesta*, PL 214:xvii–xxi = Gress-Wright, pp. 1–4; Michel Andrieu, *Le pontifical romain au moyen âge*, 2: *Le Pontifical de la Curie romaine au XIII* siècle (Vatican City, 1940) = Studi e testi, 88:267; Alain Boureau, *La Papesse Jeanne* (Paris, 1988), pp. 104–5; Robert T. Ingoglia, "'I have Neither Silver nor Gold': An Explanation of Medieval Papal Ritual," *Catholic Historical Review*, 85 (1999): 531–540. For a discussion of Roger of Hoveden's account of the election, see Helene Tillmann, *Pope Innocent III*, trans. Walter Sax (Amsterdam, 1980), p. 9, n. 11; and for a general account of the election see Maria L. Taylor, "The Election of Innocent III," in *The Church and Sovereignty, c. 590–1918: Essays in Honour of Michael Wilks* (Oxford, 1991), pp. 97–112.

[2] The following account of Innocent's life before he was elected pope is based mainly on Michele Maccarrone, "Innocenzo III Prima del Pontificato," *Archivo della*

tle of Gavignano, just below Segni, he entered the world well placed. His father, Trasmondo, was of the comtal family of Segni,[3] and his mother, Clarice, was from the Scotti, a patrician family of Rome. Family wealth was to make possible an excellent education for Lotario, in Rome, Paris, and Bologna, and then to enable him as a cardinal to refurbish churches in central Italy. For Lotario, as for everyone else of his day, family connections were the measure of one's place in the world and the instrument for improving that place. His brother Richard grew up to be a leading Roman citizen and a reliable agent for Pope Innocent III. His sister, whose name we do not know, provided a good connection through her marriage to Peter Annibaldi, a Roman who was to play important roles in both papal and urban government.[4] Lotario's cousin Octavian occupied important posts in the curia, both before and after Innocent made him a cardinal in 1206.[5] The many references in Lotario's papal letters to his nephews—including Stephen Conti, made a cardinal in 1216[6]— show a typical successful family of the time at work, in an age before nepotism was thought a vice.[7] At whatever point he and his family chose for him a clerical career, these connections began to work toward his advancement. He had probably received minor orders and had been chosen to be a canon of St. Peter's basilica before he left to study in Paris while still in his teens.[8] The prebend at St. Peter's meant that the young student would have, from that point on, a regular income in addition to the wealth of his family.

R. Deputazione romana di Storia patria, 66 [9 of n.s.] (1943): 59–134. See also Edward Peters, "Lotario dei Conti di Segni becomes Pope Innocent III: The Man and the Pope," in *Pope Innocent III and His World*, ed. John C. Moore (Aldershot, 1999), pp. 3–24.

[3] Maccarrone says that Trasmondo was one of those members of the communal government of Segni, members called "counts" there, "dukes" or "judges" elsewhere ("Innocenzo III Prima," p. 63).

[4] Marc Dykmans, "D'Innocent III à Boniface VIII. Histoire des Conti et des Annibaldi," *Bulletin de l'Institut Historique Belge de Rome*, 45 (1975): 27–31.

[5] Werner Maleczek, *Papst und Kardinalskolleg von 1191 bis 1216* (Vienna, 1984), p. 163; Reg. 1:554.

[6] Maleczek, *Papst und Kardinalskolleg*, pp. 195–201.

[7] See Constance M. Rousseau, "Pope Innocent III and Familial Relationships of Clergy and Religious," *Studies in Medieval and Renaissance History* 14 (1993): 107–148; Sandro Carocci, *Baroni di Roma: Dominazioni signorili e lignaggi aristocratici nel duecento e nel primo trecento* (Rome, 1993), pp. 371–381, with map and genealogical table. Carocci says that by the end of Innocent's pontificate, the Conti were probably the dominant aristocratic family in the region (p. 28).

[8] Maccarrone, "Innocenzo III Prima," pp. 67–68, citing the *Gesta*.

Lotario received an excellent education, and he did not forget his teachers. His early education in Rome was directed by Peter Ismaele, abbot of the Benedictine monastery of S. Andrea al Celio, whom Lotario later made bishop of Sutri, just as he was to make Peter of Corbeil, one of his university professors, first bishop of Cambrai and then archbishop of Sens.[9] At S. Andrea al Celio, Lotario took his first steps toward the trenchant Latin prose of his maturity. There he began to build up the store of biblical stories and allusions that were to fill his later writings, and there he developed the talent for liturgical chant that would distinguish him as pope.[10]

Lotario's early years also provided weighty lessons outside of the classroom.[11] In the year before his birth, a Roman cardinal, calling himself Pope Victor IV, found security on Segni's hill and glared across the plain at Anagni where his rival the Sienese cardinal Roland Bandinelli took refuge as Pope Alexander III. Alexander was to be pope for the first twenty-one years of Lotario's life, but neither Alexander nor his rival popes were able to spend much time in the rebellious city of Rome. The great secular princes of the day were often on the move, but they moved by choice, for their own convenience. Alexander's sojourns in Sens, Genoa, Messina, Anagni, Tusculum, and Veroli were forced upon him. His exile included a stay in Segni, when Lotario was about 13.[12] Whether in Segni or in Rome, the young Lotario was surely learning how insecure the life of the bishop of Rome was.

The Roman citizens showed great enthusiasm for keeping in the city the papal curia and the wealth it brought with it, but they showed equal enthusiasm for expelling popes for the sake of an independent Roman republic and senate. But even when the pope and the city government were on good terms, peace in the city was not

---

[9] *Gesta*, PL 214:ccxxiv–ccxxv = Gress-Wright, pp. 352–353. He also interceded to obtain a prebend for a poor friend of Peter (Reg. 2:49 [51]).

[10] Maccarrone, "Innocenzo III Prima," p. 69, citing the *Gesta*.

[11] The following account of the pontificate of Alexander III is based mainly on Ferdinand Gregorovius, *History of the City of Rome in the Middle Ages*, trans. from the German 4th ed. by Annie Hamilton, 4/2 (London, 1905): 563–608. For more recent general treatments, see Colin Morris, *The Papal Monarch: The Western Church to 1250* (Oxford, 1989) and I. S. Robinson, *The Papacy: 1073–1198: Continuity and Innovation* (Cambridge, 1990).

[12] Gregorovius, *History*, 4/2:597. He cites Jaffé (n. 1) to indicate that Alexander canonized Thomas Becket while in Segni, on 4 February. For Jaffé, see below, n. 29.

guaranteed. Quarrelsome and powerful noble families built their fortifications throughout the city, making it a forest of towers. Towers sprouted even from the tops of triumphal arches and other ancient monuments.

Should pope, senate, and noble families find themselves at peace, there was still Frederick Barbarossa, king of the Germans and emperor of the Romans. He was determined to be emperor of the Romans in fact as well as in name: "Since . . . I am . . . Roman Emperor, I would be merely the shadow of a sovereign and bear but an empty title without substance, if authority over the city of Rome were taken from my hands."[13] Even when he was in far-away Germany, his presence loomed above the city like a smoking volcano.

Lotario grew up in a violent world. When he was about seven years old, in the spring of 1167, a great army of Roman citizens sallied forth with the pope's blessing to take the nearby fortress of Tusculum from the imperial forces that had occupied it. The German soldiers, led by the warrior archbishops of Mainz and Cologne, inflicted upon them the most humiliating and destructive defeat that a Roman army had suffered since antiquity. A few weeks later, in more bloody fighting, the forces of the emperor invaded the Vatican, captured the fortified basilica of St. Peter, and probably would have taken the entire city had not malaria driven them away.

Twelfth-century popes were, then, very vulnerable to local violence, but they had nonetheless become very important to the rest of Christendom. A century before, a group of radical reformers had gravitated toward the papacy and had made the pope the center and principal agent of an attempt to change drastically the world around them. They wanted to see a world organized according to the principles of Christianity, united in faith, secure in peace, harmonious in love and justice. And these changes could only be achieved through the vigorous leadership of those who best understood Christian faith, peace, love, and justice: the clergy, headed by the pope. In some ways, they were similar to Marxist revolutionaries, working toward a one-party state for the good of mankind. These Gregorian reformers (so-called after Pope Gregory VII, 1073–1085) challenged a system in which powerful aristocrats routinely appointed most clerical

---

[13] Quoted by Thomas Curtis Van Cleve, *The Emperor Frederick II of Hohenstaufen* (Oxford, 1972), pp. 3–4.

officials—bishops, abbots, ordinary parish priests. By Lotario's day, the Gregorian offensive had been remarkably successful. Most clerical officials were elected by other clergy, although the aristocrats continued to be very influential—often controlling—in those elections. The Gregorian reformers had also set out to enforce the old rule of celibacy, and again, to a remarkable degree they had been successful. There were still married priests, there were still bishops with concubines, but these practices were no longer accepted as normal. They called for concealment.

The prestige and influence of the popes had grown steadily since Gregory's day. Urban II had preached the first crusade in 1095, and that expedition had recaptured the holy city of Jerusalem from the Muslim infidel. Throughout the twelfth century, papal legates moved through Christendom enforcing Gregorian reforms, actually unseating bishops whose offices had been improperly obtained. In 1123, 1139, and 1179, prelates from all over Christendom traveled to Rome to attend great councils presided over by the pope at the Lateran basilica. These councils were part of the growing acceptance throughout Christendom that the papacy was the supreme legislative and judicial office for church affairs.

But where did church affairs end and non-church affairs begin? The Gregorian party had precipitated a spectacular struggle with the emperor; but for the most part, Gregorian reforms progressed without overt conflict with the secular authorities, aristocrats of various levels. Popes and bishops were themselves usually drawn from aristocratic families, and cooperation between secular and ecclesiastical authorities was the rule rather than the exception. But secular princes were also expanding their power throughout the century, and an underlying tension was always there, occasionally breaking out, usually at the expense of the clerical official. The martyred Thomas Becket and a number of exiled popes are the best known examples, but there were many more. The power of ecclesiastical authorities was growing at the same time that they remained extremely vulnerable to violent attack, therein providing one of the great paradoxes of the twelfth century. Nowhere was it more apparent than in Rome.

Lotario was to have a second home, away from the violence of Rome and the Via Casilina: Paris. Probably at about the age of fifteen, he followed the road that many other young aristocratic Romans had taken in the twelfth century in pursuit of an education that would enhance their clerical careers.[14] Paris stood in striking contrast to Rome; it was a city of peace. No factions there dared challenge the authority of the king of France; and scholars gathered to pursue learning and to enjoy the food, wine, and security they found there in abundance. For a Roman cleric, there was no foreign region more secure than the kingdom of France. For nearly a century, exiled popes had found refuge there, as did Thomas Becket, the exiled archbishop of Canterbury. In the mid-1170s, when Lotario arrived in Paris, the master of the city was the pious King Louis VII, who had given shelter to Pope Alexander III and to Thomas Becket. Louis was very different from Frederick Barbarossa and Henry II, the ferocious princes who had sent the pope and archbishop into exile. So Lotario had very good reason to revere the kingdom of France and to recall fondly his student days in Paris.[15] He also had good reason to be solicitous of the French monarch. The one he was to know best was Louis's son Philip. In August, 1179, a year before Louis's death, the ailing king had the fourteen-year-old boy crowned king, and thus began a reign that was to last until 1223. It encompassed part of Lotario's student days and all of his pontificate.

* * *

Whereas King Louis provided a model of the pious Christian prince, his enemy Henry II of England (and Anjou) had demonstrated how dangerous the fury of a secular ruler could be to the clergy. His angry remarks had led, in 1170, to the murder of the archbishop of Canterbury, and the horror of that act was felt acutely throughout Christendom. Only three years later, Alexander III declared Thomas Becket a saint. Lotario may have been present at the canonization, since the ceremony took place in his home town.[16] In Paris, the fate of Becket was much discussed,[17] and everyone there was surely aware of King Louis's visit to the martyr's tomb in 1179.[18] Lotario himself made the pilgrimage some time during his days at

---

[14] Gregorovius, *History*, 4/2:640.

[15] Tillmann, *Pope Innocent III*, p. 11, n. 25, citing Reg. 1:171, 2:188 (197), 7:43 (42).

[16] Gregorovius, *History*, 4/2:597.

[17] Phyllis Barzillay Roberts, *Studies in the Sermons of Stephen Langton* (Toronto, 1968), p. 135.

[18] Maccarrone, "Innocenzo III Prima," p. 78.

Paris. Years later, he recalled the hospitality he had received en route from a venerable old man at the monastery of Andres in Flanders.[19] He no doubt also remembered the lesson of Thomas Becket, the same lesson taught by the experience of popes in Rome: unarmed clergy were extremely vulnerable before secular powers.

Lotario pursued his studies amid the dust of construction and expansion. The walls of the great cathedral of Notre Dame were slowly rising, and the young King Philip began an extensive program of construction—covered markets, water conduits, fountains, walls—although Lotario left too soon to enjoy the paved streets that replaced the smelly thoroughfares of his student days. The schools of Paris in the 1170s had not yet coalesced into a single entity, but the masters and students of the cathedral school overflowed from the Île de la Cité across the Petit Pont to the left bank of the Seine and mingled with the scholars of the schools of the abbeys of St. Victor and Ste. Geneviève. The association of all the faculty became the university and was formally recognized by the king in 1200. In France, unlike in Italy, the faculty were all clergy. In this way, too, France seemed a friendlier environment for clerics and their concerns.[20]

Lotario's stay in Paris probably lasted six to ten years, giving him time to complete his studies in the liberal arts and to pursue courses in theology. He may also have had an introduction to canon law. It was taught at Paris, and even the theology faculty were likely to have a familiarity with law and legal proceedings.[21] But first, he studied the liberal arts, which meant literature and logic. Students studied classical literature through the grammars of the day, which offered extensive quotations from classical authors to illustrate points of grammar. Lotario's later writings frequently quote classical writers such as Horace and Ovid. The logic of Aristotle had swept the schools of Paris and of France since the days of Abelard and his pupils, a generation or two earlier; but the passion for logic, which distracted

---

[19] *Willelmi Chronica Andrensis*, MGH SS 24:738.

[20] John W. Baldwin, *Masters, Princes, and Merchants: The Social Views of Peter the Chanter and His Circle* (Princeton, 1970), 1:64–65, 72; Stephen C. Ferruolo, "*Parisius-Paradisus*: The City, Its Schools, and the Origins of the University of Paris," in *The University and the City from Medieval Origins to the Present*, ed. Thomas Bender (New York and Oxford, 1988), pp. 22–43.

[21] Peter the Chanter, an influential Paris theologian, used Roman law in his theological writings, and he had experience as a papal judge-delegate. Baldwin, *Masters*, 1:7, 99–100, 335. Much of this discussion of the schools of Paris is based on this work by Baldwin.

scholars from literature and the Bible, was distrusted by many, especially the theologians.[22] It seems not to have lured Lotario away from traditional studies; his later writings do not display a strict application of formal logic. Still, the rigorous clarity of thought and expression he exhibited in later years is an indication that logicians were not the only scholars at Paris who respected the rules of logic.

Having become a master of arts in about six years, a cleric planning an ecclesiastical career would not be likely to dally in the long program of study leading to a master's in theology, but Lotario spent at least some time as a student of the theologian Peter of Corbeil. Few of Peter's writings have been found;[23] but the works of many other Paris masters give us a good idea of their interests and their methods. They were one in their dedication to the study of the Bible. The long years of study in the liberal arts, the study of the great Fathers of the church—Sts. Augustine, Ambrose, Jerome, Gregory— were all seen by the theologians primarily as means to understand the Bible.

The theology faculty adopted and applied a method of scriptural analysis that dated from antiquity. Its first basic principle was that the Bible was the inspired word of God and therefore an unfailing source of truth. But equally important was the principle that every line of the Bible had allegorical or "spiritual" meanings in addition to its literal meaning; and the task of the theologian was to discover and reveal those meanings.[24] The masters would read the text to their students (*lectio*) and then offer their commentary. Their explanations gave allegorical meanings not only to a story in general, but also to minor actions or objects within the story. For example, in the book of Exodus, Aaron wears a breastpiece decorated with twelve precious stones arranged in four rows. In Lotario's treatise on the mass, he points out that prelates are dressed similarly, thereby making the connection between the priesthoods of Old and New Testaments. He said that the four rows represent justice, fortitude, prudence, and temperance, and that the twelve stones each represent one of twelve virtues.[25]

---

[22] Baldwin, *Masters*, 1:81–83, 97–100.

[23] Baldwin, *Masters*, 1:18, 46.

[24] Beryl Smalley, *The Study of the Bible in the Middle Ages* (Notre Dame, 1964), passim.

[25] PL 214:785, referring to Exodus 28:15–22.

Difficulties arising in the interpretation of Scripture might be the subject of public discussion or debate or of extended analysis by a lecturer or author (*disputatio, questio*), leading toward a resolution of the difficulty (*solutio*).[26] This practice too appeared in Lotario's later writings.

Interpreting scripture was therefore a matter for specialists. There were in Europe at the time lay people who were barely literate but who nevertheless read the Bible, explained it to one another, and preached the gospel in city streets. For Lotario and his highly-trained peers, that would be roughly the equivalent of a modern person's practicing surgery or dentistry without any formal education—laughable if it were not so dangerous.

Sometime in the mid-1180s, Lotario moved from Paris to Bologna to continue his studies.[27] Bologna was the premier center for the study of law, Roman and canon, and no student in Bologna could remain impervious to its pervading influence or to the intellectual excitement that the study of law was creating throughout Europe. During the twelfth century, in an age when disputes were still commonly settled by stone, iron, and flame, Europeans rushed to make use of new legal procedures provided by princes and popes, procedures that offered reason as an alternative to violence. Young men who had studied Roman or canon law were in demand everywhere, because they knew how to take testimony, weigh evidence, and put in writing their conclusions. They knew principles for settling disputes about property, about contracts, about marriages, principles that were the fruit of centuries of experience and thought. They knew the difference between logical arguments and specious arguments; they knew how to make fine distinctions. These skills were becoming as valuable and as much sought after as the military skills of chivalric champions. Even in England, where the common law was developing principles different from either Roman or canon law, clerics from the schools played a major role in legal development, bringing to it their preference for reason over custom and their respect for the power of the written document. For any young cleric

---

[26] Baldwin, *Masters*, 1:88–107.

[27] For a description of Lotario's movements during these years, see John C. Moore, "Lotario dei Conti di Segni (Pope Innocent III) in the 1180s," *Archivum Historiae Pontificiae* 29 (1991): 255–258.

hoping to rise in the clerical establishment, there was no better train-
ing than the study of law.[28]

The products of these schools formed an international society, men
who literally spoke the same language (Latin), knew the same literature, valued the same intellectual skills. Having spent five to ten
years together in the same schools, following the same curriculum,
absorbing the same ideas, they knew one another well. A bishop in
Scotland might feel closer to a bishop in Sicily or Germany, men
he had spent his adolescence and youth with in school, than to the
local clergy and laity, who had never been far from home.

* * *

While Lotario was pursuing advanced studies in Paris, Pope Lucius
III (1181–1185) had found the political atmosphere in Rome inhos-
pitable; and in early 1182, he left, never to return. He stayed about
two years in Campagna, then moved north, passing through Bologna
in July of 1184, and then took up residence in Verona, where he
stayed until his death. His two successors, Urban III (1185–1187)
and Gregory VIII (1187) remained in Lombardy, although Gregory
was moving toward Rome when he died in Pisa on 17 December.
Clement III, elected in Pisa two days later, was in Rome by 11
February 1188. The price he paid for his peaceful entry was acknowledging the right of the Roman commune to self-government.[29]

The tenure of the papal curia in Lombardy roughly coincided
with Lotario's studies in Bologna. A man of his background and
education now studying in the vicinity (and a canon of St. Peter's
to boot) would inevitably be known in papal circles. Three incidents
of 1187 show that his star was rising. First, he appeared at Grandmont
(near Limoges) in the company of two papal legates, presumably on

---

[28] For a general and somewhat exaggerated treatment of the importance of law
in this period, see Harold J. Berman, *Law and Revolution: The Formation of the Western
Legal Tradition* (Cambridge MA, 1983). For a more reserved view of the same developments, see Susan Reynolds, *Kingdoms and Communities in Western Europe, 900–1300*,
2nd ed. (Oxford, 1997), pp. lviii–lxi, 36–66.

[29] These itineraries are based on P. Jaffé (ed.), *Regesta Pontificum Romanorum ab
condita ecclesia ad annum post Christum natum MCXCVIII*, 2nd ed. by S. Loewenfeld,
F. Kaltenbrunner, and P. Ewald under the direction of W. Wattenbach, 2 vols.
(Leipzig, 1885–1888), 2:431–535.

papal business. Second, in mid-1187, the monks of Canterbury, who were pursuing a case in the papal court, urged their representative to try to win the support of "Lord Lotario," a man whose influence clearly made his goodwill worth having. And finally, Gregory VIII ordained him subdeacon. Gregory was elected in Ferrara on 21 October 1187 and died the following 17 December. In November, he spent several days in Bologna, and this may have been the occasion of Lotario's ordination.

In the ordination ceremony, the pope said to Lotario, "Consider whose ministry you take on. If up to now, you have been lax in serving the church, henceforth you should be assiduous; if up to now drowsy, henceforth vigilant; if up to now drunken, henceforth sober; if up to now dishonorable, henceforth chaste." He then prayed to God on Lotario's behalf: "May the spirit of wisdom and understanding rest upon him, the spirit of counsel and fortitude, the spirit of knowledge and piety. May you fill him with the spirit of your fear and strengthen him in the divine ministry, so that, obedient in deed and submissive in word, he may seek your grace."[30]

In 1189 or 1190, with the papal court now back in Rome, Clement III appointed the twenty-nine-year-old Lotario cardinal deacon of the church of Sts. Sergio and Bacco, a position the pope had once held himself. Lotario probably profited from the determination of Clement to create a large number of new cardinals from the Roman region to give the papacy a more secure base in the city.[31] On 30 March 1191, Clement was succeeded by the aged Celestine III. During the next seven years, Cardinal Lotario was an active member of the curia, participating in cases heard in Rome, although not charged with any major diplomatic mission.[32]

Throughout the 1180s and the 1190s, Lotario's education in the political facts of life in Italy continued. In January of 1185, in Milan, Frederick Barbarossa presided over the marriage of his son Henry to Constance, the heiress to the kingdom of Sicily (also called "the

---

[30] This passage is based on the prescribed ritual for the ordination of subdeacons. See Andrieu, *Le pontifical Romain*, 1:129.

[31] Robinson, *The Papacy*, pp. 55–56.

[32] Maccarrone, "Innocenzo III Prima," pp. 81 ff. See Reg. 1:267, 317; I. Friedlaender, *Die päpstlichen Legaten in Deutschland und Italien am Ende des XII. Jahrhunderts (1181–1198)* (Berlin, 1928), pp. 148–154; Wilhelm Janssen, *Die päpstlichen Legaten in Frankreich von Schisma Anaklets II. bis zum Tode Coelestins III. (1130–1198)* (Cologne, 1961), pp. 138–150.

Regno," including both Sicily and southern Italy).[33] Frederick then left Italy for good, leaving his son to pursue the Hohenstaufen ambition to dominate Italy.

No one could withstand Henry, who succeeded his father as emperor in 1190. By the end of 1194, he had defeated the anti-German forces in the kingdom of Sicily, and German dominance settled like a net over Italy. Henry's brother Philip was made duke of Tuscany. Conrad of Urslingen, besides being Henry's vicar in Sicily, became duke of Spoleto. Markward of Anweiler received Romagna, the duchy of Ravenna, the march of Ancona, and the county of Abruzzi. Dipold of Schweinspeunt became count of Acerra. The aged Pope Celestine watched helplessly, his personal feebleness a fitting symbol of the status of the papacy in Italy.[34]

The successes of the Hohenstaufen became more ominous in 1194 when Constance gave birth to a son, called Frederick. The heir to the kingdom of Sicily, he was also elected to succeed his father as Holy Roman Emperor. Henry and his infant son presented the threat of permanent Hohenstaufen domination of Germany and of Italy and the permanent impotence of the papacy. That meant, almost certainly, the undoing of the Gregorian reform.

Sporadic lay resistance to this German domination got nowhere. A conspiracy of 1195 resulted in a number of Sicilian dignitaries, including the archbishop of Salerno, being sent to prisons in Germany, where some died, some were blinded.[35] Many, including the archbishop and the family of a former king of Sicily, were still there when Innocent was elected. In 1197, the anti-German party in Sicily made one last attempt to take control of the kingdom, but the plan was discovered and Henry wreaked terrible vengeance. Men of Sicily and southern Italy were hanged, impaled, skinned alive, burned at the stake, and thrown into the sea. One with royal aspirations had a red-hot crown nailed to his skull. And the Empress Constance, whose sympathies were probably with the rebels, was required to witness the punishments. In the summer of 1197, the prospects for the old pope and his curia were dismal.[36]

---

[33] Peter Munz, *Frederick Barbarossa: A Study in Medieval Politics* (London, 1969), pp. 368–369.

[34] Daniel Waley, *The Papal Sate in the Thirteenth Century* (London, 1961), pp. 26–27; Van Cleve, *Emperor Frederick*, p. 22.

[35] *Gesta*, PL 214:xxx = Gress-Wright, p. 15; Van Cleve, *Emperor Frederick*, p. 21.

[36] Van Cleve, *Emperor Frederick*, pp. 23–24; see also his *Markward of Anweiler and the Sicilian Regency* (Princeton, 1937), pp. 65–66.

If Italian politics in the 1190s were depressing to the papal curia, major "world" events, were no better. In 1187, the same year when we find signs of Lotario's presence in the curia in Lombardy, news had reached the West of terrible reverses in the Holy Land. The Muslim leader Saladin had destroyed whole Christian armies, had taken one city after another, and had captured the relic of the true cross. In October, he took the city of Jerusalem itself after almost a century of Christian control.[37] As Lotario was returning to the curia from Grandmont, a papal letter was being prepared, calling for a new crusade. That letter, probably the work of both Urban III and Gregory VIII, sounded a note that was to be fundamental for the pontificate of Innocent III: the successes of the infidel were God's punishment for the sins of all Christians. Along with military force, repentance and reform would be necessary to regain the Holy Land.[38]

The fall of Jerusalem so shocked the West that for the first and last time, most of the great Western rulers agreed to go to the rescue: the kings of England and France, the Holy Roman Emperor, and many more. But despite the prestige of its leaders, the third crusade was an embarrassment. Frederick Barbarossa drowned in Asia Minor—a punishment, Innocent was later to remark, for his sins against the church.[39] Philip Augustus stayed only briefly before returning to France. Richard the Lion-Hearted of England, Anjou, and Aquitaine enjoyed some successes in reconquering important parts of the kingdom of Jerusalem, but the city itself remained in Muslim hands. Finally, the slightly sour odor of the whole crusade became even worse when Richard, its principal hero, became the victim not of Muslims but of Christians. He was captured by Leopold of Austria and held for ransom by the Emperor Henry VI.

The suspicion that God was withholding his support for the crusades was increased by the fate of the Latin Christians who carried the title "king of Jerusalem." Conrad of Montferrat was assassinated in Tyre in 1192; Henry of Champagne fell to his death from a tower window in Acre in 1197. In papal circles, both deaths were seen as divine retribution for incestuous marriages.[40] The whole sorry story

---

[37] Jonathan Riley-Smith, *The Crusades: A Short History* (New Haven and London, 1987), p. 86.
[38] Ibid., pp. 109–110.
[39] Pott. 4133.
[40] *Gesta*, PL 214:civ = Gress-Wright, p. 79.

seemed to drive home the need for fundamental reform and rededication, if God was to bless the efforts of western crusaders.

Even in Spain, where Christian forces had been making steady progress against the Muslims, the news was not good. Christian kings expended more energy fighting one another than in fighting the infidel; and in 1195, Muslims won a major victory that nearly allowed them to regain control of Toledo.[41]

After Frederick Barbarossa drowned, the young Emperor Henry decided to take the cross himself. Pope Celestine and his advisors could hardly oppose a Christian prince who offered to deliver the Holy Land, but their experiences of Henry in Italy had not been good, and his clear ambition to expand into the eastern Mediterranean could only mean trouble for the papacy. He claimed parts of the Balkans; the kings of Cyprus and Armenia offered to become his vassals; German crusaders paraded through Italy to depart for eastern ports. The summer of 1197, then, saw the bad news in Italy and the bad news in Palestine coalescing into an ominous, Hohenstaufen whole.

The inability of the papal curia to do much about all this bad news was evident; but the importance of the papacy for the rest of Christendom continued to grow. Pilgrims still made their way to visit the city of St. Peter and St. Paul; and papal supervision of the distant church expanded, with clergy traveling to Rome to pursue their business and papal messengers making their way to all parts of Christendom. The cases assigned to Cardinal Lotario were part of a growing flood of business. His name appears frequently among those of cardinals witnessing papal documents, as it had under Clement III, and he was used as judge delegate or auditor in some of the increasing number of cases that were making their way to Rome. As pope, he later referred to cases he had dealt with while still a cardinal.[42]

*   *   *

Lotario's life as cardinal during the 1190s is not well known. He remained in Rome and its environs. The pontificate of Celestine was unusual in that the curia never left Rome, although individual

---

[41] Joseph F. O'Callaghan, *A History of Medieval Spain* (Ithaca, 1975), pp. 242–245.
[42] See for example Reg. 1:317, 538.

members may have vacationed elsewhere. As a cardinal, Lotario wrote three short treatises, but he clearly felt pressed by his curial duties. In the prologue to *The Misery of the Human Condition*, he said that he had been able to write the work because he had taken a brief vacation from his many difficulties. In the prologue to *The Four Kinds of Marriage*, he said that the work was not what he really had intended, but only what he could manage in the face of obstructing difficulties. And in the conclusion to *The Sacred Mystery of the Altar*, he acknowledged the limitations of the work, saying, "Especially since, in my duties, I am impeded by such a rush of cases and ensnared in such a tangle of business that for a brief period I could find neither leisure for reflection nor peace for writing."[43]

The content of these works shows that Paris had left its mark on Lotario. They were all in Latin, intended for a clerical audience. They all show his intimate familiarity with the Bible. Scriptural quotations are the main ingredient of nearly everything he wrote, although the works are also seasoned with quotations from classical authors. Every phrase, indeed every word, from the Bible was the inspired word of God, capable of standing on its own without reference to its context. Lotario and his contemporaries treated the Bible like a vast quarry of glass tiles, choosing them and arranging them to form whatever mosaic came to mind. The text had not only its literal meaning but several spiritual or allegorical meanings as well, as though the tile changed colors with changing light.

In the prologue to *The Four Kinds of Marriage*, Lotario gave a different interpretation to the passage of Exodus mentioned above. He reminded his friend the priest Benedict that the Old Testament priest wore a breast-plate that was both quadrangular and double (Exodus 28:16) and that the numbers four and two had symbolic significance. The priest should discern among four things, namely truth and falsehood (lest he deviate in faith) and good and evil (lest he deviate in action). He should discern on behalf of two, priests and people, lest the blind lead the blind. Four also signified the four meanings of scripture that the priest should understand; two signified the Old and New Testaments to which that understanding was applied. Four signified the gospels of the New Testament; two the tablets on which the law of the Old Testament were inscribed.[44]

---

[43] Maccarrone, "Innocenzo III Prima," 89–91; PL 217:914.
[44] PL 217:921–922. For the "symbolist mentality," see M. D. Chenu, *Nature, Man,*

Numbered distinctions were not always coupled with allegory; they could be used as a logician would to give the different meanings or different species of a term. Lotario wrote that we seek to escape three evils: innate, acquired, and inflicted. The first we inherit (original sin), the second we commit (our personal sins), the third we suffer (punishment). We escape these evils through a triple fear: servile (fear of punishment), filial (love of justice), and in between, a mixed fear made up of both.[45] He commonly made distinctions based on conventional categories: internal-external, spiritual-carnal, spirit-letter, superior-inferior.

The allegorical view of life presumed a figurative union of all truth. Every event, every object, rested in a web of figures. Attention paid to one reverberated toward its figurative equivalents. Instead of starting with a biblical text, Lotario could begin equally well with a liturgical part of the mass or with an aspect of human marriage and move to its scriptural equivalent or to the fundamental truth that bound them together. For example, the tunic worn by the priest at mass signified the seamless garment of Christ, which in turn signified the unified doctrine of Christ, which must be preserved against heretical rips.[46]

This kind of thought provided the substance of Lotario's treatise *The Four Kinds of Marriage*. He wrote that there was the ordinary marriage between a man and a woman, two in one flesh, "historical" and carnal. There was the marriage between Christ and his church, two in one body, "allegorical" and sacramental. There was the marriage between God and the individual soul, two in one spirit, "tropological" and spiritual. And finally, the marriage between the Word of God and human nature in the incarnation of Christ, two natures in one person, "anagogical" and personal. The close observation of any one of these marriages could illuminate all the others. For example, the purpose of "historical" marriages was to produce off-spring and to prevent fornication. The purpose of "allegorical" marriage was the same, for through his marriage to the church, Christ produced many children, who are conceived through catechesis, born through baptism, and nourished through communion. And through

and Society in the Twelfth Century, ed. and trans. Jerome Taylor and Lester K. Little (Chicago, 1968, repr. 1983), pp. 99–145.

[45] SAM, PL 217:900.
[46] SAM, PL 217:788–789.

this marriage, the faithful are saved from the adultery of worshiping false gods. Similarly, in the marriage between God and the soul, the soul is like the fruitful vine, bearing good works, while being saved from the vices represented by fornication.

In an ordinary marriage, there is a betrothal, a dowry, a marriage broker, and witnesses. In the "anagogical" marriage between the divine and human natures of Christ, the betrothal was God's promise to Abraham; there was no dowry, since human nature has nothing to give to God, who has everything; the marriage broker was the angel Gabriel; the witnesses (father, mother, priest, and marriage broker) were God the Father, the Virgin Mary, the Holy Spirit, and the angel Gabriel. And, Lotario continues, just as the ordinary "historical marriage" should not be clandestine,

> [God] wants the sacramental marriage not to be clandestine, but rather manifest to all. For, "He has pitched his tent in the sun, and he comes forth from his chamber like a bridegroom" (Psalm 19:4–5). "In the sun," that is, openly. Accordingly, it is said elsewhere, "The lamp has not come so that it may be placed under a bushel, but on a lampstand" (Mark 4:21). "For the Lord has made known his salvation; in the sight of the nations he has revealed his righteousness" (Psalm 98:2). For this reason, he said to the apostles, "What I say to you in darkness, you say in the light; and what you hear spoken in your ear, proclaim from the rooftops" (Luke 12:3). "Go out and preach to every creature in the whole world. . . . And they went forth and preached everywhere, while the Lord worked with them and confirmed the message by the signs that attended it" (Mark 16:15, 20). Therefore, "their voice goes out through all the earth, and their words to the end of the world" (Psalm 19:4). Every Christian should confess this sacramental marriage, "For man believes with his heart and so is justified, and he confesses with his lips and so is saved" (Romans 10:10). For this reason, [Christ] said in the gospel, "Every one who acknowledges me before men, I also will acknowledge before my Father who is in heaven" (Matt. 10:32), and "Whoever is ashamed of me and of my words . . ., of him will the Son of man also be ashamed, when he comes in the glory of his Father with the holy angels" (Mark 8:38).[47]

Lotario's *Four Kinds of Marriage* was intended to give the reader spiritual insights into the allegorical ties that connected past, present, and future, matter and spirit, but it was also a vehicle for conveying basic orthodox doctrine.

---

[47] QSN, PL 217:943.

At worst, the allegories and distinctions could become mechanical and tedious, as happened in some of the sermons Lotario wrote after he became pope. *The Four Kinds of Marriage* shows some of these traits, and its repetitions and poor organization suggest a hasty composition. At its best, though, the method provided a fertile analytic tool as well as an integrating framework in which scriptural analysis, contemporary theology, liturgical art, and moral guidance were all connected. Lotario's two works *The Four Kinds of Marriage* and *The Sacred Mystery of the Altar* are, besides being treatments of their stated subjects, remarkably comprehensive statements of Christian doctrine.

The highly speculative character of contemporary theology appears in Lotario's writing when he occasionally departs from allegorical treatments to address questions that he had clearly encountered in the schools. For example, he points out that the marriage of the soul with Christ is not broken through apostasy, any more than the marriage between man and woman is broken through adultery. With that, he moves into a series of formal questions: Why is the marriage with Christ not broken when the soul abandons the faith? Can a baptized infant enter into this sacramental marriage with Christ when it clearly cannot contract an ordinary marriage before the age of consent? Can Christ be considered a bigamist, having married first the synagogue and then the church? Or can he be considered a polygamist because he is married to many churches and many souls?[48]

Sometimes, he seems to think that this sort of speculation is irreverent, that it goes too far in trying to subject mysteries to rational analysis,[49] particularly mysteries related to the Eucharist. Having raised the question of what happens to the Eucharist if the communicant vomits, he says, "I do not know how Christ arrives and I am ignorant of how he departs; he knows who is ignorant of nothing."[50] On the relationship between the risen Christ and his shed blood, his umbilical cord, and his foreskin, Lotario said, "It is better to leave it entirely to God than to dare to define it."[51] A favorite biblical text was "God made man right, but he has tangled himself in infinite

---

[48] QSN, PL 217:933–937.
[49] SAM, PL 217:861, 867–869.
[50] SAM, PL 217:868.
[51] SAM, PL 217:876–877.

questions."[52] On the other hand, questions like these clearly held a fascination for him; he mentions them and sometimes seems unable to resist grappling with them.

Lotario's methods of analysis were not exclusively allegorical. Sometimes he offered philological explanations, as when he compared Greek, Hebrew, and Latin versions of the word for *bread* in the Lord's prayer,[53] and when he explained the meanings of three related verbs in biblical Latin, *accingere, succingere,* and *praecingere.*[54] In his work on the mass, he showed a strong sense of historical development, frequently explaining parts of the liturgy as the product of this or that historical development, sometimes giving his sources.[55] In discussing why the pope divides the consecrated host in a distinctive way, he said, "I have heard from some that the reason for this is historical, not allegorical; but since I have been able to discover nothing in authentic sources, I have thought it better to remain silent than to make rash assertions."[56]

Lotario's masters at Paris had taught him all this, but they were no less concerned with moral problems, and there was no more central moral problem for the active prelate than that of balancing spiritual ideals with practical realities. In the twelfth century, the problem often took this form: the relative merits of the active and contemplative lives.[57] Lotario struggled with the problem both as cardinal and as pope. In *The Misery of the Human Condition,* he clearly approved of the active life rather than making the traditional monastic call for abandonment of the world;[58] and in *The Sacred Mystery of the Altar,* he said that the two lives could be combined. Here too he followed the lead of his Paris masters.[59] The cloth pallium worn around the neck by metropolitans (archbishops) bore two lines, he wrote, indicating both the active and contemplative lives. The prelate should therefore follow the example of Moses, who ascended the mountain to "philosophize" with God, and then descended to the camp to

---

[52] Eccles. 7:30; SAM, PL 217:869; MHC, trans. Howard, p. 15.
[53] SAM, PL 217:903.
[54] QSN, PL 217:953.
[55] SAM, PL 217:814–815, 849, 858, 908–909.
[56] SAM, PL 217:911.
[57] Caroline Walker Bynum, *Jesus as Mother* (Berkeley, 1982), pp. 68–81.
[58] John C. Moore, "Innocent III's *De Miseria Humanae Conditionis*: A *Speculum curiae?*" *The Catholic Historical Review,* 67 (1981): 533–564.
[59] Smalley, *Study of the Bible,* pp. 249–250.

attend the needs of the people.[60] As pope, he was to offer the same formula to others,[61] but it must not have worked so well in practice—hence his perennial complaints that the crush of business caused him to neglect his spiritual life.[62]

In another work written as cardinal, *The Misery of the Human Condition*, Lotario reviewed with impressive (and depressing) thoroughness the miserable conditions that accompany all humans as they pass through this world. The second book of this work calls particular attention to the unpleasant realities likely to confront a man living in the circles of the powerful and wealthy: avarice, the corruption of justice, gluttony, lust, the love of honors. His examples make clear that he did not need to look to the households of merchants or princes to find these vices; they flourished in the world of the upper clergy. He knew the ambitious courtier, who "pretends humility, feigns honesty, displays affability, shows off his kindness, is accommodating, is compliant, honors everyone and bows to everybody, frequents courts, visits important people, rises and embraces, claps his hand and fawns."[63] He had experienced the behavior of the proud man, who "disdains his former friends, ignores acquaintances made yesterday, is contemptuous of old companions."[64] He also knew that the rule of celibacy was broken by priests "who embrace Venus at night and then worship the Virgin at dawn.... At night they excite the son of Venus on a bed, at dawn they offer the son of the Virgin on an altar."[65]

His acute awareness of the moral dangers of the world was balanced, at least partially, by a vision of how the world should be ruled. *The Four Kinds of Marriage* is not about politics, but it concludes with an epithalamium to Christ as bridegroom and king, and it sets

---

[60] PL 217:798.

[61] Reg. 9:172 = PL 215:1007; John C. Moore, "Peter of Lucedio (Cistercian Patriarch of Antioch) and Pope Innocent III," *Römische Historische Mitteilungen*, 29 (1987): 231–232.

[62] See QSN, PL 217:921–922; SAM, PL 217:914; MHC, "Prologue," as well as Innocent's prologue to a collection of his sermons, PL 217:311–312.

[63] MHC, II, xxvi, trans. Dietz. For my argument that Lotario is thinking in particular of the curial environment, see "Innocent III's *De miseria humanae conditionis*," pp. 553–564.

[64] MHC, II, xxx, trans. Dietz.

[65] MHC, II, xxii, trans. Dietz. Innocent made the same comment as pope in Sermon I/12, PL 217:368.

forth Lotario's basic idea of what a ruler should be. He contrasted the behavior of tyrants, who are terrible, cruel, false, impatient, unfair, with that of the bridegroom, who is no tyrant but a prince (*princeps*). This king is praised for the truth of the doctrine he preaches, the gentleness of the patience he exhibits, and the justice he implements in his life. "These three things are especially necessary for those who rule, that they be truthful in speech, gentle in heart, and just in deed."[66] Here is Lotario's standard for what a ruler should be, whether he be ecclesiastical or secular. Indeed, later in the treatise, he referred to bishops as having been constituted as princes over all the land, although princes called not to dominion but to service.[67] He was setting standards for all judges, ecclesiastical as well as secular, when he said that the good judge should have constancy, lest he be impetuous, justice, lest he be unfair, prudence, lest he be indiscreet.[68]

The third work written as cardinal, *The Sacred Mystery of the Altar*, also gives us some idea of how he thought the world should be governed, but it is the most problematic of these three works. On the one hand, it is the longest and contains the most elaborate development of theological ideas; it is the only one explicitly written for a general audience rather than for a particular friend; and it shows none of the signs of hasty composition found in *The Four Kinds of Marriage*. It is also the only work where Lotario augmented his allegorical and scholastic analysis with historical explanations, based on research in the sources. On the other hand, there is evidence that the work was revised after Lotario became pope,[69] so we cannot say with certainty how much of the work reflects his thinking as cardinal. My own opinion is that the revisions were slight.[70] Nevertheless,

---

[66] PL 217:954–955.

[67] PL 217:966–967.

[68] PL 217:957.

[69] Tillmann, *Pope Innocent III*, pp. 8, 18–19, n. 92; Wilhelm Imkamp, *Das Kirchenbild Innocenz' III. (1198–1216)* (Stuttgart, 1983), pp. 47–48.

[70] The tone of the work is not authoritative as we would expect from any pope, and especially from Innocent III. The liturgy he is describing, he said, derives its authority from the custom of the Apostolic See, but he claimed no special authority for the author. On the contrary, the author is tentative, humbly asking the reader to bear with the work's shortcomings and asking him to make the necessary corrections (PL 217:914). Throughout the work, there are references to the pope's role in the liturgy without a hint that the author himself holds that office. His complaint that he has given the work too little time because of the demands

the following comments must be taken with this caveat: the passages referred to may have been added long after his election to the papacy.

In this work, Lotario provided the text of the Latin mass, with extended commentary, saying that he had set forth the present custom of the Apostolic See to be followed by other churches, since the Roman church was the "mater et magistra" of other churches.[71] Having described the six orders of the clergy, he then offered a chapter on the "primacy of the Roman pontiff." He rehearsed the biblical texts concerning Peter to demonstrate that Christ had committed to him the governance (*principatum*) of the entire church. Peter can bind others, but he cannot be bound by them. It pertains to Peter, whose faith never falters, to strengthen the others. The supreme pontiff is called to the plenitude of power; other priests are called to share in the solicitude. Peter often spoke for the apostles; he alone dared to venture from the boat when Jesus asked him to walk across the water; he alone drew a sword to defend Jesus from his captors; and he alone leapt into the sea to greet the risen Jesus on the shores of the Sea of Galilee.[72]

There is something missing here. Lotario made no mention of Peter's triple denial. It is not exactly a question of honesty, since Lotario surely knew that no member of his intended audience would fail to notice the omission. Indeed, it was a subject he would address frequently as pope;[73] in fact, he referred to it in the very first letter of his papacy. But as a junior member of the papal curia, Lotario probably thought it imprudent to refer to Peter's failings. The passage shows Lotario's elevated conception of the papacy; but it also shows that his intellectual concern for thoroughness was being tempered by the diplomat's and courtier's concern for the expedient. *Veritas*, truth, was to be a constant referent of his papacy; but so also were *utilitas* and *necessitas*.

---

of his office (ibid.), which Helene Tillmann takes to be a sign that he is speaking as pope, is quite similar to remarks in the other two works written as cardinal (*Pope Innocent III*, pp. 18–19, n. 92).

[71] PL 217:774.

[72] PL 217:778–779. It is worth noting that elsewhere in this work, Lotario says that when they receive the pallium, metropolitans receive the *plenitude* of the pontifical office (PL 217:799).

[73] John C. Moore, "The Sermons of Pope Innocent III," *Römische Historische Mitteilungen* 36 (1994): 108–109.

These works of Cardinal Lotario are strangely silent about the major crises facing the papacy during the 1190s. There are no explicit references to the Hohenstaufen threat in Italy, to Islam, to the Holy Land and the crusades, or to the major heresies of the day. Nothing in these writings anticipate the vigorous actions Pope Innocent was to take against heresy. The one exceptional reference is to Greek Christianity. He was explicit in his distaste for the "heresies" and liturgical practices of Greek Christians, who he believed were responsible for "the scandal of perpetual division" within the church.[74] As pope, he was to enjoy a great but Pyrrhic victory over these "schismatics."

His silence about other major issues of the day might be used as evidence that as cardinal he was not especially interested, were it not for the fact that the sermons he wrote as pope were to show the same characteristic: virtually no allusions to the major problems facing the papacy, excepting of course the morality of Christians in general and of the clergy in particular. It seems that he simply chose to exclude practical and temporal problems from these writings, where he dealt with questions more spiritual and more perennial than those taken up in his papal letters. They were works of the mountain, not of the camp.

*   *   *

If most of the events of the 1190s seemed a clear indication of God's displeasure with Christendom, the autumn of 1197 signaled a decided change in divine favor. On 27 September, Henry VI died at the young age of 32, leaving only a two-year old son to pursue the Hohenstaufen program. Henry's Sicilian widow, Constance, was as tired of German domination as were her compatriots, and she and they moved to bring it to an end. Then, the following January, the old Pope Celestine died. Those two deaths created an opportunity and the cardinals gathered at the Septizonium seized it. They elected Lotario. He was thrust forthwith into the camp.

---

[74] PL 217:858.

CHAPTER TWO

THE BEGINNING

On Sunday, 22 February 1198, the procession moved from the sacristy toward the main altar of old St. Peter's basilica. The cross-bearer led this army through the throngs of people, followed by cantors dispersing evil spirits with their song, by candle-bearers and incense-bearers, four archbishops and twenty-eight bishops, six cardinal-priests, nine cardinal-deacons, and ten abbots.[1] Subdeacons and acolytes came in the middle of the procession, protected by the senior clergy before and after. At the rear came the pope, surrounded by deacons and sheltered by a canopy held aloft on four poles (the canopy, Lotario had written, represented Sacred Scripture, the four poles, its four allegorical meanings).[2]

The previous day, the pope had been ordained a priest, and now he moved solemnly through the candle-light, the incense, the music, to the foot of the altar and recited the opening prayers of the mass. He climbed the steps, incensed the altar, and asked God's mercy; then he took his seat on the episcopal throne. Octavian, cardinal bishop of Ostia, prayed over him and anointed his head with holy oils. An archdeacon approached carrying the cloth stole called the pallium, and said, "Receive the pallium, that is, the plenitude of the pontifical office, to the honor of the omnipotent God, of the most glorious Virgin his parent, and of the blessed apostles Peter and Paul and the holy Roman church." He laid the pallium across Lotario's shoulders. Then once again the procession took form, as the clergy made their way to the throne, each one prostrating himself at the feet of the pope and then receiving the embrace of peace. Innocent then rose and intoned the "Gloria," the prayer of jubilation, and the mass proceeded.

---

[1] *Gesta*, PL 214:xx = Gress-Wright, p. 4.

[2] The following description of the consecration ceremony is a composite based on *Gesta*, PL 214:xx–xxi = Gress-Wright, pp. 3–4; Andrieu, *Le pontifical romain*, 2:263–269; SAM, PL 217:803–810.

At the proper time, the pope himself mounted the pulpit and
preached.[3] His text was, "Who do you think is the good and faithful servant that the lord will place over his family, that he may give
them food in time?" (Matt. 24:45). "Let us ponder the words individ-
ually," he said, "because when the words are from the Word, there
is nothing in them that does not have weight; rather all are full of
heavy meaning." He continued, speaking of the Lord:

> He has himself instituted this primacy of the Apostolic See so that no
> impudence can thwart its institution. Accordingly, he himself said, "You
> are Peter, and on this rock I will build my church, and the gates of
> hell shall not prevail against it" (Matt. 16:18). For since he is himself
> both founder and foundation of the church, the gates of hell are surely
> unable to prevail against it. The foundation remains immobile, as the
> apostle says, "The foundation has been laid; none can be laid other
> than this one, which is Christ Jesus" (1 Cor. 3:11). Therefore, although
> the boat of Peter is often tossed about by great waves at sea, espe-
> cially when Jesus is sleeping, it never sinks. Jesus commands the wind
> and the sea, and a great calm descends, so that everyone is amazed
> and says, "What kind of man is this that the winds and the sea obey
> him?" (Matt. 8:27). For this house is that sublime and stable house of
> which the Truth himself speaks, "The rain fell, the floods came, and
> the winds blew and beat on that house, but it did not fall, because it
> had been founded on rock" (Matt. 7:25)—that is, the rock of whom
> the apostle says, "The rock was Christ" (1 Cor. 10:4).
>
> It is clear, therefore, that the Apostolic See does not lack tribula-
> tion, but it so profits from the promise of God that it can say with
> the prophet, "You gave me room when I was in distress" (Ps. 4:1).
> He promised to the apostles, "I will be with you all days, even to the
> consummation of the world" (Matt. 28:20). Further, "If God is with
> us, who can be against us" (Rom. 8:31). Since therefore this institu-
> tion [of the Apostolic See] is not from man but from God, or rather,
> since it is from the man-God [Jesus], in vain does the heretic and
> schismatic labor, in vain does the perfidious wolf strive to demolish
> the vineyard, to tear the tunic, to overturn the candelabrum, to extin-
> guish the light. So said Gamaliel, the honorable teacher of the law:
> "If this counsel is from men, it will pass away; but if it is indeed from
> God, you will not be able to destroy it—you may even be found
> fighting against God" (Acts 5:38–39). "The Lord is my help, I will not
> fear what man may do to me" (Ps. 118 [117]:6).

---

[3] Sermon 4:2, PL 217:653–660. Maccarrone has argued that this sermon was
not delivered on the day of consecration ("Innocenzo III Prima," p. 133), but I am
not convinced. Tillmann also attributes it to the day of consecration (*Pope Innocent
III*, p. 40, n. 4).

> For I indeed am that servant whom God has instituted over his family; may I be faithful and prudent, so that I may give it food in time!

Innocent prayed that he would not be like any of the bad servants described in the Bible. He continued:

> I call myself servant, not lord, according to what the Lord said to the apostles, "The kings of the Gentiles lord it over them; and those in authority over them are called benefactors. Not so with you, however; rather he who is greater among you will be the servant of all, and he who leads will be like a minister" (Luke 22:25–26). So I claim ministry for myself; I do not usurp dominion—following the example of that first and special predecessor who said, "Do not lord it over those in your charge, but be examples to the flock" (1 Peter 5:3), and the example of him who said, "Are they ministers of Christ (I speak as a fool), I am more so" (2 Cor. 11:23). The honor is great, since I am instituted over the family; but the burden is heavy, since I am servant to the whole family. "I am debtor to the wise and to the foolish" (Rom. 1:14). One can scarcely be served worthily by many; how much less can all be served worthily by one.

Innocent spoke of the many worries and sorrows that he carried, but he said that Christ would support him, just as he kept Peter from sinking as he walked across the water. He then returned to the text for the day. He was the servant; now what was expected of him? "You have heard my condition; now hear my charge."

> Since I am a servant, I should be faithful and prudent, so that I give to the family food in time. God requires three commandments of me, as these words show, namely that I be faithful in heart, prudent in deed, and that I give food for the mouth. "For one believes with the heart and so is justified, and one confesses with the mouth and so is saved" (Rom. 10:10). "Abraham believed God and it was credited to him as righteousness" (Gen. 15:6). "Without faith it is impossible to please God" (Heb. 11:6). "Whatever does not come from faith is sin" (Rom. 14:23). For if I myself am not solid in faith, how can I strengthen the faith of others, a responsibility which is known to pertain especially to my office, the Lord proclaiming, "I have prayed for you Peter that your own faith may not fail; and you, when once you have turned back, strengthen your brothers" (Luke 22:32). What he prayed for he received, since for his reverence he was heard in all things. And thus, the faith of the Apostolic See has never failed in any turbulence but has remained always whole and undiminished. The privilege of Peter remains unbroken. Faith is so necessary for me that, whereas for other sins I have God alone as my judge, for a sin committed against faith I can be judged by the church. For whoever does not believe is already

judged (John 3:18). Indeed, I believe, and I believe most certainly what I believe as a Catholic, trusting that my faith must save me, according to his promise: "Your faith has saved you; go and sin no more."[4]

But "faith without works is dead" (James 2:26). Living faith, however, works through love, since the just man lives by faith (Hebrews 10:38). "For it is not the hearers of the law who are righteous in God's sight, but the doers" (Rom. 2:13). "For if any are hearers of the word and not doers, they are like those who look at themselves in the mirror" (James 1:23).

Innocent described the emblem called the "logion" worn by the pope, showing how the double quadrangle symbolized the need for prudence to tell good from evil, truth from falsehood. He continued:

Oh how great must this one prudence be! It is required . . . to resolve tangled questions, to reveal things hidden in doubt, to set forth the merits of cases, to observe the orders of judges, to expound Scripture, to preach to the people, to correct the restless, to comfort the weak, to confound heretics, to strengthen Catholics. "Who is this man, and we will praise him?" (Sir. 31:9).

Such he ought to be, the man who is instituted over the family. Indeed I have been instituted over the family; my position is most excellent—may my merit be the same! It is to the great praise of the powerful Lord that he does his will through a vile servant, so that nothing is ascribed to human virtue but everything is attributed to divine power. For who am I, or what was the house of my father, that I should sit above kings and occupy the throne of glory? For me it is said to the prophet, "I have instituted you over peoples and kingdoms to root up and to pull down, to destroy and to overthrow, to build and to plant" (Jer. 1:10). For me it is said to the apostle, "I will give you the keys of the kingdom of heaven, and whatever you bind on earth shall be bound also in heaven, and whatever you bind in heaven shall be bound also on earth" (Matt. 16:19). When he spoke with the apostles, he said to them specifically, "Whose sins you [plural] shall forgive, they are forgiven them, and whose sins you shall retain, they are retained" (John 20:23). But when he spoke to Peter alone, he said universally, "Whatever you [singular] bind on earth will be bound in heaven and whatever you bind in heaven will be bound on earth," since Peter is able to bind others, but he cannot be bound by others. He said, "I will call you Cephas" (John 1:42), which means *head*, since the plenitude of all the senses is concentrated in the head while in the other members there is some part of the plenitude. So

---

[4] The first half of this quotation is derived from Mark 10:52, Luke 17:19, or Luke 18:42; the second half from John 5:14 or 8:11.

others have been called to a share of the solicitude, but only Peter has been assumed to the plenitude of power.

So now you see who this servant is who has been instituted over the family, namely the vicar of Jesus Christ, the successor of Peter, the anointed of the Lord, God of Pharaoh (Ex. 7:1), set between God and man, this side of God but beyond man, less than God, but greater than man; he judges all but is judged by no one, saying with the voice of the apostle, "who judges me is the Lord" (1 Cor. 4).

The title "vicar of Christ" had been in use occasionally for about a century, but with Innocent, it was now to become standard.[5] Heady stuff, to be sure, and Innocent warned himself. Quoting the many scriptural passages demanding humility, he reflected on the thought that from the one to whom much is given, much is expected. He will be called to give account for all those in his charge.

There then remained the final phrase of the scriptural passage: to give food to the family in time. Peter had been charged by Christ to "feed my sheep," and Innocent was to fulfill that charge with the example of his life, with the word of his doctrine, and with the sacrament of the Eucharist. And this food was to be given "in time," that is, in the proper order: first the food of example, then the food of word, so that he would then be worthy to give the food of the sacrament. For if his actions do not conform to his words, then the preaching is in vain. If the preacher's life is despised, his preaching certainly will be too. Then he concluded:

> Behold, brothers and sons, I have set forth for your repast food from the table of Sacred Scripture, expecting this compensation, asking this return, that without hesitation you will raise pure hands to the Lord and ask him in faithful prayer to make me worthy to fulfill this office of apostolic service—which is too much for my weak shoulders—for the glory of his name, for the salvation of my soul, for the well-being of the universal church, for the utility of the entire Christian people— Jesus Christ our Lord, who is the blessed God over all things, now and forever. Amen.

When the mass was completed, the procession moved through the doors of St. Peter's, and Innocent, wearing the papal crown, mounted a horse for the trip across the city to the basilica of St. John Lateran. The congregation had joined the entourage, which now included the urban prefect and the senator of Rome, together with all the other

---

[5] See Michele Maccarrone, *Vicarius Christi: storia del titolo papale* (Rome, 1952).

important nobles and officials of the city. Songs and incense "crowned the city," and Innocent stopped from time to time to throw the customary gifts of money to the crowds who hailed him with branches and flowers. At the Lateran, he entered his major residence, called the Leonine, and distributed the customary gifts of money—curiously called "priests"—to secular and ecclesiastical officials; and then the crowd of dignitaries sat down to a great banquet. Lotario dei Conti of Segni was now fully pope.

Not that the new pope had waited for this day to begin his pontificate. The Biographer, who described Lotario's election, depicted him as resisting, as weeping at the prospect of assuming the burden of being pope. Perhaps he did. To be chosen pope, to take Christ's place on earth, to take on the responsibility for the whole world, would make any sensible man quake. But his actions thereafter leave no doubt that he accepted the office with remarkable self-confidence. Instead of proceeding to his consecration on the Sunday following the election, as was customary,[6] he postponed it for more than six weeks, choosing 22 February, the feast of the Chair of St. Peter. It was an appropriate day for the consecration of the vicar of St. Peter, but in a century when more than one anti-pope had arisen to challenge the legitimacy of this or that pope, it was an act of extraordinary boldness.[7]

A bishop-elect, including the pope, could legally exercise the jurisdictional (not the sacramental) powers of his office before he had been consecrated;[8] but no one could remember anything quite like this, a man not yet forty presiding over Christendom for six weeks without even being a priest, much less a consecrated bishop. Between his election and his consecration, his letters bore only half a seal, that is, a seal imprinted on only one side. This expedient was to cause considerable loss of time and money, since he had later to

---

[6] Andrieu, *Le pontifical romain*, 2:264–265.

[7] Maria Taylor points out that custom required Innocent, who was not a priest, to wait for his ordination to the priesthood until February 21, the first day of Tempora ("Election," p. 111); but I am not convinced that Innocent could not have departed from that custom had he so desired. For a list of popes with the dates of their election and consecration, see Robinson, *The Papacy*, pp. 525–526.

[8] Wilhelm Imkamp, "'Sicut Papa Verus'; Der Anfang der Primatialgewalt beim noch nicht zum Bischof Geweihten Elekten in Theorie und Praxis Papst Innocenz' III," *Apollinaris* 49 (1976): 128–132; Robert L. Benson, *The Bishop-Elect: A Study in Medieval Ecclesiastical Office* (Princeton, 1968), pp. 163–167. See also Innocent's sermon, PL 217:663, 665.

explain it in a special letter to all the prelates in Christendom,[9] but in practice the half seal did not indicate a pope hampered by lack of authority. On 9 January, the day after his election, the clerks of the curia began to turn out his letters announcing the election. Innocent, "bishop-elect of the Apostolic See, servant of the servants of God," greeted archbishops and bishops as equals, as brothers; he greeted abbots and other prelates as subordinates, as sons, and extended to all his apostolic benediction.[10]

In this interim period, he sent out one papal order after another, acting as though the only limitation on the papal office had been the old age of its previous occupant, as though the intransigent world would now give way before youth and vigor and self-confidence. He gave the bishop of Paris the unenviable task of pressuring King Philip of France to restore his spurned queen.[11] He gave unequivocal support to King Imre of Hungary, ordering the king's brother and rival Duke Andrew to depart for the Holy Land and summoning one of Andrew's clerical supporters to Rome to account for his actions.[12] Not yet a priest himself, he deposed an archbishop.[13]

Not yet a priest, he excommunicated an entire city government. Peter cardinal-deacon of St. Maria in Vialata arrived in Rome after an extended legation in Poland and reported that he had traveled to the far reaches of Christendom without injury, only to return to Italy to be clubbed from his horse and robbed by Margrave William Pallavicino, together with some citizens of Piacenza. The cardinal's complaints in Piacenza had been met with shrugged shoulders. Innocent excommunicated all the officials of the city and issued threats he could certainly not make good. He warned them that if reparation was not made within a month, he would forbid all Christians to do business with Piacenza and would see that the goods of Piacenzan merchants throughout the world were sequestered. By April, he had broadened this offensive to include Parma as well as Piacenza.[14]

---

[9] Reg. 1:83, p. 121.

[10] Reg. 1:1, fn. 1.

[11] Reg. 1:4.

[12] The king's delegation left Rome with these and several other letters to the king's advantage: Reg. 1:5–7, 9, 10.

[13] Of St. Severina: Reg. 1:16–18.

[14] Reg. 1:3, 1:121–123.

The same inflated notion of his power prompted him to repudiate an alliance that had been painfully knit together by two experienced cardinal-diplomats Pandulf and Bernard. During the previous
year, they had brought into existence a "Tuscan League" of cities
allied with the pope against the Hohenstaufen. It had become a reality in November, 1197, with Pope Celestine's approval. What the
pope had approved, the pope-elect rejected, saying that the agreement
was neither useful nor honorable because the member cities had not
explicitly acknowledged that Tuscany belonged to the papacy.[15] The
cities of Viterbo and Perugia were told to hold back from the Tuscan
League until they received further instructions from the pope.[16]
Innocent would later realize that the cardinals had gotten as much
as could be gotten: an alliance, but not submission.

Despite his confidence, he knew that others might have misgivings about his age, and he was right. A year or two later, a German
poet complained:

> I heard the hermit in his cell,
> His plaintiff cry he sent to God,
> "Alas the pope is much too young,
> Please help, dear Lord, your Christian folk."[17]

In the letters announcing his election, Innocent anticipated this attitude . He reminded the world that the silver cup had been found
in the sack of Benjamin, the youngest of Joseph's brothers, even
though there were others of greater age, rank, and merit.[18] The old
are called to their reward and the young take over. God transfers
the luster of antiquity to a new childhood. The church is consoled
over the death of a father by the succession of a son, and God takes
praise from the mouths of suckling infants.[19]

Only the plight of the Holy Land seemed to inspire in Innocent
some hesitation. There the failures of the crusaders to retake Jerusalem
seemed to be God's punishment for the sins of Christians every-

---

[15] Reg. 1:15, 35–36; John C. Moore, "Pope Innocent III, Sardinia, and the Papal
State," *Speculum* 62 (1987): 85–86.

[16] Reg. 1:34.

[17] Walter von der Vogelweide; my version is based on the text and translation
provided by W. T. H. Jackson, *The Literature of the Middle Ages*, (New York, 1960),
pp. 268–269.

[18] Reg. 1:1.

[19] Reg. 1:11, 12.

where, a scourge laid upon the whole church. He urged the hierarchy of the kingdom of Jerusalem, as well as the German prelates and princes who were in the Holy Land as crusaders, to persevere, to put their trust in God rather than in their own strength. He offered the guarded promise that he would work to help them—insofar as God permitted.[20] This sense of limitation was to prove well-founded.

But if divine favor was uncertain in Palestine, God seemed to be showering his gifts on the papacy closer to home. The death of Henry VI greatly simplified things. The emperor's man in the city, the urban prefect Peter of Vico, was now without an emperor, and he offered his fidelity to the pope. Innocent accepted the fidelity and invested him as urban prefect—but with the provision that he would resign whenever the pope so decided.[21] As for the Roman population, Innocent had not wanted to hand out to them the traditional gifts of gold, silver, food, and drink that they expected. He had ordered a secret inventory of papal resources and the results were not encouraging.[22] But peace in Rome seemed worth the price, and he got his peace.

In Italy outside the city, the prospects were even more promising. After the death of Henry, angry Italians rose up against his German captains. Henry's brother Philip fled from Tuscany and only with difficulty made his way back to Swabia.[23] In their desperate hope to hang on to their principalities, some Germans even offered submission to the pope. Ironically, Innocent could not easily accept their submission without conferring on them legitimacy and thereby turning Italian anger against himself.[24] Conrad of Urslingen, excommunicated and surrounded by opposition, submitted to the pope and returned to Germany, leaving the duchy of Spoleto open for a new papal administration.[25] Markward of Anweiler also tried in vain to hang on to his principalities, the duchy of Ravenna and the March

---

[20] Reg. 1:11–13. Failures of crusades were widely believed to be the consequence of the sins of Christians. See Elizabeth Siberry, *Criticism of Crusading: 1095–1274* (Oxford, 1985), pp. 79–84 et passim.

[21] Reg. 1:23; 2:275.

[22] *Gesta*, PL 214:xxii = Gress-Wright, p. 5.

[23] For this, see Waley, *Papal State*, pp. 30–34, 40.

[24] *Gesta*, PL 214:xxii–xxiv = Gress-Wright, pp. 6–7.

[25] Reg. 1:356.

of Ancona, but by the end of the year he had moved south into southern Italy to try to find a new base there. The legates of Pope Celestine had been busy making ties with Italian authorities throughout central Italy, and Italian support now seemed to be there for the taking. Delegations from various Italian princes and towns, like Monteveglio, near Bologna, began to appear in Rome to offer their allegiance to the pope.[26]

For Innocent, submission of Italian authorities meant the expansion of papal authority and, therefore, of papal independence. In February, Innocent wrote the bishops of the province of Ravenna:

> Ecclesiastical liberty is no where better served than where the Roman church holds full power both in temporalities and in spiritualities. For since the Apostolic See is mother and teacher of all churches, inasmuch as it should restrain especially the peoples subject to its temporal jurisdiction from injuring churches and ecclesiastics, so much more would it redound to its own injury and to the prejudice of all churches if it did not preserve in the state of due liberty the churches in its own patrimony. Since therefore among the things our brothers and we are undertaking are these, to recall the exarchate of Ravenna, the March [of Ancona], and Tuscany to our domain, to which they belong, and then to make no slight effort to secure the immunity of your churches, you ought to take up the energetic pursuit of this matter . . . and work effectively for the . . . realization of our intention.[27]

This letter has sometimes been taken as a declaration of his intention to subject all Christendom to the temporal rule of the pope. If so, it would have been repeated and would probably have made its way into the body of canon law. Rather, it was an assertion of ancient claims of popes to be temporal rulers of central Italy, claims based on real or imagined donations made by princes dating back to Constantine. It was also an assertion of the self-evident proposition that the churches in central Italy, including the bishopric of Rome, were less likely to suffer from lay intrusions if the ancient claims were made good and the temporal prince in the area was the pope himself.

These early successes in Italy were, however, somewhat deceptive. For most Italian cities and princes, offering submission to the pope was really a way of gaining greater independence for themselves.

---

[26] *Gesta*, PL 214:xxiv–xxv = Gress-Wright, pp. 7–8; Reg. 1:47.
[27] Reg. 1:27, pp. 40–41.

They rightly saw the pope as less able to control them than the emperor and his German soldiers had been able to do.

Although Innocent certainly was determined to be the secular ruler of the Papal State, he had more modest expectations for the rest of Italy. There were certain political facts that he took as given. There would always be someone with the title Roman emperor, and that emperor would inevitably understand his title to give him some authority in Italy. There would always be a kingdom of Sicily to the south. This kingdom, the Regno, included southern Italy as well as the island of Sicily itself. The popes themselves had played a major role in its creation and had always seen its prince as a counterweight to the Roman emperor to the north. Generally speaking, the kings of Sicily had been reliable allies of the popes.[28] The reign of Henry VI, however, had been a disaster for popes and for other Italian powers, in that Henry had joined both titles in himself: Roman emperor and Sicilian king. Now Innocent had to keep that from happening again. The fact that Henry's son and heir was only three years old gave Innocent time. The fact that the boy's Sicilian-born mother disliked her husband's German friends gave Innocent opportunity. The trick was to use that time and that opportunity to keep the two titles separated, to keep the empire and the kingdom of Sicily out of the hands of one individual.

A secondary goal for Italy was to see that the emperor and the king of Sicily would acknowledge and respect the independence of the Papal State in central Italy. For well over a century, the popes had been convinced that they must be the independent rulers there to function properly, that a secular prince dominating central Italy would end up dominating the papacy. They were probably right. These two goals, then, were the heart of Innocent's policy for Italy: keep the Roman Empire and the Kingdom of Sicily separate and keep independent the Papal State that separated them.

* * *

Once news of Innocent's election had reached outlying provinces, monasteries, chapters of canons, and others began to dispatch delegations to Rome to have their traditional rights and privileges

---

[28] G. A. Loud, "Royal Control of the Church in The Twelfth-Century Kingdom of Sicily," *Studies in Church History* 28 (1982): 147–159.

confirmed by the new pope and to present whatever new business they had at hand. In mid-April, the curia moved from the Lateran to St. Peter's, where the business accelerated, as delegations arrived and sought their papal documents. Curial clerks drew up drafts and then prepared the final versions, to be signed by the pope and sometimes by cardinals, and to be authenticated with the leaden bull or seal of the pope and perhaps with those of the cardinals. Some of the letters were copied into the official register, either because the document seemed important enough to save or because the petitioner requested—and presumably paid—to have a copy registered. The monasteries of St. Vaast in Arras and of Vézelay, the canons of Tournai and of Prémontré, were all represented in Rome at the time; together they accounted for some twenty-six registered documents.[29] May was a busy month. Many of the letters cannot be dated precisely, but approximate dating of registered letters shows about forty letters from March, about sixty-two from April, and about one hundred one from May. How many more letters were issued without being registered we cannot say, but a reasonable estimate is that only about one out of five papal documents was entered in the registers.[30]

The papal clerks who managed this correspondence were not especially systematic about their business. Many papal letters of major importance were not registered at all. We know of them because they exist in other forms or because they are referred to in other letters that survive. Those that were registered are not in chronological order. It seems that the drafts would stack up, sometimes for weeks, until someone decided to enter them, with no particular attention to the order. A letter could be registered months after it had been issued.[31] Drafts of letters that were never registered might still be available for later consultation.[32] From mid-July to mid-October, Innocent was moving around central Italy, and the order of the registered letters from that period suggests that the clerks waited until

---

[29] Reg. 1:137–142, 1:148–150, 1:155–159, 1:160–163, 166, 1:196–200, 202, 203.

[30] Othmar Hageneder's estimate is eighteen percent. See "Die Register Innozenz' III." in *Papst Innozenz III.: Weichensteller Der Geschichte Europas*, ed. Thomas Frenz (Stuttgart, 2000), pp. 91–101, at p. 92.

[31] Reg. 1:296 was dated March 13, but was registered after Reg. 1:295, which was dated June 23.

[32] See Reg. 1:279, where Innocent quotes from an earlier letter, although it had not been registered.

they returned to Rome to register them, again without paying much attention to the order.[33] And occasionally they registered letters that were not from the pope but had been sent to him.[34]

A staple of papal business was disputes between two parties, one or both of them commonly clergy. Problems brought to Rome by appeal from some local jurisdiction might be settled there if both parties were represented, by themselves or by proctors. The pope would hear the case, consult with his "brothers," the cardinals present at the time, and give his decision. He could also consult with legal experts present in the curia.[35] Sometimes the pope assigned cases to be heard first by one or more auditors, who might be able to present a resolution to the pope for his approval. A complicated dispute among the clergy of Perugia had been settled in this way, with cardinal deacon Gerard of S. Adriano acting as auditor and mediator.[36]

More often, Innocent was presented with only one side of an issue, or he had no way of deciding between conflicting stories. He would then commonly refer the matter back to churchmen in the vicinity of the problem, making them papal judges-delegate. Theoretically, they were empowered to settle the matter, but in fact, their judgments could be appealed. Well-informed litigants had long known that cases could be kept alive and open for years by simply appealing to Rome again and again. In April, Innocent was presented with a dispute between two Spanish bishops that had first appeared in the papal court more than ten years earlier.[37]

The system of appeals was easily abused. This possibility was brought to Innocent's attention—not that he needed to be told—by Bishop John of Limoges who complained that clergy in his diocese were using appeals to Rome to protect themselves in all sorts of mischief—illicit business dealings, usury, consorting with concubines, forbidden recreation.[38] Litigants had their own reasons, good and bad, for using the system, but so also did the proctors. Appeals very much

---

[33] See Reg. 1:316 and 318–387.

[34] For example, the letter from the consuls and people of Montveglio, offering submission to the pope (Reg. 1:47).

[35] In July, Innocent referred to one of his subdeacons as a legal expert (Reg. 1:314, p. 446).

[36] Reg. 1:46.

[37] Reg. 1:71.

[38] Reg. 1:330. See the same complaints from the bishop of Modena: Reg. 2:13.

expanded the business of proctors. Moreover, if the proctor conducted himself well in Rome, he might fare as well as Master Peter
Chalboini, the proctor of the archbishop of Rouen, who so impressed
the curia that Innocent awarded him a prebend in Limoges.[39]

Innocent knew the disadvantages of the system, but he never was
able to reform it. Indeed his willingness to receive all manner of
appeals contributed to the problem. His own descriptions of some
of these cases should have been embarrassing to him. Toward the
end of his first year as pope, he reviewed a dispute between the
canons of Spello, near Spoleto, and their prior, Alberic, concerning
the legitimacy of Alberic's election. Innocent had first committed the
case to three cardinals to settle. Since they were preoccupied with
more important political matters, acting as papal legates in the March
of Ancona, they turned it over to two judges in Spello, who in turn
handed it over to the bishop of Spoleto and another judge. When
no progress was made there, two other cardinals, presumably assigned
to the matter by Innocent, committed the case to the bishop of
Perugia. Innocent approved of that commission, but Alberic appealed
to the pope, and Innocent appointed still another cardinal (Girard)
to settle the matter. The case was argued in Girard's presence and
he gave judgment that Alberic was to be removed from office.
Innocent confirmed the judgement, but we cannot be sure that the
matter ended there.[40]

Finding the truth was difficult enough when opposing parties were
being reasonably honest; but honesty was not always the rule. One
man persuaded a papal notary to lend him a draft of a papal letter not yet approved for use. He made off with the draft, and
Innocent had to warn the local bishop not to accept the draft as
valid.[41] Another cleric managed to cut a page from the official papal
register and carry it off to Hungary.[42] A Spanish monk in Rome
was caught trying to counterfeit Innocent's seal, and the bishops back
in Spain had to be warned to beware of spurious papal documents.[43]
A letter sent in May to the entire Christian hierarchy spoke of a
gang of counterfeiters discovered in Rome. Innocent attached to his

---

[39] Reg. 1:304.
[40] Reg. 1:542 (545).
[41] Reg. 1:68.
[42] Reg. 1:537.
[43] Reg. 1:129.

letter both a genuine and a counterfeit seal to help the bishops tell the difference.[44] In September, even Innocent was impressed by a forged papal document, to which had been cleverly attached a genuine papal seal.[45] The problem was to be endemic. The count of Flanders, later to be a Christian hero and the first Latin Emperor of Constantinople, almost certainly defrauded the pope himself with the clever use of a forged papal document.[46]

It is worth noting that few of the people arriving in Rome had been summoned. They were not there in response to papal ambitions or to curial plans to expand papal influence. They were there because they saw their own needs, legitimate or not, to be well served by the papacy. They believed the pope to be the highest ecclesiastical authority and also the closest thing there was to a universal Christian authority, so his stamp of approval on the rights, privileges, or properties they claimed was the best form of authentication available to them. For politically sophisticated clergy and laymen throughout Christendom, papal authority was one more tool, one more weapon, to be used for any number of purposes. For many, papal authority was their last hope for defense against some local injustice.

* * *

The early successes of Innocent's Italian policy can be seen in his actions of the summer of 1198. At the end of June, he wrote to tell all the authorities in south and central Italy to go to the defense of the Holy Land.[47] The death of Henry VI had produced a stream of Germans returning to Germany not only from Italy but also from the Holy Land, and Innocent wanted to recruit replacements. He clearly thought that the Hohenstaufen threat in southern Italy was fading; otherwise he would not have been urging Sicilian knights to depart for Palestine. Then, he decided to tour part of the Papal State. In late June, he commented on the summer heat in Rome,[48] and about mid-July, the curia escaped to the cool, hill-top town of

---

[44] Reg. 1:235.
[45] Reg. 1:349.
[46] John C. Moore, "Count Baldwin IX of Flanders, Philip Augustus, and the Papal Power," *Speculum* 37 (1962): 78–89.
[47] Reg. 1:302.
[48] Reg. 1:289.

Rieti, northeast of Rome. Popes in transit were not uncommon, but usually they traveled as exiles from a rebellious Rome. In this case, Innocent toured as a secular prince inspecting his domain. His party remained in Rieti until about mid-August and then proceeded to a stay of several weeks in Spoleto. That city had been suffering from a water shortage, and while Innocent was there, the citizens discovered a new spring directly beneath their walls. They called it the Papal Fountain, a good omen indeed. By mid-September, the curia was in Perugia. In early October, they made their way home by way of Todi, Amelia, Orte, and Cívita Castellana.

Throughout the tour, Innocent consecrated churches and altars, while the curia continued to turn out papal letters for all parts of Christendom. From Todi, he gave notice to the cities of Spoleto, Rieti, Foligno, Assisi, Gubbio, Perugia, Città di Castello, and Todi that henceforth, Gregory, cardinal-deacon of S. Maria in Aquiro, would act as rector and papal legate, exercising complete secular and spiritual authority in the area. He was, in effect, replacing the secular government of Conrad of Urslingen, now returned to Germany. Gregory's appointment was the first step toward the creation of an administrative system for the Papal State according to which secular princes and city governments were placed under the supervision of a regional ecclesiastical rector.[49] In these first months of his papacy, Innocent probably expected to impose a similar government further north, in the duchy of Ravenna and the march of Ancona, and perhaps even in Tuscany, but the local powers in those regions were to be less cooperative.[50]

*   *   *

Outside of Italy, Innocent's world was vast and less familiar. It can be thought of as shaped like an American football, an east-west ellipse with Rome as its center. The southern half was in Muslim hands, from southern Spain to the Holy Land (and beyond). The northern half of the ellipse outside of Italy was dominated by dozens

---

[49] *Gesta*, PL 214:xxv–xxvi = Gress-Wright, p. 9; Reg. 1:356; Waley, *Papal State*, p. 37. For a detailed description of the administration of the Papal State, including individual rectors, see Christian Lackner, "Studien zur Verwaltung des Kirchenstaates unter Papst Innocenz III.," *Römische Historische Mitteilungen* 29 (1987) 127–214.

[50] Waley, *Papal State*, pp. 33–38.

of Christian princes, each one of whom was constantly maneuvering to expand his power at the expense of his neighbors, each one of whom was inclined to see church offices and church lands as part of his arsenal. In Spain, there were the kings of Castile, León, Navarre, Aragon, and Portugal. In France, there were, in addition to the king, great princes who rivaled him in power. The most powerful was the duke of Aquitaine and Normandy and count of Anjou and Poitou, Richard the Lion-Hearted, who was also king of England. In the German-speaking areas—by far the largest of any of these regions—besides the Hohenstaufen emperors there were the great principalities, dominated by men like the dukes of Saxony and the archbishops of Mainz. To the north were the Scandinavian kings of Denmark, Sweden, and Norway. To the east lay the Slavic duchies of Poland and Bohemia, then, further south, the kingdom of Hungary. Further south still were the Balkans, that perennial battlefield, where Serbs, Croats, Greeks, Bulgars, Hungarians—to name only some of the participants—would fight for breathing room from that day to this. And at the passage-way from Europe to Asia Minor lay Constantinople, the largest Christian city in the world, the proud capital of the ancient Roman Empire, the seat of the schismatic Greek Orthodox church, the dike standing against the Muslim flood. Further south, in the Holy Land itself, Latin Christian principalities were like islands reclaimed from the Muslim sea, but islands whose coasts were now being washed away by the currents of Islam.

Far beyond these limits were distant Christian outposts. In the summer of 1198, Innocent wrote the people of Iceland, urging them to reform and assuring them of his interest in them, despite their remoteness.[51] And the limits were expanding. In 1198, there was already a colony of German merchants and clergy in the valley of the Dvina River, trading with the people of Livonia and trying to convert them. In a few years, German warriors would provide the muscle to turn Livonia and Estonia into Christian territory.[52] Further east, the Mongol and Tartar hordes were not to appear on the papal horizon until a few years after Innocent's death.

---

[51] Reg. 1:320–321.

[52] Jerzy Kloczowski, "Innocent III et les pays chrétiens autour de la mer Baltique," in *Horizons marins. Itinéraires spirituels (V^e–XVIIIe siècles)*, ed. Henri Dubois et al., 2 vols. (Paris, 1987), 1:163–170; James A. Brundage, introduction to his translation of *The Chronicle of Henry of Livonia*, (Madison, 1961), pp. 3–16.

In theory, Innocent could easily define his role in this world. He
was to shepherd his church to salvation. He was to offer his family
the food of good example, of sound doctrine, of sacramental suste-
nance. But this charge could only be realized, of course, through his
fellow clergy. To fulfill properly their functions, the clergy, from the
cardinals down to the humblest parish priest, had to be chosen and
governed properly. And the principal obstacle here, in Innocent's
mind, was the interference of lay powers who inserted their favorites
into ecclesiastical positions, using church lands to endow their relatives and other supporters. Innocent's pastoral mission, then, required
him to champion the "freedom of the church" from lay control and
lay intimidation. It required him to prod the clergy to be sound in
word and example. It also required him to defend the flock from
Satan, that "enemy of the human race" whose conspicuous instruments were the infidel in the southern half of his world and the
heretic in the northern half. The pope was armed with a shepherd's
staff, sharp at the end so that he could jab the slow and fat sheep,
straight in the middle so that he could support the sick and infirm,
curved at the top so that he could regather those who strayed.[53]

Putting the theory into practice, however, was exceedingly complicated. It was not simply a matter of defining goals, of devising
and implementing strategies, because the rest of the world was not
waiting. The business of the papal curia increased at an accelerating
rate after Innocent's election, with letters leaving Rome for every
part of Christendom, dealing with matters of the highest and low-
est magnitude. A Parisian priest was given permission to continue
as a priest, despite the fact that he had emasculated himself (a physician had advised this drastic treatment when leprosy was suspected).[54]
Another priest in France claimed he had been wrongly suspended
from his office because he was a suspect in a murder case.[55] A group
of canons in southern Italy complained about their bishop's failure
to maintain their church.[56] In the very week of Innocent's consecration, judgments were given in two matrimonial disputes.[57] In Dalmatia,
a priest in danger of death had entered a monastery; now he had

---

[53] PL 217:410.
[54] Reg. 1:19.
[55] Reg. 1:20.
[56] Reg. 1:21.
[57] Reg. 1:48, 29.

recovered and sought papal permission to resume his priestly career so that he could support his aging parents.[58] A monastery in Aragon sought protection from a violent enemy.[59] The patriarch of Antioch was chastised for transferring a man from an archbishopric to a bishopric, something only the pope could do.[60] The archbishop of Armagh in Ireland was told that women were not bound by the Mosaic law temporarily excluding them from church services after child-birth, but that the practice was not forbidden to pious women who wished to observe it.[61]

Much of this business consisted of isolated cases to be dealt with, without much bearing on over-all policy. But one theme that tied much of it together was Innocent's determination to supervise all clergy, to see that they observed the requirements of their calling. In these first months, he sent sharply worded orders or reprimands to the archbishops of Canterbury,[62] Milan,[63] and Monreale,[64] and to the patriarch of Antioch.[65] He told some judges delegate that if the archbishop of Trier did not behave, they were to suspend him and send him to Rome.[66] The young bishop-elect of Brixen had received permission from Pope Celestine to finish his studies of theology, but had used the time instead to study Roman law. Innocent ordered him back to his diocese lest he prove himself "as immature in deeds as he was in years."[67] He was equally caustic in a letter to the archbishop of Bourges concerning the abbot of the chapter of canons at l'Esterp. The abbot, Innocent said, was reported to fancy himself more a secular knight than a knight of Christ. He used ecclesiastical revenues to support his entourage of knights and the people in the area could scarcely hold a fair or tournament without his being there. If all the charges against him were listed, Innocent said, the reading would be tedious and the document immense.[68] In a different

---

[58] Reg. 1:36.
[59] Reg. 1:31.
[60] Reg. 1:50.
[61] Reg. 1:63.
[62] Reg. 1:111.
[63] Reg. 1:279.
[64] Reg. 1:106.
[65] Reg. 1:50.
[66] Reg. 1:70.
[67] Reg. 1:144.
[68] Reg. 1:291.

tone, the pope responded favorably to the French villagers who complained that their chaplain was requiring them to pay for funerals and marriages, in violation of canon law.[69]

Innocent's first year, then, set the pattern: the cacophony of petitions and complaints, the perennial concern for the independence and reform of the clergy. And scattered among these letters are those that addressed the other great issues that were to dominate his pontificate: the future of Italy and the Empire, the future of the Holy Land, the internal threat of heresy, and the external threat of Islam.

* * *

The vast expanse of Islam was the greatest threat to Christendom, both spiritually and physically, and there was no single person with greater responsibility than the pope to meet that threat. After his election and before his consecration, Innocent had promised vaguely to send help to the beleaguered crusaders in the Holy Land; but he had also made clear that the future of the Holy Land depended not so much on force of arms as on the spiritual health of Christendom. He could not rashly proclaim a crusade without addressing the moral failures at home that were both symptom and cause of the failures abroad. Before the Christian princes could be summoned for a holy war, they had first to rid themselves of their own demons. First, they had to stop fighting among themselves, inflicting suffering on their Christian subjects and comforting the infidel. Second, they had to reform their own lives. In Innocent's mind, a series of illicit marriages had served almost as a challenge to God, and God had responded accordingly. Innocent desperately needed these princes to support his Italian policies, to defend the Holy Land, and to rid the home front of heretics; but their hands must be reasonably clean or they would simply invite further divine retribution.

Perhaps for this reason, Innocent had not called immediately for a crusade. In April, he assigned to a close associate the monk Rainerius[70] the enormous task of forcing peace upon the kings of

---

[69] Reg. 1:220.

[70] Probably a Cistercian and probably the pope's confessor. See Christoph Egger, "Papst Innocenz III. als Theologe," *Archivum Historiae Pontificae*, 30 (1992): 62–63, and idem, "Joachim von Fiore, Rainer von Ponza und die römische Kurie," in *Gioacchino da Fiore tra Bernardo di Clairvaux e Innocenzo III*. Atti del 5o Congresso inter-

Spain so that they could present a united front against the Saracens. Rainerius was also given the related task of undoing the incestuous union between King Alfonso IX of León and his niece Berenguela, daughter of King Alfonso VIII of Castile.[71] In May, Innocent wrote directly to Philip Augustus about his marriage. warning him sternly to return his rejected queen to her rightful station.[72] By late June, he was ready to act more directly on behalf of the Holy Land. He urged Prince Andrew of Hungary to carry out his crusading vow, although the pope's motive here was as much to get the rebellious prince out of Hungary as anything else. In late June, he called on a number of prelates of Germany to protect the property of crusaders; and he began a major offensive by commissioning the prelates of Sicily and southern Italy to call on all the faithful to relieve the Holy Land.[73]

The final plans for a great new crusade were completed during the summer, as the curia toured the Papal State. On 15 August, an eloquent letter was dispatched from Rieti to all parts of Christendom, calling on everyone to join in the common effort for the Holy Land.[74] In terms well designed to touch the hearts of Latin warriors, he described the losses there and the moral and military failures of the Christians: "For behold, 'Our inheritance has been turned over to strangers, our homes to aliens' (Lamentations 5:2), 'the roads to Zion mourn, for none come to the appointed feasts' (ibid., 1:4)." He contrasted King David's captain Uriah with the Christian princes of the day. When Uriah returned home from battle, he foreswore even the licit embraces of his wife, but the Christian princes make time for adulterous embraces and abandon themselves to pleasures and riches. They attack one another and seek revenge for past injuries, while no one cares about the wrongs done to the Crucified. They are mocked, he said, by their Muslim enemies:

> Where is your God, who can free neither you nor himself from our hands? Behold, we have now profaned your sacred places. Behold, we have now laid hands on your precious things. With our first attack,

---

nazionale di studi gioachimiti San Giovanni in Fiore—16–21 settembre 1999. Ed. Roberto Rusconi. Pp. 136–137.

[71] Reg. 1:92.

[72] Reg. 1:171.

[73] Reg. 1:302.

[74] Reg. 1:336. For a translation of the letter, see Andrea, *Contemporary Sources*, pp. 9–19.

we violently invaded those places where you claim that your superstition had its beginning, and we now hold them against your will. Now we have weakened and shattered the lances of the French; we have repulsed the efforts of the English; for a second time we have now restrained the Germans; we have subdued the spirited Spanish. And when you led forth all your strength, stirred up against us, you scarcely achieved anything. So where is your God? Let him rise up now and help you and let him be a protector for you and for himself.

The papal call to arms was followed by specifics. The crusade was to be supervised by Cardinals Soffredus of St. Praxed and Peter Capuano of St. Maria in Vialata. (In a separate letter, Innocent told the prelates of France that although he might like to fly to all parts of Christendom "in the blink of an eye," just as the prophet Habbakuk was transported to comfort Daniel in the lion's den, the limits of the human condition forced him to rely on papal legates.)[75] Cardinal Peter was being dispatched to form a peace between the kings of England and France, Cardinal Soffredus to Venice to seek support for the crusade. Cities and princes were to supply warriors for at least a two-year effort, beginning the following March. All clergy were to support the effort by sending warriors and money.

All who went in person or supported others in their stead were to receive a full indulgence for sins truly repented and confessed. Those making lesser contributions would receive indulgences in proportion to their donations and their fervor. The property of those who took the cross would be under the protection of the pope and other clergy; and crusaders would be absolved from all payment of interest. Finally, each archbishop was told to choose one knight Templar and one Hospitaler to work with him in carrying out the papal program.

The letter was eloquent indeed, but it would take more than a single letter to move the Latin West. The physical and financial obstacles were enormous; the spiritual and diplomatic were no less so, as can be seen in tasks faced by several papal representatives. The monk Brother Rainerius was still in Spain, trying to turn the quarreling kings against the Muslims rather than one another. Cardinal Peter was sent to end the warfare between Philip Augustus and Richard the Lion-Hearted and at the same time to force Philip to

---

[75] Reg. 1:345, referring to Dan. 14:33–39 in the Vulgate, Bel 1:33–30 in the Apocrypha.

unite with his discarded wife.[76] A papal chaplain and a papal notary were dispatched to Constantinople to enlist the support of Emperor Alexius III. Their task was not made easier by the tone of Innocent's letter, which scolded the emperor for not supporting the Holy Land and for being in schism from the Roman church,[77] though he adopted a milder tone in a letter a year later.[78] Because of these and other obstacles, the following March came and went, but no crusading army took shape.

*   *   *

Innocent wanted to turn military force against Islam; he intended no gentler treatment for the enemy within. On 21 April of his first year, he dispatched a letter introducing the two Cistercian monks Rainerius and Guido to all the religious and secular authorities in southern France.[79] The authorities were to receive the monks cordially and support them in their efforts against heresy. Heretics would be, if possible, recalled from the error of their ways; but if they refused, they were to be driven out. Innocent would back up any measures the monks adopted and would enforce any penalties they imposed on those who failed to cooperate. Those who did cooperate were to receive the same indulgence as those who visited Rome or Compostella.

The power of papal documents in the hard-nosed world of the day is not always easy to assess. But there can be no doubt that these pieces of parchment marked the beginning of decades of suffering for the people of Languedoc. For the present, however, their religious dissenters may have been under less pressure than poor Rainerius himself.

The heretics of southern France were in no immediate danger, and the same could be said for many other areas. Innocent seemed reluctant to give Italian authorities the harsh and peremptory orders he was sending to southern France. In Italy, religious dissent combined with local politics. Some cities may have found it useful to have heretics in positions of authority because they were impervious

---

[76] Reg. 1:345–348, 355.
[77] Reg. 1:353.
[78] Reg. 2:202 (211).
[79] Reg. 1:94.

to threats of excommunication from the pope or bishops. Soon after his election, Innocent sent Cardinal Gregory of S. Maria in Portico to northern Italy to address the heresy problem there.[80] In April, the cardinal presided over a council of clergy at Verona, and it was agreed that heretics should be excluded from all municipal elections in Lombardy. The archdeacon of Verona was charged with obtaining compliance from city officials in Lombardy.[81] Mere exclusion from municipal elections was a far cry from confiscation of property and exile, but it seems to have been the best the pope's agents could get.

* * *

Throughout this first year, Innocent remained conscious of the magnitude of his responsibilities. In late May, he wrote several leading monastic houses, asking extra prayers that he not be overwhelmed. He reflected on the significance of the title he used for himself in every letter, "servant of the servants of God," and saw that God would require him to render account not only for his own soul but for those of all the faithful. The words of the psalmist came to mind, "I have come into deep waters, and the flood sweeps over me."[82] He routinely referred to his unworthiness to exercise his office. In late July, he wrote to the Cistercians gathered in general chapter, asking for their prayers. He was, he said, almost overwhelmed by the business of others—clarifying obscure matters, settling difficult cases, restraining the evil and protecting the humble—and could scarcely bear the burden if their prayers did not make up for his defects.[83]

Still, everything seemed to be going so well that most of 1198 must have been an exhilarating time, one of great expectations. The most formal documents that left Innocent's curia had inscribed at the bottom a "rota" consisting of two concentric circles with a cross in the center, the latter added by Innocent's own hand. Between the two circles was inscribed Innocent's motto, "fac mecum domine signum in bonum," "Show me, Lord, a sign of thy favor," an adaptation of Psalm 86 (85):17, "Show me a sign of thy favor, that those

---

[80] Reg. 2:27.
[81] Reg. 1:298.
[82] Reg. 1:176, quoting Psalm 69:2.
[83] Reg. 1:358.

who hate me may see and be put to shame because thou, Lord, hast helped me and comforted me."[84] The signs of God's favor seemed so strong during those first months that at the end of May, he spoke of visiting France himself to adjudicate the dispute between the kings of France and England.[85] In August he confidently issued the universal call for all Christians to take the cross.

Toward the end of the year, however, things began to go wrong. As the situation in southern Italy became more ominous, his optimism became more restrained. It was not just the short, cold days of January that prompted him to write in 1199, "These times, especially, abound in iniquity and the charity of many grows cold under pressure of sin."[86]

---

[84] Cheney and Semple, pp. xviii; 147, n. 10; and 182, n. 15
[85] Reg. 1:230.
[86] Reg. 1:530 (532), 549 (552).

CHAPTER THREE

THE GREAT PRINCES (1198–1200)

In 1198, Innocent had seemed to secure an ideal relationship with the kingdom of Sicily, he had enjoyed a triumphant tour of the papal possessions in central Italy, and he had called for a great crusade. But Constance, the queen-mother of Sicily, died in November and the German nemesis began to rise again, led by Markward of Anweiler. The deadline for the crusaders to gather, March 1199, came and went, but no crusading armies appeared. There were no triumphant tours in 1199, not even an escape from the Roman summer. Innocent stayed in Rome. The disorder in Italy was so threatening that in mid-summer, the king of Dioclea and Dalmatia said that he was reluctant to send emissaries to Rome because he feared for their safety.[1] In October of 1199, Innocent told the people of the Papal State that he was so preoccupied with business well beyond the usual that he would have to send a deputy.[2] About the same time he urged clergy in the Holy Land not to give up, despite the discord in the west that was delaying help for the Holy Land.[3] Even his health was bad, taking away the vigor expected from a young pope.[4]

In the midst of Christmas season of 1199, another letter went out to the prelates of Europe, bemoaning the sorry state of the Holy Land.[5] Responding to the urgency of the situation, Innocent announced that he was placing a ten percent tax on his own income to provide support for the Holy Land. He also announced that he was levying an unprecedented income tax on nearly all the clergy of Christendom, 2.5 percent of their annual revenues to be paid in support of the crusade. He assured the clergy that he was not estab-

---

[1] Reg. 2:167 (176).
[2] Reg. 2:194 (203).
[3] Reg. 2:180 (189).
[4] Reg. 2:198 (207).
[5] Reg. 2:258 (270). For a translation, see Andrea, *Contemporary Sources*, pp. 26–32.

lishing a precedent, perhaps being unduly optimistic that the crusade he was trying to organize would solve the problem of the Holy Land once and for all. The innovation was not well received, and Innocent was complaining bitterly a few months later that the tax was not being paid.[6]

The real heart of his problems, though, was his inability to restrain and direct the princes of Christendom. An energetic pope in the Gregorian tradition could not get along without these secular powers. Obviously and immediately, Innocent needed the princes for the crusade. Unless they cooperated, there would be no flow of knights to the Holy Land. Moreover, the connection between domestic peace and the crusade was obvious. Within months of his election, Innocent was asked to release Hungarian warriors from their crusader vows because the king needed them to resist the rebellion of his brother.[7] Less obviously, he needed not only men and money from the princes, but virtue as well. Innocent was like many of his contemporaries in seeing misfortune as the punishment for sin, the judgment of God. He frequently stated his belief that the greatest misfortune then suffered by Christendom, the loss of Jerusalem to the Muslims, was the direct consequence of illicit and immoral marriages of princes.

Innocent needed the cooperation of princes to guarantee the "liberty of the church." He was committed to the Gregorian program calling for the independence of the clergy from secular rulers. He never had the slightest doubt about these principles: princes were not to select prelates, they were not to bring them before their secular courts, they were not to lay hands on their persons or their property. And although he always acknowledged the legitimacy and ordinary autonomy of secular authorities, he could always find a reason for demanding obedience from them on any matter he thought really important for the spiritual health of Christendom. This program ran so contrary to the inclinations and the practices of the princes that a certain amount of conflict was inevitable. In some cases, a great deal of conflict. In the very first year of his reign, Innocent was faced with the "tyranical" King Swerri Sigurdsson of

---

[6] Pott. 1045, dated April–May, 1200; text in *Gesta*, PL 214:cxxxii–cxxxviii = Gress-Wright, pp. 164–174.

[7] Reg. 1:270.

Norway, who had chased nearly all the bishops from his kingdom
and was ignoring the excommunication and interdict levied against
him. Only the death of Swerri in 1202 ended the standoff.[8]

Even if there had been no crusade in the offing, even if the princes
had been content to accept clerical immunity and the "liberty of the
church" as defined by Innocent and canon law, questions of marriage and divorce would still have created problems for pope and
princes. Over the previous century the clergy had expanded their
jurisdictional claims over marriage, and Innocent doggedly tried to
implement these claims. Both the theologians and the canon lawyers
of the time were developing explicit definitions as to what constituted a valid marriage. Both insisted that flagrantly and notoriously
invalid marriages should not be permitted to stand and that valid
marriages could not be dissolved.[9] The only legitimate form of divorce
was an annulment, an ecclesiastical judgment that the marriage had
been invalid in the first place. Innocent accepted these principles
without question, as well as the belief that it was the clergy's responsibility to enforce the principles.

He also took to heart the scriptural requirement that he respond
to appeals from the weak, so when the king of France rejected his
wife Ingeborg, when the duke of Bohemia rejected his wife Adela,[10]
it was very difficult for Innocent to ignore the cries that came from
these women. Had he done so, moralists from that day to this, not
to mention his own conscience, would have condemned him.[11]

A few centuries earlier, the princes of Latin Christendom could
have gotten along very nicely without the pope, ruling "their" clergy
as they pleased. But by Innocent's time, intelligent princes and their
clerical advisers knew that papal authority was a given in their world.
They knew that the pope and the legal system he headed could not
simply be ignored or rejected; but they also knew that time and real
power were usually on their side. The princely courts learned how
to frustrate and manipulate the authority of the pope. It is remarkable that a priest in Rome had as much influence as he did over

---

[8] Kloczowski, "Innocent III et les pays chrétiens autour de la mer Baltique,"
1:164–165; Reg. 1:282–284.
[9] James A. Brundage, *Law, Sex, and Christian Society in Medieval Europe* (Chicago,
1987), pp. 260–278, 288–289, 319–341, et passim.
[10] Reg. 2:179 (188).
[11] Reg. 5:48 (49).

the bellicose princes of Christendom; but it would have been miraculous indeed if that influence had been decisive very often.

* * *

Whereas Innocent had a very clear idea of the obedience owed him by both secular and spiritual authorities, and whereas the princes were determined to play by their own rules whenever possible, the clergy throughout Europe found themselves in the middle. On the one hand, prelates and pope had close ties. They were usually the products of the same educational system, trained in the same religious doctrine and the same legal system. Because bishops, or their clerical advisers, were responsive to arguments based on theology and canon law, the momentum of papal ideology was difficult to resist. The Gregorian reform movement had gotten as far as it had precisely because the arguments were persuasive to educated clergy, and they became more so as the schools of Europe turned out a growing number of young men trained in a system that made the papacy the supreme court of Europe.

Those prelates unimpressed by the theory still had to take it into account. A bishop who ignored the order of a papal legate was gambling. Maybe nothing would come of it; but then again, maybe that legate would be followed by others, by papal letters to other bishops of the area. Secular or ecclesiastical rivals of such a bishop could take advantage of the papal position to promote their own interests; so conciliation with the pope might be the safest course. When Conrad, bishop of Hildesheim, transferred himself to the bishopric of Würzburg, he probably thought that at worst, Rome would protest but then move on. He was, after all, the former chancellor of the empire, no man to treat lightly. There followed, however, several years of agitation ending with Conrad prostrate before the feet of Innocent in Rome. The legal arguments advanced by the pope were persuasive in Germany; and the persistence of the papacy kept the case and the arguments from being quietly forgotten.[12]

Archbishop Hubert Walter of Canterbury no doubt believed that Rome would lose interest in the complaints from the monks of Christ

---

[12] Kenneth Pennington, *Pope and Bishops: The Papal Monarchy in the Twelfth and Thirteenth Centuries* (Philadelphia, 1984), pp. 31–33, citing *Gesta*, PL 214:lxxxvii–lxxxviii and Vat. lat. 12111, fol. 13r–13v (quoting the latter).

Church of Canterbury. He was continuing his predecessor's plans for new buildings and a chapter of canons at Lambeth, near London. The monks of Christ Church, who were the electing chapter of Canterbury, were afraid that they were about to be displaced. They kept a steady stream of complaints going to Rome. The archbishop, other bishops, and agents of the king all pressured the monks to give in, but they stubbornly persisted, putting all their hopes with the pope. When Innocent was elected, he took up the case and pursued it aggressively, finally deciding in favor of the monks. He ordered the archbishop to disperse the canons and destroy the buildings. The matter dragged on, however, with appeals, charges, and counter-charges, until everyone involved settled for a kind of compromise (one set of buildings was razed, but another erected). The papal directives had not been as effective as Innocent would have liked; but both the spiritual and secular authorities in England had been forced at least to bend to papal authority.[13]

On the other hand, the ties between prelates and princes were also strong. Generally speaking, they came from the same kind of aristocratic families, and they often joined together to promote the interests of those families. The princes usually had a strong sense of religious propriety that required rituals and ceremonies to stay on the right side of God, and they looked to the prelates to take care of such matters.

The princes were susceptible to advice from clergy, whether it be on a high level, telling them that as good knights they should defend the honor of Christ, their Lord and King, or on a lower level, urging them to curtail the activities of Jews or heretics. But the princes were very little inclined to cede authority to priests of any level. Advice, ministrations, clerical service, yes. Orders and commands, no. Commands should be backed by secular authority and, especially, force of arms, and that was generally not the province of clergy. A hundred years earlier, the *Song of Roland* could portray Archbishop Turpin as one of the Christian heroes breaking the heads of Muslims, but in the romances of Innocent's days and on real battle fields, warrior-bishops had become rare.

The mediating role of the clergy—between princes and pope—is evident in the language princes used in their letters to popes. It was

---

[13] Christopher R. Cheney, *Pope Innocent III and England* (Stuttgart, 1976), pp. 208–220.

provided by clerical advisers who knew what the pope expected to hear. When a prince wanted something from the pope, diplomacy required that his rhetoric reflect papal language about the authority of the papacy. The language in this situation was respectful, even deferential. On other occasions, the tone could be somewhat more curt. But very rarely did princely anger or contempt pass unabated through the filters of clerical advisers and scribes.

The prelates were tied, then, to both princes and pope, but Innocent wanted it to be very clear that they were ecclesiastical officers, not agents of the princes. He tried to forbid bishops from serving in royal government, requiring Hubert Walter of Canterbury to resign the office of justiciar of England.[14] The vigor with which he pursued the case of Lambeth may have been partly the result of the fact that the archbishop was a close adviser of the king. Similarly, he hounded Conrad, former bishop of Hildesheim, for transferring himself to the bishopric of Würzburg without papal permission. The right to translate bishops was for Innocent a jealously guarded papal prerogative, but the fact that Conrad had been chancellor of the Emperor Henry VI made it all the more important that Innocent not look the other way.

* * *

Innocent dealt with hundreds of powerful noblemen in his lifetime, and we must beware of imposing modern political structures on thirteenth-century Europe, looking only at the kings of what would become modern nations. There were not yet well defined kingdoms of Spain, England, France, and Germany. Still, we must admit that Innocent thought of the peoples of Europe according to these general categories, even in the twelfth century. When he issued his general call for the crusade, this is how he portrayed the speech of Muslims ridiculing Christians for their failures: "We have weakened and shattered the lances of the French; we have repulsed the efforts of the English; for a second time we have now restrained the Germans; we have subdued the spirited Spanish."[15] So to group people this way is to see things as Innocent saw them.

---

[14] Cheney, *Innocent III and England*, p. 19.
[15] Reg. 1:336.

Who were these princes the pope needed? To begin with, always most important for crusading, were the princes of France.

When Innocent became pope, the most formidable prince in France was not King Philip Augustus, but the great warrior Richard the Lion-Hearted, duke of Aquitaine and Normandy and count of Anjou, not to mention king of England. Richard and his brothers had spent much of their time in rebellion against their earthly father, Henry II, and they were no more disposed to respect their spiritual father, the pope. Richard had a Christian conscience of sorts. He occasionally experienced remorse for his sexual excesses (perhaps homosexual, perhaps not), and he chose not to receive communion because he so hated the king of France, a condition that lasted for seven years.[16]

The crusades gave a man like Richard a splendid outlet for his religious sensibilities, but by the time of Innocent's election, the king had long since left the Holy Land, and his wars in France were making it difficult for anyone else to go. In the later English stories of Robin Hood, Richard acquired the reputation of "Good King Richard," but about the only basis for the legend was his magnanimity at the time of his succession: he was generous to the knights who had fought against him on behalf of his father, and he declared a general amnesty for all the prisoners in England. He was also more forgiving to his brother than John deserved.[17] But for the next ten years, he did little for England, since he was hardly ever there, preferring to make war in the Holy Land and in France. His brother John would soon succeed him, but John had so far distinguished himself mainly for treachery and incompetence—not someone for whom Innocent could have high hopes. Like all the other princes of Europe, both brothers disliked papal action in their regions— unless of course they themselves had introduced it to serve their own purposes.

Richard's first communication with Innocent may have set the pope's teeth on edge, since it presumed to instruct the pope on his duty to serve justice without prejudice. In any case, Innocent more than once referred to that instruction when declining to do all that

---

[16] John Gillingham, *The Life and Times of Richard I* (London, 1973), pp. 43–45, 213–214. For Richard's reputation, see John Gillingham, *Richard I* (New Haven, 1999), pp. 1–14.

[17] Gillingham, *Richard I*, pp. 260–261.

Richard expected of him.[18] And Richard expected quite a lot. While returning from crusade, he had been captured by the duke of Austria and imprisoned by the Emperor Henry VI. Now free, he wanted Innocent's help in recovering the ransom. He had been a crusader, after all, under papal protection. Moreover, King Philip Augustus had attacked his possessions in France. Again, Richard claimed papal intervention on behalf of a wronged crusader.[19] He also wanted Innocent's help in obtaining money and castles promised him by King Sancho VI of Navarre as dowry when Richard married the king's daughter Berengaria. Innocent made some effort on the ransom and dowry—fruitless as it turned out—and promised, regarding the French possessions, only to give fair judgment when he had settled more pressing matters in Italy. But the firmest promise, with which he closed this letter of 21 May 1198, was to force both Richard and Philip Augustus to stop fighting each other so that a crusade could be launched. In those early, heady days of his pontificate, he even thought that he himself might visit France to settle the matter.[20]

In that month, both kings were well represented in Rome. Their emissaries were not willing to concede the pope's right to make a formal decision in their complicated dispute,[21] but each king was trying to recruit the spiritual authority of the pope against the other. Philip Augustus was a skilled practitioner of this art. Some years later, he was to object indignantly that the pope had no authority in feudal affairs; but he had himself routinely inserted that authority in feudal oaths of allegiance required of his vassals.[22] Among the letters leaving Rome in the first months of Innocent's pontificate was a set sought by representatives of the king. They quoted and confirmed an oath of fealty rendered to the king by Count Baldwin of Flanders, including the provision inserted by the king that the clergy must punish the count with excommunication and interdict if he should violate the oath.[23] If the popes of the period played an

---

[18] Cheney, *Innocent III and England*, p. 275 and n. 7; Cheney and Semple, p. 10, no. 4; Reg. 1:230.

[19] Cheney, *Innocent III and England*, p. 278.

[20] Reg. 1:230 = Cheney and Semple, pp. 3–8, no. 2; Cheney, *Innocent III and England*, pp. 273–279. Innocent's hope to visit "partes vestras" has sometime been taken as a reference to England, but the plural pronoun refers to the lands of both Philip and Richard, i.e. to France.

[21] Ibid.

[22] For example, see Moore, "Count Baldwin IX," pp. 82, 86.

[23] Reg. 1:130.

expanding role in the affairs of Europe, they did so partly at the
behest of the very princes who complained about it.

The historic ties between the papacy and the kings of France,
together with Innocent's personal memories of his student days in
Paris, should have helped the pope work with this monarch. They
were even related in some distant way,[24] and Philip himself took his
religion seriously.[25] But there was a special complication. In August
1193, Philip Augustus had married Ingeborg, the eighteen-year-old
sister of King Knut VI of Denmark. Although the young queen was
said to be both beautiful and virtuous, on the day following the marriage, at the formal coronation, the king manifested an unspeakable
aversion for his new bride and would have no more to do with her.
No one can explain the king's reaction. One theory is that he had
suffered from an unaccustomed attack of impotence and suspected
Ingeborg of sorcery. In any case, the king's discomfort was to bring
suffering to many people, not least Ingeborg, who was to spend years
isolated in various monasteries and castles in France; and it was very
much to complicate the life of Innocent III, who was at the time of
the marriage a junior cardinal in the Roman curia. Philip himself
had sought an immediate remedy. He had had his uncle Archbishop
William of Rheims annul the marriage and was before long father-
ing children from a new wife more to his liking, Agnes of Méran.
But Ingeborg was a determined young woman who was not ready
to give up easily her crown and her reputation. Unable to speak
French, she fell back on her smattering of Latin: "Mala Francia!
Roma!" She and her brother appealed her case first to Pope Celestine
III, whose legate declared the annulment invalid, and then to Innocent,
who supported her cause for years.[26] The only other support she
found was in the prayers of local clergymen.[27]

---

[24] Philip referred to Innocent as his "consanguineo" in RNI, no. 13.

[25] Jim Bradbury, *Philip Augustus. King of France, 1180–1223* (London and New
York, 1998) pp. 166–173.

[26] Robert-Henri Bautier, "Philippe Auguste: la personnalité du roi," *La France de
Philippe Auguste: Le Temps des Mutations*, ed. Robert-Henri Bautier (Paris, 1982), pp.
41–43; John W. Baldwin, *The Government of Philip Augustus: Foundations of French Royal
Power in the Middle Ages* (Berkeley, 1986), pp. 82–87; Bradbury, *Philip Augustus*, pp.
173–168; *Gesta*, PL 214:xcii–xcv = Gress-Wright, pp. 68–71.

[27] Having received her request and a small gift, the dean and chapter of Amiens
promised to pray for her. *Cartulaire du chapitre de la Cathédrale d'Amiens*, 2 vols., ed.
J. Roux (Amiens and Paris, 1905–1912), 1:137–138.

One of the first letters to leave Rome after Innocent's election had been addressed to the bishop of Paris, telling him to urge the king to restore Ingeborg and abandon Agnes. It was not an assignment the bishop would relish, and he may or may not have acted on it, even though Innocent suggested a connection between the king's marital behavior and the famine then afflicting much of France.[28] The following May, the pope wrote directly to the king, recalling fondly his own student days in France as one more reason why he was favorably disposed to the king, but still insisting that Agnes be sent out of the kingdom and Ingeborg restored as wife and queen. "No matter how much you confide in your own power, you cannot stand in the face, we do not say of ourselves, but of God, whose place we take on earth, however unworthy we may be. . . ."[29] Nothing happened. Innocent may have had his student days at Paris in mind at the time because the Danish emissary sent to Rome on behalf of Ingeborg was Anders Sunesen, a man who had been a fellow student in Paris and who would become in 1201 the archbishop of Lund.[30]

When the pope launched his call for a major crusade in August 1198, he was quite explicit in linking the misfortunes in the Holy Land to the sexual offenses of Latin Christian princes.[31] Cardinal Peter Capuano was commissioned to go to France to organize the crusade there; but an essential part of that effort was to force Philip and Richard to end their war and to force Philip to restore Ingeborg. The king was to be given a month to accept her, and the legate was to apply an interdict if the king resisted.[32] Both Philip and Richard were threatened with interdicts if they failed to make peace and give their support to the crusade.[33]

Cardinal Peter enjoyed some success at peace-making. A five year truce was agreed to in January 1199. But Richard went off to his southern provinces to fight other battles and caught a bolt from a

---

[28] Reg. 1:4.

[29] Reg. 1:172.

[30] Kloczowski, "Innocent III et les pays chrétiens autour de la mer Baltique," p. 165; Tore S. Nyberg, "Skandinavien und die Christianisierung des südöslichen Baltikums," *La cristianizzazione della Lituania: atti del Colloquio internazionale di storia ecclesiastica in occasione del VI centenario della Lituania cristiana (1387–1987)*, Roma, 24–26 giugno 1987. Ed. Paulius Rabikauskas, S.J. (Vatican, 1989), p. 239 and n. 16.

[31] Reg. 1:336.

[32] Reg. 1:345–348. For Peter Capuano's role as legate in France, see Werner Maleczek, *Petrus Capuanus* (Vienna, 1988), pp. 99–112.

[33] Reg. 1:355.

cross-bow. He died on 6 April, and everything was thrown into confusion, since it was not immediately clear who would succeed him,
and since Philip was an old hand at stirring up trouble within the
Angevin family. But Richard's brother John was soon in control,
and cardinal Peter managed to arrange still another truce between
the kings, first formed in October of 1199 and reaffirmed in January
and May of the following year.[34]

During that year-long effort at peace-making, Cardinal Peter had
remarkably little to say about his other charge, the restoration of
Ingeborg. He no doubt thought peace between the princes was more
important for the crusade. But with the truce of October 1199 in
place, he finally took action, perhaps prodded by a stern letter from
the pope to him and to all the clergy of France. Referring to Ingeborg,
the pope said that he must provide justice for those seeking it; he
must apply the hot iron to the wound.[35] A synod was summoned to
Dijon in December 1199, and the king made sure that it was well
attended, counting on the eighty or so prelates to head off the worst.
But Philip was clearly not going to restore Ingeborg as queen and
wife, so Peter placed France under interdict—although he prudently
waited until he was safely out of Dijon and the king's territory to
do so. It was declared in Vienne on 13 January 1200.[36]

Most of the bishops temporized, sending excuses to Rome. Those
who immediately observed the interdict, the bishops of Paris, Senlis,
Soissons, Amiens, and Arras, saw their churches and their possessions confiscated.[37] According to the Biographer, the king asked his
uncle the archbishop whether the pope was right, whether the annulment the archbishop had declared was worthless. The archbishop
admitted that it was. Philip responded, "Then you are a fool and a
dolt for having granted it!"[38]

*   *   *

In the summer of 1200, a new legate was dispatched to France.
Cardinal Octavian, one of Innocent's most trusted emissaries, was

---

[34] Maleczek, *Petrus Capuanus*, pp. 104–105.
[35] Reg. 2:188 (197).
[36] Maleczek, *Petrus Capuanus*, p. 108 and fn. 74.
[37] *Gesta*, PL 214:xcviii–xcix = Gress-Wright, pp. 73–74.
[38] *Gesta*, PL 214:c = Gress-Wright, p. 75.

charged with settling the matter of the king's marriage to Ingeborg and with promoting the crusade, the first being the prerequisite of the second. The results of the interdict had been traumatic. The bishops who observed the interdict were troubled physically, those who did not were troubled spiritually. At the very least, they had to worry about punishment from the pope. In fact, the failure of the bishop of Auxerre to observe the interdict was later to cost him the chance to be archbishop of Sens.[39] All the prelates who failed to observe the interdict were suspended from their offices and later had to make the long trek to Rome to have the suspensions lifted. That included the archbishop of Rheims and the bishops of Chartres, Orléans, Meaux, Auxerre, Noyons, and Beauvais.[40] Ordinary Christians found the church doors closed to their religious needs. Consequently, when Octavian arrived, there was hopeful anticipation that he would be able to solve the marriage problem, make peace between the king and his clergy, and provide once again spiritual solace to the faithful.

Precisely what happened after Octavian's arrival in France was reported to Innocent in decidedly different tones by people who were there. The bishops of Paris, Soissons, Troyes, Châlons-sur-Marne, and Chartres, as well as the archbishop of Rheims, were ecstatic. They reported that they had seen a virtual miracle. After all the suffering caused by the interdict, the king had now received the legate graciously; and at Octavian's instigation, Philip had agreed to accept Ingeborg as queen, to abandon his mistress, and to restore the churches and churchmen he had attacked. The interdict had been lifted. They acknowledged that the king had not agreed to live with Ingeborg as wife, despite their and the legate's best efforts, but he had at least put aside his mistress, restored Ingeborg to regal status, and was going to accept a judicial procedure provided by the pope to settle the marriage question.[41]

Philip was a clever and calculating man, but he was also emotional and unpredictable.[42] It may be that the legate and other clergy had convinced him that his violence against bishops was endangering his salvation; it may be that his tears of repentance were genuine. But the marriage was another matter, as was clear from the very

---

[39] Pott. 1043.
[40] *Gesta*, PL 214:ciii = Gress-Wright, p. 78.
[41] Reg. 3:13–14.
[42] Bautier, "Philippe Auguste: la personnalité du roi," pp. 32–58.

different story sent to Rome by Ingeborg. She complained bitterly
to the pope that she was still being kept in isolation, that the king
had agreed to consider her as queen for only seven months, and
that the king's promise not to dismiss her without judgment of the
clergy was good for only six months.[43]

The letter from Octavian himself filled out more details, describing with some enthusiasm how well he had been received by the
king.[44] But Innocent could tell that the cardinal had cut some cor-
ners. The precise charge had been that Octavian could lift the interdict only if the king would expel his mistress from the kingdom and
also restore the queen to her royal dignity, so that she could move
about freely and be received as queen by the prelates and princes.
In fact, however, Agnes had been removed from royal estates but
was still not too far away in the kingdom, and Ingeborg's circumstances were only slightly improved. The castle to which she had
been led had been a customary residence for former queens, but it
was still not Paris or some other city where she could be received
properly as queen.

Innocent had also told Octavian that, once the interdict was lifted,
he was to make a prolonged and sustained effort to persuade the
king to accept Ingeborg fully as wife. Only after this effort had failed
was he to give the king six months to begin legal proceedings against
the legitimacy of the marriage. That prescribed sequence had not
been followed. The pope wrote dryly, "Just how diligent and how
frequent were your warnings and exhortations, we leave for you to
decide, since on the very day, practically the very hour, at which
the restitution was made and the sentence of interdict was relaxed,
you assigned to the parties the time within which the case was to
be pursued." Innocent reassured Octavian of his love and support,
but he left no doubt that the original conditions must be fulfilled.
It would be tragic for the reputation of the Apostolic See, he said,
if "the mountains would strain and give birth to a mouse."[45]

Ingeborg was never fully accepted by the king, but the death of
Philip's mistress Agnes in August of 1201 removed the most humiliating symbol of Ingeborg's position. The death also made it easier

---

[43] Reg. 3:11, 16.
[44] Reg. 3:15.
[45] Reg. 3:16.

for the pope to make peace with Philip. The queen no longer had a rival, and the king was no longer jeopardizing the crusade by challenging God with his illicit union. At Philip's request, Innocent legitimized the king's children by Agnes. But the matter remained a minor irritant for many years. Philip continued to seek an annulment and he did not really care what the justification would be. He sought it "on the basis of affinity, or of witchcraft, or because of her entering a religious order, or for any other reasonable cause by which marriages are customarily dissolved." Innocent continued to protest that he was powerless to annul the marriage without due process and a legitimate reason.[46]

By late 1202, Philip had not accepted Ingeborg, and the good relations between King John and Philip Augustus had come to an end. Philip began an all-out effort to drive his rival from the continent.[47]

* * *

Like great lords elsewhere, the lay and ecclesiastical princes of Germany jostled one another for territory and dominance, often forming themselves into two major alliances, the Welfs concentrated in the north and the Hohenstaufen group concentrated in the south. But their fortunes were very much complicated by their connection to one of the strangest institutions in European history, the medieval Roman empire. Four hundred years before the accession of Innocent, another pope had welcomed a "king of the Franks" in Rome and had placed a crown on his head, while those present proclaimed him to be the "emperor of the Romans." The pope had done so because he needed a protector from enemies in Italy, and Charlemagne seemed the most promising candidate for that role. Innocent never tired of saying that the "business of the empire" belonged to the pope in its origin and in its purpose, *principaliter et finaliter*, because the Roman church had transferred the empire from Greece to the west for the defense of the papacy and because the emperor always received his imperial crown from the pope.[48]

---

[46] Raymonde Foreville, *Le Pape Innocent III et la France* (Stuttgart, 1992), pp. 302–3.
[47] W. L. Warren, *King John* (Berkeley, 1978), pp. 73–76.
[48] See for example Innocent's letter to the princes of Germany, RNI, no. 31, p. 97.

In the following centuries, Charlemagne's Frankish empire had been fragmented, and the title came to be associated with the eastern part, the kingdom of the Germans, rather than the western part, modern France. This peculiar empire, later to be known as the Holy Roman Empire, had ill-defined boundaries and ill-defined authority. The traditional way a man obtained the title was to be elected king of the Germans by the major secular and ecclesiastical princes of Germany. He was then crowned king of the Germans by the archbishop of Cologne at Aachen. At that point, he would begin to call himself king of the Romans and could proceed to Rome to be crowned emperor of the Romans by the pope.

The two emperors Innocent had known before his election, Frederick Barbarossa and Henry VI, considered themselves to be in no way dependent on the papacy. They were Roman emperors, after all, and they expected to dominate Rome and Italy. Henry's accession to the Sicilian throne as well made that goal all the easier. Both men treated with disdain the claims of the popes to be independent rulers of the papal Patrimony in central Italy. They expected to dominate Italian prelates, including the popes, just as they dominated German prelates. For the popes of the Gregorian tradition, this practice was the worst example of a perverted system wherein laymen chose and gave direction to priests. The popes, who had once seen the emperor as the principal protector of papal independence, had come to see him as the principal threat. Some forty years before, a former curial official had succinctly expressed the papal attitude: "the Germans were always most treacherous to the papacy and ready to oppress it on the slightest pretext."[49]

But the hand of God had given Innocent an unforeseen opportunity. The dreaded Henry VI died, the man who had united the German, imperial, and Sicilian crowns in his own person. He left a two-year old as his successor. Innocent made the most of that opportunity. In Italy, there was wide-spread revulsion among Italians against their German rulers, and Innocent was able to replace German princes in central Italy with his own representatives. He obtained from Queen Constance, the infant's mother, important agreements

---

[49] John of Salisbury, *Memoirs of the Papal Court*, translation and commentary by Marjorie Chibnall (London, 1956), p. 76. For the policies of Frederick I and Henry VI, see Horst Fuhrmann, *Germany in the High Middle Ages, c. 1050–1200*, trans. Timothy Reuter (Cambridge, 1986), pp. 135–186.

about the future of the kingdom of Sicily. Both the pope and the queen wanted to end once and for all the German imperial connection to southern Italy and Sicily, so when the three-year old was crowned on 17 May 1198, it was not as king of the Romans, the preliminary title of the emperor of the Romans, but as king of Sicily. Constance reaffirmed that her son held his kingdom as a fief from the pope, seeing this traditional arrangement as the most likely barrier to imperial claims. She even abandoned long-held privileges of the Sicilian crown that had circumscribed papal authority in the kingdom, namely, the right of the crown to intervene in episcopal elections, to exclude papal legates, to prevent appeals to the papacy, and to control clerical councils within the kingdom.[50] Before she died, on 27 November 1198, she also named the pope as the boy's guardian.[51]

Before his death, Henry had persuaded the princes of Germany to swear their loyalty to this child who was to succeed him as German king and Roman emperor; and the child's uncle Duke Philip of Swabia (Henry VI's younger brother) did try to hold together German support for his nephew. It was soon clear, however, that Hohenstaufen interests could only be defended by an adult king, present in Germany. The Welf enemies of the Hohenstaufen, led by Adolf, archbishop of Cologne, began to plan immediately for the election of an adult of their own choosing. Faced with that possibility, on 8 March 1198, Philip of Swabia permitted himself to be elected king of the Germans by an assembly of princes meeting at Mühlhausen in the upper valley of the Rhine. The Welf princes then met at Cologne with representatives of Richard the Lion-Hearted; and there, on 9 June, they elected Otto of Brunswick. Otto was the youngest son of the former Welf leader Henry the Lion, duke of Saxony and Bavaria. Otto's second main asset was that he was a favorite of his uncle, Richard the Lion-Hearted, who had made him count of Poitou in France.

The Welf princes saw in Otto, together with his formidable uncle Richard, a likely barrier to Hohenstaufen ambition, and Richard saw Otto and the Welfs as a valuable counterweight against Philip

[50] *Gesta*, PL:214:xxxii = Gress-Wright, p. 16; Loud, "Royal Control of the Church," pp. 147-159.

[51] Van Cleve, *Emperor Frederick*, pp. 36-37.

Augustus. This configuration of a Welf-Angevin/English alliance against a Hohenstaufen-French alliance had turned up before and it was to last for years.[52] It created an exceedingly difficult diplomatic situation for the papacy, since the popes generally saw Welf candidates as less threatening to their position in Italy while they also saw French kings and nobles as papal protectors and the mainstay of the crusades. The problem was to stay on good terms with each side without alienating the other.

Innocent had played no part in producing rival candidates in Germany; but the double election gave him the chance to try to extract guarantees from the candidates. Before he crowned a candidate, he wanted promises that the emperor would not try to regain the Regno (the kingdom of Sicily) and that he would acknowledge the papal claims to central Italy. Innocent had every reason to believe that Philip would continue the Hohenstaufen policies he had implemented as a collaborator with his brother Henry VI, and that expectation was confirmed when Otto agreed to Innocent's terms and Philip refused. By refusing to give his support to Philip, Innocent enabled Otto and his allies to remain contenders. The impasse served to keep both candidates out of Italy, but the civil war in Germany meant that his crusade would get little help there and that Innocent would be charged with trying to destroy the empire.[53]

Late in 1198, however, the full promise of the opportunity seemed to escape Innocent's grasp. In August, German power in Italy had seemed so small a threat that Innocent had encouraged Italian knights of the Regno to take the cross and depart for the Holy Land.[54] But then a Hohenstaufen champion emerged in Italy to threaten the pope's plans. Markward of Anweiler, one of Henry VI's most trusted lieutenants, had been made duke of Ravenna and the Romagna and margrave of Ancona. When Constance died in November, Markward moved south, gathering together those Germans still in Italy and declaring himself the defender of the Hohenstaufen cause. Innocent levied excommunication and interdict against him and tried to organize all of Italy to oppose him. He sent an army under Cardinal John to take Markward's lands to the north, and chided the men

---

[52] Ibid., pp. 28–33.
[53] RNI, no. 1, p. 4.
[54] Reg. 1:343–344.

of southern Italy for being faint-hearted.[55] He called on Tuscany to provide two thousand knights, plus foot soldiers and archers. He even offered those who opposed Markward the same benefits given crusaders—in effect, proclaiming a crusade against a Christian prince, as Celestine III had done against the king of León.[56] He said that since Markward was preventing them from going on crusade, they aided the crusading effort by fighting him.[57]

In mid-1199, Markward entered into an uneasy peace with Innocent, who removed the excommunication and urged Markward to take the cross as penance for his sins—and to get him out of Italy.[58] But in the fall of 1199, Markward abandoned all pretense of making peace with the pope. In October, he crossed over to Sicily, and Innocent again tried to rally the forces of Italy against Markward ("another Saladin") and the Germans.[59] This crisis was one of the things keeping Innocent "busier than usual," as he remarked in a letter at the end of January of 1200.[60]

Markward's successes conformed to similar Hohenstaufen good fortunes in Germany. In the spring of 1199, Innocent informed the princes that in view of their inability to present a single candidate, he would have to step in to settle the matter.[61] But at almost the same moment, the death of Richard the Lion-Hearted deprived the Welfs of a major source of support. In May, a formidable group of princes and prelates sent word from Germany that they supported Philip of Swabia and Markward his agent in Italy. The pope's claimed right to pass judgement on the two candidates was not accepted and he was warned to avoid injuring the rights of the empire and to give his support and good will to Philip and to Markward.[62]

During 1200, two more major players emerged in the Regno. In the spring Walter of Brienne, a French aristocrat who had married

---

[55] He earlier said that the people of Sicily had been corrupted by "effeminate leisure and too much peace" (Reg. 1:26).

[56] Elizabeth Kennan, "Innocent III and the First Political Crusade: A Comment on the Limitations of Papal Power," *Traditio* 27 (1971): 231–249.

[57] Reg. 1:554–9 (557–65).

[58] Reg. 2:158 (167), 159 (168).

[59] Reg. 2:212 (221), 217 (226), 268 (280).

[60] Reg. 1:543 (546), p. 787.

[61] RNI, no. 2; Tillmann, *Pope Innocent III*, p. 111. For a translation of this letter, see C. R. Cheney, "The Letters of Pope Innocent III," *Medieval Texts and Studies* (Oxford, 1973), pp. 21–20.

[62] RNI, no. 14; Tillmann, *Pope Innocent III*, p. 112.

a Sicilian princess, arrived in Rome seeking papal aid in reclaiming certain principalities in southern Italy on behalf of his wife. Backing Walter was a risk, since the princess's ancestry might be used to claim young Frederick's crown; but desperate for help in the face of Markward's successes, Innocent agreed. Walter of Brienne returned to Champagne to recruit troops and raise money. He mortgaged all of his lands to the count of Champagne for seven hundred pounds of silver in April of 1201 and was back in Italy in May.[63]

In the meantime, the Sicilian court, dominated by its chancellor, Walter of Palear, decided that they would be better off dealing with Markward than with the pope and his French ally. They had, after all, risen to their comfortable position under Hohenstaufen rule, and the chancellor was furious at the pope for having blocked his chance to be archbishop of Palermo.[64] In the fall of 1200, they agreed that Markward would control all of the island of Sicily except Palermo (where the child Frederick remained) while Walter of Palear would control the mainland part of the Regno. But the next year, Markward took the last bite of Sicily; he captured Palermo and the six-year-old King Frederick in November of 1201. The year ended with Walter of Palear dominating southern Italy, Markward dominating the island, and neither much disposed to pay any attention to the pope.[65]

Despite his role as guardian and feudal overlord of the boy-king, Innocent was never able to control events in the Regno. Even the death of Markward in the fall of 1202 changed very little. Others stepped in. One German, William Capparone, assumed control of the young king and Sicily; another, Dipold of Acerra, duelled with Walter of Palear and Walter of Brienne on the mainland, until he finally managed to kill the latter in June of 1205.[66] On the other hand, the turmoil in the kingdom of Sicily did give Innocent something of a free hand in central Italy.

The turmoil in Germany had the same effect. Neither Philip of Swabia nor Otto of Brunswick had an impregnable claim to suc-

---

[63] Theodore Evergates, trans. and ed., *Feudal Society in Medieval France: Documents from the County of Champagne* (Philadelphia, 1993), pp. 83–84; *Gesta*, PL 214:xlvi–xlvii = Gress-Wright, pp. 26–27.

[64] *Gesta*, PL 214:liii = Gress-Wright, p. 36.

[65] Van Cleve, *Emperor Frederick*, pp. 41–49.

[66] Ibid., pp. 49–51.

ceed Henry VI as king of the Germans; the election of each had
been slightly irregular. Indeed, there was no clear, generally accepted
standard for deciding what was a legitimate election. In fact, in 1196
Henry VI had almost persuaded an assembly of princes to abandon
elections altogether in favor of a hereditary monarchy.[67] In any case,
Philip had much more support among the German princes and had
the greater military strength; but he was unwilling to promise Innocent
that he would leave alone the Patrimony and the Regno. Otto had
less support, and probably for that reason was willing to promise
that papal claims would be respected.[68] During the year 1200, there
was sporadic warfare and intense diplomatic activity in Germany, as
the rival candidates and their allies sought the advantage. Emissaries went to and from Rome, with Innocent indirectly promoting the
candidacy of Otto, the weaker but more agreeable candidate. Around
the end of 1200, the curia produced an internal policy paper in
which all the pros and cons for Otto, Philip, and young Frederick
were reviewed. The memorandum concluded that Philip was altogether unacceptable and that the papal legate should try to get the
princes either to agree on a "worthy person" or to submit to papal
judgement. If they failed to do either in the very near future, the
pope would declare for Otto.[69]

In March, 1201, Innocent named Otto as emperor elect of the
Romans—to the great annoyance of the king of France.[70] Two cardinal legates were dispatched north to organize support for the decision in France and Germany, and dozens of papal letters were sent
to all the princes, prelates, and other significant people in Germany
and the Empire. The kings of England and France were notified
and urged to support Otto. Innocent claimed the right to make this
decision because the popes had responsibility "principaliter et finaliter."
He also reviewed the many sins of Philip of Swabia (who was still
excommunicate for earlier actions in Italy) and his Hohenstaufen
predecessors.[71] The matter, though, was far from settled. In 1202,

---

[67] Benjamin Arnold, *Princes and Territories in Medieval Germany* (Cambridge, 1991),
pp. 29-30.
[68] RNI, no. 3.
[69] RNI, no. 29. English translation in Brian Pullan, ed. and trans., *Sources for the
History of Medieval Europe* (Oxford, 1966), pp. 194-200.
[70] RNI, no. 63.
[71] RNI, nos. 32-49.

the lay and ecclesiastical supporters of Philip argued forcefully that the pope had no business in the imperial election; Innocent argued with equal vigor that he did.[72] The pope could obstruct the success of Philip by refusing to approve and crown him; but he could do little to advance the cause of Otto, especially after 1204, when Otto's closest allies began to abandon him, and after his uncle and ally, King John, lost a large part of his possessions in France.[73] For years the stalemate continued.

* * *

When Innocent thought of the major regions of Latin Christendom, he would not find anything inherently confusing about the political structure of England, France, or even Germany, however difficult the diplomacy might be. In each of those regions, there was only one kingdom, although there were occasional disputes about who the king was. In Spain, however, there were five Christian kingdoms and five kings when Innocent became pope, although the title of "emperor of all Spain" had been used in the past and might be resurrected again.[74] The kings of Navarre and Portugal were named Sancho (VII and I), the kings of Castile and León were named Alfonso (VIII and IX). By way of welcome relief, the king of Aragon was named Pedro (his father and brother were named Alfonso). Since the territories of these kings had for the most part been recovered from Muslim occupation in only the last century or two, the boundaries were fluid; and the intermarrying and warfare among these ruling houses resulted in their merging and separating like flights of starlings.

Despite a disastrous defeat in 1195 at the hands of the Muslim Almohads, the Spanish rulers continued to exert more energy fighting one another than fighting the infidel. They commonly made alliances with the Muslims. Celestine III had been so frustrated by this behavior that, in 1196, he not only excommunicated the most troublesome of the kings, Alfonso IX of León, but in effect declared a

---

[72] RNI, nos. 61, 62. An English translation of both documents is in Pullan, *Sources*, pp. 201–205.

[73] Tillmann, *Pope Innocent III*, pp. 117–130; RNI, nos. 32, 33, 52, 52.

[74] See Joseph F. O'Callaghan, "Innocent III and the Kingdoms of Castile and Leon," in *Pope Innocent III and His World*, pp. 317–336, and Antonio García y García, "Innocent III and the Kingdom of Castile," ibid., pp. 337–350.

crusade against him. In his own way, Alfonso tried to oblige. He made peace with his main rival the king of Castile by marrying the king's daughter, Berenguela.[75] She was, however, related to him within the prohibited degree (the second marriage of this sort that Alfonso had attempted) and the marriage was condemned by Celestine. Excommunication and interdict were levied against the king and his kingdom, although no one paid much attention to them. The invalid marriage remained for Innocent a provocation to God and a reason for Christendom's failures against the infidel. As in France, competition among princes and marital sins obstructed the crusade.

It was into this swirl of grasping and intractable princes that Innocent sent, not one of his most prestigious cardinals, but the monk Brother Rainerius.

As mentioned above, Innocent made extraordinary demands on this man. In April of 1198, the inexperienced pope told Rainerius to use excommunication and interdict to break up the illicit marriage of the king of León. He was to force the king of Navarre to respect his truce with the king of Castile and to return his occupied castles. He was to compel all the Spanish kings into an alliance against the Saracens and was to supervise their efforts. He was to collect a papal census (tax) being withheld by the king of Portugal.[76] At the same time, Innocent informed all the lay and ecclesiastical authorities of southern France that Rainerius and his fellow Cistercian Guido had been commissioned to eliminate heresy in the area.[77]

In June, another letter was sent to Rainerius, telling him to impose a peace on the kings of Portugal and Castile.[78] Innocent had already given Rainerius complete authority over Spanish prelates; in October, he authorized him to reform any churches in need of reform, wherever he might find them.[79] Rainerius actually persuaded King Sancho of Portugal to pay the census owed to the papacy; but Innocent wrote the monk in December that the payment was inadequate and that he should insist on the right amount.[80] Two weeks later, he

---

[75] Demetrio Mansilla, "Inocencio III y los reinos hispanos," *Anthologica Annua* 2 (1954): 18–19.

[76] Reg. 1:92, 93, 99.

[77] Reg. 1:94.

[78] Reg. 1:249.

[79] Reg. 1:395.

[80] Reg. 1:448, 449.

charged him, together with the archbishop of Narbonne, to supervise the resignation and replacement of the bishop of Carcasonne
and to make every effort to drive heretics from the province of
Narbonne.[81] Later, when reports reached Rome that the poor monk's
health was failing, Innocent relieved him of some of his duties.[82] It
is small wonder that when Rainerius finally made his way back to
Italy, he decided to live out the rest of his days as a hermit.[83]

Rainerius found that Alfonso of Castile was willing to take back
his daughter, but that Alfonso of León was not willing to give her
up. So Rainerius applied the excommunication and interdict as
instructed. The following spring, in 1199, a delegation from Spain
arrived in Rome, led by the archbishop of Toledo and the bishops
of Palencia and of Zamora. They discovered that Innocent would
scarcely listen to them on the matter of the marriage, so they concentrated on having the interdict lifted. It was, they said, only giving comfort to heretics and Saracens and jeopardizing the souls of
Christians. (They also said that since the laity were not making contributions to the clergy, the latter were forced to enter the service
of Jews to make a living.)[84] Rumor had it that the king's delegation
was authorized to reward a favorable response with contributions for
a crusade amounting to twenty thousand marks of silver and a force
of two hundred knights for at least a year.[85]

Innocent budged only slightly. He made the interdict perambula-
tory; that is, it applied only where the king, queen, and their major
advisers were present.[86] Unfortunately, Innocent's two goals of making peace among the kings and ending the invalid marriage were at
odds. Alfonso and Berenguela had married in the first place to settle
a border dispute between León and Castile. Several border castles
had been given by Alfonso to his bride as her marriage portion. As
long as they were married, the castles were neutral, belonging to a
woman who was the wife of one king and the daughter of the other.
But when the marriage finally ended (four children later in 1204)
and Berenguela returned to Castile, Alfonso of León went to war to

---

[81] Reg. 1:494.
[82] Reg. 5:73 (74).
[83] Frances Andrews, *The Early Humiliati* (Cambridge, 1999), pp. 95–96.
[84] Reg. 2:72 (75).
[85] Mansillo, "Inocencio III y los reinos hispanos," pp. 21–22, citing R. de Hovedon.
[86] Reg. 2:72 (75).

regain the castles. The peace that Innocent sought was not achieved until 1209. Then the combined efforts of the pope and prelates, together with the diplomatic skill of Berenguela, produced a peace treaty that helped make possible the great Christian victory at Las Navas de Tolosa in 1212.[87]

*   *   *

When Innocent called for the crusade, he did not specify a route. If the crusaders chose the overland route to the Holy Land, they would pass through two great Christian kingdoms, the kingdom of Hungary and the Byzantine Empire. Relations between Constantinople and the popes had been awkward for many years. On the one hand, the whole crusading movement had at least begun as a response to a call for help from the Byzantine emperor, and the Byzantines were still crucial allies in the war against the Muslims. On the other, Innocent considered the Greeks schismatics. Papal legates and Greek prelates had hurled excommunications at each other more than a century earlier; and Latin crusaders had never gotten along very well with the Greeks.

The king of Hungary, like the king of France, was historically closely allied to the papacy, and Innocent sought to continue that relationship. In the first year of Innocent's papacy, King Imre sought the pope's help against his rebellious brother Duke Andrew, and Innocent tried to help, though with little effect.[88]

But even if the king of Hungary and the Byzantine emperor had been perfectly disposed to aid the crusade, they could not really guarantee safe passage to a crusading army. Nearly all the Balkans was theoretically subject to one or the other of these rulers, but in fact the mountainous terrain and the diversity of peoples, with different languages and liturgies, have made the area dangerous through most of its history.

A few years before Innocent's election, the Bulgarians had rebelled against the Byzantine state and established an independent kingdom. To the west, along the east coast of the Adriatic, was a string of principalities all theoretically subject to the king of Hungary. That subjection meant very little. The northernmost principality was the

---

[87] Mansilla, "Inocencio III y los reinos hispanos," pp. 25–28.
[88] Reg. 1:270–271.

duchy of Croatia. That area, together with Slavonia farther east, was ruled by Duke Andrew, the younger brother of King Imre of Hungary. He had taken it by force of arms against the king's will and gave his brother only formal allegiance. To the south of Croatia was Bosnia, ruled by Kulin as "ban." He also was theoretically subject to the king of Hungary, but the subjection meant nothing. Farther south were Hum and then Zeta (or Duklja, or Dioclea—later Montenegro). Both were ruled by Serbian families, Greek Christian, theoretically under the "Grand Zupan" of Serbia, who was in turn theoretically under Byzantine authority. Little is known about Hum, but the ruler of Zeta was Vukan, who called himself king of Dioclea and Dalmatia. Just as Duke Andrew had created a principality for himself in defiance of his brother the king of Hungary, Vukan declared his independence of his brother Stefan "Grand Zupan" of Serbia, and then began to look around for allies. Hungary and Rome were two obvious places to look.[89]

Late in 1198, Vukan's emissaries arrived in Rome offering submission to the pope and asking that papal legates be sent to reform the church in Vukan's region—which probably meant the offer of switching allegiance from Greek to Latin Christianity. Innocent dispatched two legates, John of Casamari, a papal chaplain and Cistercian monk, and the papal subdeacon Simon. At the same time, he sent a number of letters into the area, including one to Vukan's brother the Grand Zupan, urging all to support the legates. He sent separate letters to the wives of both brothers, apparently seeing these women as being influential in the religious choices of their husbands.[90] The overture of Vukan clearly opened for Innocent the possibility of winning over substantial parts of Greek Christianity to Roman allegiance.

In the late summer of 1199, the two legates returned to Rome. Their mission had been a spectacular success. The Grand Zupan had merely sent a courteous reply, but Vukan, together with the archbishop of Antivari, could not have been more eager to cooperate with the legates. They had called a council of the province of Antivari where all the bishops of the province had agreed to a reform

---

[89] John V. A. Fine, Jr., *The Late Medieval Balkans* (Ann Arbor, 1987), pp. 17–48.
[90] Reg. 1:525–526 (527, 528).

program dictated by the legates. Ecclesiastical benefices were not to be sold, priests were to get rid of their wives, no violence was to be visited upon the persons of clergy, nor were any clergy to be required to appear before secular courts, especially for trial by hot iron or water. Clergy were not to receive churches or clerical benefices from the hands of laymen. Rules on consanguinity were to be observed, and wives were not to be dismissed without judgment of the church. Men were to be ordained priests only if they met the legal requirements: they must be thirty years old and of legitimate birth. Whatever their intentions, the archbishop and six suffragan bishops signed the document which the legates bore to Rome.[91]

With the help of his Latin advisers, Vukan himself sent an effusive and fawning letter to the pope. The holy and wholesome preaching of the legates had illumined his kingdom as the sun illumines the world. He suggested, on what grounds it is not clear, that he was in some way related to the pope. He also presented himself as the champion of orthodoxy, warning the pope that Ban Kulin of Bosnia and his family had become heretics, along with ten thousand others. The king of Hungary had sent some to Rome to be examined by the pope, but they had returned, according to Vukan, with forged letters of good standing. Vukan helpfully suggested that the pope urge the king of Hungary to expel them.[92] Innocent did in fact give that advice to the king of Hungary,[93] but Kulin seems to have preserved his reputation for orthodoxy and his rule until his death in 1204.[94]

In 1202, Vukan even succeeded in replacing his brother Stefan as Grand Zupan, raising the possibility of even greater expansion of the pope's authority, but it came to very little. By the time of Innocent's death, Vukan and his kingdom had disappeared and Stefan was once more in control of the entire area.[95]

* * *

---

[91] Reg. 2:169 (178).

[92] Reg. 2:167 (176).

[93] Pott. 1142 (11 October 1200).

[94] The editors of Reg. 2 follow other scholars in saying that Ban Kulin had made Bogomilism the state religion in 1199 (Reg. 2:167, p. 325, n. 9), whereas Fine asserts Catholic Kulin's orthodoxy (*Late Medieval Balkans,* p. 47).

[95] Fine, *Late Medieval Balkans,* pp. 47–50.

When Innocent celebrated the second anniversary of his coronation on 22 February 1200, he could look back on a great deal of diplomatic activity, of papal messengers dispatched to all parts of Christendom, but the achievements were modest, to say the least. The kingdom of France was under interdict; and the king of Navarre, the king of Norway, the de facto ruler of the island of Sicily (Markward), the leading candidate to be German king and Roman Emperor (Philip of Swabia)—all of these were under papal excommunication. The crusade called for in August 1198 had not materialized. Still, things were stirring in the provinces, in the hearts of Christians for whom the call to crusade was powerful. Fulk of Neuilly, a popular preacher in the vicinity of Paris, had expanded his message from moral reform, from attacks on concubinage and usury, and had taken up the message of the crusade. Fulk's eloquence and the miracles attributed to him touched every level of society. The poor who took the cross to redeem the Holy Land and save their souls would offer very little to the effort, but crusading fervor also reached the great nobles of France. In November of 1199, the count of Champagne hosted a large assembly of aristocrats gathered in Ecry-sur-Aisne for the pleasures of a tournament—an entertainment strongly disapproved of by the official church. Some pious spark became a blaze, as one after another took the cross: the young counts of Champagne and Blois were followed by dozens from their entourage. The tournament in Champagne had been held at the end of November of 1199, so word may have reached Innocent by the time of his second anniversary, 22 February 1200. The very next day, Ash Wednesday, Count Baldwin of Flanders took the cross in Bruges, and in the following months, news of other crusaders' vows were to reach Rome from France. Things had not been going very well, but at least the crusade was beginning to come to life.

CHAPTER FOUR

CURIA AND CITY (1200–1203)

It was a splendid scene. Before the pope stood Gerald of Wales on the one hand and on the other his rivals the messengers of the archbishop of Canterbury holding bundles of letters with dangling wax seals. The messengers proclaimed that the letters were testimonies against Gerald from all the prelates of England. Innocent called for pen and ink and said, "Thus do I cancel, discredit, and abrogate these testimonies." Then in French, he called Gerald forward and together with the cardinals consecrated him bishop of St. Davids. Gerald was then dressed in his episcopal garments, and, when they could find no crozier, the pope presented Gerald with his own. A splendid scene indeed, but it was, alas, only a dream reported by a friend while Gerald was studying at Paris.[1]

But years later, Gerald believed that the vision was about to come true. In the summer of 1199, at St. Davids on the barren and windswept coast of western Wales, he considered the dangerous course he had chosen. A tall, fiftyish archdeacon with great bushy eyebrows, a geographer, naturalist, moralist, historian, poet, a scholar who had studied at Paris, a courtier who had served in the courts of King Henry and Prince John, Gerald of Wales knew well the enemies who opposed him and the physical and political barriers that stood in his way. His aristocratic brother Philip of Barri was blunt in his warnings: Gerald was opposing himself to the archbishop of Canterbury, to the king—indeed to all of England.

Gerald had failed to achieve promotion in the English church, his first choice. He then became a belated champion of the Welsh church. He argued that St. Davids had been once and should be again a metropolitan church (archbishopric), not subject to the archbishop of Canterbury. The canons of St. Davids agreed, at least for the time being, and they elected him bishop; but King John and the archbishop of Canterbury were outraged that the election had proceeded at all without their permission or participation. Nor were

---

[1] *Giraldi Cambrensis Opera*, ed. J. S. Brewer, 1 (London, 1861), RS 21/1:170–1.

they going to tolerate a hint of Welsh separatism in the bishop of
St. Davids. Against all odds, Gerald resolved to take to the papal
curia two causes: his own election and the metropolitan status of St.
Davids. His brother Philip warned him that he should not expect
things to go any more smoothly than they had for the disciples of
Christ, who suffered chains and prisons and wounds and even death.
But, Philip told him, if he was truly moved by concern for the church
of St. Davids and not by earthly ambition, God would not desert him.

When earthly ambition and high ideals pursue the same objective, it is very difficult to separate the two. It was especially difficult
for a man as vain and as single-minded as Gerald. But encouraged
and consoled by his brother's counsel, Gerald set out in August of
1199, making his way across England to Sandwich and then across
the "Flemish Sea" to St. Omer. His sole companion, a canon of St.
Davids, fell ill there and had to be left behind, but he found two
more young men from St. Davids who were studying in St. Omer
and who were willing to accompany him for the sake of their Welsh
church. Because the count of Flanders at the time was an ally of
King John, making war against the king of France, Gerald had to
make a long detour to the east, through the "bristly and dreadful"
forest of the Ardennes, full of bandits and thieves. In Champagne
and Burgundy, he was back on public roads in the company of pilgrims and merchants. He crossed the Alps before the winter snows,
passed through Tuscany, and reached Rome and the curia in late
November, 1199, about three months after he had departed.

Gerald was graciously received by the pope, whom Gerald delighted
with an unusual gift, six volumes of works written by Gerald himself. Innocent kept the books at his side for nearly a month, showing them off to visitors and occasionally lending a volume to an
admiring cardinal. It was an appropriate gift for one Paris alumnus
to give another. Gerald told the pope that whereas others brought
money (libras), he brought books (libros).

About the same time, however, a messenger from Hubert Walter
the archbishop of Canterbury arrived, bearing letters against Gerald
for pope and cardinals. Some cleric who knew the purpose of the
letters managed to steal them and offered to sell them to Gerald.
Gerald had a look at one, but then was advised by John cardinal-
bishop of Albano to have nothing more to do with them. Gerald
returned the sample to the thief, who then sold the bundle back to
the original messenger. The case was beginning in something less
than a wholesome atmosphere.

Gerald was eager to get on with it, since expenses mounted with each passing day; but the Christmas season had begun, and Innocent suspended all consistory business until after the holy days. Finally, on 7 January 1200, the day after the Epiphany, the proceedings began with the reading of the archbishop's letter.[2]

* * *

Three times a week, Innocent sat in consistory with cardinals and clerks to hear cases that had come to the curia. He seemed to enjoy nothing more, and the enjoyment probably grew as his skill and knowledge of the law increased. Unlike the headstrong princes and unreliable prelates of Christendom, these cases could be clearly defined, could be seen as problems to be solved with reason and the skillful use of language. Here, the limitations on his power seemed less restricting. His authority was supreme, his interpretation became the law. Long-standing custom might here be abrogated if he found it "contrary to reason."[3] No one standing in his court was likely to defy him to his face. His skill at grasping the problems and at restating the arguments attracted a learned audience, whose respectful presence added to the pleasure. Visiting prelates were sometimes drawn into the process, as when the archbishop of Compostella and the bishop of Tortona, present on business, were recruited to serve as auditors in a case. They learned, at the same time, papal procedures and their own subordinate roles.[4]

There was, to be sure, something illusory about the experience, since the pope's decisions might or might not be implemented by the time they made their way back to where the case began. Months would pass, circumstances would change, and those determined to delay or avoid an unpleasant decision could often find a way to do so. But whatever their immediate impact, many of Innocent's decisions were to be binding on generations of Christians who had nothing to do with the original case. Collected as papal decretals, the

---

[2] *Giraldi*, 21/1:lxiv–lxxi, 117–120; Michael Richter, *Giraldus Cambrensis: The Growth of the Welsh Nation*, 2nd ed. (Aberystwyth, 1976), pp. 117–127 et passim. Much of the material included in this chapter about Gerald can be found in English translation in *The Autobiography of Giraldus Cambrensis*, ed. and trans. H. E. Butler (London, 1937). For an authoritative summary of the case, see Cheney, *Innocent III and England*, pp. 134–141. For a general account of the life of Gerald, see Robert Bartlett, *Gerald of Wales: 1146–1223* (Oxford, 1982).

[3] Reg. 1:462 = PL 214:433.

[4] *Gesta*, PL:214:lxxx–lxxxi = Gress-Wright, p. 61; Reg. 1:283.

decisions became church law that would be binding all the way into the twentieth century. Innocent had better reason than he could have imagined to take satisfaction in his consistory decisions.

Gerald of Wales was a more interesting suitor than most who appeared in the papal curia. Too narrowly focused to be a consummate courtier, he was nevertheless a man of learning and wit; and he had a great fund of gossip about important people in England. Innocent enjoyed his company, inviting him to spend evenings with him in the papal chambers. The jokes were sometimes at Gerald's expense—perhaps an irresistible temptation, given Gerald's pretensions—but Innocent seems to have felt a genuine affection for the archdeacon.

One evening when they were talking, Innocent called for the register in which all metropolitan churches were listed, together with their suffragan bishoprics. Innocent turned to the kingdom of the English and there found listed the suffragans of Canterbury. The churches of Wales, including St. Davids, were there, but they had been inserted separately in the rubrics. Somewhat derisively, Innocent said, "There, you see, the church of St. Davids is listed."

Gerald noted a grammatical difference and replied, "Yes, but not like the English suffragans, not in the accusative case."

"Good point," said the pope. "And there is one more thing going for you and your church. Things inserted like this in the register have been added only when there has been a transfer, from one kingdom to another or one metropolitan to another."

Gerald took this as evidence that the Welsh churches had originally been independent of Canterbury, that they had at some point been illegitimately transferred to Canterbury from their rightful place in the province of St. Davids.

The pope responded encouragingly, but cautiously, "Well, you know one thing: our register is not against you."

After further discussion, Innocent told him to put his arguments in writing. They would proceed as soon as representatives of the archbishop arrived.

Gerald had high hopes. The curia seemed friendly to him and to his cause. In one of his evening visits, Innocent greeted him by saying, "Come in, elect of St. Davids, come in." Gerald took that to be tantamount to official confirmation of his election; but then the pope smiled and told him that his casual manner of speaking was not to be mistaken for a serious confirmation. But after the archbishop's representatives arrived announcing that a second election to St. Davids had taken place and that there was now a rival candidate, Innocent assigned the question of the election to judges-delegate in England instead of deciding immediately in Gerald's favor. He was clearly not eager to antagonize the king and the archbishop simply on the word of a single Welsh archdeacon. Gravely disappointed, Gerald was convinced that the archbishop's bribery was at work throughout the curia.

In the hope of keeping alive his other cause, the metropolitan status of St. Davids, Gerald asked that a similar commission of judges-delegate be appointed for that; but Innocent said the evidence did not warrant such a step. Perhaps in an effort to console Gerald, the pope offered to appoint him as administrator of the diocese of St. Davids until the matter of the election was settled. To Innocent's annoyance, Gerald said that if he could not have the commission, he would not take the job of administrator. Later, when Gerald changed his mind and asked for a letter making him administrator, Innocent curtly told him, "You won't get now what you rejected earlier."

Gerald, the accomplished courtier when he chose to be, replied, "But my lord, if a father offers his son bread and the son insolently and foolishly refuses the gift, does that mean that the son is to be forever denied bread?" The pope relented.[5]

Gerald was allowed to search the papal registers for evidence to support his case for the metropolitan status of St. Davids. He was encouraged by what he found and by the continuing friendliness of the curia. In another of his evening visits to the pope, Innocent greeted him as "archbishop." Gerald didn't notice, thinking he had said "archdeacon."

Cardinal Hugolino, who was sitting with Innocent, said to Gerald, "Didn't you hear what the pope called you?"

Gerald said, "Archdeacon?"

"On the contrary," Hugolino said, "he greeted you with the name archbishop." Gerald prostrated himself and kissed the pope's feet, saying that the word in the mouth of so great a pontiff must be prophetic.

---

[5] *Giraldi*, 21/3:183–184.

It was a rather cruel joke, given Gerald's obsessive pursuit of both the office and the metropolitan status; but Gerald made the most of it by tying the pope's greatness to the accuracy of his prophecies. In any case, having examined the evidence Gerald had discovered, Innocent did agree to set up a commission on the status of St. Davids and also agreed to begin canonization procedures for a Welsh holy man later to be known as St. Caradoc. When Gerald made his way back to England in the summer of 1200, he could feel that he was at least holding his own.[6]

* * *

The concrete results of Gerald's visit were a set of papal documents dispatched for England. The pieces of parchment that moved back and forth between the curia and other areas could be objects of great power. In earlier centuries, the order and stability of communities depended upon memory. The rights of individuals, the rights of families, the ways in which people could expect to be treated by others—all this was regulated by remembrance of the way things had always been done. But by the time Innocent became pope, European society was changing rapidly. The regulating power of writing had always been present in the Bible and in the liturgy, but in the twelfth century, written documents were gaining on memory as the standard regulating society. Lay and ecclesiastical princes were sending out written documents that changed custom; clerics in the service of those princes were poring over texts of Roman and canon law for guidance on how to do things, regardless of custom; towns as well as monasteries were having their rights secured in written form, since memory was not enough. By Innocent's day, even ordinary people tried to protect their rights by having them enshrined in charters.

A graph showing the increasing number of surviving letters from the courts of the popes, the kings of England, the kings of France during the twelfth century is a steeply rising cliff. The amount of wax used to seal documents in the English royal chancery was to increase tenfold in the mid-thirteenth century.[7] Government bureau-

---

[6] *Giraldi*, 21/3:165–184.
[7] Michael T. Clanchy, *From Memory to Written Record: England, 1066–1307* (Cambridge MA, 1979), pp. 41–46.

cracies had begun, those great machines for producing paper—although animal skin, parchment, was the preferred material for these documents until the late thirteenth century.

* * *

The proceedings in Innocent's curia and the carefully framed documents that left his chancery were expressions of order and rational control in welcome contrast to life outside in the city of Rome itself. There, peace and stability were preserved with difficulty because Roman citizens were pulled in two directions. On the one hand, they could not forget the republican ideals that had first made the city great in antiquity and that were very much in style in the towns of twelfth-century Europe, especially in Italy. In this light, Rome should be ruled by her citizens, not by a pontiff, no matter how supreme. On the other hand, the papacy was a source of prestige and wealth for these same citizens. It was not in their interest to weaken or humiliate the pope or to drive him out of Rome. Nor could they ignore the unpleasant fact that republican government often meant great instability, government by this or that faction at the expense of the others. So around these rival ideals, groups rallied, seeking popular support for their own factional or familial goals.

Clearly Innocent had swung the balance far in the pope's favor. In previous years, Rome had fluctuated between an urban government of only one senator and one of multiple senators. After his consecration, Innocent arranged that there would be only one senator, appointed by a mediator, who was in turn appointed by the pope.[8] Innocent extended his authority over territories around the city, particularly Sabina and Marittima, that had recently been under the city's administration. There is no sure way to decide from history who had the greater rights in these matters, on whose side justice lay. The political history of urban and papal government had been fluid enough through the centuries to provide precedents and arguments for many different positions. But John Pierleone and John Capoccio, two former senators, could reasonably argue that Innocent

---

[8] For a brief history of the Roman Senate during this period, see Robert Brentano, *Rome Before Avignon: A Social History of Thirteenth-Century Rome* (New York, 1974), pp. 95–97.

was despoiling the Roman republic, "as a falcon plucks its prey."[9]
They, and others whose power had declined as Innocent's increased,
looked for opportunities to change the balance.

Their task was not easy. In 1201 and 1202, Innocent's leadership
(and his brother Richard's money) helped the Romans defeat a superior force led by Viterbo. That victory led to the restoration of the
bronze doors of St. Peter's, which the Viterbese had taken in the days
of Frederick Barbarossa. It also enhanced the prestige of the pope
and enabled him to keep one step ahead of his Roman rivals.[10]

* * *

When Gerald of Wales returned to the curia in Lent of 1201, he
found a pope for whom things were going rather well, at least in
comparison with the previous year. The city was at peace, the promotion of the crusade was proceeding nicely, and Innocent had
found—or thought he had found—a pliable imperial candidate in
Otto of Brunswick. Dozens of letters flowed from the curia to all
parts of Germany, ordering lay and ecclesiastical authorities to support Otto.[11] In May, the papal cause in the Regno was fortified by
the return of Walter of Brienne with an army. The pope and the
curia could attend to Gerald and his causes without undue anxiety
about the state of Rome and the world.

The same could not be said for Gerald. By this time, the canons
of St. Davids had abandoned him for Walter the Cistercian abbot
of St. Dogmaelis, the rival candidate to be bishop of St. Davids.
The canons, the abbot, and the archbishop of Canterbury all had
their representatives in Rome. The case of the election was assigned
to Cardinals Peter Capuano and Soffredus as auditors, and the key
questions were how many elections had taken place and in what
order. The debates were vigorous and bitter. Gerald was convinced
that Cardinal Peter was favoring the archbishop's party, allowing
them to submit written depositions that conflicted with their earlier
oral testimony. Gerald himself was able to produce a number of witnesses because there was in Rome at the time a flock of Lenten pilgrims from Wales. Finally, the opposition claimed that they needed

---

[9] *Gesta*, PL:214:clxxviii = Gress-Wright, p. 324.
[10] *Gesta*, PL:214:clxxxiii = Gress-Wright, p. 329.
[11] RNI, nos. 32–48.

time to produce their own witnesses and to obtain further authorization for the archbishop's proctor, who had been authorized to deal only with the election, not with the status of St. Davids.

Innocent reluctantly granted the delay, but in deference to Gerald's concern that witnesses in England were subject to intimidation, he said that the witnesses must appear in Rome. He also required the archbishop to pay at least half of Gerald's expenses. He said, "If we could render judgement based on our inclinations rather than on the law, certainly no delay would be granted." And to Gerald, he said, "And you, brother, however difficult and expensive it may be for you, I hope you will return to us at the set time; indeed, if you do return, unless we hear something new, in fact something very new, you will go home not as a man authorized to be consecrated but as one already consecrated." The pope apparently did not have similar encouraging words about the status of St. Davids, but the vision of Gerald's consecration seemed closer to realization.[12]

Gerald accompanied the entire curia as it escaped the heat of the city in early July 1201 and went to Segni. He remained there throughout the month, fortifying himself with papal letters—letters to various people confirming Gerald's rights as administrator of St. Davids and letters warning the king and archbishop not to interfere with his movements. When the archbishop's proctor fell ill and died in Segni, Gerald may have seen it as a good omen. Once again, he could return home with hope, despite the delays, the expense, and the formidable opposition.[13]

The curia remained in Segni until the end of September 1201 and them moved on to Anagni. It was a leisurely and secure period, when Innocent could feel confident about papal success on all fronts. His candidate for the imperial crown seemed to be gaining support; Walter of Brienne was making progress in southern Italy, even capturing some of the more notorious German captains, and the city of Rome was completely under Innocent's control.[14] The curia lingered in Anagni into the winter. The Romans then received a cruel reminder of the importance of papal wealth to the city. Food shortages throughout Italy brought Innocent back to Rome in February

---

[12] *Giraldi*, 21/3:195.
[13] *Giraldi*, 21/3:188–195, 66–70.
[14] See Innocent's report to his legates in Germany, RNI, no. 56.

1202. The Biographer says the pope fed more than eight thousand people himself and urged the wealthy to be equally generous. Even in ordinary times, Innocent devoted one tenth of his income to alms. Not all of his charitable work had political rewards—the sheltering of abandoned infants, for example. But those who received money for food and clothing, those impoverished families whose daughters received dowries, those indigent nobles to whom he gave a kind of food-stamp, all these beneficiaries would be slow to join a protest against papal government. If the curia was driven from the city again, a fairly large number of people would feel its absence immediately and acutely.[15] Even those who did not receive anything directly from the pope still profited from his presence. The litigants who came to Rome, together with their entourages and proctors, inevitably brought considerable wealth with them.[16]

But Roman life was always volatile. In Roman politics, petty legal disputes could mix with constitutional issues. At one point, Lando Collis de Medio and his brothers seized some property held by another noble family, and when their rivals took the matter to Innocent's court, Lando and his brothers refused to appear. Innocent had his brother Richard the marshal seize the property and return it to the plaintiffs. Having lost the property they had recently seized, Lando and his brothers united their case with the republican cause by claiming the land was not only theirs, but that it was held from the former senators; and they joined the senators' supporters in stirring up opposition to Innocent's government of the city. Innocent met their bet and raised it: he destroyed their crops, cut down their trees, and seized their livestock. The cries of injustice became so great that Innocent was forced to call a public meeting and to use all his oratorical skills to calm the crowd.[17]

* * *

---

[15] *Gesta*, PL:214:cxcvi–cciii = Gress-Wright, pp. 343–345. For Innocent's charitable activities, see Brenda M. Bolton, "Hearts Not Purses? Pope Innocent III's Attitude to Social Welfare," in *Through the Eye of a Needle*, ed. Emily Alba-Hanawalt and Carter Lindberg (Columbia MO, 1994), pp. 123–145, and Bolton, "'Received in His Name': Rome's Busy Baby Box," *Studies in Church History*, 31 (1994): 152–167 repr. in *Innocent III: Studies on Papal Authority and Pastoral Care* (Aldershot, 1995), art. XVIII and art. XIX respectively. The famine of 1202 is described in *Annales Ceccanenses*, MGH SS 19:296.

[16] For examples, see Cheney, *Innocent III and England*, p. 110.

[17] *Gesta*, PL:214:clxxx–clxxxi = Gress-Wright, pp. 327–328.

The summer of 1202 was relatively uneventful in Rome. Diplomatic business continued. There was continuing friction with the archbishop of Canterbury and the king of England over various things, and with the king of France over his marriage. A crusading army was finally gathering in Venice and Innocent dispatched cardinal Peter Capuano with instructions for it. In late July, the curia left for an extended stay at the Benedictine monastery of Subiaco.

Subiaco took its name—*sub lacu*, beneath the lake—from the lakes built by Nero to decorate his villa there. Some five hundred years later, St. Benedict had lived as a hermit in a cave high above Subiaco, had then come part way down the mountain to found one of his first monasteries, called in Innocent's day the monastery of Subiaco, today the monastery of St. Scholastica of Subiaco. Since the monks there were not strictly observing the monastic rule and were neglecting their traditional work of caring for the sick,[18] the papal court combined the work of a pastoral visit with a country vacation.

The papal party arrived at the monastery in early August and pitched camp around the building. The pope's small tent was near the winding road climbing to the monastery from the west. Next came tents that housed curial officials and their pack animals. In the same vicinity was a large tent, elegantly painted with scenes from nature, that served as a hall for official business. To the south of the monastery, on the downward slope, were the cooks' tents; and to the east, the apothecary was camped, with his constantly grinding mortars and vials of urine. To the north, on the up-hill slope, local farmers gathered each morning to wake everyone with their noisy bargaining. Far below the monastery, the waters of one of Nero's lakes reflected the greenery of the opposite hill, making the lake seem a placid meadow. In the heat of the day, the papal chaplains frolicked in the lake and the pope strolled paths winding among islands and rivulets, refreshing himself in natural basins, washing and gargling with the water.

The scene is described to us in a sardonic letter written by one of the curial clerks, a man used to the comforts of the city and unenthusiastic about the rustic surroundings, for all their natural beauty.[19] The noise of cicadas and crickets, the shouting of peasants

---

[18] Reg. 5:81 (82).
[19] Karl Hampe, "Eine Schilderung des Sommeraufenthaltes der römischen Kurie unter Innozenz III. in Subiaco 1202," *Historische Vierteljahrschrift* 8 (1905): 509–535.

and cooks, the moaning of the sick who came to the monastery for treatment—all these disturbed his afternoon and evening sleep. The flies were so thick that it was hard not to swallow them when eating. The lake could be refreshing briefly, but it was also like the torture of Tantalus. It was tempting to go down to the cool waters of the lake, but the exhausting trip back up left one worse off than before. Although the clerk acknowledged the refreshing breezes and splendid vistas, he was nevertheless maneuvering to get the pope to send him elsewhere.

The tone of the letter is mildly irreverent. He wrote that the tent that served as papal hall was so solidly erected that if Samson were to rise from the dead, he could achieve another triumph equal to his first by knocking it down. He referred to the pope as "the third Solomon," "our most holy father Abraham." He wrote that the only thing that sustained the curia in their rough life at camp was spiritual guidance from "the fountain of living water, the vicar of Jesus Christ, in whom are found treasures of all wisdom and eloquence." Still, he seemed more than willing to forego these blessings if he could escape to more comfortable surroundings.

The kind of wisdom and eloquence Innocent provided can be sampled in a sermon he preached to the monks at Subiaco (if not during this visit, then in 1201 or 1203).[20] His text was "Blessed are the clean of heart, for they shall see God" (Matt. 5:8). He first discussed the various meanings of "clean of heart" and then distinguished between the blessed still living in the world and those in heaven.

The pope turned to the second clause of the sentence and asked, can anyone truly see God? Many scriptural passages suggested that no one could see God, while others seemed to say the contrary. Nor could one say that "seeing" here refers merely to seeing God incarnate in Christ, since many saw him who were certainly not saints: Herod, Pilate, Judas, Caiphas. Rather, one must distinguish among three kinds of vision: corporeal, enigmatic, and comprehending.

---

[20] PL 217:589–596. Migne identifies the sermon as having been given on All Saints Day (November 1). Innocent's text was Matt. 5:8, which is from the liturgy for that day; but Innocent might have used that text on some other day. In any case, he was certainly not in Subiaco 1 November 1202, though he could have been in 1201 or 1203.

Corporeal is in the senses, enigmatic is in the imagination, and comprehending is in the intellect. Of the first it is said, "Mine eyes have seen thy salvation" (Luke 2:30). Of the second, "Now we see through a mirror, in an enigma" (1 Cor. 13:12). Of the third, it is added, "Then, however, we will see face to face" (ibid.). With corporeal vision, no one has ever been able to see the deity, nor ever will, since God is not corporeal but spiritual. With enigmatic vision, however, God is seen in the present in a way, not face to face, but through faith, not fully but imperfectly. But God is seen with comprehending vision by the holy angels and the blessed souls, who know as they are known. Therefore it is true that "No one has ever seen God" (John 1:18), but this refers to corporeal vision. What God says is also true: "No one will see me and live" (Exodus 33:20); but he means in this mortal life.

When Christ said, "Blessed are the pure of heart, for they shall see God," he used the future tense, "shall see," not the present. God will be seen fully and perfectly in the future.

Nevertheless, he is seen in the present through the effect of inspiration, contemplation, prayer, meditation, reading, preaching—through which the soul is raised to the perception of God.

This kind of vision, he said, required one to be free from secular cares and earthly occupations. Zechariah was unable to see Jesus because he was too short, and he was surrounded by a crowd, representing earthly cares. Only when he escaped the crowd and climbed a tree could he see, the tree representing faith in the cross.

The mind withdraws itself from all earthly matters, in which are vanity and affliction, and rises to seek out celestial things, in which are true happiness and perfect blessedness. It considers and admires in that high court the orders of the angels, the assembly of the patriarchs, the chorus of the prophets, the crowns of the apostles, the palms of the martyrs, the maniples of confessors, the fruits of virgins—all resting in peace, all rejoicing in praise, all shining in light; all secure without fear, all at rest without labor, all joyful without sadness. . . . And if the mind is carried up to pursue these things with a certain taste of sweetness, then it is contemplating. And how sweet it is so to contemplate, he knows well who has tasted it.

In the next life, though, the vision will be complete.

Certainly, the one who sees God has whatever he desires. If you take delight in wisdom, you will have what you want if you see God, since God is the most perfect wisdom. . . . If you take delight in beauty, you will have what you want if you see God, since God is the most perfect beauty. . . . If you take delight in peace, you will have what you want if you see God, since God is the most perfect peace. . . .

If the monks took delight in light, or fortitude, or sweetness, or any other thing, they would have it if they saw God, in whom was the plenitude of all good things.

Perhaps the sojourn in Subiaco gave Innocent the chance to climb the tree with Zechariah, to taste the sweetness of contemplation, but he could not completely escape the crowd of worldly concerns. Problems from all over Christendom followed the curia wherever it went. One pitiful man named Lomberd had traveled all the way from Scotland and made the final trek from Rome to Subiaco. He came to seek absolution for the sin of having cut out the tongue of the bishop of Caithness. He had been forced to commit the crime by some of his fellow soldiers; but he had done it, nonetheless, and he now sought forgiveness. Innocent sent him home with the instructions that he was to parade for fifteen days through the region with his tongue protruding and a string tied from it to his neck. He was to live during that period on only bread and water. He was to have himself scourged in front of the bishop's house, and then he was to go to the Holy Land for three years. Even more pitiful was Robert, who had, on orders from Muslim captors during a famine, killed his own daughter and eaten her. He had also killed his wife, but could not bring himself to eat her. He was sentenced in Subiaco to a lifetime of celibacy and fasting and he was required to wander barefoot for three years, then to return to the pope for absolution. The letter the pope gave Robert also urged all he met to treat him with compassion.[21]

In the second week of September, the papal party broke camp and moved on to the more comfortable surroundings of Velletri. There the pace of temporal business picked up, as Innocent pressed the German bishops to support Otto, even ordering several to Rome to be chastened properly.[22] Innocent prodded Walter of Brienne and other princes of southern Italy to move against Markward, placing at their disposal all the regional revenues that the pope commanded as the young king's guardian.[23] By the end of the month, the death of Markward came as a welcome sign that God had not abandoned

---

[21] Reg. 5:78 (79), 79 (80); PL 214:1062–63, 1063–64.
[22] RNI, nos. 70–74.
[23] Reg. 5:84–87; PL 214:1070–73.

Innocent's enterprises, and the pope was soon back at the Lateran palace.[24]

* * *

Back in Rome, rivalries between the family of Innocent's mother, the Scotti, and the family of Celestine III, the Boboni branch of the Orsini, mixed in with the other tensions.[25] Our source is the Biographer, for whom Innocent was always in the right, so the account must be taken with a grain of salt, but this is the story he tells. The Boboni held land from the papacy. As papal control of Rome expanded, their fear grew that Innocent would try to reclaim their land. They therefore became militant republicans. In the fall of 1202, after Innocent had moved on from Subiaco to Velletri, the Boboni seized the homes of a number of Innocent's cousins. Innocent returned immediately to Rome and supervised a peaceful settlement.

What happened next, according to the Biographer, was not the work of Innocent. First, the pro-papal senator Pandulf de Subuxa took matters further than Innocent had intended. He required both sides to surrender their towers and temporarily to leave the city (the Boboni to St. Peter's, the Scotti to St. Paul's outside the Walls). He then began to tear down one of the Boboni towers as a penalty for their actions. At the same time, one of the Boboni who had been on fairly good terms with one of the Scotti decided to go speak with him at St. Pauls. It may have been a peace-making mission, but some of the Scotti decided he was up to no good. On the broad, flat road between the city and St. Pauls, in the hot-headed manner made famous by the Montagues and Capulets, they attacked and killed him.

As soon as the news reached the rest of the Boboni, they rushed into the city, recaptured all the towers, and began to tear down those of the Scotti. They recovered the body of the murdered man, hoping to incite popular opinion by parading it through the city and displaying it in front of the home of Innocent's brother Richard and at the palace of the pope. By then, the papal allies had rallied and things reached a stalemate. Tensions remained high in 1202.

[24] Reg. 5:88 (89); PL 214:1076–76.

[25] For an excellent description of the aristocratic families of Rome during Innocent's time and the following century, see Brentano, *Rome Before Avignon*, pp. 173–209.

Innocent's control over the Patrimonium was no better. He could not prevent warfare between two cities of Umbria, the warfare that left Francis, a young dandy from Assisi, to spend a year in prison in Perugia.

* * *

Meanwhile, far to the north, Gerald was pursuing his quixotic quest in Wales and England, finding virtually no support for his cause. He excommunicated some of his enemies and placed his hope once more in the pope. Having been declared a traitor and an enemy of the king,[26] he sneaked around England as a fugitive before he finally found transit to the continent. Hounded by opportunists who obstructed his movements in order to extort money, he finally made his way through the winter snows of the Alps and the Apennines and arrived in Rome in early January of 1203. The archbishop of Canterbury and the rival candidate for St. Davids were already well represented there with proctors and supporting witnesses.

After the feast of the Epiphany (6 January), the consistory took up the case once again. It was, perhaps, a welcome distraction to the pope, who had recently received two very disturbing pieces of news. The bishop of Würzburg had been murdered, and the men of Duke Philip of Swabia were prime suspects.[27] Even worse, the crusade had taken a disastrous turn. The force that departed from Venice in the fall of 1202 had captured and sacked the Christian city of Zara on the coast of Dalmatia. The very act of attacking a Christian city meant that all the attackers, almost the whole crusading force, were now excommunicated. The entire crusade was in jeopardy, and it was not at all clear that Innocent could get it back on track. The case of Gerald and his bishopric was, in contrast, both manageable and entertaining.

Gerald began by vilifying the opposing witnesses with his usual gusto. He scored at least one solid hit when he showed that one of the men presenting himself as a well-informed canon of St. Davids could not describe the church and its environs.[28]

A side show developed when a Welsh monk—probably financed

---

[26] Richter, *Giraldus Cambrensis,* p. 119.
[27] Reg. 5:133 (134), 154 (155).
[28] *Giraldi,* 21/3:196–249.

by the archbishop's money—appeared before the papal chamberlain and accused Gerald of stealing his horse in Wales. He claimed that Gerald had ridden the horse to Rome and he demanded its restoration. The chamberlain was apparently responsible for minor security matters in the papal household, and Gerald soon found himself in the day defending his bishopric before the pope and in the evening defending his horse before the chamberlain.

Gerald insisted to the chamberlain that he had not stolen the horse. Rather, as archdeacon, he had confiscated a horse from this renegade and excommunicated monk. But the confiscated horse had been a broken-down nag, not the fine specimen now stabled in Rome—though he did concede that they were the same color. At this point, Gerald's other opponents rallied around and supported the testimony of the renegade monk. The chamberlain had the horse sequestered until the matter could be settled. Gerald found a way to end the annoying distraction. The next evening, he had one of his companions appear before the chamberlain and declare that the horse confiscated in Wales had been a gelding, whereas the sequestered animal was a stallion. The monk immediately objected that the horse stolen in Wales had definitely been a stallion, that he had intact all the parts a good stallion ought to have. Gerald asked that the monk's testimony—that the stolen horse was a stallion—be entered in the record. The chamberlain then dispatched men to the stable to examine the sequestered horse. They returned shortly with this report: "My lord, we have followed your orders but did not find what we were looking for. The monk himself came with us. He closely inspected the parts in question, examining and testing with his eyes and with his hands, but all he found was a useless staff and an empty wallet." The proceedings broke up in laughter. When the story reached Innocent the same night, he was greatly amused and ordered the horse returned to the archdeacon; and the next day the whole court was laughing, to the great embarrassment of Gerald's opponents. Gerald was sure that his major cases had been helped.[29]

While the cases were still in process, probably on a warm day in March, the pope retired to one of his favorite retreats, the Maidens' Fountain, a short ride south of the Lateran. It was a lovely fountain, enclosed with stone-work so that it sent out clear, cold rivulets across a field laced with footpaths—perhaps a small scale version of

---

[29] *Giraldi*, 21/3:249–52.

the Villa d'Este now in Tivoli. Gerald and other suitors followed. There the pope distanced himself from the crowd, sitting with a few of his household, as if in a kind of room enclosed with streams of flowing water. He sent for Gerald so that they could relish the story of the monk and the horse. Gerald told them that if the monk had been like the horse, lacking witnesses (*testes*), he might have pursued religion instead of litigation. He also reported that the monk had been teased by one of the his own colleagues, reminding him that throughout much of his life witnesses (*testes*) had given him trouble, and now he had been undone by the "witnesses" of the horse. Innocent laughed and said, "Are these the kind of witnesses they produce against you?" That set Gerald off on another diatribe, vilifying the opposition and bemoaning the corrupting power of the archbishop's money. Innocent gently urged him to concentrate more on preparing his case and less on the vices of his opponents. "In the Roman curia," he said, "the unshakable justice of cases always comes out in the end, regardless of the merits of persons." Then he turned the conversation to more amusing subjects. "But now let's talk about your archbishop's grammar and sermons." Gerald's stories of Hubert Walter's ignorance of Latin and theology were favorites in Rome.[30]

As they sat there in the garden, Gerald could take heart from the pleasant camaraderie with the pope, and in the curia he found his cases going very well. He was certainly pleased with his own defense. Others complimented him, and the pope continued to treat him warmly. But as Lent wore on, he saw that some of the cardinals seemed to be giving a favorable ear to the opposition. He had no doubt that the archbishop's silver was corrupting the curia—including the pope. The archbishop was later to say that the case had cost him eleven thousand marks, and Gerald took that as proof of corruption in the curia.[31]

Gerald's cases were consuming a great deal of time. Innocent warned him of the dangers of the summer heat in Rome and urged him not to prolong matters by impugning the character and credibility of every opposing witness. Nor, he said, did Gerald need to respond to all the accusations made against his own character. The pope did not believe them. Against his better judgment, Gerald

[30] *Giraldi*, 21/3:252–4.
[31] *Giraldi*, 21/3:254–264.

agreed. Whereas Gerald had no doubt that he could make all fair-minded people see things as he saw them, Innocent was apparently concluding that taking hours to let the two sides vilify each other would result in nothing.

It was now Holy Week of 1203. Innocent had received letters against Gerald not only from King John but also from Otto, John's nephew and Innocent's preferred candidate for emperor. Innocent assured Gerald that the opinions of princes did not affect decisions in consistory. Gerald answered that if the curia began to believe witnesses like these princes, then more than one subdeacon would suffer—indeed more than a few archbishops would have to be deposed and degraded. The pope smiled at Cardinal Hugolino and nodded. But while Gerald was oblivious to everything that did not bear directly on his case, the pope had more to worry about than the St. Davids cases and the approaching summer heat.

The factional unrest in Rome had not ended.[32] During lent the discontent took on a religious guise. Despite prohibitions from the pope, the anti-papal party stripped down and carried crosses in processions from church to church, linking their own oppression with the suffering of Christ. The popular agitation became so great that on Easter Monday, 7 April, the papal liturgy at St. Peter's was disrupted, and Innocent had to make his way back across the city to the Lateran in the face of cat-calls and insults. Many of his entourage were injured in the scuffling. As the violence swelled, crowds attacked the senator's palace on the Capitoline hill and the senator was forced to flee. The city was becoming dangerous.[33] The chaos in Rome was, moreover, echoed in the wider world. Virtually the entire crusading army, still in Zara, was excommunicated, and Innocent had yet to hear whether the crusaders would accept his terms for absolution.

* * *

A week after Easter, on Tuesday, 15 April, the pope gave his judgment on the elections of St. Davids.[34] He canceled both elections and called for a new one. Since the canons of St. Davids had long

---

[32] *Giraldi*, 21/3:264–7.

[33] *Gesta*, PL 214:clxxxvi–clxxxvii = Gress-Wright, pp. 333–334.

[34] Reg. 6:74 and p. 103, n. 7.

since abandoned Gerald, the pope's decision meant the end of his candidacy. Gerald was crushed; his opponents were delighted. But Gerald bounced back gamely and asked the right to continue as champion of the status of St. Davids. The pope and the cardinals retired to discuss the matter, then summoned Gerald. Innocent gave him permission to pursue the case and, perhaps trying to give him some hope, said he would appoint judges delegate from outside the jurisdiction of the archbishop of Canterbury—provided Gerald could show that the canons of St. Davids had abandoned that cause because of duress. Privately, Innocent commended Gerald for his efforts and his spirit, contending against kings and princes and an archbishop, struggling for his own right and the right of his church. He said that God would surely reward him. Gerald was not greatly consoled, and he never lost the feeling that the pope had betrayed him.[35]

In early May 1203, Innocent and the curia abandoned the strife-ridden city and took to the Via Casilina.[36] Gerald soon followed and joined them at Palestrina. There the pope again offered consoling gestures: he lent him money (Gerald was already in debt to Cardinal Octavian); he absolved him from his old vow to take the cross; and he promised him that at least part of his expenses would be paid by the archbishop of Canterbury. By mid-May, the curia was ensconced in Ferentino, where Gerald remained through June, building an arsenal of papal letters to protect him and his rights when he returned home.[37]

Gerald had no money to pay chancery fees for all these letters and he still owed money to Cardinal Octavian and the pope. He had earlier borrowed from money-lenders from Bologna, and he hoped to be able to satisfy them now by borrowing elsewhere. But the Bolognese money-lenders in the environs of Rome had spread rumors about him—or so he believed—so that no one else would lend to him. Gerald was in fact a much worse credit risk now that his election had been quashed. The Bolognese lent him more money, but they forced him to change the terms of the existing loan, which originally was to be paid at the markets of Troyes (where Gerald probably hoped to refinance the loan). Now he would have to repay

[35] *Giraldi*, 21/3:267–271.
[36] *Gesta*, PL 214:clxxxvii = Gress-Wright, p. 334.
[37] *Giraldi*, 21/3:272–86.

the entire loan in Bologna, with heavy interest, before he had even crossed the Alps and where he would still be dealing with the same hard-eyed money-changers. As a final indignity, they required him to hand over as security almost all of his possessions, including the papal letters.[38]

Gerald was gradually realizing the hopelessness of his position. He took his leave of the pope in Ferentino. "It is time, father, for us to go home," he said, solemnly slipping into the formal "we." "But this time, we do not ask permission to return as we have done before. We make our final farewell to the curia, never to return."

"Surely not," answered the pope. "For what will become of the dignity of St. Davids? We are sure you won't abandon the case of its status."

Gerald answered boldly that the same person who had quashed his election had for all practical purposes ended the other case as well. He had sought to be bishop of an impoverished church only to restore its ancient dignity, he said; the result had been only immense labor and unmeasured martyrdom. "Up to now, we have looked to the interests of the curia; now we will look to our own interests and our own peace. But we would never have abandoned the case of the status if the curia had not first abandoned us. Our rod and our staff are broken; we cannot cling to clouds."

Innocent was touched. He urged Gerald to believe that God was looking after him, that God had mercifully delivered him from the long litigation perhaps with something better in store for him in the future. Gerald said he was confident that God would reward his good intentions in the next life if not in this. Then he took the Via Casilina to Rome and proceeded on to Bologna to face his creditors.[39] Innocent and his curia soon moved on to Anagni.

When Gerald of Wales finally arrived home in late 1203, he pursued his vision for a while longer; but finally, when a new election produced a new bishop-elect of unimpeachable character, he gave up. He came to terms with the king and the archbishop of Canterbury, who did in fact pay half of the expenses of litigation. Gerald presented a charter to the archbishop in which he promised, "In whatever position I shall be I shall never raise the issue of the

---

[38] *Giraldi*, 21/3:286–7.
[39] *Giraldi*, 21/3:288–9.

status of the church of St. David's against the church of Canterbury, nor shall I give counsel or help to anybody else who would like to raise it, but I shall oppose, as much as I can, anybody who would raise it, in order to protect the liberty and the dignity of Christ Church, Canterbury." In return, he received an annual income of sixty marks; the archbishop arranged that Gerald's nephew could succeed him as archdeacon of Brecon; and he arranged to have Gerald returned to the king's good graces.[40] Gerald lived quietly for many more years, pursuing his studies and his writing. But he knew that the archbishop's money had won.

But the money may not have won in the way Gerald believed. Archbishop Hubert Walter was a man of limited learning, but he knew enough to have excellent canon lawyers in his employment.[41] The eleven thousand marks he spent in the case could have been entirely legitimate expenses (though we might wonder about some of the witnesses who vacationed in Rome at his expense). Few scholars have been willing to share Gerald's belief that anyone who did not agree with him was corrupt, though many are willing to believe the worst of the Roman curia. How do we evaluate the ubiquitous charges of venality in the curia?

Innocent had set a high standard for himself, when he wrote as a cardinal:

> Woe to you who have been corrupted by pressure or bribery. . . . You pay no attention to the value of a case, but to the value of a person; not to laws but to bribes; not to justice but to money.[42]

The Biographer assures us that Innocent adhered to that standard:

> Who can enumerate the great multitude of cases he settled between different churches and persons, with their various and difficult points, always following the royal way, never straying to the right or to the left, not giving preference to persons and not accepting gifts?[43]

But Gerald apparently gave Innocent a valuable gift of six bound volumes, and neither he nor the pope seemed to think anything wrong was being done. Part of the problem was that they had not

---

[40] Richter, *Giraldus Cambrensis*, p. 126; *Giraldi*, 21/1:lxxxvi.

[41] Charles R. Young, *Hubert Walter, Lord of Canterbury and Lord of England* (Durham, N.C., 1968), pp. 7–8, 57, 63.

[42] MHC, II.iv (trans. Dietz).

[43] *Gesta*, PL 214:lxxxvi = Gress-Wright, pp. 63–64.

yet completely abandoned the "gift-giving" culture of an earlier era, when giving gifts was not only good manners but a sign of the importance of the giver. The gift could not be lightly refused. In modern politics and business, the line between a gift and a bribe is still not easily drawn, and it is drawn in very different ways in different modern cultures. The line was even more obscure in Innocent's day. Innocent faced that difficulty when the bishop of Hildesheim came to Rome as a repentant sinner and suitor, humbled himself before the pope, but then gave him a splendid silver vase. The pope did not wish further to humiliate the bishop by rejecting the gift, but neither did he want the impending favorable judgment to seem bought. So he accepted the silver vase and sent the bishop a gold one.[44]

I doubt that Innocent was corrupted by bribes or gifts. The Biographer not only testifies to the probity of his judgments, but he also reports that Innocent tried to reduce the level of luxury in the curia, replacing gold and silver and ermine with wood and glass and wool. What seems likely is that even the necessary fees charged for services seemed extortionate to people like Gerald. Moreover, small gifts were common in Rome, and it is probable that people in the papal orbit occasionally turned that practice into extortion. They also may have claimed to be doing so on behalf of the pope. Innocent's efforts at reform, as reported by the Biographer, show that there was indeed a problem when he became pope; but my guess is that there was less of that petty extortion under Innocent than under many other popes.

But even if we grant the honesty of Innocent, the integrity of his judgments can still be questioned. There was no division of powers in papal government. A modern citizen might legitimately give a gift to a congressman or to a president, but a gift to a judge or regulator having direct authority over a citizen's business would obviously be seen as wrong and illegal. The pope, however, was many things. Suitors could not give a gift to their spiritual father without also giving it to their judge. With the most principled of popes, rumors of judicial corruption would continue until contained by a system of salaried judges and uniform court fees.

---

[44] *Gesta*, PL 214:lxxxviii = Gress-Wright, pp. 65–66.

Popes could not give away their services gratis. As much as Innocent may have wanted to avoid worrying about money, it was never far from his mind. The military efforts against the Germans in the south, his promised subsidy for the crusades, the very substantial needs of the papal curia, in Rome or elsewhere, all these were expensive. When he visited towns in his territories, he was expected to present gifts. The Biographer, obviously writing with a register of these gifts before him, lists dozens of churches that received silver chalices, gold-plated crosses, money for repairs. The merchants supplying the curia with chasubles of red samite trimmed with gold, to be used as gifts, made a very good living indeed.[45]

Papal government had expanded enormously in the previous century or so, but the papal right to tax had not expanded with it. The popes were still dependent mainly on revenues from papal territories. When the curia had been in exile in France, separated from papal estates, the popes had turned to a new device. Instead of paying curial officials, the popes arranged to have them appointed to local ecclesiastical offices so that they could receive the attached incomes (prebends). The officials may have even performed some of the functions associated with those prebends while they were in France, but the practice continued when the curia was back in Italy, officials holding prebends from churches in France and elsewhere.[46] From one point of view, it was a reasonable solution, asking local churches throughout Christendom to share the cost of papal government. But from another, it was an ominous precedent, moving the entire church toward a system of absentee pastors on every level. The rebellious career of Martin Luther was launched by the successful attempt of a young German nobleman to be absentee bishop of more than one bishopric.

Quite apart from money, however, Innocent's impartiality could be compromised in other ways. His office combined both executive and judicial functions, and the two could get in each other's way. Placing the worst construction on his actions, we find him merely

---

[45] *Gesta*, PL 214:cciii–ccxi = Gress-Wright, pp. 345–352. On these gifts, see Brenda M. Bolton, "*Qui fidelis est in minimo*: The Importance of Innocent III's Gift List," in *Pope Innocent III and His World*, pp. 113–140.

[46] A. Graboïs, "Les séjours des papes en France au XIIe siècle et leurs rapports avec le développement de la fiscalité pontificale," *Revue d'histoire de l'église de France*, 49 (1963) 5–18.

leading Gerald on, knowing that ultimately he would not decide in his favor because he did not want to antagonize the archbishop of Canterbury, the king of the English, and the king of the Germans— all for one eccentric Welsh archdeacon. That is, I think, too harsh a judgment. On more than one occasion, after all, Innocent took on the very powerful when he might have found an easier way. But at the very least, Innocent must have felt relieved to be able to find an easy way out, quashing Gerald's election and calling for a new one, even though he was certain that it ended Gerald's hopes. The pope had come to know that Gerald's temperament did not make him an ideal candidate for bishop; he knew that Gerald's growing Welsh loyalties could never be reconciled with the interests of the English crown. However much he liked Gerald, he must have been relieved that the threats and promises of powerful people had wiped out the support for Gerald at home, so that even the canons of St. Davids were against him. An impartial judge might not have cared about these things, but the pope had to.

* * *

In early June of 1203, however, Innocent's greatest concern in Ferentino was not the plight of Gerald of Wales, stranded without funds with the curia, or even the disorder in the city of Rome. It was the crusading host. They were still excommunicated for their sack of Zara, and they still had not responded to his terms for absolution. Would they submit to papal authority, or were other Christian cities in danger? With the spring weather, the crusaders had probably set sail from Zara, but where they were or what they intended, he did not know.

CHAPTER FIVE

THE FOURTH CRUSADE (1203–1204)

On his first trip to Rome in the late fall of 1199, Gerald of Wales passed through Champagne. Had he lingered there a little longer, he might have witnessed the first flames of crusading fervor among the French chivalry of the day. In November, at his castle at Écry-sur-Aisne, Count Thibaut of Champagne played host to a tournament. Present were his cousin Count Louis of Blois, Simon de Montfort, Renaud de Montmirail, Walter of Brienne, Geoffrey de Joinville (seneschal of Champagne), Geoffrey de Villehardouin (marshal of Champagne), Bishop Garnier of Troyes, and dozens of other well placed aristocrats from northeastern France. The two cousin-counts were in their twenties. They were both nephews of the king of France as well as of the king of England. Thibaut's mother Marie of Champagne had maintained in her court poets who celebrated the courage and prowess of warriors but also the force of romantic love, sometimes empowering, sometimes disabling.

The presence of all these nobles, including clergy, at a tournament shows the limited influence of clerical authorities when their rules ran contrary to the strong preferences of the powerful, for tournaments were a forbidden past-time. They endangered lives for frivolous reasons, and those killed in a tournament were therefore denied Christian burial. Tournaments flourished, nonetheless, and there are few signs that the consciences of the participants were much troubled by the condemnations of clerical authorities. The aristocrats loved the display of horses and weapons and heraldry. They loved the rituals of etiquette, the affirmations of their superior status. They loved the prestige that came from performing well and honorably in mock combat—mock, but still potentially lethal.[1]

But this tournament took a different turn. It is not clear what moved the count on 28 November at Écry, but he suddenly announced his intention to take the cross, to commit himself by oath to go to

---

[1] Maurice Keen, *Chivalry* (New Haven, 1984), pp. 83–101.

the rescue of the Holy Land. Such a splendid and heroic gesture could hardly be ignored by the other nobles in attendance, and soon a formidable assembly of aristocratic warriors had cloth crosses attached to their shoulders.

The oath of the young count came from an emotionally charged environment. Sporadic famine in northern Europe had for some years given warning that God was angry.[2] Popular rumor in France had it that the anti-Christ had been born in "Babylon" (Cairo) and that the end of the world was near.[3] Innocent's crusading letter of 15 August 1198 had elicited no immediate response, but the ferment continued. The popular preacher Fulk of Neuilly had gone through the countryside calling for repentance, attacking usury and lust—especially among the clergy. Innocent commissioned him to use his talents to preach the crusade.[4] Thibaut himself came from a long line of crusaders, his brother having recently died as king of Jerusalem. Geoffrey of Villehardouin refers to the preaching of Fulk and to the "generous terms" of the pope's indulgence: all who took the cross and served for one year would obtain "remission of any sins they have committed, provided they have confessed them."[5] The political atmosphere was also right. The efforts of Cardinal Peter Capuano had produced a truce between the kings of England and France in October, and his interdict on France because of the king's marital problems was still a month in the future.

In the following months, in spite of—or perhaps because of—the interdict on France, more princes followed the example of Thibaut and his colleagues. The counts of Flanders, Perche, and St. Pol took the cross, bringing with them great Flemish and French aristocrats, together with their noble entourages. But the crusaders soon discovered that the spirit that moved them to begin the enterprise did not also provide a plan for accomplishing it. Sometime in 1200, the

[2] Bolton, "Hearts Not Purses?," pp. 123–124; Michel Mollat, *The Poor in the Middle Ages: An Essay in Social History*, trans. Arthur Goldhammer (New Haven, 1986), pp. 61–62.

[3] Rigordus, *Gesta Philippi Augusti*, in *Oeuvres de Rigord et de Guillaume le Breton*, ed. François Delaborde, 2 vols. (Paris, 1882–1885) 1:141.

[4] Reg. 1:398. For Innocent's use of preaching to recruit for this crusade, see Penny J. Cole, *The Preaching of the Crusades to the Holy Land, 1095–1270* (Cambridge, MA, 1991), pp. 80–97.

[5] *The Conquest of Constantinople*, in *Joinville & Villehardouin: Chronicles of the Crusades*, trans. M. R. B. Shaw (Baltimore, 1963), p. 29.

major princes met at Compiègne where, after much discussion, they agreed, or seemed to agree, on two points. First, they would move their army by sea, rather than risk the hazards of passing through Hungary, the Balkans, and the Byzantine empire. Second, they would place entire responsibility for making the arrangements in the hands of six men to be chosen, two each, by the highest ranking princes of the crusade, the counts of Champagne, of Flanders, and of Blois. Included in this commission of six was Geoffrey of Villehardouin, the marshal of Champagne, whose later account tells us much of what we know about the fourth crusade.

Since only Genoa, Pisa, and Venice were capable of moving such an army by sea, and since the Genoese and Pisans were exhausting themselves fighting each other, the delegates proceeded to Venice, arriving there in the first week of Lent of 1201. They presented their credentials—letters from the counts of Champagne, Flanders, and Blois, binding themselves to whatever arrangements the envoys should make.[6]

*   *   *

By 1201, Venice was the most powerful force in the eastern Mediterranean, but it had not reached that position without reversals. Thirty years before, Venice had suffered one of the greatest disasters of its history. Worried by the power of Venice throughout the eastern Mediterranean, the emperor of Constantinople had arranged that all Venetians in the city be suddenly arrested. Thousands of Venetians filled Byzantine prisons, and all their goods and ships were confiscated. The doge of Venice then led a great fleet to Greece, where they were met by envoys of the emperor, who assured the doge that justice would be done and the prisoners freed if he would only send his own envoys to Constantinople to work out the details. The Venetians sent their envoys to Constantinople, but the emperor toyed with them for weeks. In the meantime, plague ravaged the Venetian fleet moored at Chios. The doge led the sorry remnants of the fleet back to Venice, bringing the plague with them. As more Venetians fell victim to disease, an angry mob killed the doge.[7]

---

[6] Donald Queller and Thomas Madden, *The Fourth Crusade: The Conquest of Constantinople, 1201–1204*, 2nd ed. (Philadelphia, 1997), pp. 1–8; *Joinville & Villehardouin*, pp. 29–32. This chapter depends heavily on the careful and balanced analysis provided by Queller and Madden.

[7] John Julius Norwich, *A History of Venice* (New York, 1982), pp. 104–106.

Among the envoys who had been humiliated at Constantinople in 1171–1172 was a man named Enrico Dondolo.[8] By 1201, he was old, he was blind; he should have been, if not in the grave, at least in retirement. Instead, he was the doge who greeted Geoffrey of Villehardouin and his fellow emissaries from France. He was a man of such power and energy that historians have had difficulty believing that he was as old and blind as Villehardouin says, but even putting him at 75 instead of 85 makes him no less remarkable. And even if he had forgotten the events of 1171–1172, the current Byzantine emperor, who followed a consistent anti-Venice policy, had given Enrico fresh reasons to dislike the Byzantine state.[9]

A few days after their reception in Venice, the French envoys went to the splendid palace of the doge (since rebuilt) and addressed the doge and his Council of Six:

> My lords, we have come to you on behalf of the great barons of France, who have taken the cross to avenge the outrage suffered by our Lord, and, if God so wills, to recapture Jerusalem. And since our lords know there is no people who can help them so well as yours, they entreat you, in God's name, to take pity on the land overseas, and the outrage suffered by our Lord, and graciously do your best to supply us with a fleet of warships and transports.[10]

The doge asked a week's time to consider the request. On the appointed day, the envoys returned and were told that the doge and the Small Council had themselves approved the enterprise, but that they would need also the agreement of the Great Council and the Popular Assembly. After some negotiations, the envoys agreed to these terms, which had yet to be put to the Great Council: the Venetians would build ships to move forty-five hundred knights and their horses, nine thousand unmounted squires, and twenty-thousand foot soldiers. They would supply provisions for horses and men for

---

[8] The idea that this early experience permanently embittered Dandolo and made him eager for revenge is effectively rebutted by Thomas F. Madden, "Venice and Constantinople in 1171 and 1172: Enrico Dandolo's Attitudes towards Byzantium," *Mediterranean Historical Review*, 8 (1993) 166–185. It still seems likely to me that a residue of ill-will would inevitably remain. The Greek historian Nicetas Choniates also thought that Dandolo was moved in part by the desire for revenge. See Jonathan Harris, "Distortion, divine providence and genre in Nicetas Choniates's account of the collapse of Byzantium 1180–1204," *Journal of Medieval History*, 26 (2000): 31.

[9] Charles M. Brand, *Byzantium Confronts the West: 1180–1204* (Cambridge MA, 1968), pp. 199–204.

[10] Villehardouin, in *Joinville & Villehardouin*, pp. 32–33.

a year. The total cost would be eighty-five thousand silver marks of Cologne.[11] In addition, the Venetians would provide fifty armed galleys of their own, provided that they would receive half of anything acquired by the crusade.

In the following days, the Great Council of Forty gave their agreement. Then the Popular Assembly gathered in the basilica of St. Mark where, after mass, Geoffrey of Villehardouin addressed them and the six envoys knelt to plead for their support. Geoffrey later described the scene like this:

> Thereupon the six envoys, in floods of tears, knelt at the feet of the assembled people. The doge and all the other Venetians present also burst out weeping, and holding up their hands towards heaven, cried out with one accord: "We consent! We consent!"[12]

The terms were soon set in writing and sworn to by both parties. The crusaders were to gather in Venice in the spring of 1202 for a departure in the early summer. It was also agreed—secretly—that instead of sailing directly for the holy land, the crusade would attack Cairo. The leaders believed that Egypt was the basis of Muslim power in Jerusalem, but they also believed that the ordinary crusaders might not understand the wisdom of this strategic detour.

The envoys borrowed two thousand marks for a down-payment on the fleet and then split up, some going to Genoa to recruit support, while Geoffrey of Villehardouin and a colleague went north to report their success. As he passed through Mont Cenis pass, Geoffrey met Walter of Brienne and his force of knights, on their way to join papal forces in southern Italy. They parted company with the happy expectation of meeting again in Venice the following year, but as Villehardouin remarked, "in the end, they [Walter and his knights] no longer found it possible to rejoin the army."[13] Geoffrey would survive the crusade to write his memoir; but in June of 1205, Walter would die in southern Italy as German swords struck at him under his collapsed tent.

* * *

---

[11] Queller and Madden, p. 11. I am indebted to Thomas Madden for explaining to me the discrepancy between Queller and Madden's figures and those in the Shaw translation of Villehardouin (a matter of variant manuscripts).

[12] Villehardouin, in *Joinville & Villehardouin*, p. 34.

[13] *Joinville & Villehardouin*, p. 36. For the amount borrowed, see Queller and Madden, p. 16.

For Innocent, these developments were a mixed blessing. He had been disappointed that his call for a crusade in 1198 had not produced a crusading army the following spring, and he was glad to hear that something was now taking shape. On the other hand, he had appointed two cardinals, Peter Capuano and Soffredus, to act as leaders of the crusade, and he had sent Cardinal Octavian to France in 1200 with several missions, among them, the promotion of the crusade. But papal representatives were conspicuously missing from the actual planning in France and Venice. The French and Venetian leaders presented him with a fait accompli. The Biographer says he approved their agreement "cautiously," stipulating that the crusaders were not to attack any Christians except for "just and necessary cause," and even with that cause they were to act only with the concurrence of a papal legate. It took no great prescience on Innocent's part to be concerned that a horde of men under arms could represent a threat to Christians whose territory they entered or that the Venetians might try to use the gathering force against some of their regional enemies. He was nervous about the absence of his representatives. He had even greater reason to be nervous when the Venetians rejected the provision requiring the legate's approval.[14]

From the very beginning, the crusade was developing outside of papal control, and its path continued to take unforeseen turns. When Villehardouin returned to Champagne in 1201, he found Count Thibaut on his sick bed. Within a month, the crusade had lost a young leader, and the other princes now sought to find another.[15] Villehardouin and others approached first the duke of Burgundy and then the count of Bar-le-Duc to assume leadership; both refused. Finally, the great princes accepted Villehardouin's suggestion that they offer the post to Marquis Boniface of Montferrat in northern Italy. Boniface was received by the princes at Soissons rather like a conquering hero, and he accepted the leadership. From there, he went to another meeting at Cîteaux, where were gathered not only Cistercian abbots at their annual general chapter, but also a great assembly of nobles. The preacher Fulk of Neuilly was also there, preaching the crusade, and many Burgundian nobles took the cross.

A man of about fifty, Boniface seems to have been the model Christian prince, equally at home in the company of Cistercian

---

[14] *Gesta*, PL 217:cxxxi = Gress-Wright, pp. 163–164.
[15] Regarding the "leadership" of Thibaut, see Queller and Madden, p. 24.

monks or troubadour poets.[16] He had many family attachments to
the east. His brothers had married into the ruling families of Constan-
tinople and Jerusalem, and he was the vassal of the Hohenstaufen
Philip of Swabia, who was also married to a Byzantine princess.
Shortly after accepting the leadership of the crusade, in late 1201,
Boniface paid a visit to Philip at Hagenau.

Again, Innocent had some reason to be concerned. On the plus
side, Boniface was admired as much by clerical reformers as he was
by courtly poets, and he had close ties to the city of Genoa, where
support for the crusade would be useful. But his ties to Philip of
Swabia were awkward, since by this time Innocent had given his
support to Philip's rival for the German and imperial crowns, Otto
of Brunswick. Innocent might well have preferred Count Baldwin of
Flanders, who had already taken the cross and who had in recent
years been allied with Otto and the kings of England; but the crusaders passed over him in favor of a candidate who was tied to
Philip of Swabia and who was approved by Philip's ally, Philip
Augustus.[17]

Boniface's visit to Philip of Swabia at Hagenau at Christmas of
1201 had raised another complicating possibility. He found there
Philip's brother-in-law, a young Byzantine prince named Alexius.
Alexius had recently escaped from Constantinople, where his father,
Isaac, had been overthrown as emperor and blinded by his own
brother, who had become the new emperor Alexius III. Philip and
the young Alexius raised with Boniface the possibility of routing the
crusade through Constantinople. If they restored the overthrown
emperor, they would then receive Byzantine help for the crusade.
Boniface left Hagenau and went to Rome to consult with Innocent.
At some point, young Alexius also came to Rome. There, before
the pope and a distinguished gathering of cardinals and Roman aristocrats, he gave his version of the unseating of his father. Innocent
now opposed the idea of diverting the crusade to Constantinople.[18]
There were so many western interests in the Byzantine empire that
he could easily foresee that the crusaders might be stalled there and

---

[16] See the editor's introduction to *The Poems of the Troubadour Raimbaut de Vaqueiras*,
ed. and trans. Joseph Linskill (Hague, 1964), pp. 8–10, 13–15, 18–20.

[17] Queller and Madden, p. 25.

[18] *Gesta*, PL 214:cxxx–cxxxi = Gress-Wright, pp. 160–163; Reg. 5:121 (122).

forget about the Holy Land. And he could not welcome closer ties between the Hohenstaufen and Constantinople.[19]

In the spring and early summer of 1202, crusaders began to trickle into Venice, where they were ferried out to the Lido to pitch their camps. A total of 33,500 crusaders was expected, too many to shelter safely within the city proper. The original plan had been to depart at the end of June, but this was not a disciplined modern army. Large numbers of crusaders, ignoring warnings from the pope,[20] decided to take different routes and departed from Marseilles, Genoa, and Apulia. A fleet that had set sail from Flanders was supposed to go to Venice, by way of the straits of Gibraltar; but after many delays, its leaders decided to proceed directly to the Holy Land. Others did not feel bound by any particular timetable. Boniface of Montferrat, seeing no reason to leave the comfort of his own territory until the army had assembled, did not arrive until 15 August 1202.

In the meantime, the Byzantine prince Alexius had taken up residence in Verona, and his envoys were lobbying the leaders of the crusade to look toward Constantinople. They argued that the prince's father could easily be restored and that then all the wealth and resources of the Empire would back the crusade. The leaders had good reason to consider the plan. The throng of men on the Lido, speaking a variety of French, Italian, and German dialects, was growing restless; and it had become clear that their numbers were not going to increase. Only about one third of the 33,500 men had arrived and their resources fell far short of the money promised to the Venetians.

But so far as the pope knew in mid-summer of 1202, there were no serious problems with the crusade. It was running a little behind schedule, but it was taking shape nonetheless, and with a leader of high character. Innocent had no great reason to be concerned; and in early August, 1202, before open violence had broken out between

---

[19] There is abundant scholarly literature on whether or not there were from the beginning conspiracies or plans by which some or all the leaders of the crusade were committed to diverting the crusade to Constantinople. For an introduction to the literature, see Charles M. Brand, "The Fourth Crusade: Some Recent Interpretations," *Medievalia et Humanistica* 12 (1984) 33–45. Brand believes there was such a plan; I agree with those, notably Queller, Madden, and Maleczek, who see the decision to go to Constantinople arising out of the circumstances the crusaders found themselves in first in Venice and then in Zara. See Queller and Madden, passim, and Maleczek, *Petrus Capuanus*, p. 150.

[20] Queller and Madden, p. 48.

the Scotti and Boboni in Rome, he led his curia from the heat of Rome for the visit to Subiaco that was described in the previous chapter.

*   *   *

While the pope enjoyed his late summer excursion, the crusade in Venice ran into serious trouble. The Venetians had turned all their efforts to meeting the terms of the agreement. A fully equipped fleet lay bobbing in the harbor; but the crusaders, after pooling all their resources, were still thirty-four thousand marks short of what was owed. The French envoys had grossly overestimated the men and money they could muster; and the Venetians were angry. The doge told them,

> Lords, you have used us ill, for as soon as your messengers had made the bargain with me I commanded through all my land that no trader should go a-trading, but that all should help prepare this navy. So they have waited ever since and have not made any money for a year and a half past. Instead, they have lost a great deal, and therefore we wish, my men and I, that you should pay us the money you owe us. And if you do not do so, then know that you shall not depart from this island before we are paid, nor shall you find anyone to bring you anything to eat or drink.[21]

The threat was an empty one. The fleet had already been built, and starving 11,000 crusaders on the Lido would do nothing to recoup the investment. What could be done?

*   *   *

The city of Zara (modern Zadar) stood on the eastern coast of the Adriatic, about 290 km. southeast of Venice, and it had long before been brought under Venetian control. But for some twenty years, the city had found freedom from the Venetians by offering allegiance to the king of Hungary and by seeking ties with Pisa. Venice had tried several times in vain to retake the heavily fortified city. The doge now proposed that the crusaders help Venice to do so. In

---

[21] Robert of Clari, *The Conquest of Constantinople*, tr. Edgar Holmes McNeal (New York, 1979 repr. of 1936), p. 40.

return, the balance of their debt would be postponed, to be paid out of the booty of later conquests.

The crusaders faced a hard decision. Zara was a Christian city that claimed allegiance to the Christian king of Hungary, who was himself a sworn crusader. Even if Venetian claims to the city were legitimate, it was an awkward course for a crusading army, and it clearly ran contrary to the pope's prohibition against attacking other Christians. On the other hand, if the great army lingering on the Lido broke up and went slinking back home, it would be to the eternal disgrace of its leaders, and Jerusalem would remain in the hands of the infidel. Reluctantly, those leaders agreed to go to Zara, but not without sharp disagreements among themselves. Although they decided to tell the army only that the Venetians had agreed to postpone payment, without mentioning the attack on Zara, rumors soon circulated. Crusaders at every level debated the legitimacy of the plan; many were tempted to use it as an excuse to return home, their crusading fervor having been burned out on the hot beaches of the Lido. Some high-level clergy thought they should abandon the crusade rather than be associated with an attack on Christians. The papal legate Peter Capuano, without approving the diversion to Zara, told others that they must stay with the crusade.[22] In the end, some defected, but the greater part of the army formed the splendid armada that set sail in the first week of October 1202.[23] Zara was the destination.

News of the plan probably reached Innocent in Ferentino or Rome in October. Peter Capuano had done what he could to keep the army together; but his authority over the venture as papal legate had been rejected by the Venetians, so he went immediately to report to Innocent. Boniface of Montferrat and his adviser Peter the Cistercian abbot of Lucedio carried the same news to the pope. Innocent personally forbad Boniface to join the attack on Zara and dispatched Abbot Peter with a letter to the crusaders, forbidding the attack.[24]

---

[22] Queller and Madden, p. 63, present the cardinal as a hard-nosed realist, invoking "necessity" and approving the diversion to Zara as a necessary evil, but the sources do not go that far. See Alfred J. Andrea and John C. Moore, "A Question of Character: Two Views on Innocent III and the Fourth Crusade," in *Innocentius Papa III: Urbis et Orbis*. 2 vols. Ed. Brenda Bolton and Werner Maleczek (in press).

[23] Queller and Madden, pp. 68–71.

[24] For the disputed chronology of these events, see John C. Moore, "Peter of Lucedio," pp. 242–243. There I have the two visiting Rome in "1202 about

The letter, read to the crusaders beneath the walls of Zara by another Cistercian abbot, once again presented the barons with a moral dilemma. The papal prohibition was clear; still they had given their word to the Venetians. The city stood before them as a necessary means for continuing the crusade. A substantial number of the crusaders refused to have any part of the attack, some finding immediate passage to the Holy Land;[25] but in November 1202 the assault began and Zara was taken, with much bloodshed and looting. Since winter made sea passage dangerous, the expedition settled in for the winter, not without serious friction between the Venetians and the rest of the crusaders, now forced to live together in close quarters.

* * *

In the very month when the crusaders were occupying and despoiling Zara, and before Innocent knew that they had disregarded his prohibition, a remarkable confluence of envoys from the Balkan area was present in Rome pursuing related interests. The envoys of King Imre of Hungary were in Rome seeking papal approval for a number of things, and Innocent was trying to accommodate, even defending the king's rights against the Hungarian hierarchy.[26] To the king's request that he be excused from carrying out his crusading oath, however, Innocent was more resistant. If his kingdom was actually threatened by the troublesome Kulin, ban of Bosnia, he might delay his crusade; otherwise he should proceed. Innocent did not mention Zara; he probably did not know whether the crusaders had obeyed his order not to attack the city. But the possibility of their disobedience was certainly in his mind when he told King Imre that perhaps he had already offended God not only by delaying his crusade but also by attacking other Christians.[27] Should the crusaders take the city, Imre might see it as divine retribution rather than a crusade gone awry.

Kulin, ban of Bosnia, had his own representatives there, including the archbishop of Ragusa. They were responding to complaints

(made by the king of Hungary) that heretics were flourishing in the
ban's territories. They denied that the people in question were heretics
and invited the pope to send representatives to examine them.
Innocent did so, saying that he did not seek the death of sinners,
but rather their conversion and life.[28]

At about the same time, the papal messenger Dominic (a Greek
archpriest from Brindisi) returned from his journey to the Bulgars
and Vlachs, bearing messages from the "Emperor" Johanitsa Asen—
also known as Kalojan—and his familiars. Kalojan's own envoy, having come by a different route, had not yet arrived. Kalojan sought
an imperial crown from the pope, implicitly claiming equal status
with the Latin and Greek Roman emperors. Kalojan's claims were
based on strength; he and his forces of Vlachs, Bulgarians, and
Cumans had recently come close to capturing Constantinople itself.[29]
Innocent responded by dispatching as legate the papal chaplain John
of Casamari, charged with examining "old books and other documents" concerning Kalojan's claim to the imperial title.[30]

And finally, representatives of the Byzantine Emperor Alexius III
were in Rome. Alexius had not only Kalojan to fear. He knew that
his own nephew Alexius was in the West seeking support, and he
urged Innocent to oppose him, especially because of his connection
to the Hohenstaufens. Innocent responded that the young Alexius
had in fact been making every effort to recruit the pope, the
Hohenstaufens, and the crusaders to support his father's restoration
to the Byzantine throne. Most recently, the crusaders had sent
Cardinal Peter Capuano to Rome to obtain papal judgment on the
plan. Innocent told the Greek emperor that his own ruling "should
be pleasing to you"—though many urged support for the plan, given
the fact that the Greek church was in schism from the Roman
church. The pope clearly did not want Alexius to feel too secure
that the diversion to Constantinople was a completely dead letter.
Innocent warned Alexius to respond with deeds rather than words.[31]

These dignitaries and their business do not appear in the papal
registers for December 1202. For the remainder of the month,
Innocent was occupied with matters large and small touching on

---

[28] Reg. 5:109 (110).
[29] Robert Lee Wolff. "The 'Second Bulgarian empire.' Its Origin and History to
1204," *Speculum* 24 (1949): 189.
[30] Reg. 5:114 (115)–119 (120), especially Reg. 5:115 (116).
[31] Reg. 5:121 (122).

many different parts of Europe. Generally, things were looking very good. The rulers of Greek and Bulgar territories to the east were represented in his court as petitioners. The death of three prominent enemies in the Regno heartened him, giving him hope that he could now turn his full attention to establishing his candidate in the empire.[32] He called on all the German princes to observe a one-year truce, beginning at Easter, during which they should establish a final peace in the empire. He suggested that they convene in Rome where they could work together to restore tranquility to the empire.[33] He was even considering calling a general council to address all the problems facing the church.[34]

But this heady atmosphere was soured by the news that arrived, probably in the second half of December. The Christian citizens of Zara had hung crucifixes from the wall, trying to stave off the attack, but in vain. The crusaders had taken and despoiled the city, attacking Christians and violating the rights of the city's crusader lord, King Imre of Hungary. Innocent wrote a bitter letter of recrimination, telling them that they had already incurred excommunication by their actions and warning them to restore to the city and the king all that they had taken.[35]

In January of 1203, a delegation led by Bishop Nivelon of Soissons arrived from Zara seeking forgiveness for the crusaders. In his response, Innocent stressed again the gravity of the offense, that "soldiers of Christ" who had taken the cross on behalf of Christ had then turned their arms against him; but Innocent also rejoiced that they had repented. He warned them sternly to restore everything they had taken from Zara and to seek the forgiveness of the king of Hungary. He dispatched Cardinal Peter Capuano to remove the excommunication they had incurred, but he was to do so only after the leaders of the crusade had committed themselves in writing to carry out the papal orders. The pope repeated his earlier instruction that they were to refrain from any further attacks on Christians,

---

[32] Markward of Anweiler, Conrad of Urslingen, and Otto von Barkenstein. RNI, no. 80, p. 219.

[33] RNI, no. 79.

[34] RNI, no. 80, p. 219.

[35] Reg. 5:160 (161); Queller and Madden, pp. 76–78; Andrea and Moore, "Question of Character," (in press); Othmar Hageneder, "Innocenz III. und die Eroberung Zadars (1202): Eine Neuinterpretation des Br. V 160 (161)," *Mitteilungen des Instituts für Österreichische Geschichtsforschung*, 100 (1992): 197–213.

"unless perchance they wrongly impede your way or unless some other just and necessary reason should arise"—and in those cases they should act only in consultation with papal authority.[36]

The exact state of the crusaders remained rather murky. Many of them had refused to participate in the attack on Zara, and Boniface of Montferrat had not been present, having rejoined the army only after the city had been taken. These crusaders could assume that they were not excommunicated. Those who had taken part in the assault had probably assumed rightly that they were, but they had also been absolved, illegally, by some of the clergy present. Moreover, Cardinal Peter never made it to Zara to lift the excommunication, sending his messenger instead while he himself proceeded to the Holy Land.[37] For their part, the Venetians showed no sign of repentance whatsoever.

In the early months of 1203, while Gerald of Wales pursued the defense of his church and his gelding, while the Roman factions gave Lent a political flavor, and while Innocent expressed his confidence that the imperial question would soon be settled,[38] the crusaders wintering in Zara faced still another cruel decision. A delegation from Philip of Swabia arrived to push the cause of his brother-in-law, young Alexius of Constantinople. The crusading army had been weakened by further defections; the contract bound the Venetians for only one year, and months were being eaten up by the winter stay in Zara. The delegation presented an attractive offer: if the crusaders would proceed to Constantinople to restore young Alexius and his father to power, then the Byzantine government would guarantee that the Greek church would accept the authority of the pope (thus ending the schism) and that the Greeks would give support to the crusade in the form of supplies, two-hundred thousand marks, and ten thousand soldiers. The crusaders were given the impression that they would be received in Constantinople as liberators, so that there would be little need to shed Christian blood.[39]

The offer was bitterly debated, with clergy and laity on both sides of the issue. As things stood, the crusade seemed to be falling apart.

---

[36] Reg. 5:161 (162).

[37] Maleczek, *Petrus Capuanus*, pp. 141, 148.

[38] RNI, no. 84, p. 226. Writing to Cardinal Guido, he wrote, "quoniam, quod credimus, in breui terminabitur labor tuus ad exaltationem apostolice sedis, augmentum imperii et tue fraternitatis honorem."

[39] Maleczek, *Petrus Capuanus*, pp. 149–150.

If Alexius could deliver on his promises, the crusade would receive an enormous boost and Christianity would be delivered from a scandalous schism between Greek and Latin. But could he deliver? And for those whose consciences were already raw from the diversion to Zara, how could another diversion, against another Christian city, be justified? For the Venetians, the decision was not difficult. Their consciences had not been troubled by the sack of Zara, and the diversion to Constantinople offered weighty advantages beyond those sought by the crusaders: the Venetians would improve their chances of getting paid by the crusaders and they would gain an advantage over Genoa and Pisa, their commercial rivals in Constantinople. Finally, Boniface of Montferrat, the other major leaders, and the Venetians agreed. But as many as two thousand crusaders balked and set out by various routes directly for Jerusalem. Villehardouin believed that these crusaders, together with another group that had sailed from Flanders and wintered at Marseilles, without ever going to Venice and Zara, outnumbered those who followed their leaders to Constantinople.[40]

About the same time that this was going on, in April of 1203, the non-Venetian leaders decided to give the pope the required promise of obedience and dispatched a messenger for Rome. Boniface included his own message, telling the pope that he had suppressed the papal bull excommunicating the recalcitrant Venetians because he was afraid that its publication would lead to the dispersal of the force. The crusaders now asked for further instructions from the pope, probably knowing full well that instructions would not arrive in time to hamper any plans they might make.[41]

For his part, Innocent knew nothing definite about the crusaders' plans. He did receive a message from Peter Capuano about this time, written before Peter had left Italy for the Holy Land. In his response, dated 21 April, Innocent told Peter that if the entire force refused to repent the sack of Zara, he should abandon the crusade and condemn the entire force. If the non-Venetians should repent, he should absolve them and accompany them to the Holy Land. And if the non-Venetian crusaders balked at some of the pope's stipulations, Peter should do as the spirit of God moved him—pre-

---

[40] Queller and Madden, pp. 82–93.
[41] Reg. 6:99, 100. These letters are discussed further below.

sumably meaning he should make the best deal he could. That was all Innocent could say in April, as he waited to see whether he was going to have to abandon and condemn his crusading force for their sins at Zara.

*   *   *

However anxious Innocent may have been for news from Zara, the rest of the world did not sit back and wait. The papal letters continued to pour forth from Rome to Italy, France, Germany, England. A notable series went to Sardinia, where Innocent was trying to make good his claim that Sardinia belonged to the Patrimonium. As part of that effort he successfully placed Biaggio, one of his curial clerks, as archbishop of Torres.[42]

In May 1203, the papal court moved on to Palestrina and then Ferentino, followed by a crowd of suitors, including the discouraged and impoverished Gerald of Wales.

At Ferentino, the cathedral where Innocent prayed still stands, still boasts a tile floor said to have been given by him. It rises from the very summit of the town, part of the acropolis that rests on a foundation of enormous stones of irregular size and shape, stacked long before the ancient Romans arrived. A pagan temple once stood there; now only the bases of the columns remain, lying in submission near the cathedral. Down narrow twisting streets can be found the market stalls of antiquity, sheltered by a barrel vault, and the modest three-story stone house said to have been Innocent's residence.

Centuries before, Horace advised, "If you like quiet and late sleep in the morning, and if dust, clattering wheels, and hotels annoy you, then go to Ferentino, I urge you."[43] The piazza in front of the cathedral overlooks the neatly laid out fields far below to the south and west. To the east lies a series of rounded hills, each a little higher until the most remote seem to blend with the distant sky. In May, the cool, clear mountain air is full of the perfume of blossoming trees and the whistling of swallows circling above the red-tiled roof tops. Innocent did his part to add to the beauty of the place that summer by commissioning a beautiful new fountain.[44]

---

[42] Moore, "Pope Innocent III, Sardinia," pp. 89–91.
[43] *Epistolae*, 1.17.8.
[44] *Gesta*, PL 214:clxxxvii = Gress-Wright, p. 334.

Here Innocent had his last conversations with Gerald; but it is surprising that the pope had any time for him at all, because the suitors that followed to Ferentino were as numerous and persistent as the swallows in the air. During the summer, Innocent was most concerned with two things, the division within the empire and the needs of the Holy Land,[45] but many other weighty matters pressed upon the curia. Innocent threatened King John of England with excommunication and interdict because of his mistreatment of both the archbishop of Dublin and the bishop of Séez.[46] He pressed John and Philip Augustus to make peace with each other (for the sake of recruiting support for the faltering crusade).[47] He gave judgment in a centuries-old dispute over the boundaries separating several Spanish bishoprics.[48] He scolded—once again—King Alfonso of Castile for the incestuous marriage of his daughter to the king of Léon,[49] and he attended to a number of lesser matters emanating from Spain[50]— including the case of the man who had made his way to the papal court to confess to having sexual relations with his mother-in-law.[51] About this time, a letter from Ingeborg arrived, complaining bitterly of her treatment by Philip Augustus. She was, she said, a prisoner at Étampes, unable to communicate with the outside world or even to pray as she wished. Her plight was one more problem that would not go away, and Innocent tried again, sending the Abbot Gerald of Casamari to console the queen and writing another letter to Philip, urging him to treat her decently.[52] The French monarch seemed to regard Ingeborg about the same way as a certain woman in Spain regarded her first husband. Her case reached Ferentino about this time, and she is quoted as saying that she would rather become a Muslim and lose her soul than be forced to return to him.[53]

In June, the long-awaited messenger arrived from the crusading princes, and once again, Innocent was faced with a painfully ambiguous situation. He had insisted that they commit themselves and their

---

[45] RNI, no. 87, p. 232.
[46] Reg. 6:63, 6:73.
[47] Reg. 6:68, 6:69.
[48] Reg. 6:75.
[49] Reg. 6:80.
[50] See Register entries for May and June, 1203.
[51] Reg. 6:92.
[52] Reg. 6:85–86.
[53] Reg. 6:108.

heirs to reparations to Zara and the king of Hungary if they were to be freed from excommunication. Because the Venetians had made no pretense of repentance, he had sent a bull formally excommunicating them. Now he received the letter from the counts of Flanders, Blois, and St. Pol affirming that they and a few other leaders accepted his terms and promised to obey his will in the matter of reparations. They bound themselves and their heirs to do so, and they had received absolution from the messenger of Cardinal Peter Capuano.[54] But from the same letter, and from the separate letter from Boniface of Montferrat,[55] Innocent learned that the bull excommunicating the unrepentant Venetians had been held back by Boniface for fear that its publication would disrupt the crusade. Boniface had suppressed the bull despite the fact that Innocent had explicitly rejected such an idea when it had been proposed by the messenger of the princes the previous January.

The princes did not cast these letters in defiant terms; on the contrary, the princes asked for further instructions from the pope. But since they were following a course of fairly consistent defiance of papal orders, they were probably in no hurry to receive any more of those orders. Their messenger was a low-level functionary[56] not qualified to do any more than deliver the letters to the pope, and he was probably told to take his time in even doing that. It was a tactic worthy of Count Baldwin of Flanders, a man who had already proven himself to be a skillful manipulator of papal authority.[57]

Innocent's ambivalence is abundantly clear in his response. comparing the crusaders to the biblical Jews fleeing Egypt:

> Since you set out from Egypt under the strong hand and extended arm [of God] so that you might offer yourselves in sacrifice to the Lord, we have mourned not a little, and we still mourn, that you flee before the pharaoh, or rather, you follow the pharaoh, who, under the appearance of necessity and a cloak of piety is trying in the same old way to subject you to servitude under the yoke of sin. We have mourned, as we said, and we still mourn, equally for ourselves, for you, and for the whole Christian people.

---

[54] Reg. 6:99, Andrea, *Contemporary Sources*, pp. 54–57.

[55] Reg. 6:100, Andrea, *Contemporary Sources*, pp. 57–59.

[56] My understanding of "simplicitatem huius nuntii." Andrea translates it, however, as "the directness of this message" (*Contemporary Sources*, p. 59).

[57] See Moore, "Count Baldwin IX," pp. 79–89.

We mourn for ourselves. We thought that what we had sown in tears through our legates and letters to you and to others—often with a certain bitterness of heart and considerable physical anxiety, setting forth the word of the Lord and urging the bearers of the name "Christian" to avenge the injury to Jesus Christ—we thought that with shouts of joy we would reap what we had sown. Suddenly, the enemy has sown weeds on top of our sowing and has so spoiled the crop that the wheat seems to have turned into darnel.

We mourn for you. When you had discarded the old leaven and were thought to have completely cast off the old man and his ways, a small measure, a tragic measure, of the old leaven has again corrupted the whole mass. You have not kept your garments white, but have put on the old garment again. You have withdrawn your hand from the plow, and with Lot's wife, you have looked back. As the apostle says, you do not seem ready for the kingdom of God.

We have mourned and we still mourn for the Christian people. They have been humiliated where they thought they would be exalted. For when many who had preceded you to . . . the Holy Land heard that you had set sail, they departed for their homelands, confident of your arrival. The Saracens, however, doubtful about your arrival but certain of the others' departure, have taken up arms against Christians. We do want to repeat how they have prevailed against them (the wages of sin), since it is known almost everywhere.

Innocent told them that he rejoiced that they had seen the error of their ways, had met papal terms for absolution, and had agreed to abide by papal orders in the future. But he was clearly uneasy about the sincerity of their submission. He said that he hoped their repentance was sincere and that they would beware of committing the same sin again. To do so would be like a dog returning to its vomit. He continued:

Let no one of you carelessly delude himself into thinking that it is licit to occupy or plunder the land of the Greeks because it is not subject to the Apostolic See or because the emperor of Constantinople usurped the government from his brother, having deposed and blinded him. Clearly, regardless of how much the emperor and those under his jurisdiction are delinquent in these and in other matters, it is not for you to judge their crimes. You have not taken the cross to avenge that injustice, but rather to avenge the shame of the crucified one, to whose service you have been especially appointed.

Therefore, we warn you, we urgently exhort you, and by apostolic letter we authoritatively command you that you neither deceive yourselves nor permit others to deceive you, so that under the appearance of piety you do those things—God forbid—that may lead to the destruction of your souls. Rather, we command you to put an end to the frivolous excuses and pretended necessities and go the aid of the Holy Land and avenge the injury of the cross. Take from the enemy those spoils which you might otherwise, should you delay in Byzantine territory, take from your brothers. Otherwise, we certainly do not promise you the grace of remission of sins—nor can we nor should we.

Innocent reminded them of his earlier letter in which he had forbidden them, under threat of excommunication, to invade or injure the lands of Christians without just cause and without the approval of a papal legate. And he ordered them to deliver immediately to the Venetians the bull of excommunication.[58]

The letter containing these demands was a formal one, intended to be seen by all. Next to it in the papal register is another message, a separate note sent without the papal seal, giving secret instructions to the princes. It probably accompanied the formal letter. In it, Innocent advised the princes that if the Venetians repented, all well and good; but if they persisted in their sins, as seemed likely, they remained excommunicated. Lest the princes should feel bound to avoid their company, Innocent explained in some detail that given their circumstances, the princes were permitted to communicate with the excommunicated Venetians until they reached the Holy Land. At that point, however, they should not join them in battle against the Saracens for fear that the presence of excommunicates in their ranks would turn God against them. He also told the princes that he was writing the emperor of Constantinople to remind him of his promise to provide supplies to the crusaders; and he defined the way the crusaders could requisition supplies if the emperor should renege on his promises.[59]

* * *

By June, when the letters to which Innocent was responding had reached him in Ferentino, however, the crusading fleet had moved on, with the young Alexius in tow. In May, at the island of Corfu, the crusaders had continued their debate over the diversion to

---

[58] Reg. 6:101, Andrea, *Contemporary Sources*, pp. 59-64.

[59] Reg. 6:102. For the dating of this document, see Alfred J. Andrea and John C. Moore, "The Date of Reg. 6:102: Pope Innocent III's Letter of Advice to the Crusaders," in *Medieval and Renaissance Venice*, ed. Ellen E. Kittel and Thomas F. Madden (Urbana, 1999), pp. 109-123. For a discussion of its contents and context, see Andrea and Moore, "A Question of Character," (in press).

Constantinople, with the majority in opposition. The leaders, who had already committed themselves to Alexius, finally persuaded the others to go to Constantinople by guaranteeing them that if things did not go as smoothly as predicted, those who wished could proceed directly to the Holy Land.[60]

When Innocent dispatched his replies to the crusading princes in June, forbidding them to attack the lands of the Greeks, he had no idea where they were. In fact, their fleet was already maneuvering within sight of Constantinople. The crusaders did not find the welcome they expected from the supporters of young Alexius; but in the following weeks, their attacks upon the walls of the city created disunity within the city. Frightened by enemies within and without the city, the reigning emperor fled. The officials he left behind wisely removed Isaac II, the father of young Alexius, from his prison and restored him to his throne. By 1 August, it appeared that the diversion to Constantinople had been successful. All that remained was for Isaac and his son to fulfill the young man's promise: two-hundred thousand marks of silver, provisions for one year, ten thousand men to serve for one year, and a permanent garrison of five hundred knights in the Holy Land.[61]

As of August 1203, Innocent had not yet received this news, but he had heard from the Holy Land. A delegation from the church of the Holy Sepulcher arrived bearing letters that made two things clear: first, that the bitter divisions among Christians there, especially in the vicinity of Tyre, was proving an intractable problem that was wearing down Cardinal Soffredus, and second, that despite his resistance to the idea, the canons of the Holy Sepulcher wanted Soffredus as their new patriarch. Soffredus had heard of the diversion to Zara and had heard reports of even worse to come. Innocent wrote at length to Soffredus, offering consolation and urging him to accept the office of patriarch—in vain as things turned out. He assured the cardinal that even if the crusaders were diverted to Constantinople, Innocent would persevere in his efforts to get them to the Holy Land.[62]

---

[60] Queller and Madden, pp. 98–99; Thomas F. Madden, "Vows and Contracts in the Fourth Crusade: The Treaty of Zara and the Attack on Constantinople in 1204," *International History Review*, 15 (1993): 441–442.

[61] Queller and Madden, pp. 108–134.

[62] Reg. 6:130–135.

Meanwhile, as the crusaders had worked their victorious, if not glorious, way around the edges of the Balkans, the papal legate John of Casamari had worked his equally victorious way through the center. He had visited the lands of Kulin of Bosnia and the kingdom of Hungary, and about the beginning of September, reports of his progress reached the pope. While in Bosnia, John had taken stock of the religious situation. He had obtained an oath of submission to Rome from a religious group there, previously thought to be heretics. He also reported that the kingdom itself needed new bishoprics, since it took ten days to cross and there was but a single bishopric. John had not yet completed his mission of visiting Kalojan, the king of the Vlacs and Bulgars, but he expressed his intention to continue through Hungary to do so.[63]

About the same time, September, 1203, Innocent received a letter directly from Kalojan himself. The letter continued an exchange that had been drawn out over several years because of the difficulty of communication. In blunt terms, Kalojan informed the pope once again that he was interested in union with Rome, but for a price: the title of emperor for himself and the title of patriarch for his archbishop of Trnovo (Zagoro). To motivate the pope, he made the incredible claim that Constantinople had offered him both titles, but that he preferred alliance with the pope.[64] Innocent encouraged Kalojan and his archbishop to submit to Rome and told them that John of Casamari was on the way to Bulgaria, where he would look into the claims made for the imperial and patriarchal titles—though Innocent continued to speak of Kalojan only as "Lord of the Bulgars," not even yet conceding the title of "king."[65]

The prospects for Latin expansion in the Balkans were very promising. King Imre of Hungary seemed to be supporting papal negotiations with Kalojan—promising to permit messengers to pass back and forth through his kingdom.[66] In his letter to Kalojan, Innocent urged him to make peace with Vukan, prince of Dalmatia and Dioclea (who was already an ally of Imre).[67] If the king of the Bulgars,

---

[63] Reg. 6:140.

[64] Reg. 6:142.

[65] Reg. 6:143–144; Wolff. "The 'Second Bulgarian empire,'" pp. 190–195.

[66] Reg. 6:140. For a thorough treatment of Innocent's diplomacy in this area, see James Ross Sweeney, "Innocent III, Hungary and the Bulgarian Coronation: A Study in Medieval Papal Diplomacy," *Church History* 42 (1973): 320–334.

[67] Fine, *Late Medieval Balkans*, pp. 43–46.

the king of the Hungarians, and the prince (or "Grand Zupan") of Dalmatia and Dioclea could all be brought within the Roman orbit and all be persuaded to make peace with one another, the strength of Latin Christendom, vis-a-vis Islam, would be very much enhanced. This prospect would have been in the mind of Innocent and his advisers when news first reached them that the Latin crusaders had taken control of Constantinople.

Then all the grandiose plans seemed ready to disintegrate in October when the pope fell seriously ill. His brother Marshal Richard and Walter of Brienne both suspended their military campaigns in the south to come to his sick bed in Anagni. Soon, reports of the pope's death swept through Italy, and southern cities and nobles rebelled against the agents of papal authority, showing how fragile was the allegiance they had sworn to the pope. In Germany, supporters of Duke Philip of Swabia actually reported that a new pope, named Clement, had been elected, and they presented bulls purported to be from the new pope in support of their case against Otto. The reports, however, were false. Innocent soon informed the world that the same God who had struck him down had now fully restored him to health.[68] In the last weeks of 1203, Innocent was back to his routine, issuing a letter in which he bitterly criticized Philip Augustus for keeping Ingeborg sequestered in quarters like "a peasant's hut in a cucumber field."[69] Other letters initiated a new diplomatic offensive to organize support for Otto in Germany and northern Italy.[70]

The last weeks of 1203 also produced a very different kind of letter. A few days before Christmas, the curia issued one of the longest letters of the year, but it was a letter without political import. John of Bellesmains, an old man who had once served as bishop of Poitiers and then as archbishop of Lyons, had retired to the monastery at Clairvaux. He had recently written the pope a letter asking about certain minor anomalies in the liturgy, and Innocent wrote a wide-ranging response dealing mainly with the Trinity but touching on the nature of angels and of humans, and on the way liturgical prayers

---

[68] *Gesta*, PL 214:lxvi–lxvii, clxxxvii–clxxxviii = Gress-Wright, pp. 52, 334. Tillmann, *Pope Innocent III*, p. 126. See Innocent's description of his illness: RNI, no. 91, p. 238, no. 96, p. 251.

[69] Reg. 6:182.

[70] RNI, nos. 92–105.

had grown in response to heretical movements. At one point, he reined himself in "lest we seem to be dictating a book rather than writing a letter." There is a gentleness about the letter that does not often appear in the papal registers. Innocent commended the old man for his piety, and urged that any failures in his response be attributed to the pressing obligations that occupied him, as they did Martha. He was so burdened with red-eyed Leah, he said, that he could rarely touch the loveliness of Rachel—that is, the press of practical matters kept him from the beauty of prayerful contemplation.[71]

* * *

Whether the news from Constantinople had anything to do with his illness, we do not know. We do not know when Innocent first heard that the Latins had taken Constantinople and had installed an emperor offering submission to the papacy, and we have no record of his immediate reaction. We also do not know when news reached Innocent of subsequent troubles in Constantinople. In August, the same month in which young Alexius IV was installed, there were riots between Greeks and Latins, and a fire carelessly begun by Latins destroyed major parts of the city. Alexius IV was trying to fulfill his agreement with the crusaders, but the more he tried to raise money, the more bitter the resistance he faced from his own people. He probably saw the pointlessness of a vain attempt to steer the Greek church toward Rome. The crusaders for their part were eager to proceed to the Holy Land, but they needed the promised support. They were therefore soon involved in Alexius's attempts to subdue his empire. Again, after bitter debate among the crusaders, they agreed to delay their departure for the Holy Land, this time until the following March.[72]

Whether or not reports of all this reached Innocent earlier, in late January of 1204, he received official notices, written the previous August. A letter from the crusaders triumphantly proclaimed their success in Constantinople, and a letter from young Alexius IV offered submission to the Roman church.[73]

---

[71] Reg. 6:193. On John of Bellesmains, see Charles Duggan, "Bishop John and Archdeacon Richard of Poitiers. Their Roles in the Becket Dispute and its Aftermath," in Duggan, *Canon Law in Medieval England. The Becket Dispute and Decretal Collections* (London, 1982).

[72] Queller and Madden, pp. 140–147; Brand, *Byzantium*, pp. 242–250.

[73] Reg. 6:210–211.

The papal register for February 1204 reveals sharp differences within the curia about the proper response.[74] Some argued that the crusaders had in fact been justified, that they had sought to unite the Greek and Latin churches out of reverence for the Holy See. Others argued that the crusaders had simply defied the pope again and perjured themselves in the process, and that the unification of the two churches was only an excuse. Innocent showed his own uncertainty when he wrote letters that castigated the crusaders for the diversion, but that said only that he was "afraid" that they had again incurred excommunication. The letters also reflect the delicacy required in dealing with the situation in Constantinople. On the one hand, Innocent wanted to rebuke the crusaders for their disobedience to papal commands; on the other, he did not want to make so much of their sinfulness that they would abandon the crusade or that the Greeks would repudiate the promises of Alexius.[75] Innocent expressed the not very optimistic hope that something would come of Alexius's promises and urged the crusaders to repent and proceed to the Holy Land.

Innocent may have been ambivalent about the capture of Constantinople and the deposition of the emperor, but he had some reason to see the hand of God at work. He wrote to Otto in January 1204 that Otto's successes seemed to show that God approved the pope's choice for emperor.[76] Could not the fall of Constantinople be another sign of God's favor? The sudden prospect of a united Christendom stretching through the Balkans and the Byzantine Empire, all acknowledging papal authority, was very appealing.

An immediate benefit of the capture of Constantinople was the impression it would make on others in the area. When a delegation from Kalojan, king of the Bulgarians, arrived at the papal court in Anagni in early 1204, Innocent had a new diplomatic weapon. The delegation repeated Kalojan's offer to submit to the pope and to bring his people into communion with the Latin church, provided Innocent would concede to him the title of emperor and to the arch-

---

[74] Reg. 6:229 (230)–231 (232). These letters contain several references to differing opinions held by "certain people" or "many," and Innocent refers to what "seems" to have taken place, rather than making flat assertions.

[75] For an interpretation of these letters, see Andrea and Moore, "A Question of Character," (in press).

[76] RNI, no. 107, p. 266.

bishop of Trnovo the title of patriarch. Innocent wrote with t. confidence that now Kalojan had before him the disturbing specta cle of what happened to rulers who were at odds with the pope. Biblical references to "destroying" and "tearing down" now took on ominous new meaning in the wake of the capture of Constantinople. This new situation may also have been the stimulus for Innocent's eloquent statement in his response to Kalojan of the majesty of the papal office:

> The king of kings and lord of lords, Jesus Christ, forever priest of the order of Melchisedech, in whose hands the father has placed all things and under whose feet all things are cast, to whom belongs the earth and its plenitude, the orb and all its inhabitants, before whom indeed every knee bends in heaven, on earth, and in hell—he has established over nations and kingdoms the supreme pontiff of the Apostolic See and Roman church. Through Blessed Peter, he ordained the pontiff as his vicar, conferring upon him the power to root up, to break down, to destroy, and to overthrow, to build and to plant [Jer. 1:10]. . . . In order to draw in his sheep that were not of the this flock so that there would be one flock and one shepherd [John 10:16], the blessed God has established the foundation of the universal church in himself, who is above all things, and has conferred upon Peter, the prince of his apostles, *magisterium* and primacy, saying to him, "You are Peter and upon this rock I will build my church, and the gates of hell will not prevail against it, and I give to you the keys of the kingdom of heaven" [Matt. 16:18–19]. And then he added, "Whatever you bind on earth will be bound in heaven, and whatever you loose on earth will be loosed in heaven." And after his passion, about to ascend into heaven, he committed and commended to Peter his flock, that is, the church, in all things, and said to him, "Feed my sheep" [John 21:17]. He repeated it three times, thereby showing clearly that those sheep do not belong to his flock who contumaciously deny that they have been committed to and are subject to blessed Peter, who refuse to be instructed with his doctrine and to be subject to his *magisterium*. Indeed, the church is that ark in which a few souls were saved, the others perishing in the flood. Just as all those not taken in the ark perished in the flood, so will all those found outside the church be damned in judgment. For the ark prefigures the church, the deluge prefigures judgment, and Noah, the captain of the arc, prefigures Peter the shepherd (*pastor*) of the church. Noah, it is written, walked with the Lord; but Peter, it is written, came to the Lord across the waves of the sea, which there signifies the world.
>
> It should be noted that it was not some particular church that was committed especially to Peter, but rather the whole world and the general church. For just as the many waters are the many peoples, so also does the great and spacious sea signify the entire world. Whence,

having called others to a share in the solicitude, the Lord raised Peter
to the fullness of power when he said to him, "You will be called
Cephas," [John 1:42] which means Peter and head, in order to show
Peter to be the head of the church.... In the head the plenitude of
the senses flourishes, but some part of the senses is channeled to the
members. Moreover, when Peter asked if, as often as his brother sinned
against him, he should forgive him even up to seven times, it is written that the Lord answered, "I do not say to you seven times, but
seventy times seven" [Matt. 18:22]. Clearly, since all time is included
in the number of seven days, when multiplied by seventy in this context, it means all the sins of all people, since only Peter is able to forgive not only all offenses but the offenses of all people. For it was to
him and not to another that we find the Lord saying, "Follow me"
[Matt. 8:22], that is, imitate him in the true office of shepherd and
the fullness of ecclesiastical power, since the Lord had substituted him
as his vicar in office and his successor in *magisterium*....

Since therefore we, although unworthy, occupy the place on earth
of him who rules in the kingdom of men and who bestows it upon
whomever he wants, so that kings reign and princes rule through him;
since we know that it was said to Peter and his successor and to us
in him, "I have asked on your behalf, Peter, that your faith may not
fail; and when you have turned again, strengthen your brethren" [Luke
22:31]; and since by the precept of the lord we are bound to feed
his sheep, wishing now in paternal solicitude to provide both spiritually and temporally for the Bulgar and Vlac peoples, who have long
been separated from the breasts of their mother, we have, with the
authority of him though whom Samuel anointed David king, established you as king over them. Through our beloved son Leo, cardinal priest of S. Croce, legate of the Apostolic See ..., we send to you
the scepter of the kingdom and a royal diadem, to be placed upon
you with his hands as though with ours. He will receive from you
your sworn oath that you will remain devoted and obedient to us and
our successors and to the Roman church, and that you will preserve
all the lands and peoples subject to your authority [*imperio*] in obedience and devotion to the Apostolic See.[77]

Innocent also granted the archbishop of Trnovo primacy in the kingdom. Even though there was no mention of the two crucial titles,
emperor and patriarch, the Bulgars seemed to have moved within
the Roman orbit.

As for the curia's debate over the right response to Alexius and
the crusaders, their soul-searching was all in vain. Even as they struggled with the problem, young Alexius IV was being deposed in Con-

---

[77] Reg. 7:1. See also Reg. 7:2–15; *Gesta*, PL 214:cxxv–cxxx = Gress-Wright, pp.
111–160; Fine, *Late Medieval Balkans*, pp. 55–56.

stantinople. A new emperor, Mourtzouphlus, had arisen, who repudiated all the promises made by Alexius and who defied the crusaders. Alexius was soon strangled in his prison. Innocent's crusading army now faced more hard decisions in a hostile Greek world.[78]

*　*　*

The departure of the pope from Rome the previous May had not ended the intrigue there. The republican forces won agreement that there should be fifty-six senators instead of just one; but the factionalism was so great that ultimately, the senators could not even agree on a time and place to meet. A growing number of people began to think fondly of the firm hand of the pope. The delegations leaving periodically to seek the pope's return became larger and weightier, and finally, in March of 1204, Innocent returned to the city.

Innocent restored the regime of one senator and, in a conciliatory gesture of some magnitude, chose John Pierleone as mediator to choose that senator. The citizens approved the choice; and when John chose as senator Gregory Pierleone, they approved of that too. The Biographer concedes that Gregory was a good man but adds that he was not tough enough "for the maliciousness of the time." John Capoccio, the leader of the anti-papal party, began to rebuild his tower. Pandulf, a former senator and a leader of the pro-papal party, objected, and when John continued, Pandulf and his allies began to prepare for war. Once more the Easter season was the time for violence. On Easter Sunday of 1204, John Capoccio and his partisans ran through the streets of Rome, calling on the populace to rise up against papal domination. Pandolfo's forces also took to the streets and ruled the day. Then an arms race began as both sides threw up fortifications wherever they could. Pandolfo's efforts were financed by Richard the marshal and were further reinforced with towers built by Innocent's brother-in-law Peter Annibaldi. Petraries and mangonels were built, archers and cross bowmen were recruited. Men fought in the streets; stones and arrows rained down from towers. As the tide slowly turned against the republicans and they lost popular support, they complained that the money of the pope was fighting against them.[79]

---

[78] Queller and Madden, pp. 161–171.
[79] *Gesta*, PL 214:clxxxix–cxciv = Gress-Wright, pp. 335–339.

Innocent tried to mediate. He proposed that four good men be chosen to arbitrate the differences dividing the city. After more fighting, the proposal was accepted, and the citizens elected four men to settle the problems. They immediately acknowledged the pope's right to establish the senate, but noting that there was no single person who could be trusted by everyone, they suggested a senate of fifty-six rather than one. Innocent predicted more faction-alism but reluctantly agreed. The division in the senate made for an impotent government, as Innocent had predicted, and popular sen-timent soon shifted in favor of a single senator. For the time being, relative order was restored.[80] It is not surprising, though, that Innocent's extensive building program in Rome included walls surrounding the papal palace at St. Peter's with towers raised high above the gates.[81]

* * *

In the last weeks of Lent in April 1204, this disorder in the "first Rome" was nothing compared to what took place in the "second Rome," Constantinople. In their war against the new Emperor Mourtzouphlus (Alexius V), the crusaders had taken the city. They believed that they had experienced one betrayal after another from the Greeks. The months of anxiety and frustration, together with the sudden exhilaration of victory, now turned the army into a rav-aging mob. They terrorized the civilian population of the city with murder, rape, and pillage. Anything that could be stolen was stolen, with special preference for sacred relics and liturgical objects. The loot was loaded on pack animals within the churches themselves.[82] The city was taken and the Latins elected a new emperor from among their number. Count Baldwin IX of Flanders thus became emperor of Constantinople.

News of all this may have reached Innocent before the official let-ter of Baldwin, which a knight Templar probably delivered in late October 1204, but if so, there is no early sign of the news in the papal register. As late as 23 September, Innocent was referring to Baldwin merely as count of Flanders.[83] In Baldwin's letter, however,

---

[80] *Gesta*, PL 214:cxciv–cxcvi = Gress-Wright, pp. 339–342.
[81] *Gesta*, PL 214:ccxi = Gress-Wright, p. 351.
[82] Queller and Madden, pp. 193–194.
[83] Pott. 2285, PL 217:115.

Innocent was presented with a lengthy account designed to make the unexpected events seem as both the work of God and the inevitable and necessary consequences of the treachery of the Greeks. The clerical advisers who composed this masterful letter for Baldwin knew exactly how to present it to the pope. Baldwin told the pope that after the crusaders had installed the young Alexius in his rightful place as emperor, they had voluntarily withdrawn from the city to avoid any incidents. Alexius had then betrayed them, abandoning his obligations. Alexius had in turn been treacherously replaced by Mourtzouphlus, who also betrayed and attacked the Latins. Finally, in self-defense, the Latins captured the city. Mourtzouphlus and his supporters fled, leaving vast treasures for the crusaders. The crusaders had agreed on an electoral body, which had then elected Baldwin as the new Latin emperor of Constantinople. All this, Baldwin assured Innocent, was not the work of man; rather, the hand of God had brought about things neither hoped for nor foreseen by the crusaders. "More than all other wonders, this is wonderful in our eyes."[84] Baldwin repeatedly emphasized that all that had happened served the cause of delivering the Holy Land from the hands of the infidel. He invoked the possibility of a great general council to be held in Constantinople under the presidency of the pope. He wrote:

> Sound your priestly trumpet in Zion, most beloved father; call the assemblage; gather the people; bring together the old men and the suckling infants. Sanctify this day as the day acceptable to the Lord for establishing unity and peace and for confirming our courage, which we preserve in the Lord. For however much we may be lacking in ourselves, we dare to hope in the Lord that the joy of the Lord may be our courage for undoing the humiliation of the cross and for subduing on earth every power that raises itself against the Lord and his Anointed.

Baldwin closed with a discreet commendation of his Venetian allies, who were still excommunicate.[85]

We have no record of how the curia responded to this news from Constantinople. The near unanimous judgment of modern historians has been that the crusade was an utter disaster. It had been out

---

[84] "A Domino factum est istud: et est mirabile in oculis nostris" (Ps. 117 [118]:23).

[85] Reg. 7:152, Andrea, *Contemporary Sources*, pp. 98–112. For this and related documents, see also W. Prevenier, ed., *De Oorkonden der graven van Vlanderen (1191-aanvang 1206)*, 3 vols. (Brussels, 1964), 2:542–5 (no. 260), 591–601 (no. 274).

of control from the beginning; it had gone from the conquest of one Christian city to the conquest of another. It had now come to its scandalous conclusion, not in the recapture of the Holy Land, but in a frenzy of looting and appropriation in the Christian empire of Constantinople.

Such thoughts were probably almost unthinkable in the curia. How could such a thing be? How could God allow the complete corruption of an army raised to avenge his honor, to return to Christian hands the holy places that Christ had sanctified with his presence and that were now desecrated by the feet of the infidel? When such terrible thoughts passed through the minds of those in the curia, they must have avoided one another's eyes; they must have turned again and again to Baldwin's letter hoping to soothe their own consciences with the eloquent balm of Baldwin's clerical advisers. And they succeeded.

Innocent and his curia were especially hungry for some sign of God's favor because the fortunes of their .imperial candidate had taken a decided turn for the worse. Otto's prospects depended on the support of his uncle King John; and during the summer of 1204, John had lost all of Normandy to Philip Augustus, the ally of Philip of Swabia. Archbishop Adolf of Cologne, who had originally crowned Otto, had now defected to Philip of Swabia. Whereas less than a year before, the success of Otto could be seen as a sign of divine favor, there were now distressing setbacks. Could God have turned against papal policy in both the western and the eastern empires? On the contrary, in October, Innocent reassured himself and others with the recent return to obedience to the Apostolic See of Greeks, Vlachs, Bulgars and Armenians.[86]

Innocent's letter to Baldwin, dated 7 November, congratulated him for his victory and election, but even more for his humility in recognizing that his success was more the work of God than his own. The capture of Constantinople was "the just judgment of God." God had acted for the praise and glory of his name, for the honor and profit of the Apostolic See, and for the utility and exaltation of the Christian people. Innocent promised his support so that the secure possession of Constantinople could lead to the recovery of the Holy Land. It was a subdued letter, closing with a warning that

---

[86] RNI, no. 113, p. 280.

Baldwin should protect ecclesiastical property, so that there be no confusion between what belongs to Caesar and what belongs to God.[87] A different kind of letter was to be issued six days later.

This may not have been the best time for an ordinary suitor to approach the pope on lesser matters. On the same day that Innocent's letter to Baldwin was dated, an English lawyer-monk arrived in Rome to defend the independence of his monastery from the jurisdiction of the local bishop.[88] The monk Thomas of Marlborough met with the pope and presented him with a valuable silver cup. Some time later, Innocent told Thomas that before the matter proceeded, he was to go find his abbot, detained somewhere between England and Rome. When Thomas responded with an impertinent remark, the pope ordered him to be quiet and get out. Thomas did as he was told.

In the letter of 13 November to Constantinople, Innocent wrote at length to all the clergy accompanying the crusading army. It was an elaborate argument, like one of his sermons, offering an allegorical interpretation of the scriptural story of Mary Magdelene going to the empty tomb. She represented the Jews, he said, who did not understand that Jesus was God. Perplexed by the empty tomb, she rightly went to Peter and John for enlightenment. John represented the Greek churches. He arrived first at the tomb, since the Gospel first reached the Greek world, but did not enter, since he did not understand the full doctrine of the Trinity, that the Holy Spirit proceeded from the father *and the son*. Peter, however, represented the Latin church; and he entered the tomb, because the Latin church would have the full doctrine of the Trinity.

> Behold, now, brothers and sons, you can clearly conclude that God has finally fulfilled through you and in us that sacrament which he foresaw from all eternity and presaged in the Gospel. You may understand that God has brought about this mystery through your ministry not like some chance occurrence but as something issuing from his high counsel, so that now there may be one flock and one shepherd. According to his foreknowledge, the creator of times has so arranged all times that when the fullness of the gentiles has entered into the faith, then even all of Israel will be saved.

---

[87] Reg. 7:153.
[88] For the following account, see *Chronicon Abbatiae de Evesham ad annum 1418*, ed. W. D. Macray, Rolls Series, 1863; Cheney, *Innocent III and England*, pp. 196–199.

Innocent had adopted and expanded the version presented in Baldwin's letter and had borrowed prophetic ideas from Abbot Joachim of Fiore concerning the conversion of the Jews.[89] So fortified, he had convinced himself that the outcome of his crusade was not a disaster. It was rather a sacrament, the mysterious working out of God's plan, anticipating the final conversion of infidels and Jews. It was wonderful in his eyes.[90]

---

[89] Egger, "Joachim von Fiore, Rainer von Ponza and die römische Kurie," pp. 129–162, especially 146.

[90] Reg. 7:154. Most clerical historians of the following decades were to see the capture of Constantinople as providential, just as Innocent did. See Alfred J. Andrea, "Cistercian Accounts of the Fourth Crusade: Were they Anti-Venetian?" *Analecta Cisterciensia*, 41 (1985) 3–41. For a survey of recent treatments of this crusade, see Thomas F. Madden, "Outside and Inside the Fourth Crusade." *International History Review*, 17 (1995) 726–743.

CHAPTER SIX

JEWS AND HERETICS (1205–1207)

In January of 1205, seven years after Innocent's election, an objective observer of his papacy might have found its record mixed. The campaign against heresy was achieving little and things were not going well in Germany—worse even than Innocent knew at the time. The support for Otto was evaporating. That very month, Philip of Swabia was being crowned a second time in Aachen. Not only had the archbishop of Cologne who had crowned Otto switched sides,[1] but Philip could now count nearly a dozen bishops and princes as new recruits for his cause. Otto's brother Henry, the count palatine of the Rhine, had abandoned him[2] and his uncle King John could not be persuaded to pay him the legacy left him by King Richard.[3] If Innocent had any doubt of Philip's hostile intentions, Philip took care of that by sending an imperial army into Italy—led by a bishop! In March the pope would dispatch a slew of letters intended to reestablish support for Otto.[4]

On the other hand, Innocent had recently enjoyed some impressive successes. In November, Pedro II king of Aragon (and lord of Montpellier) had arrived in Rome in regal splendor, bringing with him in five galleys the archbishop of Arles, the provost of Maguelonne, and assorted other dignitaries. He had been escorted by all the lay and ecclesiastical dignitaries of Rome to Innocent's presence at St. Peter's. Three days later, Innocent had crowned Pedro and received his oath of submission to the pope, making the kingdom of Aragon a tributary (*censualis*) of the papacy and the recipient of papal protection.[5]

In Italy, after a rocky year, Innocent's plans seemed to be going reasonably well. The force sent into Italy by Philip of Swabia had

---

[1] RNI, nos. 113, 116.

[2] Paul B. Pixton, *The German Episcopacy and the Implementation of the Decrees of the Fourth Lateran Council, 1216–1245: Watchmen on the Tower* (Leiden, 1995), pp. 131–133; Van Cleve, *Emperor Frederick*, p. 51.

[3] RNI, nos. 49, 69, 132.

[4] RNI, nos. 113–120.

[5] *Gesta*, PL 214:clix–clxi = Gress-Wright, pp. 306–309.

been rebuffed by papal forces, and its leader, Bishop Liupold of Worms, had returned to Germany.[6] A modest victory had been won in southern France, where, in 1203, the leaders of the city of Toulouse had promised their support to Innocent's legates working to combat heresy, although the promise was not to mean much.[7] The most welcome news was coming from the eastern end of Christendom. The Bulgars and Vlachs had been led by their king Kalojan into at least nominal submission to Rome. As a sign of that submission, the king sent two boys to Rome, Basil and Bethlehem, so that they could learn Latin and then bring their skills back to help the king in his communication with the pope.[8]

But for Innocent, the defining event was the miracle at Constantinople. Innocent's acceptance of the Latin conquest grew into a broader vision of where he stood in history. Around Christmas of 1204, a delegation from Constantinople arrived in Rome. They sought approval for the treaty made before the conquest between Venetians and the other crusaders concerning the distribution of power and wealth. In late January 1205, Innocent sent his responses to Emperor Baldwin, to the Venetian doge, and to all the clergy in Constantinople. Innocent accepted the election of Baldwin, and he accepted the nominee for the new patriarch (while rejecting the Venetians' claimed right to nominate him). But his letter to the clergy in Constantinople was also an elaborate commentary on this text from Luke 5:

> Getting into one of the boats, which was Simon's, he [Jesus] asked him to put out a little from the land. And he sat down and taught the people from the boat. And when he had ceased speaking, he said to Simon, "Put out into the deep and let down your nets for a catch." And Simon answered, "Master, we toiled all night and took nothing! But at your word I will let down the nets." And when they had done this, they enclosed a great multitude of fish; and as their nets were breaking, they beckoned to their colleagues in the other boat to come and help them. And they came and filled both the boats, so that they began to sink. But when Simon Peter saw it, he fell down at Jesus' knees, saying, "Depart from me, for I am a sinful man, O Lord." For astonishment overwhelmed him, and all who were with him, at the catch of fish which they had taken. . . ."

---

[6] Waley, *Papal State*, pp. 47–49.
[7] John Hine Mundy, *The Repression of Catharism at Toulouse: The Royal Diploma of 1279* (Toronto, 1985), pp. 17–18.
[8] Reg. 7:230–231.

In the manner of one of his sermons, he used this text to lay out his vision of the world and of history, again drawing on the ideas of the Calabrian abbot Joachim of Fiore.[9]

> We learn from evangelical scripture that Jesus climbed into one boat belonging to Simon and asked that it be moved a little from the land. He sat down and taught the crowd from the boat. The sea stands for the world, the boat stands for the church, and the net stands for preaching. Therefore the boat of Simon is the church of Peter, which is rightly called "one," since the catholic church is one. Christ committed it to Peter to be ruled, so that unity may prevent division. Jesus climbed into the boat of Simon in effect when he made the church of Peter to rise, as has been clear since the time of Constantine. Whence it is worthwhile to ask who it was who was able so to govern that he was leading more gently through requests than through commands [Jesus *asked*, not commanded, that Simon move the boat from shore], and to what extent they moved the boat a little from the land, that is, they moved the church a little further from earthly custom, closer to heavenly custom—or rather from literal to spiritual doctrine. Sitting down, he taught the people from the boat. That is, he has thereby given Peter a secure seat, at the Lateran or at the Vatican, and he has made him teach, since from this, the teachers began to multiply in the church of Peter—Leo, Gregory, Gelasius, Innocent, and many others after them.
>
> After a while, he ceased speaking. . . . He said to Simon, "Put out into the deep and let down your nets for a catch" (Luke 5:4). The boat is then taken into the deep, meaning that the church is lifted to lofty teaching or is moved to a better state.

At this point, Innocent interjected a personal aside, using the first person singular instead of his usual "we": "As to whether during these days the boat has been put out into the deep, I prefer to remain silent, lest I seem to commend myself, but I do boldly affirm this one thing, that I have let down the nets for a catch." He continued, sometimes referring to himself as "we," sometimes as "I":

> Simon, therefore, being truly obedient, taking the *request* of the master to be a *command* [*praeceptum*], said to him, "Master [*praeceptor*], we toiled all night and took nothing, but at your word I will let down the nets."

---

[9] Reg. 7:203, Andrea, *Contemporary Sources*, pp. 131–139; Egger, "Joachim von Fiore, Rainer von Ponza und die römische Kurie," pp. 146–148. A similar view of events was presented by Gunther of Pairis in his *Historia Constantinopolitana*, written around 1218. See Andrea, "Cistercian Accounts of the Fourth Crusade," pp. 20–31, 40–41.

The night of adversity has certainly been an obstacle. Although my predecessors have toiled greatly they have taken virtually nothing. But where I have let down the net at the word of the Lord, my brothers and I have enclosed a great multitude of fish: in Livonia, by converting pagans through preachers sent there for the faith; in Bulgaria and Vlachia, by leading divided peoples back into unity; in Armenia, by seeking out those long lost peoples through dispatching legates to them.

But what is the meaning of what follows: "their net was breaking"? Is it not that heretics are trying to undo apostolic preaching so that some fish may escape from the nets? (Even though a few have flourished, they will not prevail finally, since the gates of hell will not prevail against it).

But when they had enclosed a great multitude of fish, they beckoned to their colleagues in the other boat to come and help them. The other boat was the Greek church, which made itself "other," since it presumed to alienate itself from the unity of the universal church. Indeed we have beckoned to them, since we have warned them through our letters and messengers that they should come and help us, that is, that turning back they should resume part of our solicitude, as coadjutors of the duties laid upon us.

They have come, however, through the grace of God. In these days the empire of Constantinople has been transferred from the Greeks to the Latins, and the church of Constantinople has returned to obedience to the Apostolic See, like a daughter to her mother, like a member [of a body] to the head, so that henceforth one undivided society may endure between them and us.

Indeed, we call them brothers, colleagues, and friends, since, although we hold the office of prelate over them, this prelacy leads not to dominion, but rather to service. For the Lord said to the apostles: "The princes of the gentiles have dominion over them, and those who have power are called benefactors; but not so with you. Rather let him who is greater among you be the server of all, and the foremost be like a servant" (Luke 22:25–26). And blessed Peter the apostle said, "Not as domineering over the clergy but from the heart being made a model for the flock" (1 Peter 5:3).

Therefore, our colleagues have come . . . so that what follows may be fulfilled: "And they filled both the boats so that they were almost sinking." Certainly, each boat is to be filled, since those who had withdrawn themselves from obedience to each are returning to the Roman See and to the church of Constantinople. And each is almost sinking, since it is necessary that scandals come. But God is faithful; he does not allow his faithful to be tempted beyond their strength.

When Simon Peter saw this, however, he fell down at Jesus' knees and said, "'Depart from me, for I am a sinful man, O Lord.' For astonishment overwhelmed him, and all who were with him." I, too, seeing that these things are now beginning to be fulfilled, I too should go in humility and devotion to the knees of the savior, so that I can give thanks to him for so great a gift. And I can say that since I am a sinful man I am not worthy to enjoy his brilliant presence. I am indeed overcome with great astonishment, and all those who are with me, because of the unexpectedness of so great a miracle that has occurred in these times.

But, lest perhaps I be confounded by too much amazement, I should note carefully what Jesus said to Simon, "Do not be afraid, since henceforth you will be a catcher of men"; as if he were saying, be assured that after you have caught fish (that is, after you have regained Christians), then you will catch men (that is, you will convert Jews and pagans).

For the fish, who live in the water, stand for Christians, who are born again from water and the spirit. The people, however, who live on the land, stand for the Jews and pagans, who covet and cling to earthly things. But after all Christians shall have completely returned to obedience to the Apostolic See, then the multitude of peoples will enter the faith, and so all Israel will be saved.

Behold, therefore, our colleagues come to help us. The church of the Greeks is returning to obedience to the Apostolic See, so that with their help, the Apostolic See may free its two sisters, the churches of Alexandria and Jerusalem, who are held captive under the yoke of the king of Egypt.

In March and May of 1205, dozens of letters left Rome for Constantinople, aimed at arranging and consolidating the gains made there. Since a representative of the "Franks" had acquired the imperial title, the Venetians considered it their right, by prior agreement with the Franks, to monopolize the office of patriarch. Their candidate, Thomas Morosini, was well known to the pope, and Innocent ordained him and consecrated him patriarch. But when Thomas went from Rome to Venice for transport to his new see, he found himself at the mercy of his Venetian compatriots. He needed to get to his new office (and its income) to pay the debts he was accumulating, but the Venetians refused to transport him until he promised to appoint only Venetians to the electing chapter of St. Sophia in Constantinople. Once again, Innocent had to contend with the strength their navy gave the Venetians, doing what he could to prevent the patriarch and cathedral chapter of St. Sophia from becoming a Venetian preserve.[10]

---

[10] Robert Lee Wolff, "Politics in the Latin Patriarchate of Constantinople, 1204–1261," *Dumbarton Oaks Papers*, Number 8 (1954), pp. 227–242.

In May, Innocent informed the bishops of France that the Emperor
Baldwin had called for a new kind of crusading force, this one to
be made up of women as well as men, people of every social status, to share in the spiritual and material benefits of the crusaders.
With Constantinople so fortified with Latin colonists, Baldwin would
lead an army into the Holy Land. Innocent ordered the bishops to
do as the emperor requested, promising the new crusaders the usual
crusader indulgence.[11] The colonization was to be a thorough one,
penetrating the culture of the Greek world. Innocent called on the
clergy to send missals, breviaries, and other books, all, of course, in
Latin. He urged the scholars of the University of Paris to go themselves to Constantinople to reform the educational system there. With
the scholars as with the other potential recruits, he emphasized the
vast wealth that would be available to them in the Byzantine world.[12]

*   *   *

The schism between Latins and Greeks had been healed—or so
Innocent hoped. There now remained pagans, Jews, and heretics.
To all appearances, the problem of pagans or infidels was being
addressed successfully. Since his election, Innocent had supported the
German (and Christian) expansion on the shores of the Baltic. He
had approved a new order of monastic knights called the "Livonian
Brothers of the Sword" and had most recently called on the clergy
and laity throughout the province of Bremen to join in common
efforts to subdue and convert the pagans of Livonia. He even allowed
some crusaders to fulfill their vows there without going to the Holy
Land.[13] And now, thanks to the miraculous intervention of God at
Constantinople, the united Latin and Greek churches could soon
move to regain Jerusalem and Alexandria. Neither the pope nor the
new Emperor Baldwin believed that the crusaders who had captured
Constantinople had thereby fulfilled their crusader vows, and Inno-

---

[11] Reg. 8:69 = PL 215:634.
[12] Reg. 8:70–71 = PL 215:636–638. English translation in Lynn Thorndike, ed.,
University Records and Life in the Middle Ages (New York, 1944), pp. 24–25.
[13] Reg. 7:139. For the crusade in Livonia, see *The Chronicle of Henry of Livonia*,
passim; Eric Christiansen, *The Northern Crusades: The Baltic and the Catholic Frontier,
1100–1525* (Minneapolis, 1980), pp. 93–94, 122–124, et passim; Michele Maccarrone,
"I Papi e gli inizi della Cristianizzazione della Livonia," in *Gli inizi del cristianesimo
in Livonia-Lettonia* (Vatican City, 1989), rpr. in Michele Maccarrone, *Nuovi Studi su
Innocenzo III* (Rome, 1995), pp. 369–416.

cent clearly expected the crusaders, now fortified with their Greek connections, to proceed to the Holy Land.[14]

The "multitude of peoples" were therefore being attended to, but Jews and heretics were another matter. They seemed to be flourishing within the boundaries of Latin Christendom, especially in France. What about them?

* * *

Jews and heretics fell into two very different categories. Traditional Christian society had created a unique place for Jews. Christians believed that the Jews who refused to become Christians had first refused to accept the good news Jesus brought them and had then been responsible for his death. Jews who rejected Jesus should therefore not enjoy the same status as those Jews and Gentiles who had accepted the gift of faith, and they certainly should not be allowed to do anything that would weaken the faith of Christians. On the other hand, Christian thinkers had long believed that God's plan included the survival of the "perfidious" Jews until the end of time, when they would ultimately be converted. In the meantime, they should live as a marginal people, tolerated, with certain minimal legal protections, but disdained.[15]

As the twelfth century progressed and the economy flourished, Jewish communities became larger and richer. Jews owned property within and around towns, rented additional property from Christians, and employed Christian servants. Money lent to Christian churches resulted in church lands and expensive liturgical utensils being forfeited into Jewish hands. Engaged in commerce, but prevented from entering many kinds of economic activity by required Christian oaths, they came more and more to engage in money-lending. The annual interest rate when Innocent became pope could be as high as 65%, and the sums could be very large indeed. In 1207, a monastery in Champagne owed a Jewish money lender seventeen hundred pounds (at 65%) and was forced to sell land in order to retire the debt. Of course much of the profits went to the great princes within whose land the Jews lived, and beginning in 1198, many of those princes

---

[14] Brundage, *Medieval Canon Law*, p. 123, citing *Annales Colonienses maximi*, MGH, SS, 17:818 and Reg. 6:136, PL 215:699–702.

[15] Jeremy Cohen, *The Friars and the Jews: The Evolution of Medieval Anti-Judaism* (Ithaca, 1982), pp. 19–22.

entered into agreements whereby each prince promised not to permit the Jews from the lands of other princes to settle in his land, thereby offering mutual protection from the loss of their Jewish subjects.[16]

Innocent gave voice (and legal reinforcement) to the traditional attitude of protecting but restraining in a "constitution" dated 15 September 1199. He wrote:

> Although the Jewish perfidy is in every way worthy of condemnation, nevertheless, because through them the truth of our own faith is proved, they are not to be severely oppressed by the faithful. . . . We, following in the footsteps of our predecessors . . . grant their petition and offer them the shield of our protection.
>
> We decree that no Christian shall use violence to force them to be baptized as long as they are unwilling and refuse, but that if anyone of them seeks refuge among the Christians of his own free will and by reason of his faith, (only then,) after his willingness has become quite clear, shall he be made a Christian without subjecting himself to any calumny. For surely none can be believed to possess the true faith of a Christian who is known to have come to Christian baptism not willingly, and even against his wishes.
>
> Moreover, without the judgment of the authority of the land, no Christian shall presume to wound their persons, or kill (them) or rob them of their money, or change the good customs which they have thus far enjoyed in the place where they live. Furthermore, while they celebrate their festivals, no one shall disturb them in any way by means of sticks or stones, nor exact from any of them forced service, except that which they have been accustomed to perform from ancient times. In opposition to the wickedness and avarice of evil men in these matters, we decree that no one shall presume to desecrate or reduce the cemetery of the Jews, or, with the object of extorting money to exhume bodies there buried. If any one, however, after being acquainted with the contents of this decree, should presume to act in defiance of it . . ., he shall suffer loss of honor and office, or he shall be restrained by the penalty of excommunication, unless he shall have made proper amends for his presumption.
>
> We wish, however, to place under the protection of this decree only those (Jews) who have not presumed to plot against the Christian Faith.[17]

---

[16] Emily Taitz, *The Jews of Medieval France: The Community of Champagne* (Westport CN, 1994), pp. 45–46, 115–116, 126–131, 154–155.

[17] Reg. 2:276 (302). Trans. Solomon Grayzel, *The Church and the Jews in the XIIIth Century* (Philadelphia, 1933), pp. 92–95.

Except for the last sentence, the constitution merely repeated provisions that had been issued by previous popes, and the addition of that sentence was ominous.[18] As time passed, Innocent's attitude toward the Jews seemed to grow more harsh, probably reflecting the growing number of complaints coming from France. In 1205, he wrote Philip Augustus, assuring him it was the will of God that Jews should live under catholic kings and Christian princes. But the same letter made clear that some people in France were angry at what they saw as Jewish presumption and that they found in the pope a sympathetic listener. The reports were that Jews were collecting not only usury, but "usury on usury" (compound interest or fines for late payments), and in doing so they were even confiscating ecclesiastical goods that had served as collateral. Moreover, in defiance of canon law, they had Christian servants. In some legal cases, the testimony of Jews was being given preference to that of Christians. Jews had built a new synagogue in Sens whose size and location seemed to threaten a nearby Christian church, and they openly challenged and ridiculed Christian belief. Innocent even repeated the perennial charge that Jews had murdered someone and hid the body in a latrine. Finally, he ordered Philip to restrain the presumption of the Jews and to punish the guilty.[19]

Christian belief concerning Jews has been a source of great suffering for Jews throughout the centuries. But in its ambiguous ground combining toleration and disapproval, it also made for awkward, inconsistent, and divisive policy among Christians. In France and elsewhere, Jews had gradually been excluded from nearly every occupation other than money-lending at interest, the one area where there was not supposed to be any Christian competition. In this regard, Jews provided a useful—if resented—service to borrowers; and they also provided a valued source of income for the lay lords who taxed the profits of the Jewish money-lenders. Philip Augustus himself had abandoned his earlier policy of expelling Jews from his territories in order to benefit from their presence.[20] Therefore, when Innocent

---

[18] On this point, see Robert Chazan, "Pope Innocent III and the Jews," in *Pope Innocent III and His World*, pp. 187–204.

[19] Reg. 7:186. For an English translation, see Robert Chazan, *Church, State, and Jew in the Middle Ages* (New York, 1980), pp. 171–173.

[20] See William Chester Jordan, *The French Monarch and the Jews: From Philip Augustus to the Last Capetians* (Philadelphia, 1989), pp. 31–45.

granted to all who took the cross an exemption from any further
interest payments on loans, he provided a welcome relief to some
debtors but also reduced the incomes not only of Jews but also of
some very important Christians.

One such man was Eudes, duke of Burgundy, who protested the
policy. The king, like, many other Christians before and after, had
occasionally found in the persecution of Jews a simple-minded form
of piety that was dramatic, satisfying, and often profitable without
being too inconvenient to himself. In this case, he was willing to
accommodate the pope in the matter of the crusaders' exemption
from interest, and he wrote Eudes telling him so. Eudes wrote back
complaining that the king should not permit papal intrusion in matters that properly belong to the king and his men. The king should
not permit "anyone to institute anything new in your kingdom which
had not been instituted or ordained or which had not been the usage
in the times of your predecessors."[21] What actually happened to the
debts of individual crusaders is difficult to say, but in 1206, the king
issued an ordinance governing Jewish money lenders. Like Eudes,
he was unwilling to forgo the income he derived from taxing Jewish
money lenders, so he regulated their operations. His ordinance,
adopted by other barons and applied throughout the regions the
king had recently taken from King John, required record keeping of
Jewish loans, forbad compound interest, limited annual rates of interest to a maximum of 43%, and forbad the use of ecclesiastical property for collateral on loans.[22]

But despite the royal ordinance, princes' use of Jews to collect
high rates of interest continued to generate complaints from France,
and Innocent continued to respond. In January of 1208, he wrote
Hervé, count of Nevers, reviewing the charges being reported to the
pope—generally that Hervé was supporting Jewish usurers to exploit
the people of the area so that "widows and orphans [are] robbed
of their inheritance, and churches [are] defrauded of their tithes and
other regular sources of income, since the Jews maintain themselves

[21] *Layettes du trésor des chartres*, ed. Alexandre Teulet et al. (Paris, 1863–1909),
1:292–293, no. 768.
[22] The document is in *Recueil des Actes de Philippe Auguste*, ed. M. H. François
Delaborde, 2 (Paris, 1943), pp. 550–1, no. 955. See also Chazan, *Church and State*,
pp. 205–207, Robert Chazan, *Medieval Jewry in Northern France: A Political and Social
History* (Baltimore, 1973), pp. 76–81; Jordan, *The French Monarchy and the Jews*, pp.
56–72.

in seized castles and villas and utterly refuse to respond to prelates of the churches." He told Hervé that "blasphemers of the Christian name ought not to be aided by Christian princes to oppress the servants of the Lord, but ought rather to be forced into servitude, which they brought on themselves when they raised sacrilegious hands against him who had come to confer true liberty upon them, thus calling down his blood upon themselves and upon their children."[23] Innocent was to continue the traditional ambiguous policy toward Jews and, in his last years, he made it worse.

* * *

For the most part, Jews were easily recognized in Innocent's society, and insofar as they were a problem, they were a small and well defined problem. The same was not true of heretics.[24] Religious fervor was taking new forms in the twelfth century. Previously, the dominant religious image in Europe was that of Christ the king and judge, a lord presiding over subject peoples, a judge sitting above the church door, separating the saved from the damned. The best way to please that judge was to adopt the life of the monk, a life of prayer, poverty, chastity, and obedience in the isolation of the monastery. For the layman, the best way to please the divine king was to place one's sword in his service against the infidel. Those themes certainly continued, but in the twelfth century, growing literacy and the emergence of urban life made possible the blossoming of different religious ideals. It became easier for people to recognize and identify with the historical Jesus and his disciples. They found in the New Testament men and women who were neither royal judges nor cloistered monks, but rather ordinary working people who met together to pray and who wandered from place to place preaching the good news. That image of "evangelical poverty," poverty as exemplified by Jesus and the apostles in the gospels and in the *Acts of the Apostles*, provided awkward contrasts with the lives of many of the wealthy clergy of the day. The image could easily bring its advocates into conflict with well-to-do ecclesiastical authorities, with both

---

[23] Reg. 10:190; English translation in Chazan, *Church, State, and Jew*, pp. 174–176.

[24] The following account is based largely on Herbert Grundmann, *Religious Movements in the Middle Ages*, trans. Steven Rowan (Notre Dame, 1995), and Malcolm Lambert, *Medieval Heresy: Popular Movements from the Gregorian Reform to the Reformation*, 2nd ed. (Oxford, 1992).

sides suspecting that their opponents had abandoned the true faith.

In mid-century, a wealthy businessman in Lyons heard a moving sermon on the life of St. Alexius and decided to live a life of evangelical poverty. His name was Waldes (later called Peter Waldo). Not well educated himself, he had sections of the Bible translated into French so that he could use them as the basis of sermons. Jesus sent out the seventy disciples to preach; Waldes considered himself and the followers he attracted to have received the same commission. Their preaching, in the language of ordinary people and backed up by exemplary lives, was well received.

But preaching, like the learned professions in modern societies, was considered by ecclesiastical authorities to be a professional occupation, to be engaged in only by those who were properly trained and licensed, that is, by the ordained clergy. From the point of view of clerical authorities, the Waldensian advocacy of poverty was legitimate, even if sometimes embarrassing to the wealthy clergy; but their claim to have the right to preach was tantamount to the uneducated today presenting themselves as doctors or lawyers. It was intolerable. After some friction, Waldes agreed to preach only with the permission of local ecclesiastical authorities; but his followers soon came to find that limitation to be in conflict with what they considered their commission to "teach all nations." Jesus told them to preach. Worldly bishops told them not to. It was a short step from this point to the conviction that the bishops and other clergy, by the extravagance of their lives and by their opposition to lay preachers, had forfeited their rights to be pastors and ministers of the gospel, that a good laymen was a more reliable minister of Christ than a sinful bishop. That short step was the step into heresy, and many Waldensians took it.[25]

Waldensians were not the only ones who searched the New Testament for models of Christian life. The impulse to emulate the lives of Jesus, the apostles, and other early Christians was felt throughout Europe. Some lay people and clergy in northern Italy formed confraternities dedicated to simple lives of work, charitable activity, and poverty. They came to be called *Humiliati*, "humble ones." Like

---

[25] Lambert, *Medieval Heresy*, pp. 62–65; Walter L. Wakefield and Austin P. Evans, ed. and trans., *Heresies of the High Middle Ages: Selected Sources* (New York, 1969), pp. 200–235.

the Waldensians, lay people among the *Humiliati* were led by their fervor to preach the gospel and they too soon found themselves accused of heresy.[26]

The beliefs of Waldensians and *Humiliati* were not drastically different from those of most other Christians, but one reason why they were mistrusted was that in their outward lives they were similar to other groups whose beliefs departed radically from traditional Christian faith. These other groups, known variously as Patarines, Cathars, and Albigensians, believed in two deities, the evil god of the Old Testament (Satan), who had created all material things, and the good god of the New Testament, who created only spiritual things. Matter was evil; spirit was good. Therefore Jesus had never really had a body, had never really died, and had therefore never risen. Procreation was evil, since it imprisoned a good spirit in an evil body. Moreover, all the church ceremonies involving material things, including the Eucharist, with its bread and wine, were to be rejected, as were all the clergy who provided and defended the whole evil system. The leaders of these groups, the *perfecti* or "perfect ones," lived lives of strict asceticism. So a poor preacher who quoted the gospel, rejected material comforts for himself, and who explicitly or implicitly criticized the wealthy clerical establishment could be a *Humiliatus* who was perfectly orthodox—or a Cathar who rejected the whole belief system of the established church. Or he could be a St. Francis of Assisi.

Deeply held religious beliefs certainly account for the growth of these movements, but there were other motives as well. Any movement that challenged an unpopular bishop might find adherents, and Catharism offered a rather painless escape from the moral demands of Catholicism. Ordinary Cathar believers, as distinguished from the *perfecti*, lived in the knowledge that everything they did was sinful anyway, so there was no point in going to great effort to be virtuous until a final repentance at the point of death. It was a comfortable alternative for those who disliked the penitential practices of Catholics or Waldensians.[27] It was an attractive alternative for the Christian money-lender, for the man who resented paying tithes to

---

[26] See now Andrews, *The Early Humiliati*, pp. 38–63. She warns against identifying the early *Humiliati* with any particular social or economic group.

[27] Mundy, *Repression*, p. 9.

the clergy, and it seems, at least in Toulouse, to have been an outlet for a growing sense of lay and urban independence.[28]

But for most Europeans, heresy was a dreadful sin and a fearsome charge. In the eyes of many, heretics were the medieval equivalent of drug-pushers or child-molesters. According to the widely shared
beliefs in Innocent's world, heretics jeopardized not only their own
eternal salvation but also the salvation of all those they infected.
Nearly every cathedral church had an image of the last judgement,
where Christ consigned the damned to the tortures of hell. There
was no surer way to end up in hell than to betray the Lord by corrupting the true faith he had bestowed and by leading others astray.
"It would be better for him if a millstone were hung round his neck
and he were cast into the sea, than that he should cause one of
these little ones to sin" (Luke 17:2). To the risk of damnation in the
next world was added the risk of chaos in this. Many of those studying the gospel decided that they would no longer take oaths because
Jesus had said, "Do not swear at all,. . . . Let what you say be simply 'Yes' or 'No'; anything more than this comes from evil" (Matt.
5:34). For a society glued together largely with oaths, this was a
radically disruptive position.[29] Innocent wrote, "We execrate people
of this sort who oppose the orthodox faith while living and, if we
are able, we prevent them from destroying the vineyard of the Lord.
But also after their death, we condemn their memory, so that the
skillful investigation by catholics can hunt out those hidden behind
the imitation of the Christian life, superficially worn, especially to
terrify those who suffer from a similar disease."[30] Moreover, a whole-
sale rejection of the established clergy, as proposed by some heretical groups, was sufficiently revolutionary in itself to make many a
secular prince determined to stamp out heresy. Innocent's young
ward Frederick II was to become, in his adult years, the first secular prince formally to outlaw heresy, even though he himself was
certainly no model of religious orthodoxy.

---

[28] Malcolm Barber, *The Cathars: Dualist Heretics in Languedoc in the High Middle Ages*
(Harlow, 2000), pp. 34–70; John H. Mundy, "Urban Society and Culture: Toulouse
and Its Region," in *Renaissance and Renewal in the Twelfth Century*, ed. Robert L. Benson
and Giles Constable (Cambridge MA, 1982), pp. 229–247. See also the five social
conditions Mundy lists as conducive to heresy in southern France in his *Society and
Government at Toulouse in the Age of the Cathars* (Toronto, 1997), pp. 3–4 et passim.
[29] Grundmann, *Religious Movements*, pp. 35, 42.
[30] Reg. 9:213 = PL 215:1057.

The elimination of heresy was first of all the responsibility of the bishops. In 1184, Pope Lucius III issued the bull *Ad abolendum* requiring all bishops to seek out heretics in their dioceses; but as in all other matters, bishops responded with varying degrees of interest, and popular religious movements suspected of being heretical continued to grow. Archbishop Berengar of Narbonne, for example, seemed to be completely indifferent to the heresy flourishing in his territory, one of the many lapses that ultimately led Innocent to depose him.[31] In the neighborhood of Toulouse, Cistercian preachers as well as secular lords tried to restrain the growth of heresy in the last decades of the twelfth century, but to no great effect.[32]

From the earliest months of his papacy, Innocent considered it his responsibility to organize spiritual and secular authorities in response to the danger, especially in southern France. In April of 1198, he wrote the archbishop of Auch to drive heresy from his province. If necessary, he was to recruit the physical power of the princes and people of the area to bring this about.[33] A few weeks later, Innocent issued letters addressed to all the prelates, clergy, princes, and people throughout the region of southern France and northeastern Spain, telling them that he was sending Rainerius and Guido into their area to combat heresy and invoking their full cooperation. Innocent had learned that those "who are called Waldensians, Cathari, Patarines, and others, whoever they are and by whatever names they are called, are entangling innumerable peoples with their snares and are corrupting them with the yeast of falsehood." Innocent hoped that preaching, investigations, spiritual sanctions like excommunication and interdict, and expulsions would meet the need. He expected that some would heed the warning and return to the Lord; others would be driven out.[34] Expulsion was the task of secular rulers. Innocent always believed that the elimination of heresy was a basic function of secular government, as he made clear to the king of Hungary in 1200.[35]

Pious groups that were heretical—or that might be heretical— were not limited to southern France. The towns were fertile seed

---

[31] See Reg. 2:114, fn. 4.
[32] Mundy, *Repression*, pp. 11–16.
[33] Reg. 1:81.
[34] Reg. 1:94. See also Reg. 1:165 and 1:484.
[35] Reg. 3:172.

beds, and the trade routes were seed-bearing breezes. In 1199, Innocent was informed by the archbishop of Sens that heresy was spreading into areas of northern France where it had previously been absent.[36] It was an embarrassing fact that heresy seemed to be thriving even within the papal territories. In late March of 1199, Innocent wrote everyone in Viterbo, warning them to deprive all unrepentant heretics of their legal rights in the community. Adding something new to canon law, he prescribed that the goods of the guilty should be confiscated, just as the goods of traitors were confiscated under Roman law.[37]

Although concerned about the growth of heresy, Innocent was at first reluctant to use too heavy a hand. In 1199, he was careful to see that a clergyman in Nevers charged with heresy should be guaranteed due process,[38] and in the same year he chastened the archpriest of Verona for excommunicating indiscriminately pious laymen called *Humiliati*. Innocent said he had no desire to punish the harmless with the harmful, and he cautioned prelates to investigate the beliefs of the people in question before levying penalties, giving them a chance to show their orthodoxy or even to repent their heterodoxy.[39]

Also in 1199, Innocent addressed the problem of restless lay piety in the city of Metz. In a general letter to all the people of the diocese, he wrote that the bishop had informed him that lay groups had been meeting secretly, using their own French translations of parts of the Bible, and that they were even giving sermons based on their texts. When told that preaching was the prerogative of clergy, they mocked the ignorance and incompetence of the clergy. Innocent sent the people of Metz scriptural arguments against secret meetings and warned them that even simple priests should be respected. He closed with the warning: "if you do not receive humbly and devotedly our correction and paternal warning, we will pour on not only oil but wine, applying ecclesiastical severity so that those who do not wish to obey spontaneously may learn to do so against their

---

[36] Reg. 2:91.
[37] Reg. 2:1 = the decretal *Vergentis*, X 5.7.10.
[38] Reg. 2:60 (63). See also Pott. 1124.
[39] Reg. 2:219 (228). See Raoul Manselli, "I vescovi italiani, gli ordini religiosi e I movimenti popolari religiosi nel secolo XIII," *Vescovi e Diocesi in Italia nel Medioevo (sec. IX–XIII): Atti del II Convengno di Storia della Chiesa in Italia* (Padua, 1964), pp. 316–317.

will."[40] Innocent intended to eliminate heresy and contain pious movements within the bounds of orthodoxy. The soothing oil of conciliation was the preferred treatment; but painful disinfecting with wine would be used if necessary. In either case, the treatment depended on accurate diagnosis, and Innocent confessed to the clergy of the area that since he was not well informed in the matter, he and they needed to investigate carefully before acting.[41]

Many people accused of heresy found refuge by appealing to papal authority. A troop of men and women from La Charité-sur-Loire came to Rome to defend themselves against charges of heresy levied against them by the bishop of Auxerre, and they found protection in papal procedure.[42] In 1205, Innocent defended a group of pious men and women from being bothered by the bishop of Bologna—and this despite the fact that the men and women themselves believed that they had been possessed by the devil. The symptoms, uttering "profane and blasphemous voices" while experiencing the sensation of mice running between their flesh and their skin, clearly indicate a form of ergot poisoning. Innocent's diagnosis, that of some form of madness rather than diabolical possession, was probably right, and he offered his protection to the afflicted group.[43] Papal procedure might even protect the guilty. Innocent received complaints from the bishop of Verona that local heretics—including laymen and clergy involved in usury—were using appeals to Rome to protect themselves from the bishop's authority.[44] A man from Auxerre, excommunicated for heresy by his bishop, managed to mislead Innocent's curia and obtained a letter that led to the removal of the excommunication.[45]

Consistent with this legal restraint was Innocent's general interest, greater than that of his predecessors, in trying to accommodate the new religious movements, to keep those that he could within the fold. In 1200 and 1201, extensive negotiations with *Humiliati* of

---

[40] Reg. 2:132 (141).

[41] Reg. 2:133 (142). On Innocent's response to the situation in Metz, see Leonard M. Boyle, O. P., "Innocent III and Vernacular Versions of Scripture," in *The Bible in the Medieval World: Essays in Memory of Beryl Smalley*, ed. Katherine Walsh and Diana Wood (Oxford, 1985), pp. 97–107.

[42] Reg. 5:35 (36); Reg. 6:66.

[43] Reg. 8:157. See Mary Kilbourne Matossian, *Poisons of the Past: Molds, Epidemics, and History* (New Haven, 1989), pp. 9–14.

[44] Reg. 5:32 (33), 33 (34).

[45] Reg. 10:206 = PL 215:1312.

northern Italy showed the wisdom of his efforts. They remained submissive to his authority, and in return, they acquired the right to
preach, so long as they restricted themselves to moral exhortation
and avoided doctrinal instruction. The settlement satisfied Innocent's
sense of order by providing an informal rule governing the several
different groups among the *Humiliati*: celibates living in community,
married couples living in community, and married couples living in
their own homes. Innocent's acceptance of these groups gave them
legitimacy and protection[46] and he was still actively supporting them
in 1214.[47]

Innocent never abandoned his efforts to incorporate new religious
movements into the existing structure of the church, but as time
passed, in 1203 and 1204, he seemed to become less patient, and
his letters show less concern with restraining those making charges
of heresy. He warned the archbishop of Mainz to be more aggressive in searching out heresy in his diocese.[48] He scolded Archbishop
Berengar of Narbonne for neglecting his pastoral duties, thereby permitting heresy to flourish in his province.[49] In January of 1204, he
chastened the archbishop and all the other clerical authorities in the
area for not supporting the Cistercian monks Peter of Castelnau and
Raoul, the new papal legates sent into the area to combat heresy.
In February, the pope supported the legates when they suspended
from office the bishop of Béziers because of his failure to move
against heresy.[50] Whereas earlier, Innocent had protected people
charged with heresy from the bishop of Auxerre, in February of
1204, he prodded the bishop to look closely for signs of the heretical
disease among his people, because he was, after all, their physician.[51]

In May 1204 he stepped up his campaign, calling on clerical and
lay authorities to play their necessary roles. He ordered all the ecclesiastical authorities in southern France to support the Cistercian le-

---

[46] Andrews, *Early Humiliati*, pp. 64–98 et passim; Frances Andrews, "Innocent III
and Evangelical Enthusiasts: The Route to Approval," *Pope Innocent III and His World*,
pp. 229–241, Brenda Bolton, "Innocent III's treatment of the *humiliati*," *Studies in
Church History*, 8 (1971): 73–82; Michele Maccarrone, "Riforme e innovazioni di
Innocenzo III nella vita religiosa," in *Studi su Innocenzo III* (Padua, 1972), 284–290.
[47] Pott. 4945.
[48] Reg. 6:41 (about 9 April 1203).
[49] Reg. 6:81 (30 May 1203).
[50] Reg. 6:241 (242).
[51] Reg. 6:238 (239).

gates.[52] He commissioned the legates to investigate and perhaps even depose Berengar of Narbonne,[53] and he gave the archbishop a serious slap on the wrist by depriving him of the office of abbot that he held in Spain so that he could better attend to the problem of heresy in his province.[54] At the same time, he offered lay warriors who took up arms against the heretics of southern France the same spiritual benefits as those received by crusaders seeking the recovery of the Holy Land.[55] He wrote to Philip Augustus:

> For the protection of his spouse, that is to say the universal church, the Lord instituted the pontifical and the royal dignities, the one which brings up sons, the other which battles enemies; the one to shape the lives of its subjects with word and example, the other to restrain the jaws of the evil with rein and halter lest they perturb the peace of the church; the one that loves her enemies and prays for those who persecute her, the other that wields the material sword for the punishment of evil-doers and the praise of the good, that shelters ecclesiastical repose with weapons. It is therefore useful that the spiritual authority and the secular power, attending to the reason for their respective creations, come together for the defense of the church, with the one supporting the other so that the secular arm compels those whom ecclesiastical discipline cannot recall from evil, and spiritual punishment pursues those who, trusting in their own ferocity, do not fear the material sword.

He urged Philip, either through his son Prince Louis or through some other suitable leader, to force the counts and barons of the south to move against heretics, to confiscate their goods and proscribe their persons. If any counts, barons, or citizens refused, they were to suffer the same punishment. By so aiding the Cistercian legates, the king would receive not only temporal glory but the same forgiveness of sins as granted to crusaders to the Holy Land.[56]

Philip Augustus, however, was fully engaged in his war with King John, and he showed no more interest in Innocent's admonition in this matter than he did for the pope's intervention for Ingeborg.

---

[52] Reg. 7:77.
[53] Reg. 7:75.
[54] Reg. 7:78.
[55] Reg. 7:76.
[56] Reg. 7:79. Yves Dossat believes that it was the tolerance by the secular authorities more than the negligence of the clergy that accounted for the progress of heresy in the south. See "Le clergé méridional à la veille de la Croisade Albigeoise," *Revue historique et littéraire du Languedoc* 1 (1944) 263-278, especially pp. 277-8. Repr. in Dossat, *Église et hérésie en France au XIIIe siècle* (London, 1982).

In January of 1205, Innocent repeated his instructions of the previous May, urging the king to use the material sword to support the
anti-heresy efforts of the legates in the south. Innocent had hoped
that their words and example would have an impact, but they had
reported that the heretics of the south had no interest in sound doctrine and no fear of the spiritual sword.[57] At the same time, Innocent
offered consolation to the discouraged Cistercians, who were clearly
longing for the peace of the cloister, the life they had, after all, originally chosen. Innocent told them that although meritorious, the
monastic life was not as useful as the active life, where the trials and
reversals of the world strengthened virtue. He reminded them that
God rewards effort, not results.[58]

*   *   *

But the Cistercians were not the only ones experiencing disappointment and frustration. As the year 1205 progressed, intractable problems within Christendom wore on Innocent, and his almost apocalyptic
optimism of January seemed to fade. In March he expressed his frustration over warfare among Christians in the Holy Land itself.[59] In
Germany, nearly all the major princes and bishops were supporting
Philip of Swabia, while individual bishoprics were riven with civil
war as rival factions sought to install their own candidates as bishop
and looked to Welf and Hohenstaufen powers to support their causes.
A contemporary declared that "hardly a bishopric, hardly an ecclesiastical dignity, or hardly even a parish church exists that has not
been disputed."[60] Even individual bishops seemed torn asunder. The
bishop of Treves was summoned to Philip's court to participate in
the coronation of Philip's queen. He dared not ignore the summons,
but he was equally afraid of the pope, who could deprive him of
his offices. So he took to the road but deliberately fell off his horse
and retired to Münster to "recuperate." When Innocent heard the
news, he said it was a "happy fall"—a wry allusion to Adam's sin,
called a happy fault or fall, "felix culpa," because it resulted in the
coming of Christ.[61]

---

[57] Reg. 7:212.
[58] Reg. 7:210.
[59] Reg. 8:1 = PL 215:555.
[60] Pixton, *German Episcopacy*, p. 100, quoting Burchard of Ursperg.
[61] "Gestorum Treverorum continuatio IV," MGH SS 24:391.

Neither of the pope's two cherished goals, reform or crusade, could flourish in that environment.[62] His attempts to form a peace between the kings of England and France had failed. Philip Augustus had taken all of Normandy and was demanding oaths of fealty from bishops who had customarily given those oaths to the duke of Normandy, hitherto the king of England. They asked advice, and in March 1205, Innocent could only profess ignorance of the situation and advise them to do what seemed best.[63] In May, he criticized the king of Castile, who seemed to be favoring Jews in his kingdom to the extent that "the synagogue increases and the church decreases, the slave girl is given preference over the free woman."[64] In the same month, he wrote his former teacher Peter, archbishop of Sens, that the world was growing old, and that "in this evening of the world, we are troubled more than usual and are burdened even more than before."[65] His July letter to Ingeborg confessed that he had been unable to move Philip Augustus to show her marital affection.[66] Perhaps it was the weight of these burdens that kept him in Rome, away from his summer retreats, throughout the summer of 1205, for the first time since 1200. Even petitioners fled the unhealthy heat of Rome that year.[67]

It is a shame that the pope did not know that his church was at the time enjoying one piece of extraordinary good fortune, or perhaps rather a blessing from above. The young dandy from Assisi, despite his misadventure in 1202 that made him a war prisoner in Perugia, had set out to join the army of Walter of Brienne. This was an opportunity to win the kind of glory his beloved chivalric tales presented. But along the way, Francis had a vision that put him on an altogether different road to glory, and he turned back to Assisi. He did not share the fate of Walter in Apulia, but lived to found the Franciscan Order, that great bulwark to Innocent's church. But in the summer of 1205, Innocent knew nothing of that.

Innocent's efforts to contain heresy were bearing little fruit, and that fact was especially galling when heresy flourished in his own

---

[62] Pixton, *German Episcopacy*, pp. 181-3 et passim.
[63] Reg. 8:7 = PL 215:564.
[64] Reg. 8:50 = PL 215:616.
[65] Reg. 8:52 = PL 215:618.
[66] Reg. 8:113 = PL 215:680.
[67] *Chronicon abbatiae de Evesham*, p. 151.

back yard. The citizens of Viterbo may have borne the brunt of his pent-up frustration, perhaps aggravated by the unusual prospect of a hot summer in Rome. They elected some Patarines as consuls of the city, and in June of 1205, Innocent wrote to the Viterbese with a fury unsurpassed in any of his other letters.

> If the earth should rise up against you, and the stars of the heavens should reveal your iniquity and manifest your stains to the whole world, so that not only humans but the very elements themselves would join together for your destruction and ruin and wipe you from the face of the earth, sparing neither sex nor age, even that punishment laid upon you would still not be sufficient and worthy. Neither fearing God nor dreading man, failing to distinguish between the profane and the holy, you have taken light for darkness and darkness for light; you have called evil good and good evil. You have disdained to seek good reputation, which fattens the bones, and good name, which brings many riches. Rather you have been indifferent to infamy, since you have shamelessly assumed the impudent face of the prostitute. You have rotted in your sins, like a beast in its dung. The fumes and the filth of your putrification have already infected the surrounding regions, and we believe that the Lord himself is moved to nausea.

Innocent declared the Patarines worse than Jews and pagans. The Jews at least recognize God as creator while the Patarines believe the visible creation to be the work of Satan. The pagans damage the bodies of Christians, but the Patarines kill their souls.

The letter is a masterpiece of vilification, culminating with the threat of military assault if the Viterbese did not reform their ways.[68]

In July, Innocent adopted a similar angry tone concerning the "insolence" of the Jews in France. He had learned, he wrote the archbishop of Sens and the bishop of Paris, that the Jews were showing the same appreciation for hospitality extended to them by Christian princes as—quoting a popular proverb—a mouse in the wallet, a snake on the lap, or a flame in the clothing. Among their "detestable and unheard of" offenses, they were not only violating canon law by taking Christian servants and wet nurses, they were requiring the wet nurses for three days after having received communion to cast their milk into a latrine. For Christians to permit such behavior was to risk provoking divine indignation.[69]

What was probably most burdensome and frustrating to Innocent

---

[68] Reg. 8:85 = PL 215:654–657. See also Reg. 8:105 = PL 215:673.
[69] Reg. 8:121 = PL 215:694.

was that the wondrous conquest of Constantinople no longer seemed quite so wondrous, and the promise of a united effort of Greeks and Latins against the Muslim world was dissolving. During July, 1205, Innocent wrote a letter that clearly reveals a sense of desperation about the situation in the East.[70] It urges an unnamed prelate to convey to the king of France the precarious nature of the Christian outposts in the Holy Land, and it does so bluntly, without any rhetorical flourishes or biblical illusions. The personal tone of the letter, written to someone closely trusted and someone in the position to make the case with Philip Augustus, makes Guy de Paray (Guido de Paredo) the likely recipient. A former abbot of Cîteaux, Guy had been, as cardinal bishop of Palestrina and papal legate, one of Innocent's most trusted and effective diplomats in the matter of the empire, and in 1204 he had been installed as archbishop of Rheims.[71] Now Innocent urged him to seek help from the king, saying ". . . in so great a crisis of need, we should not rest at all, nor should we spare any solicitude of heart nor labor of body until we are able to succor the Holy Land."

In his letter, Innocent bemoaned the fact that unless something was done soon, the present Christian holdings in the Holy Land would be jeopardized—never mind expanding them. By July, Innocent knew that the capture of Constantinople had led to a mass exodus of people from the Holy Land to Constantinople, leaving the province of Jerusalem undefended. There was no leadership left because the patriarch and the king of Jerusalem had both recently died, as had the king's son and heir; and the two cardinal legates had joined those rushing to Constantinople. The count of Tripoli and the king of Armenia (both Christian) were fighting with each other over the principality of Antioch with the two military orders taking sides, the Templars favoring the count and the Hospitalers favoring the king. The Saracens, frightened by the Latin occupation of Constantinople, had put aside their differences and were entering into a confederacy to oppose the Christians. The king of the Vlachs and Bulgars (only recently having declared his submission to Rome) was now entering into alliances with Cumans, Turks, and Greeks to fight the Latins. Finally, Cardinal Peter Capuano—incredibly—had released

---

[70] Reg. 8:125 = PL 215:698–699.
[71] Reg. 7:116; Maleczek, *Papst*, pp. 133–4.

the Latins in Constantinople from their crusaders' oaths, thereby eliminating the hope for help from that quarter. Hence the desperate need for help from Philip Augustus.

About the same time, Innocent vented the same frustration in a letter to the two cardinal legates. He wrote Peter Capuano sharply upbraiding him and Cardinal Soffredus for abandoning their responsibilities in the Holy Land and leaving the province of Jerusalem without leadership. He bitterly criticized Peter for presuming to absolve the Latins in Constantinople from their crusader's oaths, although Peter may have recognized that the position of the Latins in the Greek world was so insecure that they could not possible leave for the Holy Land. By this time, stories of the sack of Constantinople and its many atrocities had reached Innocent, and the reality of the situation was hitting the pope full force. He reviewed the course of the crusade and said,

> For how will the church of the Greeks, so afflicted and persecuted, return to ecclesiastical unity and to devotion to the Apostolic See when it sees in the Latins only an example of perdition and works of darkness? With reason, the Greek church abhors the Latins more than dogs.

The Latins had turned their swords against Christians, he said, sparing no one regardless of religion, age, or sex; they had committed incest, adultery, and fornication, victimizing matrons and consecrated virgins. They had stolen sacred objects from the churches.[72] These reports caused great consternation and extensive discussion in the curia,[73] and Innocent's conviction of a few months before that all this had been God's work was clearly weakening.[74] Publicly he stuck to his confident pose in a letter dated 16 August, as he again summoned all the faithful to a new effort to relieve the Holy Land.[75] But even more bad news followed. He soon learned that Kalojan, king of the Bulgars and Vlachs, had defeated an army of the Latins

---

[72] Reg. 8:126 = PL 215:699–702, Andrea, *Contemporary Sources*, pp. 162–168 (numbered Reg. 8:127 [128]).

[73] *Gesta*, PL 214:xcli–cxlii = Gress-Wright, pp. 212–213.

[74] In a letter to Boniface of Montferrat, probably written the following August, Innocent said that the capture of Constantinople "seemed" to have been a divine judgement. Reg. 8:133 = PL 215:713, English translation in Andrea, *Contemporary Sources*, pp. 171–176. Other letters show that Innocent did not believe that the Latin hold on Constantinople was secure, frequently referring to the state of flux there. See for example his letter to the patriarch: Reg. 8:24 = PL 215:578.

[75] Reg. 8:130 = PL 215:706.

from Constantinople. Emperor Baldwin himself was now Kalojan's prisoner.[76] That Innocent realized the fragility of the Latin Empire can be seen in a later letter to the bishop of Soissons (December 1206), newly elected as archbishop of Thessalonica. Instead of requiring the bishop to give up the Soissons see, Innocent permitted him to hold both "until the status of the empire in Constantinople is solidified."[77] It had become much more difficult to find in the Latin Empire a sign of God's favor.

*   *   *

After news of Baldwin's capture reached the pope, probably in late August 1205,[78] the papal registers show no sustained effort against Muslim, heretic, or Jew. The letter from Baldwin's brother Henry asked the pope to make an all out effort to organize all of Christendom in support of Constantinople,[79] but a dispirited Innocent responded with an unusually brief letter, merely urging Henry to try to make peace with Kalojan, king of the Bulgars and Vlachs.[80] Instead of major initiatives on any subject, the registers for the following months show the usual flow of petty business, much of it concerned with Christian conflict with Christian rather than non-Christian or heretical enemies. The grandiose assertions of papal authority that abounded in the letters of his early years became less common.[81] The summer in Rome in 1205 seems to have left Innocent with little enthusiasm for grand plans.

The registers from the summer of 1205 to the summer of 1206 also show that the princes who might have been organizing the crusade or leading the attacks on heretics, seemed to be more interested in fighting among themselves and oppressing their local clergymen. Besides the fact that the Christian emperor of Constantinople was

---

[76] Reg. 8:129, 131, 132 = PL 215:705, 706, 710. Innocent's letters on the capture are undated, but their position in the register and the fact that the capture is not mentioned in his general letter of 16 August suggest that they were written in late August.

[77] Reg. 9:200 = PL 215:1037.

[78] On 16 August, Innocent sent a letter to all the faithful, suggesting that if people trying to go to Constantinople in response to his May appeal found difficulty finding transport, they should come through southern Italy so that he could help. It makes no mention of Baldwin's capture. Reg. 8:130 = PL 215:706.

[79] Reg. 8:131 = PL 215:706–710.

[80] Reg. 8:132 = PL 215:710.

[81] Cheney, "The Letters of Pope Innocent III," p. 35.

a prisoner of the Christian king of the Bulgars and Vlachs, the kings of England and France were still at war with each other, as were the rival candidates for the office of Roman Emperor (and Innocent's candidate was clearly losing).[82] In September, the clergy of Cologne sent Innocent a plaintive appeal for help. The allies of the deposed archbishop of Cologne were ravaging their property and the new archbishop had been captured and imprisoned by Philip of Swabia.[83] King John of England was for Innocent a constant irritant on many fronts. He was interfering in the election of the bishop of Winchester[84] (as he had done in earlier years in Ireland[85] and Normandy),[86] and he was refusing to pay the legacy left by his brother Richard for Otto, Innocent's imperial candidate.[87] Waldemar king of the Danes was holding the bishop of Slesvik in prison.[88] Even King Pedro of Aragon, who seemed at least to be making an effort against the heretics, had to be warned about meddling in ecclesiastical elections.[89]

What energy Innocent had for things other than routine business, he gave to the imperial controversy and to building the Patrimony. In March and in September 1205, he sent letters to Germany intended to reverse the flow of defectors from Otto to Philip. He put pressure on the German bishops to toe the papal line, and he actually deposed Archbishop Adolf of Cologne, who had abandoned Otto for Philip.[90] Closer to home, Innocent also pursued aggressively his claim that Sardinia belonged to the papal Patrimony. Challenging the claims of Pisa to the island, he had already placed one of his papal clerks as archbishop of Torres and was now arranging to marry his own cousin Trasmondo to the heiress to Gallura.[91] But apart

---

[82] Theo Holzapfel, *Papst Innozenz III., Philipp II. August, König von Frankreich und die englisch-welfische Verbindung 1198–1216* (Frankfurt am Main, 1991), pp. 120–121.

[83] Leonard Emnen and Gottfried Eckertz (eds.), *Quellen der Stadt Köln*, 2 (Cologne, 1863): 22–23, no. 20.

[84] Reg. 8:5 = PL 215:562; Reg. 8:104 = PL 215:674; Reg. 8:209 = PL 215:792.

[85] Reg. 1:367; Reg. 6:64 (63, 64); Reg. 7:171.

[86] Reg. 6:73.

[87] RNI, nos. 129, 132.

[88] Reg. 8:192–193 = PL 215:768–773.

[89] Peter was apparently gaining territory previously under the control of heretics (Reg. 8:97 = PL 215:667; Reg. 8:94–95 = PL 215:666). The warning is in Reg. 8:9 = PL 215:568.

[90] RNI, nos. 116–129.

[91] Moore, "Pope Innocent III, Sardinia," pp. 81–101.

from a few letters about heretics in northern Italy,[92] little effort was made against heretics, infidels, and Jews.

Routine curial business continued. Thomas of Marlborough, who had annoyed the pope in 1204, was back in Rome in the summer of 1205, and his case finally came before Innocent late in the year. This time it was Thomas' opponent who annoyed the pope. His long and erudite preamble was cut short. Fixing the advocate with a stern look, Innocent told him, "We don't want an introduction of that sort; get to the matter at hand." When the same advocate complained that Thomas had hired all the legal talent in Rome, the pope responded with a smile, perhaps a sad smile, that there was never any shortage of lawyers in the Roman curia.[93]

In December 1205, Innocent devoted a remarkable amount of time to Thomas's case on behalf of the monastery of Evesham. He became engrossed in the details and may have again found relief in dealing with a judicial matter he could master more easily than the intractable world of politics. With great confidence, he issued a magisterial judgment on Christmas eve, a judgment that was to be incorporated into canon law. But the confidence was misplaced; the judgment of modern scholars is that "the pope was no match for the monks." His decision in favor of the monastery was based on forged documents and he left untouched one of the most corrupt abbots in Christendom.[94] The discussion of peripheral matters continued into January of 1206. It was then that Innocent made his celebrated remark when a lawyer opposing Thomas claimed that he and the other English masters taught a certain legal principle. Innocent said, "You and your masters were surely drinking too much English ale when you taught that."[95]

Whether the registers of 1205–1206 actually reflect a mood of discouragement or disappointment is difficult to say with certainty, but we do know how Innocent would have addressed such a mood. In early 1206, the bishop of Cagliari in Sardinia asked for permission to resign his bishopric, and Innocent wrote a long and thoughtful letter urging the bishop to remain at his post.[96] He argued that

---

[92] Reg. 9:7–8, 18–21 = PL 215:813–815, 819–822.
[93] *Chronicon abbatiae de Evesham*, pp. 152–153.
[94] Cheney, *Innocent III and England*, p. 199.
[95] *Chronicon abbatiae de Evesham*, p. 189.
[96] Reg. 9:1 = PL 215:801–810.

the contemplative life should not be preferred to the active life, despite the fact that Jesus said that Mary had chosen a better way than her sister Martha. He said:

> Consider a man who wants to give up his office, who has administered it laudably in time of prosperity, with fortune smiling..., but, when time of adversity threatens, he is anxious that if anything bad happens it could be attributed to his negligence. Clearly, if this is his reason for resigning, he can compare himself to the improvident sea captain, who steers the ship with little effort on tranquil seas, but when the storm rises he deserts it and abandons it to the depths. ....
>
> There is an impious opinion that a bishop, because of worldly occupations and secular concerns, is not able to exercise his pontifical office without sin. We reject and condemn it, since the church venerates many saints who administered both spiritual and temporal things. .... You should not think that Martha chose an evil part, being busy about many things, just because Mary chose the best. ... Although Mary's role is more secure, Martha's is more fruitful; although Mary's is sweeter, Martha's is more useful, since in producing offspring, the weak-eyes of Leah are preferred to the beauty of Rachel. You can be simultaneously contemplative and active, following the example of the legislator [Moses], who at one moment ascended the mountain so that he could there perceive more freely the glory of the Lord, and at another descended into the camp, so that he could more usefully provide for the needs of the people. ... Do not refuse the labor of pastoral rule; cast your thoughts upon the Lord ... who sees you as necessary for his people. ...

In May 1206, the curia left Rome for the first time since March 1204, and moved to the cool mountain air of Ferentino, followed as usual by the crowd of suitors and petitioners. In July of 1206, Innocent wrote to the abbots of the Cistercian order who would soon be meeting in general chapter, and described his own experience trying to handle his fishing boat. He had taken to sea to put out his nets, he said, but the sea was great and expansive and full of dangers. In this unusual letter, with hardly any biblical references except for the basic figure of himself as fisherman, Innocent went on at great length about the waves, the winds, the sea-monsters, the pirates. Even after he had taken his ship into such dangerous waters and had managed to gather fish into his net, some had escaped as the nets broke and reverted to heresy. Faced with all this, Innocent earnestly asked for their prayers.[97]

---

[97] Reg. 9:119 = PL 215:940.

The summer of 1206 in Ferentino was relatively uneventful. A minor act of generosity was remembered by one chronicler, who noted that while Innocent was there, he did not require the local churches to provide fodder for his entourage because the imposition would be too burdensome.[98] The pope gave considerable attention to arrangements being made in Constantinople regarding clergy and church property and to the authority there of the new patriarch.[99] The most promising development of the period was a conciliatory letter from Philip of Swabia, offering to make peace on several issues. Innocent, now seeing little hope of a victory for Otto, commissioned Woflger, the patriarch of Aquileia, to try to mediate a peace between Otto and Philip and wrote Otto encouraging him to accept the idea.[100]

* * *

In September, the curia returned to the Lateran. For several years to come, letters against heresy regularly left the curia, and in some of them, we find not only condemnations but also reasoned argumentation against heretical beliefs and also an acknowledgment that corrupt clergy were a major source of heresy. In December of 1206, he wrote to several clergy in the dioceses of Nantes and St. Malo in Brittany, commissioning them to investigate the problem in their area. He wrote that now that peace had come to their area (the war between King John and Philip Augustus being in hiatus), men wearing the appearance of piety but not its substance were waging a war of their own, going into homes and leading away young women in the shackles of sin. When their neighbors are sick, they visit them before the priest does and urge the sick persons not to confess their sins to the priest, "saying that a confession made to priests is worthless for salvation, since the priests are weighted down with their own sins." They condemn marriage, and many other things taught by the Catholic faith. They fail to recognize that the relation between the priest and the sacrament is the same as that between the doctor and his medicine.

> Just as the illness of a doctor does not impede the strength of his medicine, so also, the crime of the catholic priest does not impede the

---

[98] *Annales Ceccanenses*, MGH SS 19:296.
[99] *Gesta*, PL 214:cxliv–xclv = Gress-Wright, pp. 239–254.
[100] RNI, nos. 136–139.

force of the sacrament—although the life ought to be in harmony with the teaching, lest perchance he who is being corrected by speech will be corrupted by example.

This concern about the morals of the clergy, and perhaps the discouraging course of events in recent years, led Innocent in February of 1207 to introduce drastic changes in the curia, imposing on himself and his associates a new discipline. The Biographer wrote:

Because there was such an excess of extravagance in the world, especially among prelates, he reduced himself to moderation so that he could more freely rebuke those prelates and recall them to the example of him who first so acted and taught.

His gold and silver vessels he replaced with wood and glass. He discarded his precious vestments, his ermine and miniver furs, in favor of white wool and lamb skin. He limited his meals to three dishes, except on special occasions, and replaced his lay servants with religious. It was as though he would make his court a replica of a Cistercian monastery.[101]

Judging from Innocent's letter to Brittany, the heretics there were apparently closer to Waldensian beliefs than Cathar. His understanding of Catharism can be found in a letter to the podestà, consuls, and people of Treviso (21 April 1207) in northern Italy:

The glory of your name would be shining far and wide were it not that the smoke of heretical perversity obscures it, since, according to the apostle, a small measure of leaven can corrupt the whole mass just as well as a large measure. Why therefore, worthy citizens, do you permit the Catholic faith (through which you have been reborn from water and the Spirit) to be corrupted by certain lawless and unlearned men, seduced and seducers, who neither understand sacred Scriptures nor recognize divine power? They hide the rapacity of a wolf under the pelt of a sheep so that they may lead the unwary to drink venom from the golden cup of the dragons (cf. Rev. 17:4). Expel therefore the old leaven, so that you may be a new baptism, an unleavened bread, not in the leaven of malice and iniquity but in the unleavened bread of sincerity and truth, avoiding those false prophets who come to you in sheep's clothing but inside are rapacious wolves. Especially to be avoided are the impious Manicheans, who call themselves Cathars

---

[101] *Gesta*, PL 214:ccxxv–ccxxvi = Gress-Wright, p. 353; Bolton, "*Qui fidelis est in minimo*," pp. 120–121.

or Patarines, whose madness the apostle Paul foresaw in the Spirit as something to be avoided, writing to Timothy, among other things:

> Now the Spirit expressly says that in later times some will depart from the faith by giving heed to deceitful spirits and doctrines of demons, through the pretensions of liars whose consciences are seared, who forbid marriage and enjoin abstinence from foods which God created to be received with thanksgiving by those who believe and know the truth. For everything created by God is good, and nothing is to be rejected if it is received with thanksgiving; for then it is consecrated by the word of God and prayer (1 Tim. 4:1–5).

Behold how the apostle Paul . . . expressly and manifestly says he did not receive or learn this from men but only through the revelation of Jesus Christ. He condemns and rejects the wild dogma of the perfidious Manicheus which is thoroughly alien not only from the truth of the orthodox faith but also from the judgment of natural reason. Indeed the Manichean dogma, together with its followers, teaches that corporeal food was created not by God, but by the Devil, whom it calls the prince of darkness and by whom, it says, all corporeal and visible things were created. But faith teaches that food was created by God and should be accepted as such by the faithful with signs of thanks. The Manichean dogma prohibits marrying, damning matrimony and asserting that it is no greater sin to have intercourse with your mother or daughter than with a non-relative or stranger. Faith commends marriage, asserting it to be a great sacrament in Christ and the church, according to which the first man awakened and prophesied, "This at last is bone of my bones and flesh of my flesh" (Gen. 2:23). "For this reason a man shall leave his father and mother and be joined to his wife, and the two shall become one flesh" (Ephes. 5:31). Therefore he [St. Paul] says that it is better to marry than to burn. But why should we dwell on things like this when among all the madness, there is this great madness, and among all the errors there is this one more horrible, which not only attacks the evangelical truth but also overthrows that philosophical doctrine which teaches that there is one author of all things, both visible and invisible?

Flee, therefore, flee the error, damnable and damned, indeed ruinous and ruining, which induces interior darkness in order to produce exterior darkness. And do not be darkened with those who fancy themselves to have been created by the principle of darkness; rather, be illuminated with those who confess themselves to have been created by the father of lights, with whom there is no darkness. For we pledge on your behalf before Christ Jesus, who will come to judge the living and the dead, that what the Apostolic See teaches is the true and right faith, according to apostolic and prophetic doctrine. Although unworthy, we preside over that see, and on the last day of strict judgment we wish to respond before Christ's tribunal . . . on your behalf, interceding for you with the tribunal of the divine majesty, before whom finally you will stand according to merit.

Spurning and detesting the false dogma of heretical depravity, may you embrace and pursue the true doctrine of the Apostolic See, founded on the firm rock with immovable solidity. Remember that formerly you promised us, taking an oath in the hand of our venerable brother the bishop of Ferrara, when, with paternal devotion, we restored to you the grace of communion that had long been removed from you through his ministry.

Concerning all this, we warn and exhort your devotion, ordering you through apostolic letter that you give credence to our venerable brother your bishop. We have given him orders that he strictly correct the excesses of the clergy whose depraved example disturbs you, and we warn and exhort you to take comfort in those who are redolent of honest morals and who know the orthodox faith. Do not permit your souls to be scandalized by the fact that certain men do not live as they teach. Just as the sickness of the physician does not impede the force of his medicine, neither does the iniquity of the priest annul the power of the sacrament.[102]

The connection between heresy and corrupt clergy was a recurrent theme in Innocent's letters and sermons. He faced the problem directly many times, but never in such dramatic form as in Berengar, archbishop of Narbonne, in the very heart of Cathar country. A Spanish abbot who served as archbishop of Narbonne from 1190 to 1212, Berengar seemed to be everything a bishop should not be. Until 1204, he preferred to live in his abbey of Monte Aragon in Spain, and when he did visit Narbonne, his accusers said, he cared only for money. He extorted payments at every opportunity, he was completely indifferent to the spiritual and material needs of the faithful, and he routinely ignored all papal directives.[103] Innocent had deprived him of his abbey in 1204, but that seems to have had no effect on his behavior. After papal legates sent the pope depositions taken against Berengar, the archbishop was summoned to Rome. After considerable delay, he appeared there as a repentant sinner in the spring of 1206. He was old and feeble in body, he had been deprived of his abbey, he had suffered the difficult trip to Rome, and Innocent took pity on him. Innocent ordered him to seek profit not in money but in souls, to engage himself not in illicit exactions

---

[102] Reg. 10:54 = PL 215:1146–1148.
[103] Foreville, *Le Pape Innocent III et la France*, pp. 176, 178–179; Bolton, "Hearts Not Purses?," pp. 129–132.

and crooked business deals but in hospitality and piety, to be generous to pilgrims and the impoverished. He told him to visit his province, to hold councils, to eliminate heresies, and to correct the many excesses in the province.[104] A year later, however, in May of 1207, Innocent was instructing new commissioners to look into charges that Berengar had returned home only to find new ways to violate his trust.[105] Berengar was to avoid a final reckoning for years to come.

Not that Berengar was alone. In the summer of 1207, the citizens of Le Puy sent messengers to the pope complaining that their bishop was extorting money from them for weddings and funerals. Innocent ordered the bishop to make reparations while urging the citizens to respect his legitimate authority.[106]

* * *

The battle against heresy needed conscientious and reputable bishops, but Innocent also called on the secular arm to help. Count Raymond VI of Toulouse was the most obvious ally needed, but Raymond was not interested. In May of 1207, at the same time that Innocent was beginning a new investigation of Berengar, he sent an exceedingly angry letter to the count, confirming the excommunication the legates had already laid upon him and excoriating him for his failures to move against heretics. Not only was Raymond supporting heretics and placing Jews in public office, he had seized the property of clergy and had driven the bishop of Carpentras from his bishopric.

> Alas! What pride swells your heart, what madness captures you, oh pestilent man? You disdain to make peace with your neighbors, and abandoning divine law, you join yourself to the enemies of the Catholic truth. Is it not enough for you to pester men; must you also pester God?

Innocent reminded him that the Lord of life and death could send him to eternal torment and that even in this life, God might afflict him with leprosy, paralysis, or any number of other incurable diseases. And he concluded with a threat to call on all the surrounding princes to rise up against him as an enemy of Christ and persecutor

---

[104] Reg. 9:66 = PL 215:883.
[105] Reg. 10:68 = PL 215:1164.
[106] Reg. 10:85 = PL 215:1181–82.

of the church, with the understanding that they might keep whatever land they could take from him.[107]

It was a fearsome threat, but not so easily carried out. The two
most powerful of the "surrounding princes" were the kings John and
Philip Augustus, but they continued to be problems in their own
right. In April of 1207, still another plaintive letter had been sent
to the French king, asking him to treat Ingeborg decently.[108] In May,
the same month of Innocent's fierce letter to Count Raymond, the
pope was threatening ecclesiastical censures against the king for despoiling the diocese of Auxerre after the death of the bishop.[109]

As for King John, Innocent had long tried to keep the king from
intervening in episcopal elections, and John had long considered it
his prerogative to do so. The death of Hubert Walter in 1205 had
set the stage for what was to be a prolonged and painful struggle
over the succession to the archbishopric of Canterbury. The monks
of Christ Church had the right to elect the new archbishop, but the
suffragan bishops of the province claimed a role, and the king expected
his candidate to be selected. Two candidates emerged, and after a
series of delegations to Rome from the interested parties, Innocent
declared both elections invalid and summoned a delegation of monks
to his presence to hold a new election. In December 1206, they
elected Stephen Langton, an Englishman and distinguished scholar
from Paris, who had only recently been appointed cardinal by the
pope. King John did not take the news well. His envoys told the
pope that he would not accept Stephen for several reasons: he was
unknown to the king, he had been living in France among the king's
enemies, the king's consent had not been sought. Innocent found no
merit in any of these objections and urged the king to comply.[110]

In Germany, the division between Otto and Philip was crippling
the entire society. In a letter of May 1207, Innocent included a long
list of evils the civil war was bringing to Germany, among them,
the loss of faith and the growth of heresy.[111]

If heresy was to be restrained, both ecclesiastical and secular
authorities would have to do a good deal more that they had to
date. That was about to happen.

[107] Reg. 10:69 = PL 215:1166–68.
[108] Reg. 10:42 = PL 215:1135.
[109] Reg. 10:71 = PL 215:1169.
[110] Reg. 10:219 = PL 215:1327 = Cheney and Semple, pp. 86–90, no. 29.
[111] RNI, no. 141.

CHAPTER SEVEN

DEFENSE OF THE CHURCH (1207–1212)

The apparent unification of Greek and Latin Christianity had encouraged Innocent to expect similar successes in dealing with Jews and heretics. But in this endeavor, like many others, he was frustrated by the indifference or opposition of the secular rulers of Europe. Between 1207 and 1212, however, he seemed once again to experience a cycle of apparent success, optimism, and confidence followed by reversals and discouragement. His confident disciplining of King John of England turned the situation in England into a running sore, with the upper clergy in exile and the pastoral needs of the people left unattended. Apparent successes in Italy, in the empire, and in the heretical regions of southern France were also followed by reversals, by disappointments, and—worst of all—by a new Muslim threat advancing in Spain.

* * *

But the summer of 1207 was, for Innocent, a blessed one, a time when his vision of a harmonious and peaceful Christian society seemed to be realized in the Papal State, the one place where the spiritual and temporal swords were not in conflict, at least for the time being. There, both swords were in the hands of the pope. In 1205, Innocent had railed against Viterbo for permitting heretics to flourish in their city. He had smarted from the criticism of others that the pope attacked heresy elsewhere but allowed it to flourish in his own Patrimony. "Physician heal yourself," they said; "first remove the beam from your own eye, then remove the speck from the eye of your brother."[1] So in June of 1207, instead of taking his customary route on the Via Casilina, Innocent led the curia north to Viterbo, arriving like a king and his court.[2]

It was at Viterbo that William of Andres, a monk from Flanders,

---

[1] *Gesta*, PL 214:clxi–clxii = Gress-Wright, p. 310.
[2] *Gesta*, PL 214:clxii = Gress-Wright, pp. 310–314.

found Innocent. He had come to Italy with business for the curia[3] and had gone to Viterbo, where he said he found "Rome." He hoped to make his case about his own election as prior and about the independence of his monastery from its mother house. Viterbo was a city better suited to handle the crowds of clerics, laymen, and pilgrims that followed the curia than were the hill-top cities along the Via Casilina. William said that Innocent chose it out of consideration for others as well as for himself (his body could not tolerate the summer heat of Rome). Viterbo was blessed with abundant supplies of bread, wine, hay, grass, barley, as well as wholesome hot springs, vineyards, and forests. Every bodily need of humans and horses could be met there at moderate cost.

There were weighty matters for Innocent to deal with in Viterbo (the monks of Canterbury were there to choose an archbishop), but one day after his afternoon nap, he received William to hear his petition in private. To William's great delight, the pope embraced him and invited him to sit at his feet, show his documents, and make his case. Innocent said he would do all he could in fairness, since he had enjoyed the hospitality of William's monastery when he was a student at Paris, traveling to England to visit the shrine of Thomas Becket. But in fact, William's case was to drag on and require him to make two more visits to the papal court.

The curia remained in Viterbo for the entire summer, except for a brief and satisfying visit to Montefiascone. It was the former fortress of Philip of Swabia and was now in the hands of Count Hildebrand, a former lieutenant of Philip. In the presence of a great crowd of ecclesiastical dignitaries, Hildebrand abandoned Philip and swore homage to the pope.[4]

When Innocent chose Viterbo for his summer residence, he had more in mind than the convenience of pilgrims and petitioners. It provided an opportunity to attend to heretics there and to hold a grand parliament for central Italy. The heretics of the city fled before his arrival, and after an investigation, Innocent had their homes torn down. Then in response to his summons, delegations from all over the Patrimony arrived in Viterbo in September. Innocent presided over a great gathering, a parliament of the Papal State, and issued

---

[3] For the following, see *Willelmi Chronica Andrensis*, MGH SS 24:737–8.
[4] *Gesta*, PL 214:clxvii = Gress-Wright, p. 316; PL 217:298–299.

laws to provide for the entire Patrimony.[5] He wrote to all his "fideles" throughout the Patrimony of St. Peter:

> Since counts and barons, podestàs and consuls have sworn to observe peace and justice and security, strictly adhering to our command, we command all of you that, observing true peace, you will never commit an offense against one another—not community against community, not person against person, not community against person, except bandits and robbers, outlaws and traitors. In order to punish this sort, the rectors of the Apostolic Patrimony will offer opportune assistance as often as you require it.
>
> If any one suffers an offense, he will not immediately strike back in kind, but he will first give warning so that the offender may make amends. And if an argument breaks out over the appropriate settlement, the matter will be referred to the judgment of a rector of the Apostolic Patrimony, unless it can first be settled by someone else. Otherwise, let the rector impugn the malefactor as a public enemy.
>
> When a controversy begins between anyone, let it be terminated by agreement or judgment. Let the judgment be in the hands of the competent judge, always saving the legitimate appeals made or to be made to us or to a rector of the Apostolic Patrimony. If indeed anyone within the Patrimony of St. Peter disdains to observe this, he is to be compelled to do so by all, according to the command of the rector of the Apostolic Patrimony.
>
> If anyone, by his own authority accepts plunder or has it accepted by others, if he steals something or has it stolen, then both he and the one who knowingly buys it shall restore the plunder and stolen goods in twofold as punishment. Whoever buys plunder or stolen goods unknowingly shall restore it entirely, with none of it claimed or to be claimed in compensation, although the buyer may take legal action against the seller.
>
> All these things we have enjoined on the counts and barons, the podestàs and consuls, bound by oath, so that they will observe them faithfully and see that others do the same.[6]

In another letter to all laymen and clergy throughout the Patrimony, Innocent invoked both his spiritual and his temporal authority to render null and void all "evil constitutions" passed by laymen at the expense of churches and churchmen. And in another, he set forth the provisions for dealing with heresy throughout the Patrimony:

> So that the filth of heretics may be eliminated altogether from the Patrimony of Saint Peter, we decree by law to be observed forever,

---

[5] See Tillmann, *Pope Innocent III*, p. 176, n. 184.

[6] Reg. 10:132 = PL 215:1228.

that any heretic, and especially any Patarine, found within the Patrimony is to be seized immediately and handed over to a secular court to be punished according to legitimate sanctions. All his goods are to be confiscated, so that one part is paid to the person who captured him, a second part to the court that punishes him, and a third part set aside for the construction of the walls of the land in which he was captured. The house in which the heretic had been received is to be thoroughly destroyed, and let no one presume to rebuild it. Rather let what was a hiding place for the perfidious become a sordid space.

Moreover, let defenders and supporters of heretics be punished with a fourth of their own goods, which is to be set aside for the use of the republic. But if any of those punished in this way should relapse again into a similar crime, let them be expelled entirely from those places and never return, except by command of the high pontiff, appropriate satisfaction having been performed. [Legal] pleas and appeals of persons of this sort shall not be heard. No one shall be forced to respond to them in any [legal] case, but they shall be forced to respond to others. Judges, advocates, and notaries shall bestow office on none of them, and they shall be deprived in perpetuity of any office. Clergy are not to administer ecclesiastical sacraments to pestilential people of this sort and they are not to accept alms or oblations from them. Hospitalers and Templars and members of religious orders are to follow the same rule; otherwise they will be deprived of their office, to which they shall not be restored without special grant from the Apostolic See.

The letter continues, spelling out every possible way that heretics and their supporters, protectors, and defenders can be cut off from every aspect of society, in life and in death. Innocent concluded by requiring all officials to swear annually to observe the rules, and by ordering any official who failed to observe them to lose his office and to pay a hundred pound fine to whomever the pope designated.[7]

The world, as Innocent would have it, would be one free from violence, a world of law and peaceful resolution of conflict. But he clearly saw heresy as the most dangerous of crimes, and in his attempts to make heresy unthinkable for the people of the Patrimony, he seemed to bypass all his precious legal procedures in favor of a kind of martial law that punished even those loosely connected with the crime, although he held back from prescribing capital punishment for anyone. In any case, during his stay at Viterbo in the summer of 1207, Innocent had the satisfaction of seeing his vision of a Christian society becoming a reality, at least in the Papal State.

---

[7] Reg. 10:130 = PL 215:1226–27.

During 1207, Innocent intensified efforts to move the world out-side the Patrimony. In May of 1207, shortly before the curia departed for Viterbo, Innocent had issued bold new letters to England, France, and Germany, all intended to restore right order in Christendom and to recall princes to their proper roles. On 26 May 1207, Innocent wrote King John of England concerning the Canterbury election, warning him that "to fight against God and the Church in this cause for which St. Thomas, that glorious martyr and archbishop, recently shed his blood, would be dangerous for you."[8] Three days later, Innocent addressed the previously mentioned angry letter to Count Raymond VI of Toulouse, calling him the "enemy of Christ and persecutor of the church" and warning him to change his ways or have neighboring princes turned against him.[9] As for Germany, Innocent sent notice to the secular and ecclesiastical princes there that he was sending a new and prestigious delegation—Cardinals Hugolino and Leo—to address the schism there created by the rivalry between Otto and Philip.[10]

Once in Viterbo, the mood remained confident. Shortly after his triumphant entry into the city, and despite the objections of King John, the pope consecrated Stephen Langton archbishop of Canter-bury.[11] From Germany came signs that a settlement of the imperial problem might be in the offing,[12] and that in turn had ramifications in Italy. Pisa was a perennial ally of emperors against popes, but now that the pope was on the verge of an agreement with Philip of Swabia, a delegation of Pisans appeared at Viterbo offering coop-eration with the pope's policies in Sardinia and Sicily.[13] Another unexpected bonus came with a messenger from the archbishop of Lund, telling the pope that the entire population of Livonia had now been converted to Christianity, with not a single soul left unbaptized.[14]

In November, on his way back to Rome, he wrote Philip of Swabia congratulating him on no longer being excommunicated.[15] Negotiations in Germany were clearly going well.

---

[8] Reg. 10:219 = PL 215:1327; English trans. by Cheney and Semple, p. 89, no. 29.
[9] Reg. 10:69 = PL 215:1166-68.
[10] RNI, no. 141 = PL 216:1140-41.
[11] Pott., entry for 17 June 1207, p. 266, between nos. 3120 and 3121.
[12] RNI, no. 140.
[13] Reg. 10:117 = PL 215:1215-16; Moore, "Pope Innocent III, Sardinia," pp. 93-94.
[14] Gesta, PL 214:clxiv = Gress-Wright, p. 315.
[15] RNI, no. 143.

* * *

Back in Rome, at St. Peter's, Innocent returned to the matter of Raymond of Toulouse. The count of Toulouse was in a complicated position.[16] As one of the great princes of France, he owed allegiance to the king of France, but for various holdings in the south, he also owed allegiance to the king of Aragon, the Roman emperor, the duke of Aquitaine (who was also king of England), and the pope. Although everyone of those overlords was interested in expanding his authority (at the expense of the count of Toulouse), they were all much preoccupied elsewhere. Philip Augustus of France and John of England and Aquitaine each had the other to worry about, as did the two candidates for the empire. King Pedro of Aragon had his Christian and Muslim opponents to hold his attention.

As for Innocent, he might also have put Toulouse far down on his list of priorities, were it not for the burgeoning growth of heresy in and around the count's lands. Raymond had clearly shown himself an unreliable instrument for eradicating heresy. The angry letter to Raymond in May 1207 had been written in the hope that he would finally be moved by severe warnings and threats. By November 1207, Innocent had decided that the time had come to make good on those threats, and he called once again on the princes of France, including the king, to take arms against the heretics of southern France. He offered them the same benefits as those extended to crusaders bound for the Holy Land, and in doing so instituted what has come to be known as the Albigensian crusade.[17] He wrote:

> The long-standing seduction of heretical depravity, which grows vigorously in the region of Toulouse, does not cease to produce monstrous off-spring. They in turn channel the corruption of their own madness into others. Then revives the detestable succession of the damned, who glory in the inventions of their own vanity and spurn the dogmas of the true faith. . . . Therefore, since wounds that do not respond to the treatment of a poultice should be cut away with a knife, and since those who despise ecclesiastical correction should by restrained by secular power, we have determined to call upon your help so that the injury done to Jesus Christ may be punished.[18]

---

[16] Much of the following is based on Austin P. Evans, "The Albigensian Crusade," *A History of the Crusades*, vol. 2: *The Later Crusades: 1198–1311* (Madison, 1969), pp. 277–314; Foreville, *Le Pape Innocent III et la France*, pp. 217–270; and Michael Costen, *The Cathars and the Albigensian Crusade* (Manchester, 1997).

[17] Reg. 10:149 = PL 215:1246–48.

[18] Reg. 10:149 = PL 215:1246–47.

There was little enthusiasm for this new crusade at first. Philip Augustus made clear that he would need more help against King John before he could commit forces to another front in the south. He was also troubled by the idea of permitting crusaders to confiscate the lands of a Christian prince who had not formally been found guilty of heresy. Perhaps the latter consideration restrained lesser princes and nobles as well. But early in 1208, a single bloody act gave a new intensity to the southern situation. On 13 January, the papal legate Peter of Castelnau attended a negotiating conference with Raymond of Toulouse. It came to nothing but ill-will. The very next day, an assassin murdered the legate.

The news was slow to reach Rome, perhaps delayed by winter weather. But by early March 1208, Innocent had received a detailed account of the murder. A spear had been thrust between Peter's ribs, and Peter had died offering forgiveness to his assassin. Buoyed by the successes of the previous year, confident that Philip of Swabia was about to become a cooperative emperor, and stunned that a legate had been struck down while on a papal mission, Innocent threw himself into a campaign to restore proper order in southern France once and for all. The self-assurance Innocent showed in 1207 hardened into aggressive determination in 1208. A flood of letters soon left Rome for every part of France, calling on all to join in a common effort against Raymond of Toulouse, whom, the pope said, the devil had stirred up as his minister. Innocent wrote the clergy:

> The count has already been struck with the sword of anathema [excommunication] for many and great disgraceful actions. He is now presumed from several indications to be guilty of the death of this holy man. Not only did he publicly threaten his death, he also, as it is asserted, admitted the murderer into his close friendship and rewarded him with many gifts.

The count was once again to be excommunicated, this time solemnly, with bell and candle. And since no one was to associate with a man so sentenced, all those bound to him by oaths or other ties of allegiance were to be released from those ties.[19]

Innocent's letter to the prelates did not show the cold fury that sometimes characterized his letters. The murder of Thomas Becket

---

[19] Reg. 11:26 = PL 215:1354; English translation in Peter of les Vaux-de-Cernay, *The History of the Albigensian Crusade*, trans. W. A. and M. D. Sibly (Woodbridge, 1998), pp. 31–38.

was much on his mind, as it had been when he wrote King John the previous summer. Faced with the reality that any cleric doing God's will could suffer the fate of St. Thomas, Innocent spoke of the martyrdom of Peter of Castelnau, and offered sober theological reflection to encourage the clerical recipients, reminding them it was necessary for grain to die and go into the ground in order for it to bear fruit. He wrote to his legate the Cistercian Arnaud Amalric that the death of Peter should not inspire fear in him but should rather enkindle love, for Peter had now, through his death, earned eternal life.[20]

Innocent's letters to the secular princes, however, were different. To the king of France, he wrote,

> Rise up, then, knight of Christ! Rise up most Christian prince! Let the mourning cries of the holy universal church move your most religious breast! Let pious zeal inflame you to vindicate such a great injury to your God! May you hear the voice of the blood of a just man calling to you, and may you take up the shield of protection on behalf of the church against the tyrant and enemy of the faith!

He called on Philip to join his secular sword to Innocent's spiritual sword. St. Peter had told Jesus at Gethsemane that there were two swords, and Jesus had replied, "It is enough," indicating that the secular and spiritual swords were to help and support each other. Innocent warned and exhorted Philip to extend his arm against heresy, whose adherents were worse than Saracens.[21] In nearly the same terms, he called for support from the "counts, barons, and all people throughout the kingdom of France."[22]

The heretics, he said, were worse than the Saracens. Innocent was here following the lead of the Third Lateran Council of 1179. The prelates there had lumped together the heretics and the bands of mercenary soldiers of southern France and then offered Christians who made war against them the same benefits as those given to Christians who fought against Muslims:

> . . . on all the faithful we enjoin, for the remission of sins, that they oppose this scourge with all their might and by arms protect the Christian people against them. . . . Those who in true sorrow for their

---

[20] Reg. 11:32 = PL 215:1361.
[21] Reg. 11:28 = PL 215:1358–59.
[22] Reg. 11:29 = PL 215:1359–60.

sins die in such a conflict should not doubt that they will receive forgiveness for their sins and the fruit of an eternal reward.[23]

Innocent expanded on that, making more explicit the fact that those who took the cross for southern France would receive the full benefits of a crusader to the Holy Land. In the letters of March 1208, the crusaders were offered full remission of their sins for which they had offered "contrition of heart and confession of mouth" and the crusaders were authorized to occupy the lands of the count and especially of heretics.[24] Letters sent out from Ferentino in October of 1208 also gave the crusaders to the south exemption from all payments of interest (usury) and called for clergy and laity in the homelands of their crusaders to pay a ten-percent tax for one year to support the crusaders, saying that "those acting in the public interest should be supported by public taxes."[25] In February of 1209, he wrote the faithful, "Up to now, you have perhaps fought for transitory glory; fight now for eternal glory. You have fought for the body; fight now for the soul. You have fought for the world, fight now for God."[26] At the same time, he placed the crusaders and their possessions under papal protection.[27]

During this same period, in late 1208 and early 1209, there were more peaceful victories over heresy. Durand of Huesca, a Spanish priest who had been a Waldensian, made his peace with Rome and brought with him his followers, thereafter called the "Catholic Poor" or "Poor Catholics." In the spring of 1209, Innocent took what may have been the most successful anti-heresy action of his life. About a dozen rag-tag men, led by Francis of Assisi, arrived in Rome to seek papal approval of their unusual way of life. All laymen, they lived lives of extreme poverty, spent their time repairing decaying churches and wandering around preaching the gospel. Fortunately for them, the bishop of Assisi had a good opinion of them and was in Rome at the time. The bishop in turn was a friend of Cardinal John of St. Paul, who recommended them to Innocent, who gave them his

[23] Tanner, 1:225. For this point and for Innocent's understanding of this crusade, see Foreville, *Le Pape Innocent III et la France*, pp. 249–264.

[24] Reg. 11:26 = PL 215:1356–7.

[25] Reg. 11:158 = PL 215:1469–70.

[26] Reg. 11:230 = PL 215:1545.

[27] Reg. 11:231 = PL 215:1546.

blessing.[28] He probably thought little of it, despite later legends, but within fifty years of his death, there would be hundreds of Franciscan friars throughout Europe.[29] The simplicity of their lives and of their preaching rivaled that of heretical groups, and their religious work in cities probably did as much to combat heresy as any of the oppressive measures sponsored by Innocent and his successors.

Earlier calls for a crusade against the heretics of southern France had been ignored, but this time, the knights of France (if not the king) responded. In June of 1209, while Innocent and his court were again summering in Viterbo, a great force of knights from northern and central France gathered at Lyons. It included a number of dignitaries: the duke of Burgundy, the counts of Nevers, St. Pol, and Boulogne, the archbishops of Rheims, Rouen, and Sens. Presiding were the papal legates Milo and Arnaud Amalric, abbot of Cîteaux. Faced with this gathering force, Raymond sought desperately to find an out. He was reconciled with the pope in June through the agency of the legate Milo, took the cross himself, and joined the crusading army moving south in the hope of directing it away from his lands and toward those of his nephew and rival Raymond Roger. Those lands included the cities of Béziers and Carcassonne. The citizens of Béziers resisted the crusading army, and when the city fell on 22 July 1209, it paid a terrible price for its resistance. The legates reported to the pope that the crusaders had "fed into the mouth of the sword nearly twenty thousand people, without regard to status, sex, or age."[30] However inflated the number, the massacre was certainly a reality.[31] Carcassonne was taken shortly thereafter, though this time the surviving occupants were allowed to leave unharmed. Oaths of submission were offered by cities and nobles throughout the area, a few heretics were burned alive—the first of many—and

---

[28] Frances Andrews, "Innocent III and Evangelical Enthusiasts: The Route to Approval," in *Pope Innocent III and His World*, pp. 231–233.

[29] See C. H. Lawrence, *The Friars: the Impact of the Early Mendicant Movement on Western Society* (London, 1994), p. 103 et passim.

[30] Reg. 12:108 = PL 216:137.

[31] Evans estimated the entire population of the city to be eight or nine thousand ("The Albigensian Crusade"), p. 289, n. 14. The customs of war permitted the massacre of all the population of a city that refused to surrender. See Jim Bradbury, *The Medieval Siege* (Woodbridge, 1992), pp. 296, 302, 318–321; R. Rogers, *Latin Siege Warfare in the Twelfth Century* (Oxford, 1992), p. 248.

Milo made a point of requiring the authorities to exclude Jews from all offices in their governments.[32]

By the end of the summer, most of the crusading force believed that they had done what was necessary to earn their indulgence, and having selected Simon, earl of Leicester and lord of Montfort, to be the leader of the forces remaining, they departed. Innocent was satisfied that the Albigensian crusade, or what he routinely referred to as "the matter of peace and faith," had been a great success, albeit one that needed continuing support from the orthodox faithful.[33]

When in 1202, many crusaders had been persuaded by the Venetians to capture the city of Zara, one of the crusaders who refused to join in was this same Simon de Montfort. He had carried out his vow by leaving the main crusading force and going directly to Palestine to fight the Muslims. Now, after a more successful crusade, he found himself the ruler of the lands formerly held by Raymond Roger, who had died at the hands of the crusaders. Innocent confirmed that the conquered lands now belonged to Simon and his heirs.[34] But Simon also found himself the leader of only a tiny force as the bulk of the army went home, and for the next several years, he struggled to expand his control among his hostile neighbors, occasionally receiving reinforcements from the north. Raymond VI continued to carry on negotiations with the pope and the papal legates. In late 1209, he even went to Rome to defend himself. But he was soon excommunicate again, for "protecting heretics and sheltering mercenaries,"[35] and he and Simon were often at war. Towns and nobles shifted allegiances as seemed expedient, reinforcements for Simon from the north came and went, and many people died ghastly deaths. By the end of 1212, Simon controlled almost all of Raymond's territories except the city of Toulouse itself.

Even before the crusaders' arrival in southern France, the most forceful voice for change in the area had been the stern Arnaud

---

[32] Peter of les Vaux-de-Cernay, *History*, 51–54. The oaths of submission are found in PL 216:127–138.

[33] "Negotium pacis et fidei." See for example Reg. 12:136 = PL 216:158. The region of southern France had long been as notorious for its lawless mercenaries as for its heretics. See canon 27 of Lateran III (Tanner 1:224–225).

[34] Reg. 12:122,123 = PL 216:151–153.

[35] Pott. 4317 = *Layettes*, 1:372, no. 973 (5 October 1211).

Amalric, abbot of Cîteaux and papal legate.[36] Since 1204, Arnaud had been directing Cistercian preachers into the area. In 1206, he encouraged the bishop of Osma and a Spanish canon named Dominic to go to Rome for a commission to preach against heresy. That advice led to the formation of the Dominican Friars, soon to be a major spiritual force in southern France and elsewhere. True to the militant spirit of St. Bernard, the most famous of the Cistercians, Arnaud had no hesitation about using military force against heresy. He was the dominant leader of the crusading force as it proceeded into the South, and it was he who supposedly said of the resisting people of Béziers, "Kill them all, the Lord will know his own." He may not have used those words at the time, but they are consistent with his report to the pope about the massacre at Béziers.[37]

Arnaud was determined that the lax ecclesiastical regime of the South would be replaced with something more rigorous. Acting with another papal legate, the bishop of Uzès, he saw to it that the archbishop of Auch and the bishops of Carcasonne, Rodez, and Vienne were ordered by the pope in 1211 to resign from their offices.[38] Archbishop Berengar of Narbonne, after years of eluding papal discipline, was finally deposed, and Arnaud himself was elected the new archbishop in March of 1212. The process Innocent had begun continued: gradually, prelates with local roots and a tolerance for local practices were being replaced by more rigorous men, including Cistercian monks.[39]

The Cistercians saw little hope for the conversion of Raymond, and his close association with another Raymond Roger, this one the count of Foix, did not help. This ally had both Cathars and Waldensians in his immediate family, and a Cistercian chronicler

---

[36] The following account of Arnaud's activities is based mainly on Foreville, *Le Pape Innocent III*, pp. 230–48.

[37] Reg. 12:108 = PL 216:137–141. Richard Kay has pointed out in an e-mail posting that the latter half of the quotation is from 2 Tim. 2:19. The source of this quotation is Caesarius of Heisterbach, writing forty years after the fact. An argument against the authenticity of the quotation is that another, very well informed Cistercian chronicler, writing a few years after the event, makes no mention of the remark and says that it was remarkable that the city and its inhabitants were destroyed by low-level soldiers without the knowledge of the leaders of the army. Peter also reports that the leaders were at pains to see that the same thing did not happen at Carcassonne, since a destroyed city meant lost resources (Peter of les Vaux-de-Cernay, *History*, pp. 50, 54).

[38] Reg. 14:32–34 = PL 216:408–410.

[39] Foreville, *Le Pape Innocent III et la France*, pp. 177–8.

reported all sorts of atrocities that he had perpetrated against monks, churches, and sacred objects, atrocities carried out with the aid of mercenaries and harlots.[40] But the ferocity with which Arnaud and Simon went after the count of Toulouse began to worry Innocent. Even before the campaign had begun, Philip Augustus had expressed his reservations about attacking a prince without any formal judgment. In the spring of 1212, Innocent wrote his legates Arnaud and the bishop of Uzès that since Raymond had not in fact been convicted either of heresy or of the murder of Peter of Castelnau, there was no basis for depriving him and his heirs of their lands. He wanted to reserve judgment on Raymond's punishment to himself, and he was concerned that some other authority (such as the legates) would presume to award Raymond's patrimonial lands to Simon de Montfort or other crusaders. One version of this letter to the legates ended, "be sure that in carrying out our order, you are not lukewarm or remiss, as you are said to have been up to now."[41] But from this point, Innocent was satisfied that the threat of heresy in the South had been contained.[42] From now on, his interest was to be focused on the Muslim threat, and his responses to the south tended to vacillate with whatever version of the facts he had at hand. The only real consistency in his policies regarding the disputed territories in the south of France was his desire to have the fighting stop and the remaining disputes settled peacefully through conferences and councils. Innocent wanted the militant energies of Christians to turn once again to the Holy Land and to the new Muslim threat in Spain,[43] but his desires in this regard were largely ignored by the leaders of the crusade in southern France.

*   *   *

As Innocent's struggles against John of England and Raymond of Toulouse were opening up in March of 1207, his battle against Philip of Swabia was winding down. In 1206 and 1207, Otto's support in

---

[40] Peter of les Vaux-de-Cernay, *History*, pp. 27, 103–107 and notes.

[41] Reg. 15:102 = PL 216:613–614.

[42] Reg. 15:215 = PL 216:744–745.

[43] See the excellent analysis of Innocent's policy by W. A. and M. D. Sibly in Appendix G of their edition of Peter of les Vaux-de-Cernay, *History*, pp. 313–20. In the text of the translation and in Appendix F, they provide translations of a number of Innocent's letters on the matter.

Germany had dwindled, and Philip began making conciliatory overtures to the pope.[44] Innocent had little choice but to try to find some compromise. His letter of May 1207 had introduced his two legates, the Cardinals Hugolino (the future Pope Gregory IX and a relative of Innocent) and Leo Brancaleo. He called on all the princes of Germany to cooperate with the legates so that schism and civil war could be ended, divisions that had caused unspeakable suffering to the entire Christian people and had prevented aid to the Holy Land.[45] The legates were aided by Philip's messenger Patriarch Wolfger of Aquileia, trusted by both Philip and Innocent.[46]

The rapprochement with Philip went very well, hence the letter of November 1207, congratulating Philip for having finally been absolved from the excommunication.[47] Innocent urged his cardinals to continue to work for a peaceful settlement between Otto and Philip that would be acceptable to the pope, warning them that they should not expect their negotiations to be easy, "since a great edifice cannot be brought to completion in a short time."[48] Some months later the cardinal legates could report that Philip had sworn he would follow papal orders concerning all matters for which he had been excommunicated, that he had freed the captive Archbishop Bruno of Cologne, that he had accepted Siegfried as archbishop of Mainz instead of his own candidate Liupold, that he had dispersed a great army previously gathered to use against Otto, and that he had agreed to a truce.[49] From the discussions had come a plan whereby Otto would concede the imperial title but would marry Philip's daughter Beatrice. Since Philip had no son, Otto could be soothed with the face-saving possibility—however remote—of someday succeeding Philip as emperor.[50] In early 1208, the curia was host to a bevy of Germans seeking to work out a settlement under papal supervision: two men

---

[44] RNI, nos. 136–138. For a brief summary of the Welf-Hohenstaufen conflict and a hostile description of Innocent's role, see Karl Hampe, *Germany under the Salian and Hohenstaufen Emperors*, trans. Ralph Bennet (Totowa, 1973), pp. 236–243. See also Van Cleve, *Emperor Frederick*, pp. 51–71.

[45] RNI, no. 141.

[46] See F. W. von Kries, "Wolfger von Erla," *Dictionary of the Middle Ages*, 12 (1989): 672–673.

[47] RNI, no. 143.

[48] RNI, nos. 146–147.

[49] RNI, no. 142. Concerning Mainz, see Reg. 6:38–41.

[50] RNI, nos. 153, 169, 178, 181.

claiming to be archbishop of Cologne, the archbiship of Mainz, the bishop of Worms, as well as representatives of Otto, Philip, and the city of Mainz.[51] A peaceful settlement seemed likely, and Innocent could now expect that neither Philip nor Otto would be likely to annex the kingdom of Sicily to the empire, since young King Frederick would come of age in December of 1208.

Not that Frederick was in secure possession of Sicily. Quite apart from the restless Italian and Muslim peoples of the Regno, he still had German opposition to contend with. In 1205, Dipold of Acerra had managed to kill Walter of Brienne under his collapsed tent. Since then, Dipold had continued to be an independent force in southern Italy, rarely acknowledging either the authority of the young king or that of the pope. Innocent had made great efforts to build alliances against Dipold, and in February 1208, shortly before the tenth anniversary of Innocent's consecration, his supporters achieved a major victory.[52] The combined efforts of the abbot of Monte Cassino, the papal chamberlain Stephen, Innocent's brother Richard, and Cardinal Peter de Sasso (papal rector of Campagna and Marittima) led to the capture of the city of Sora and the nearby fortress of Sorella, fortifications that controlled the northern frontier of the Regno. The whole area, wrote a local monk, had suffered for the previous seventeen years under the German yoke, while the German castellan Conrad had reduced the local nobles to beggary. But now the region had been delivered. So when, in mid-May 1208, the curia departed from Rome and took to the Via Casilina, the mood was festive.

The first stop was Anagni. While there, Innocent commissioned Guala, cardinal deacon of Sta. Maria in Portico as legate *a latere*. Perhaps in an overly-optimistic mood, the pope sent Guala to France with an extraordinary set of assignments: to find support for the Holy Land and for the Eastern Church (now supposedly reunited with Rome), to take up the perennial case between the king and Queen Ingeborg, and to look to the general reform of the church in France, that is, "to root up and to destroy, and to build and to plant" (Jer. 1:10) as he saw the need.[53] Guala was to have more

---

[51] Pixton, *German Episcopacy*, pp. 145–146.

[52] For the following, see Waley, *Papal State*, pp. 54–56; Tillmann, *Pope Innocent*, pp. 136–137; *Annales Ceccanenses*, MGH SS 19:296–297.

[53] Reg. 11:85, 86 = PL 215:1403.

luck with reform than with any of the other charges,[54] since Innocent himself had created a situation in which French warriors could get all the benefits of a crusader with a few weeks in southern France without taking on the expensive and arduous journey to the Holy Land.

After spending the first half of June 1208 in Anagni, the pope set out for a tour to the south. At Alatri, he and his entourage were joined by the count of Ceccano and a force of fifty splendidly attired knights—part escort, part parade. As they approached the fortified town of Giuliano, near Ceccano, they were greeted by the bishop of Ferentino and a great gathering of clergy in full liturgical garb, chanting a hymn beginning "Yours is the power." After papal benediction, they all retired for a rest before returning to the field outside the city for a great feast, with an abundance of bread, wine, pork, mutton, chicken, goose—served with the best of condiments: pepper, cinnamon, saffron, plus barley and herbs. For the remainder of the week, the procession proceeded leisurely through the newly liberated area. While they were at the abbey of Fossanova, an official sent by King Frederick bestowed upon the pope's brother Richard the title of count of Sora. The curia then made its way to Cassino (then called San Germano), lying at the foot of Monte Cassino.[55] The German threat had never before permitted Innocent to go that far into the Regno.

The pope remained there through most of July, and while there, he presided over another great gathering of Italian princes similar to the one held in Viterbo the year before. At Viterbo, he had acted as the supreme secular ruler of his own Papal State; now he acted as overlord of the kingdom of Sicily. King Frederick continued to face German opponents in Sicily as well as a rebellion of Sicilian Muslims. Innocent required the gathered nobles to swear that they would support the king and look to the peace and security of the kingdom. And as he did in Viterbo, he required that they not take up arms to settle private quarrels, but rather look to legitimate authorities for peaceful adjudication. Then a substantial force was dispatched to help the king.[56] These were days of great success, or at

[54] Maleczek, *Papst und Kardinalskolleg*, p. 142.

[55] *Annales Ceccanensis*, MGH SS 19:297–8.

[56] *Gesta*, PL 214:lxxiv–lxxx = Gress-Wright, pp. 58–59; Reg. 8:130–133 = PL 215:706–714.

least apparent success, even rivaling the first months of Innocent's papacy, when he had toured the Papal State in the wake of the German collapse that followed the death of Henry VI. Only the heat of the summer kept him from touring Apulia.[57]

Late the same summer, the Flemish monk William of Andres made his second trip to the curia to pursue his case against his mother abbey. He was delayed in Rome in September when one of his young companions overindulged in the autumn crop of fruit and died of dysentery, but William caught up with the curia in Ferentino. Innocent greeted him warmly, but October was a very busy month for the curia in Ferentino, and William cooled his heels for five weeks while the curia dealt with more important matters: local political matters, the crusade in southern France, and problems brought to Ferentino from Greece, Poland, Germany, France, and northern Italy.[58] The pope was invited back to Rome by the Roman nobility, and William accompanied him back to the city, where the monk was greatly impressed to see the greeting provided by the nobles and their horses in all their finery and by the people of Rome, Christian and Jew, in grand procession. After more delays, William was able to present his case in the morning consistory after mass. Things did not go well (his election as prior was quashed), but he left Rome with kind words from Innocent and with the hope that judges delegate appointed by the pope might reinstate him. Preoccupied with the great issues of all of Christendom, Innocent still found time to work in "the petitions of pitiful persons" like William.[59]

Around this time, 1207 and 1208, when Innocent was issuing legislation to establish the reign of law in his Patrimony and in the Regno, he also took steps to do the same for all of Christendom. On a small scale, he limited the number of masters of theology at the university of Paris to eight, lest, because of an excess of masters, "their office be cheapened or fulfilled less thoroughly." He did allow, however, for exceptions, should "necessity or usefulness" demand it.[60] On a much larger scale, he took a significant step to regularize the law of the universal church. Up to this point, there had been

[57] Reg. 8:131 = PL 215:706–710.

[58] See Pott. 3505–3528.

[59] *Willelmi Chronica Andrensis*, MGH SS 24:743–745.

[60] Reg. 10:151 = PL 215:1248 (14 November 1207). English translation in Thorndike, *University Records*, pp. 25–26.

no official law code governing the church. Since shortly after its composition ca. 1140, the *Decretum* of Gratian had enjoyed a quasi-official status as a compendium of canon law. After that, a number of legal scholars had made unofficial collections of papal decretals that were widely circulated and used. But now, for the first time, a pope commissioned an official collection of his decretals. The task was assigned to Peter Beneventano, a member of the curia who was later to become a cardinal. The completed work, now known as the *Compilatio Tertia*, was officially presented to the University of Bologna in 1209.[61] Innocent was formally embracing his role as legislator for all of Christendom.

In these years, Innocent was even hopeful that help for the Holy Land might soon be forthcoming. In 1208, he wrote the patriarch of Jerusalem and the masters of the Templars and Hospitallers that the plight of the Christians in the Holy Land was constantly on his mind. He told them that a new crusading army was taking shape in France and Germany, among whose leaders were the count of Eu and the duke of Austria. At the same time, substantial amounts of money were being placed at the disposal of the patriarch and masters, raised from collections in France and from the pope himself, all to be used for the defense of the Holy Land. Innocent assured them of his ceaseless efforts to establish peace in the west so that greater help could be sent to the Holy Land.[62]

The promise of these days was further enhanced when, in late July 1208, either at San Germano or at Sora, Innocent received stunning news. Once again, an assassin had struck, this time transforming the political landscape of Europe far more than the assassination of Cardinal Peter of Castelnau the previous January. Philip of Swabia, on the verge of being accepted by all parties as the Roman emperor, had been murdered, apparently by a man with a private grievance. Suddenly the forlorn Otto became the leading candidate for the German and imperial crowns, and most German princes accepted him as the only alternative to continuing civil war.

Since Innocent had been on the verge of a settlement with Philip,

---

[61] Kenneth Pennington, "The Making of a Decretal Collection. The Genesis of 'Compilatio tertia,'" in *Proceedings of the Fifth International Congress of Medieval Canon Law* (Vatican City, 1980), pp. 68–92. For the general history of the development of canon law, see James Brundage, *Medieval Canon Law* (London, 1995).

[62] Reg. 11:109 = PL 215:1427–1428.

the news required a rapid reassessment of everything, but the reassessment meant that now Innocent's most desired scenario could become a reality. The imperial title would not go to a Hohenstaufen, who might try to unite Sicily and the empire. Otto had been his favored candidate before and he became that again. A barrage of letters immediately left the curia urging all German authorities and King John to rally around Otto.[63] Within months, Otto had been elected and crowned king of the Romans. Once again, Innocent could conclude, as he did after the capture of Constantinople, that the judgment of God had intervened, presenting the pope with entirely unexpected opportunities.[64] His judgment was so swayed by signs of divine favor that back at the Lateran in December, he made a major effort to mobilize northern Italy for a crusade to the Holy Land,[65] even as he mobilized French crusaders against heresy in southern France. Nothing came of it. Even a serious illness gave way before the good news from Germany. He wrote Otto in early January, 1209, "The delightful arrival of your messengers has so consoled us while we were held in the grip of illness that, like a kind of medicinal property, the welcome reports they bring of your successes have made us revive from painful weakness to the joy of health."[66] He did not condone the murder of Philip, but he considered the sudden change in Otto's fortunes to be miraculous, and in an almost ecstatic letter he told Otto—whom he addressed as emperor-elect— that cooperation between pope and emperor now gave hope for benefits beyond imagining.[67]

In March, Otto encouraged these high hopes by taking a solemn oath at Speyer, conceding everything that Innocent demanded. The election of bishops would be free, without imperial involvement; appeals to the pope would not be impeded; the income from vacant churches would not be appropriated as it had been in the past; all the territory claimed by Innocent for the Papal State would be recognized as such; and Otto would help to see that it was placed under papal authority. In effect, Otto promised to place his imperial

---

[63] RNI, nos. 153–159.
[64] RNI, no. 155: "quem diuino judicio credimus approbatum."
[65] Reg. 11:185, 186 = PL 215:1500–1503.
[66] RNI, no. 177.
[67] RNI, no. 179. English translation in Pullan, *Sources*, pp. 205–206.

power at the service of the papacy.[68] This happy string of events, including the successes of the Albigensian crusaders, culminated in October 1209, when the triumphant Otto proceeded to Rome where Innocent crowned him emperor of the Roman people.

* * *

As the conquest of Constantinople turned sour as time passed, however, so did the election of Otto. The Emperor Otto behaved quite differently from the candidate Otto. He was surrounded by imperial officials who had not abandoned the Hohenstaufen dream of a united empire including Germany and Italy, and Otto soon embraced the old Hohenstaufen program.[69] Despite his promise to honor papal claims to the Papal State and to the Kingdom of Sicily, Otto soon appointed Dipold of Acerra as "grand captain" of Apulia and the Terra di Lavoro and named him duke of Spoleto. He began to assert his authority throughout the territories claimed by the pope, and he gave the city of Pisa commercial privileges throughout the Regno in return for the Pisans' support for a planned invasion of Sicily.[70]

Philip Augustus had long opposed the candidacy of Otto, tied as it was to Philip's enemy and Otto's uncle King John. In the heady days of 1208, when Otto was promising Innocent everything Innocent wanted to hear, the pope wrote Philip Augustus assuring him that he had no reason to fear Otto's election. With what Van Cleve calls "astonishing *naïveté*,"[71] Innocent wrote Philip, "Moved by the affection that we have for you, we have taken care to provide for your protection and that of your kingdom in this matter. We have received a certain promise from Otto himself, in writing, sealed with a golden bull and confirmed by an oath, that regarding peace and concord to be made and observed with you, he will submit to our will and command in all things . . ."[72] But by early 1210, Innocent's wishful thinking was over, and it was time for him to admit his mistake. He wrote the French king, "If only, dearest son, I had known the character of Otto who now calls himself Emperor, as well as you

---

[68] RNI, no. 189; Van Cleve, *Emperor Frederick*, p. 70.

[69] The following account is based mainly on Van Cleve, *Emperor Frederick*, pp. 72–88 and Tillmann, *Pope Innocent III*, pp. 137–149.

[70] Reg. 14:101 = PL 216:465.

[71] *Emperor Frederick*, p. 69.

[72] RNI, no. 165.

knew it! . . . It is with shame that I write this to you who so well prophesied what has come to pass."[73]

A Parisian cleric could now in song openly offer sympathy to the pope without fear of antagonizing the king:

> Otto, how does this concern you?
> What presumption had seized you?
> Stop, for your fall is imminent. . . .

The poet has Innocent exclaim, "I am wounded by the staff I made. . . ."[74]

It was awkward for Innocent to repudiate Otto after the Herculean efforts he had made to promote him, but in November 1210, after Otto actually invaded the Regno, Innocent excommunicated him. Around the end of March of 1211, the pope informed the princes of Germany that because of Otto's violation of his promises and because of the wrongs he had committed against the young king of Sicily and the Roman church, Innocent was releasing everyone from fealty owed to Otto. "We grieve for the church," he wrote, "we grieve for the empire, and we grieve for the whole Christian people." He warned them to prepare themselves to resist while there was still time.[75]

In the midst of all this, William of Andres arrived for the third time at the papal court. Finally Innocent called him aside and told him that he knew all the trouble he had taken to come to Rome, and that he wanted to save William and his monastery so much trouble and expense. He asked William if he would settle for a compromise settlement instead of a formal judgment. William said that he would, since he was a man of peace, and when he heard the terms of the settlement, he left the room and laughed and joked with his companions. After the opposition had their private conversation with the pope and came back out to the general tribunal, their long faces made clear to everyone whom Innocent had favored in the settlement. William's monastery would remain subject to the mother house but it would be free to elect its own prior.[76]

---

[73] Van Cleve, *Emperor Frederick*, p. 73. I was unable to locate Van Cleve's source for this quotation.

[74] Philippe the Chancellor, quoted and trans. by John W. Baldwin, "The Image of the Jongleur in Northern France around 1200," *Speculum* 72 (1997): 658–59.

[75] Pott. 4213.

[76] *Willelmi Chronica Andrensis*, MGH SS 24, 751–2.

But what to do about the imperial office? Philip of Swabia was dead; Otto showed no sign of repenting and adhering to the promises he had made. That left the young Hohenstaufen Frederick, king of Sicily. Innocent had made every effort to separate the imperial crown from the Sicilian crown and to avoid having a Hohenstaufen emperor in the style of Frederick Barbarossa and Henry VI, but now there seemed nowhere else to turn. In this new situation, an alliance began to form, combining the pope, King Philip Augustus of France, and a number of German princes who had been alienated by Otto, all working to advance the candidacy of Frederick and to reject Otto. The alliance was sufficiently threatening that Otto abandoned his plans to invade Sicily and led his armies back to Germany, arriving in Frankfurt in March of 1212.[77]

Prudence might have led young Frederick to reject the invitation sent to him by the rebellious German princes.[78] He was only seventeen years old, he could hardly control the kingdom of Sicily, and he had virtually nothing by way of resources to help him overcome Otto for the German crown. But apparently the lure of emulating his father and grandfather was irresistible. Despite the advice of his wife and his Sicilian advisers, he accepted the invitation. Having offered to the pope the same guarantees that Otto had offered in order to win papal support, Frederick arrived in Rome to a warm reception in April of 1212.

The difficulty of the task ahead and the importance of papal support were clear from the very beginning. It was dangerous even to leave Sicily. Dipold and his German allies were still in the south; the ships of Pisa threatened him when he took to sea; and Milan and its allies stood between him and Germany. The pope offered money and encouragement; Genoa offered protection at sea, and Milan's enemies in the north offered overland escorts. But Frederick's trip to Germany was still full of hazards and delays, and Innocent had ample reason to be concerned about its success.

* * *

[77] This alliance and its rival is examined in detail in Holzapfel, *Papst Innozenz III., Philipp II. August, König von Frankreich und die englisch-welfische Verbindung 1198–1216* (Franfurt-am-Main, 1991).

[78] The following account is based mainly on Van Cleve, *Emperor Frederick*, pp. 76–84, and Tillmann, *Pope Innocent*, pp. 147–148.

In August of 1207, in Viterbo, Innocent directed several bishops in England to lay an interdict on the entire kingdom if the king failed to accept fully the new archbishop.[79] In March 1208, a few days after Innocent sent out the letters that were to set the Albigensian crusade in motion, the bishops of London, Ely, and Worcester carried out the orders from the pope. Having failed to persuade King John to accept Stephen Langton as archbishop of Canterbury, they declared a general interdict on all England, to take effect 24 March 1208. In a sense, Innocent was now at war on two major fronts.

When Innocent consecrated Stephen Langton archbishop of Canterbury, it no doubt seemed an ideal solution to a complicated situation.[80] Hubert Walter, the former archbishop (and Gerald of Wales' nemesis), died in July of 1205, and the monks of Christ Church claimed their traditional responsibility for electing his successor. The suffragans (the bishops of the province), however, and certainly the king also expected to play a role. King John ordered a postponement of the election; the suffragans sent representatives to Rome to defend their right to participate, and the monks themselves secretly and conditionally elected their subprior, Reginald. They sent him and a delegation of monks to Rome to defend their rights. While those two parties were in Rome, King John summoned the suffragans and the remaining monks to his presence and saw to it that his choice John de Gray, bishop of Norwich, was elected archbishop. In December of 1205, John notified Innocent of these proceedings and sought his approval.

In order to straighten out this juridical mess, Innocent summoned to his court a delegation of monks authorized to hold another election, since he considered the elections up to that point to be suspect or void. In the fall of 1206, after all parties had made their cases, Innocent ruled that the suffragans had no customary right to participate in the election, that the right to elect lay solely with the chapter of monks. Innocent charged the monks then in Rome to hold a new election, but they were divided between two candidates. They then settled on a compromise candidate, Stephen Langton, Englishman, cardinal priest of S. Crisgono, and former master at Paris.

---

[79] Reg. 10:113 = PL 215:1208–10 = Cheney and Semple, pp. 91–95, no. 30.
[80] The following account is based mainly on Cheney, *Innocent III and England*, pp. 147–154, 294–325 and Ralph V. Turner, *King John* (London, 1994), pp. 147–174.

It surely came come as no surprise to Innocent that John would object. When Innocent ignored the objections and consecrated Stephen in Viterbo in June of 1207, he must have decided to have a show-down with John, once and for all, probably being unduly optimistic about John's acquiescence. Despite the fiasco with Thomas Becket, King Henry II and his sons Richard and John had continued to enjoy considerable success in controlling the election of bishops. Of the eight bishops elected under John before the interdict over Canterbury, five had been filled by royal officials and one by a member of an aristocratic family friendly to the king.[81] But the customary role these kings enjoyed in episcopal elections had not been accepted in Rome, and Innocent had earlier admonished John about his intervention in episcopal elections in various parts of his territories: Dublin, Lincoln, Séez, and Coutances.[82] From Innocent's point of view, the customary practice of the king to approve episcopal elections was at best a courtesy, certainly not a right, and the fact that John had declined to approve Stephen Langton in no way affected the validity of Stephen's election and consecration.

John was not looking for a quarrel with the pope. He seems to have had few religious scruples, but he observed the formalities of Christian ritual and charitable giving. His alliance with his nephew Otto also gave him a bond with Innocent that both he and the pope tried to maintain—more difficult for Innocent than for John, since Innocent also sought the good will of Philip Augustus, the enemy of John and Otto. But even as the case in Canterbury was coming to a climax, John was engaged in a conflict with the archbishop of York over the king's right to tax ecclesiastical property. By the end of 1207, John had confiscated the goods of the archbishop and Innocent was threatening interdict over both Canterbury and York. The interdict became a fact in March 1208. From John's point of view, the idea that an archbishop of Canterbury could be elected without the king's approval was an outrageous violation of the king's traditional rights. He forbad Stephen Langton to enter the kingdom; he exiled the monk-electors; he occupied the property (and income) of the archbishop and the monks. He wrote the pope, "All my pre-

---

[81] Turner, *King John*, p. 151.
[82] Reg. 5:160 = Cheney and Semple, pp. 50–51, no. 17 (20 February 1203).

decessors conferred archbishoprics, bishoprics and abbeys in their chamber."[83]

The interdict shut down almost all formal religious services in England, although the vagueness of the pope's orders made for considerable confusion among the English clergy. The king's anger was felt in many quarters. Roman citizens in England on business were expelled and their property confiscated. John appears to have tolerated for a while various acts of violence against individual clergymen. But most important, he confiscated the property and incomes of those clerics who were not, so to speak, earning those incomes by providing religious services, although he did permit many to redeem their confiscated property by paying substantial fines. John also adopted a clever device that had been used by some of his predecessors. To harass further the clergy who were observing the interdict, he arrested their mistresses. He was, after all, merely enforcing the church's own requirement of celibacy for priests. Having had his little joke, however, he followed his customary tendency to turn everything into money income by permitting the arrested women to go free after their men paid appropriate fines. What with the income from clerical lands and the various fines he imposed on the clergy, John found the interdict to be highly profitable.[84]

There were extensive negotiations for months thereafter, with Innocent using all his rhetorical powers of persuasion but also threatening to add excommunication to interdict if John did not accept Stephen. In a letter of 23 January 1209, the pope used medical images, as he often did, warning John against "crafty men, who do not wish to point out to you your own wound and who have skill only to smear on the oil of flattery, not to pour in the wine of rebuke . . ." He continued,

> We . . . blend threats with blandishments and blandishments with threats, like a skilled doctor varying the resources of his medical art, applying the knife when poultices are of no use and with a draught of warm water curing ailments which have not responded to drastic medical treatment . . . We should prefer, while there remains hope of such a cure, to cure you by gentle and pleasant means rather than by hard

---

[83] Quoted by Turner, *King John*, p. 155.

[84] Roger de Wendover, *The Flowers of History*, Rolls Series, 84/1–3 (London, 1886–1889) 2:47–8; trans. J. A. Giles (New York, 1968 reprt. of 1949), 2 vols., 2:246–247; Cheney, *Innocent III and England*, pp. 303–312.

and painful means: for the former leave no infection, but the latter usually leaves an ugly scar. And so lest you bring us and yourself into a worse strait—look! as a friend we request you, pleasantly we urge you, like a father we counsel you, with kindness we beg you, and in the light of divine judgment we charge you as you hope for remission of sin, without further delay to give prompt satisfaction to us and the church, or rather to God, in the matter of the church of Canterbury . . .[85]

The threat of excommunication was probably more troublesome to John's clerical advisers than to John, since they would then have to risk princely anger by refusing to associate with him or risk papal anger by continuing to do so. Princely anger was a dangerous thing, and no English bishop could forget—nor could Innocent himself— the fate of Thomas Becket forty years earlier. Innocent had also received a fresh reminder of the danger of princely anger in the previous year, when, at the other end of Christendom, Bohemond, the prince of Antioch, had imprisoned the patriarch of Antioch. The patriarch was driven by thirst to drink his lamp oil and died. But princely anger was no excuse to back away. Innocent sent as the new patriarch one of his most reliable prelates Peter of Lucedio, bishop of Ivrea in northern Italy, just as he had managed to place as patriarch of Jerusalem another reliable prelate of northern Italy, Bishop Albert of Vercelli, later a canonized saint.[86] Innocent did not hesitate to ask his prelates to place their lives in jeopardy. He told several English bishops that he himself was prepared to lay down his life for his sheep if necessary.[87]

The sentence of excommunication was published in November 1209, by which time the pope had returned to Rome from another summer stay in Viterbo and had crowned Otto Roman emperor. The battle between king and pope had already produced a steady exodus of prelates from England, and soon there were few bishops left there. Most took refuge in the lands of John's enemy Philip Augustus, further annoying the king. For several years, the stalemate persisted: the king enjoyed the incomes of the English churches and, apparently, the loyalty and obedience of the vast majority of his subjects; the archbishop of Canterbury and many of his fellow bishops

---

[85] Reg. 11:221 = PL 215:1535–37. This translation is a modified version of that of Cheney and Semple, pp. 117–120, no. 39.

[86] Moore, "Peter of Lucedio," pp. 228, 233–38.

[87] Reg. 11:141 = PL 215:1455–57.

waited in exile in France; desultory communication between king and pope continued. In the spring and summer of 1211, Innocent undertook another initiative by sending a delegation to John under the leadership of the papal subdeacon Pandulf and the Templar Durand. The message they presented to the king in August called for the complete capitulation of John in the matter of Canterbury.[88] Innocent warned John, "we purpose to make heavy our hands against you, so that one who is unmoved by kindness may at least by changed by tribulation—though you might well fear that penitence will be too late after your downfall."[89] John's throne was being threatened, but John remained unmoved. Innocent had probably expected an early solution when he consecrated Stephen archbishop in 1207, but now years had passed without progress.

It should be noted that Otto and John were not the only threatening princes during these years, and in 1210, 1211, and 1212, the behavior of princes weighed heavily on Innocent. In the spring of 1210, messengers came to Rome from the clergy of the new Latin Empire in Constantinople. The aristocrats who had so miraculously come into possession of the Byzantine empire were now, according to the clergy of the area, seizing the possessions and incomes of the clergy, Greek and Latin alike. Furthermore, they were apparently making inroads into future as well as present clerical revenues by forbidding anyone to bequeath property to the clergy. Innocent issued letters to Emperor Henry and to the prelates of the area, trying to set things right,[90] though these problems in the East were still requiring his attention in 1212.[91] Even Philip Augustus, whom Innocent claimed to hold up to other princes as a model for the proper treatment of churches, was chastised by the pope in 1210 for occupying the property of the bishops of Auxerre and Orléans.[92]

Also in the spring of 1210, the bishop of Oporto arrived in Rome. He had been so despoiled by the king of Portugal that he had been forced to flee in the dead of night. He had arrived in Rome, the pope said, "almost naked."[93] Rather than repent, King Sancho soon

---

[88] Reg. 15:234 = PL 216:776 = Cheney and Semple, pp. 125–127, no. 43.
[89] Cheney and Semple, no. 44, pp. 128–129 (14 April 1211).
[90] Reg. 13:98–117 = PL 216:296–304.
[91] See Innocent's register for May, 1212.
[92] Reg. 13:190; 14:52 = PL 216:357–359, 417–421.
[93] Reg. 13:75, 76 = PL 216:270–273.

made things even worse. According to reports that reached Innocent in early 1211, the king was despoiling churches, oppressing the clergy, and generally depriving others of their rights. When the bishop of Coimbra upbraided the king for consorting daily with a sorceress, the king destroyed the house of the bishop and canons. The bishop laid an interdict on the king's territories, but when the king threatened to rip out the eyes of clergy who observed the interdict, the bishop, to save the clergy, relented. He planned to take his complaints to Rome, but the king threw him in prison. Innocent wrote the king that he would have found all this difficult to believe had not the king sent the pope letters "full of indiscretion and presumption, accusing the pope of, among other things, paying people to say bad things about the king." "Clearly," said Innocent, "no prince, however great (unless perchance a heretic or tyrant), has tried to write so irreverently and arrogantly to us or to our predecessors." Even so, Innocent was remarkable mild in his early warnings to Sancho, merely calling on him to repent and make amends and warning him that the pope would not abandon the wronged bishop.[94] Whatever the effect of Innocent's letters, sickness and the danger of death led Sancho shortly thereafter to make peace with the pope.[95]

At other edges of Christendom, there was more of the same. In the spring of 1211, Innocent tried to restrain Duke Wladyslaw of Poland, who reportedly had occupied the treasury of the archbishopric of Gnesen, burned some of the church's villages, and caused injuries to the canons and laymen of the church.[96] About the same time, Innocent heard the latest about the on-going dispute between the king of Armenia and the Templars. Now the king had confiscated lands and houses of the Templars, and in skirmishes between the two enemies, some Templars were wounded and one killed. Patriarch Albert of Jerusalem, acting as papal legate, had excommunicated the king, and now the pope sent off a batch of letters to see that the excommunication was observed, and to see especially that neither local people nor pilgrims passing through would have anything to do with the king. The patriarch reported that the king had refused to have his disputes with the Templars adjudicated. Innocent was

---

[94] Reg. 14:8 = PL 216:383–385.
[95] Reg. 14:58–60 (May 1211) = PL 216:423–425.
[96] Reg. 14:44 = PL 216:413. See also Reg. 14:89 = PL 216:451–454.

notably concerned because the Templars' property now held by the king was "especially intended for the defense of the Holy Land."[97]

* * *

Innocent's troubles with Christian princes were discouraging enough on their own, but they seemed all the more dangerous when a new Saracen threat to Christendom appeared. In January of 1212, the bishop-elect of Segovia was in Rome seeking help for a desperate King Alfonso VIII of Castile. The previous May, a new invading force of Almohads had crossed the straits of Gibraltar under the Caliph an-Nasir (Miramamolin to the Christians) and had begun to move north toward Toledo. Only their decision to beseige the fortress of Salvatierra along the way delayed their progress. The knights of Calatrava, who staffed the fortress, were able to hold out until September before surrendering, and then Miramamolin decided to postpone his advance until the following spring. But now the spring was approaching.[98]

The message the bishop-elect brought from Alfonso in January was, Innocent said, "full of sorrow and fear."[99] The pope immediately wrote to the prelates of France, ordering them to urge the people of their areas to come to the defense of Christian Spain against the coming Muslim campaign. He wrote Alfonso, offering him encouragement and telling him of his efforts to recruit reinforcements for Spain, but the tone of his letter was not optimistic. He wrote, "But since right now almost the whole world is thrown into disorder and stuck in wickedness, we advise and warn you that if you can make an appropriate truce, do so, until a more opportune time comes for you to overcome more securely."[100] He also told the archbishops of Toledo and Compostella to use excommunication and interdict against any Spanish king who broke ranks and made alliance with Muslims against Christians.[101] Meanwhile, Alfonso sent Archbishop Jiménez de Rada of Toledo throughout Europe to convey the message that help was desperately needed.[102]

---

[97] Reg. 14:64 as well as 65–66 = PL 216:430–432.
[98] O'Callaghan, "Innocent III and the Kingdoms of Castile and Leon," pp. 328–9.
[99] Reg. 14:155 = PL 216:514.
[100] Reg. 14:154 = PL 216:513–514.
[101] Reg. 15:15 = PL 216:553.
[102] Gary Dickson, "La Genèse de la croisade des enfants (1212)," *Bibliothèque de l'École des chartes* 153 (1995): 77–78.

It may have been his own sense of desperation that led Innocent to try to mobilize the spiritual as well as the material resources of Christendom. In May of 1212, he organized the people of Rome in an extraordinary day of prayer for the crusaders who were about to meet the great force of Almohad invaders in Spain. On 16 May, the population of the city gathered at three churches: the women at Santa Maria Maggiore, the men at Santa Anastasia, and the clergy at Santi Apostoli. With church bells tolling, the three groups processed bare-foot to the square of the Lateran, where they were met by the pope and the papal court, and where Innocent preached a sermon. The men and women then divided for mass, the latter going to the church of Santa Croce and the men entering the Lateran basilica. Throughout the day, all Romans were to fast on bread and water and to give alms.[103]

There may also be a note of desperation in Innocent's letter to Philip Augustus, sent from Rome in early June 1212. Envoys from Philip had come to Rome, again seeking a dissolution of Philip's marriage to Ingeborg. Philip claimed that the marriage had not been consummated, but Ingeborg had told one of the same envoys that it had. What's more, her testimony had also been heard by the stern moralist Robert Courson, formerly a master at Paris and now a cardinal. Innocent assured the king that he had listened most carefully to the envoys and had discussed the matter thoroughly with the curia, but they could find no way to grant legitimately his request. The pope said he did not dare, on his own, to go against what Christ said, "What God has joined together, let no man put asunder" (Matt. 19:6). On the last day, he said, he would have to answer before God for Philip's soul, and if God found Philip guilty of false testimony, the souls of both the king and the pope could be lost.

> Wherefore, most prudent king, we beseech you to let this matter rest. It places your soul in perpetual danger, for the Lord, the just judge, may punish you for this, that you have sinned against him and against the queen whom you willingly accepted before God and man . . . and who has long suffered a martyrdom for observing the law of marriage. And may you not trouble us more severely over this matter, lest you appear to be trying to extort it from us by using the persecution we

---

[103] PL 216:698–99; Christoph T. Maier, "Mass, the Eucharist and the Cross: Innocent III and the Relocation of the Crusade," in *Pope Innocent III and his World*, pp. 351–360.

are presently suffering. As we do not wish to deny you anything that can be rightly granted, so do we not wish to grant you anything which should rightly be denied, especially at this time, lest we appear to stray from the path of truth because of the pressure of persecution.[104]

Some fifty years earlier, Pope Eugenius III, faced with a recalcitrant prince who would not accept his wife, had moved the prince to tears and won him over with a desperate act: "And then, bursting into tears, he hastened down from his seat in the sight of all, great as he was, and prostrated himself before the count so utterly that his mitre, slipping from his head and rolling in the dust, was found after the bishops and cardinals had raised him from under the feet of the dumb-founded count."[105] In this letter, Innocent came close to the humble posture of Eugenius.

At the same time, Innocent urged Philip to restore the possessions of the bishops of Auxerre and Orléans, for the sake of the peace of the church, "which especially at this time is greatly disturbed in many other kingdoms."[106] His tone to Philip in these letters is almost pleading. Instead of threats of further ecclesiastical penalties, Innocent merely concludes, "There is no man under heaven who does not die sometime."[107]

Philip Augustus's quarrel with the bishops of Auxerre and Orléans shows the frustrating complexity of trying to maintain an orderly Christendom. The king had confiscated the lands of the bishops, and in return, the bishops laid an interdict on the king's lands within their jurisdiction. The king then prevailed upon the archbishop of Sens to remove the interdict—to the great annoyance of Innocent. In his letter to the king, Innocent said with irony, "we are amazed at the archbishop's prudence" in lifting the interdict, and he soon wrote the bishop of Troyes to annul the archbishop's action. Still, in June of 1212, there are no grandiose statements of papal authority. Rigor had not been very productive with King John, and Innocent was not feeling very confident about his ability to compel compliance. On the contrary, he made the remarkable admission that he was exercising the office of mediator between the bishops and the

---

[104] Reg. 15:106 = PL 216:617–618.
[105] John of Salisbury, *Memoirs of the Papal Court*, pp. 81–82.
[106] Reg. 15:108 = PL 216:619–620.
[107] Ibid.

king, advising the bishops that "kings and princes are sometimes more easily conquered with gentleness than with rigor."[108] In any case, the pope could not in good conscience grant the king's request concerning Ingeborg and he could not abandon the bishops of Auxerre and Orléans. But feeling pressed on all sides, at odds with King John and Otto of Brunswick and worried about the Muslim threat, he desperately needed the good will of the king of France.

*　*　*

In late June of 1212, the papal court left Rome for a summer sojourn in Innocent's home town of Segni. Business would continue there as usual, but the mood of the curia could not have been the buoyant optimism of a few years earlier. During the heady days of 1207, 1208, and 1209, it seemed that the authority of the pope was shaping the world as God intended. It was a confident pope who gave orders to the count of Toulouse, to the king of England, and to the princes of Germany. Innocent had experienced the splendid papal parliament in Viterbo in the summer of 1207 and the triumphant tour to the south of the Papal State in the summer of 1208. He had dispatched letters and legates in the optimistic belief that he might soon send help to the Holy Land. He had received the promises first of a conciliatory Philip of Swabia and then of a submissive Otto. Even the two assassinations of 1208 had not diverted the thrust of papal policy. The murder of Peter of Castelnau had even strengthened the pope's resolve to rid the South of heresy and mercenaries and enabled him to move a crusading army into the area. The early stages of the Albigensian crusade seemed an unmitigated success.

But from mid-1210, things had once again turned sour. Otto's violation of his oaths and his invasion of Italy were bitter and humiliating blows, and the Albigensian crusade, after its initial victories, seemed to be degenerating into an ungovernable series of bloody battles having little to do with religious goals. The clergy were being abused by princes everywhere, even by Philip Augustus (not to mention his persistent refusal to accept Ingeborg). No help for the Holy Land had materialized and a new Muslim force threatened Spain, where the best help Innocent could offer the king of Castile was only advice: seek a truce. Innocent had finally been driven to back

---

[108] Reg. 15:108, 109, 123 = PL 216:619–620, 635–636.

the young Hohenstaufen Frederick as imperial candidate, but even with papal backing, Frederick had moved toward Germany more like a fugitive than a great prince. In August of 1212, five months after his departure from Sicily, he had not yet been able to reach Germany. Almost the whole world was thrown into disorder and stuck in wickedness, Innocent wrote in 1212, and he himself was suffering persecution. His inability to restrain the princes of Christendom was indicated by the fact in the summer of 1212, a low point in Innocent's pontificate, all these were excommunicate: John, Otto, Raymond VI of Toulouse, Alfonso II of Portugal, and Leo II of Armenia.[109] Even summering in Segni was not likely to lighten the mood. While at Segni, either in 1212 or 1213, Innocent charged his chaplain priests to prepare an ordinal of prayers, summarizing when certain feast days were to be observed and when certain psalms were to be said throughout the year. One of the chaplains wrote that they were given the assignment "in that arid Segni."[110] He may have been referring to the mood as well as to the climate in the summer of 1212.

The disorder and impotence among the powers of Christendom were placed in sad relief by the naive but abundant confidence in another quarter. As the papal court prepared to leave Rome for Segni in June of 1212, other processions of a very different sort were taking shape in Germany, France, and Spain. For many years, preachers had been promoting crusades—to save the Holy Land, to turn back the Muslims in Spain, to defeat the infidels along the Baltic, to drive the heretics from southern France—and equally important, to provide salvation for those who took up the cross. The same spirit that had moved common folk to follow Peter the Hermit in 1095 now led spontaneous uprisings of young people, mixed with clergy and adults, to congregate at various places in northern France and Germany, at least some of them determined to go to the Holy Land. Despite the disapproval of parents and ecclesiastical authorities, they wandered south, declaring that they were going "to God." Some made it to Italy, some apparently to Marseilles, but few of them made it to Muslim territory, with the possible exception of several

---

[109] Noted by Cheney, *Innocent III and England*, p. 327 and n. 7.
[110] S. J. P. Van Dijk, *The Ordinal of the Papal Court from Innocent III to Boniface VIII and Related Documents* (Spicilegium Friburgense, 22) (Fribourg, 1975), p. xxi.

boat-loads who were said to have been sold to Muslim slave-traders by unscrupulous merchants from Marseilles.[111] Whether any of these "crusaders" saw Innocent in Segni we do not know, but one chronicler quoted him as saying, "These children put us to shame. They rush to recover the Holy Land while we sleep."[112]

---

[111] Norman P. Zacour, "The Children's Crusade," *A History of the Crusades*, ed. Kenneth M. Setton, 2 (Madison, 1969): 325–342; Peter Raedts, "The Children's crusade of 1212," *Journal of Medieval History* 3 (1977): 279–323; Dickson, "La Genèse de la croisade des enfants (1212)."

[112] *Annales Stadensis auctore Alberto*, MGH SS 16:355, quoted by Zacour, p. 335.

CHAPTER EIGHT

RENEWAL (1212–1214)

In 1204, when Innocent's crusading force seemed completely out of control, Innocent had convinced himself that God had intervened so as to place Constantinople in Latin hands and return the Greek church to communion with Rome. It was not a disaster; it was a miracle. In the fall of 1212, another dark period was suddenly illuminated by another miraculous intervention, although this time Innocent and his familiars would find no reason to doubt that God's hand was at work. The previous year, Miramamolín had led his invading force of Almohad Muslims from Africa into Spain. The threat had led Innocent in the spring of 1212 to organize the entire city of Rome to solicit God's aid for the crusaders in Spain. In October, shortly after returning from Segni to the Lateran, he called the Roman people together once again, this time to hear a long and jubilant letter from King Alfonso of Castile.[1] Their prayers had been answered. The letter described in some detail a great Christian victory at Las Navas de Tolosa on 16 July 1212.[2] The Christian forces had united—a minor miracle in itself—and, led by Alfonso, King Pedro II of Aragon, and King Sancho VII of Navarre, they had ended the Almohad threat.[3] The Muslim forces had suffered horrendous casualties, the Christians hardly any. The pope could now present to the Roman people the trophies sent to him by Alfonso: the battle standard and tent of Miramamolín himself. As Innocent thanked God before the multitude in Rome and extolled the Christian prince who had been God's instrument, he probably experienced the grandest day of his life. It was not only a great victory; God had given him an unambiguous sign of his favor.

At the same time, the news from Germany was almost as good. Frederick had finally arrived at Constance in the late summer of 1212, almost six months after his departure from Sicily. There the

---

[1] Reg. 15:183 = PL 216:703–704.
[2] Reg. 15:182 = PL 216:698–703.
[3] O'Callaghan, *History of Medieval Spain*, pp. 245–249.

archbishop of Constance hesitated between his loyalties to Otto, who was advancing rapidly from the north, and his obedience to the pope. The papal legate accompanying Frederick's entourage warned the archbishop of the consequences of allying himself with an excommunicate against the express orders of the pope. The archbishop opened the city gates to Frederick and closed them to Otto, providing a rare instance in which papal orders seem to have had precisely the desired and decisive effect in determining the course of events. Otto retreated to the north, and German princes, especially bishops, rallied around the young King Frederick.[4]

It was a renewed and bolder Innocent who now addressed a long letter to the intransigent consuls and people of Milan, adopting a much more aggressive stance than he had taken the previous June.[5] They had continued in their support of Otto as emperor, they had broken a truce by capturing some men of Pavia who had been escorting Frederick of Sicily to the north, and they were sheltering heretics, including those driven from other areas. Faced with these infractions, Innocent adopted a tone more of sorrow than anger but nevertheless presented them with a formidable list of threats. The leaders of the city would be solemnly excommunicated. The king of France and the businessmen of France and Italy would be warned to have nothing to do with them. Mercantile goods belonging to Milanese would be impounded and debts owing to them would not be paid. He told them that they no longer deserved to enjoy the status of an episcopal city, much less a metropolitan city, and he planned to call a council of the bishops of France and northern Italy to consider the possibility of depriving them of their bishopric. And finally, he hinted at a crusade.

> You should consider that no multitude is able to resist the Lord of armies. We need not speak of the Old Testament. As in Provence over heretics, and as in Spain, where he has deigned both miraculously and mercifully to cast down countless Saracens before an army of the faithful, so is he able to reduce your city to nothing.[6]

It was a bolder Innocent who wrote the excommunicated King Leo II of Armenia in February of 1213. Leo's earlier depredations against

---

[4] Van Cleve, *Emperor Frederick*, pp. 85–88.
[5] Reg. 15:122 = PL 216:635.
[6] Reg. 15:189 = PL 216:710–714.

the Templars and the patriarch of Antioch had led the patriarch of Jerusalem to excommunicate him, and in 1211, Innocent had confirmed the excommunication and offered consolation to his old friend the patriarch of Antioch.[7] But now Innocent addressed the king directly, saying that he could no longer remain silent about all the things he had heard. He told Leo that he was writing the kings of Jerusalem and Cyprus and their barons, the Templars and Hospitalers, and all the crusaders in the area, telling them to offer him no support of any kind. And he closed: "You therefore should gather your senses like a provident man and be very careful that you do not lead yourself into that dire situation where you repent too late your failure to submit to apostolic warnings and mandates."[8] As it happened, Leo had offered to reform even before the letter left Rome,[9] but Innocent's warning would surely have called to Leo's mind the fate of Alexius III, of Philip of Swabia, and of Raymond VI of Toulouse.

Of course, less weighty matters continued to flow to Rome. In March of 1213, Innocent expressed to French prelates his dismay that it had become a general custom for men in France, either in anger or in levity, to swear not only by the hands and feet of Christ and the saints, but also by their private parts.[10] The following month he became the protector of the children of Queen Marie of Aragon, the wife of Pedro, the hero of Las Navas de Tolosa. She had arrived in Rome the previous fall, about the same time that Innocent received news of Pedro's great victory. Pedro had for some years been trying to rid himself of Marie, and like Ingeborg, she found in Innocent a reliable defender. She remained in Rome until her death in April 1213, and Innocent defended her marriage against Pedro[11] and her property against the people of Montpellier[12]—property which Pedro had mortgaged to pay for his trip to Rome in 1204. When she died, widely regarded as a saint, she placed her estate and her children under the protection of the pope.[13]

Another petitioner in Rome seeking papal protection during these

---

[7] Reg. 14:64–72 = PL 216:430–436. For the situation in Antioch, see Moore, "Peter of Lucedio," pp. 235–7.

[8] Reg. 16:2 = PL 216:784–786.

[9] Reg. 16:7 = PL 216:792–793.

[10] Reg. 16:3 = PL 216:786–787.

[11] Reg. 15:221 = PL 216:749–754.

[12] Reg. 16:23 = PL 216:811–812.

[13] Foreville, *Le Pape Innocent III*, pp. 289–292.

months was a priest from Langres, who had been accused of heresy and had failed to answer a summons from a commission appointed by the pope. He had come to Rome for direct judgment by the pope, he said, because anti-heretical feeling was running so high in Champagne that they were burning not only heretics but even people suspected of heresy. Innocent evidently did not believe the danger was as great as the priest claimed and ordered him to appear for a new hearing to be set up in France by the judges delegate. On the other hand, he did not punish the priest for his earlier failure to appear, since, he said, "We should not scatter those gathered together but rather gather together those who are scattered."[14]

* * *

During Queen Marie's sojourn in Rome, the renewed pope revived his long-delayed plan to call a general council. In 1199, he had announced plans for such a council, one at which the Greek emperor and patriarch of Constantinople would be represented and Latin and Greek Christianity would be reunited,[15] but first the Fourth Crusade and then a succession of other problems had kept the council in abeyance. Now, in April of 1213, the letters poured forth from the Lateran, going to the secular and religious leaders of all Christendom: to the prelates in Latin Christendom as well as to those in Bulgaria, Cyprus, Armenia, the Holy Land, and the empire of Constantinople (both Latin and Greek prelates); to the emperor of Constantinople and to the kings of France, Aragon, Navarre, Castile, Leon, Portugal, Cyprus, Norway, Sweden, Cork, Limerick, Connaught, and Meath—although not to the man who called himself "lord of Ireland," the excommunicated King John; to the Templars, Hospitalers, and Cistercians.[16] Not mentioned in the papal register but probably included were the kings of Bohemia, Hungary, Denmark, and Sicily.

Innocent reminded the addressees of the many kinds of "beasts" seeking to destroy the vineyard of the Lord and then continued:

> Therefore we invoke the testimony of him, who is a faithful witness in the heavens, that of all the desires of our heart we long chiefly for

---

[14] Reg. 16:17 = PL 216:801–803.

[15] Reg. 2:200, 202.

[16] Reg. 16:30 = PL 216:823–827. The text with extended commentary is also in Alberto Melloni, "*Vineam Domini*—10 April 1213: New Efforts and Traditional *Topoi*—Summoning Lateran IV," in *Pope Innocent III and His World*, pp. 63–73. Text with English translation is in Cheney and Semple, pp. 144–147, no. 51.

two things in this world, namely, that we may help bring about the recovery of the Holy Land and the reform of the universal church.

The prayer asked not just for those two goals, but that he would play a role in their attainment. He confessed that he had struggled over these two concerns and had begged God to enlighten him as to how to address them. Now, with the advice of his cardinals and other prudent men, he had made his decision:

> ... we have finally decided that, since these matters are related to the common condition of all the faithful, we should convoke a general council, following the ancient custom of the holy fathers, a council to be held at an opportune time and for the sole purpose of profiting souls.

The council would concern itself with

> rooting up vices and planting virtues, correcting excesses and reforming morals, eliminating heresies and strengthening faith, calming discord and establishing peace, restraining oppression and promoting liberty, with inducing the Christian princes and people, both clerical and lay, to offer aid and support to the Holy Land—and with other things too numerous to mention.

Those things approved by the council "for the praise and glory of the divine name, for the cure and salvation of our souls, and for the well-being and utility of the Christian people," should then be "inviolably observed."

The letter continued to lay out the preparations. Innocent announced that he was appointing prudent men in every province to see what needed to be addressed by the council and was sending out agents to make preparations for the crusade. If necessity required and the council approved, Innocent himself would direct the crusade. In the meantime, the recipients of the letter were to plan to be in Rome on 1 November 1215, leaving one or two bishops in each province to take care of local business. Those left behind were to send deputies. The prelates were warned against extravagance and were told to limit their entourages to the guidelines established at Lateran III (c. 4): forty to fifty horses for archbishops, twenty to thirty for bishops, five to seven for archdeacons. They were encouraged to settle for less, "since it is not worldly applause but spiritual progress that is to be sought in this matter." For this council, chapters of canons were also to send representatives .

In the meantime, the recipients were to examine their own regions and submit written reports to the council concerning those things in need of reform. They were to support the crusade-agents in their areas.

No excuses about the dangers of travel were to be offered—and here Innocent shared his new optimism—since the Lord was showing a sign of his favor and the disorders afflicting Christendom had begun to fade. (Innocent's motto was, "Lord, show me a sign of your favor.") Finally, he turned once again to the sea for his metaphor: "No one will ever take to the sea if he is always waiting for the turmoil of its waves to cease."

A few days after launching the call for the council and crusade, Innocent dispatched a remarkable letter to al-'Ādil, the sultan "of Damascus and Babylon [Cairo]":

> We learn from the prophet Daniel that it is God in heaven who reveals mysteries, changes times, and transfers kingdoms, so that all may recognize that the most high presides over the reign of men and that he will give it to whomever he wills. He clearly showed this when he permitted Jerusalem and its environs to fall into the hands of your brother [Saladin], not so much because of his strength as because of the sin of the Christian people, who provoked the anger of God himself. Now, however, having returned to this matter, we hope that he will have mercy on us, he who (according to the prophet), when he has been angered, does not forget to have mercy. And so we now wish to imitate him who said of himself in the gospel, "Learn from me, for I am meek and humble of heart"(Matt. 11:29). We humbly beseech your majesty that you follow a wiser course and restore these lands to us, so that your continued violent detention of them will lead to the shedding of no more blood than has already been shed. The detention of these lands may well bring you—apart from empty glory—more difficulty than utility. Once the lands are returned and the captives of both sides are freed, we may be at peace from each other's attacks. The circumstances of our people will not be worse before you, and those of your people will not be worse before us. We therefore ask that you kindly receive the bearers of this message and treat them well, and that you give them a useful and worthy response.[17]

The bearers of the message were not sent directly to the sultan, but to Innocent's trusted agent Albert patriarch of Jerusalem. Innocent explained to Albert that although Saracens were not usually responsive to the humble prayers of Christians, he and his advisers had

---

[17] Reg. 16:37 = PL 216:831–832.

taken to heart the biblical warning that God resists the proud but gives grace to the humble and had decided to write the sultan. Perhaps God would inspire the sultan with fear. Perhaps if asked kindly he will do freely what he would resist if faced with compulsion. At the same time, he urged the patriarch to try to contain the sinful dissension of quarreling Christians in his area, lest God once again be provoked to anger. Albert was to add to Innocent's delegation his own envoys to the sultan who could help support Innocent's request. And he added a personal note to Albert, who had long served him in Italy and the Holy Land and would one day be called St. Albert, "Finally, venerable brother in Christ, before the most just judge and most pious father, give me the support of your prayers, for which I am very much in need."[18]

Although the letter shows that Innocent was not irrevocably committed to war against the infidel, he was not counting on a favorable response from the sultan (although he apparently tried again sometime later).[19] At virtually the same time that these letters were leaving Rome, another batch left addressed to all Christians throughout Christendom, calling for them to take up the cross.[20] He reminded them that God was quite capable of recovering the Holy Land without them, "but since there has been a superabundance of iniquity and since the faith of many is growing cold, he has set forth this trial for his faithful so that he can awake them from the sleep of death to an eagerness for life and so that he can try their faith like gold in a furnace." God provides for them the means of salvation, so that

> those who faithfully struggle for him will be joyfully crowned by him. . . . . For if any temporal king should be ejected from his kingdom by his enemies and if his vassals failed to expend not only their goods but their persons for him, would he not, when he recovered his lost kingdom, condemn them as faithless and contrive unthinkable torments with which to destroy them? So also will the king of kings, the Lord Jesus Christ, who conferred upon you body, soul and other good things, condemn you for the vice of ingratitude and the crime of faithlessness, if you fail to give support to him who has, so to speak, been ejected from the kingdom that he bought with his own blood.

[18] Reg. 16:36 = PL 216:830–831.
[19] Pott. 5186–5187.
[20] Reg. 16:28 = PL 216:817–822.

Innocent also reminded them of their obligation to love their Christian neighbors, neighbors that were suffering under the oppression of the Saracens. He offered a brief history of the rise of Islam and predicted its approaching end:

> The Christian people possessed nearly all the provinces of the Saracens up until shortly after the time of blessed Gregory [d. 604]. Then a certain son of perdition, Machometus [Mohammed] the pseudoprophet, arose, and through worldly allurements and carnal delights, seduced many from the truth. His perfidy has persisted even up to the present time, but we have confidence in the Lord, who now has given us a sign of his favor, that the end of this beast approaches. Its number, according to the Apocalypse of John is inclosed within 666, of which now almost 600 years have been completed.

Innocent laid out the provisions for the crusade:

1. Those who took part in the crusade at their own expense and at the same time truly repented of their sins and confessed them orally would receive a full indulgence from the pope, who had received the power of binding and loosening.
2. The same benefit was to go both to those who did not go but financed others and to those who went at the expense of others.
3. To those who could only contribute financially to the effort, a similar indulgence was granted in proportion to "the amount of their contribution and the quality of their devotion."
4. The persons and possessions of every one who took the cross were to receive papal protection, enforced by all the prelates, until the crusader had returned or was known to be dead.
5. Prelates were to assure that any crusader bound by oath to pay interest on a debt had payments on both principal and interest suspended. Christian creditors who failed to observe this requirement were to be excommunicated, Jewish creditors who did so were to be denied all contact with Christians.
6. All clerical authorities and communities and all secular communities—towns, villages, and castles—were to provide a suitable number of soldiers together with financial support for three years. Groups not able to meet this requirement were to join together to provide the soldiers.
7. The same expectation applied to secular princes and authorities—and Innocent promised to do the same himself.
8. Clergy were given the unusual permission to mortgage their property for three years if this was necessary to raise their fair share.
9. Given the urgency of the situation, anyone who wanted to take the cross should be allowed to do so, without consideration of qualifications; if necessary, some vows could be commuted or otherwise dealt with later.

10. The same crusading privileges heretofore given to those going to Spain to fight Moors and those going to Provence to fight heretics were revoked, at least for the time being, since those threats seemed to have ceased. The residents of Spain, however, were still to enjoy those privileges.
11. Corsairs and pirates (who obstruct aid to the Holy Land) were to be excommunicated so that no Christian could have anything to do with them; cities were to do their best to restrain them.
12. As before, anyone supplying arms, iron, or ship-building timbers to the Saracens was to be excommunicated. Anyone sharing command of Saracen ships should suffer loss of goods and crew if captured. These regulations were to be announced publicly in all maritime cities on all Sundays and feast days.

These elaborate procedures were intended to provide the men and supplies necessary for a successful crusade. But Innocent had learned from the success of Las Navas de Tolosa that the mobilizing of spiritual resources was also essential. In the spring of 1212, he had apparently helped bring about the spectacular victory in Spain by organizing the people of Rome in prayers and processions. How much more powerful would be the prayers and processions of all Latin Christendom. Consequently, he ordered that there be processions held every month throughout Christendom to beg God to free the Holy Land and restore it to the Christian people. These petitions should be joined to prayer and fasting and special prayers were to be added to the mass.

The processions, however, were not exclusively spiritual exercises. Chests were to be placed in those churches where processions ended so that everyone could offer their donations for the crusade. Each chest was to be secured by three locks with one key given each to a priest, a layman, and a religious, a procedure that had first been set forth in 1199.[21]

For the supervision of all this, Innocent was commissioning a number of legates—prelates, Cistercian monks, academics, usually men who had served previously in papal commissions—to act in his name in their respective regions.[22]

Other letters that left the curia suggest that Innocent's preparation for crusade and council was very wide ranging. Although church

---

[21] Reg. 2:258 (270).
[22] Powell, *Anatomy of a Crusade, 1213–1221*, pp. 22–26. See this basic work for the general preparation for the crusade.

authorities had been denouncing tournaments for almost a century, Innocent could not forget that the Fourth Crusade had received its igniting spark at a tournament in Champagne. He now wrote Robert Courson, his legate in France, giving him permission (with the advice of prudent men) "to act regarding tournaments in a way that seems useful to the Holy Land, while adhering to God."[23] For the sake of the crusade, some moral flexibility seemed in order. The same impulse is seen in the permission given to his commissioners to recruit known incendiaries and men who had committed violence against the clergy, so long as they offered satisfaction for their sins. Only those guilty of the most horrendous crimes need be referred to Rome for consideration.[24]

The papal register for 1213 also suggests that Innocent's preparation for the council may have included purging the episcopate of unworthy men. During that year he took steps to remove the archbishop of Auch[25] and the bishops of Besançon,[26] Halberstadt,[27] Hildesheim,[28] Bologna,[29] Sorrento,[30] and Dax.[31]

* * *

While the confidence of Innocent was rallying in late 1212 and early 1213, the confidence of King John was flagging.[32] Whereas in late 1211, he had been bold enough to dismiss the pope's warnings, things looked very different by the spring of 1213. In the course of 1212, as John remained excommunicate and his kingdom under interdict, rumors had circulated that the pope had deposed him and released all subjects from their oaths of obedience. Although untrue, it was not an implausible rumor. The excommunication of John's nephew Otto of Brunswick had brought with it the release of his subjects from their oaths of allegiance, as was the case with John's brother-in-law Raymond VI of Toulouse. Raymond, in his desper-

---

[23] Reg. 16:32 = PL 216:827.
[24] Reg. 16:108 = PL 216:904–905.
[25] Reg. 16:5 = PL 216:789–790.
[26] Reg. 16:63, 158 = PL 216:866, 945–946.
[27] Reg. 16:71 = PL 216:872–873.
[28] Reg. 16:70 = PL 216:871–872.
[29] Reg. 16:184 (Appendix) = PL 216:966.
[30] Reg. 16:139 = PL 216:928–931.
[31] Reg. 16:140 = PL 216:932.
[32] For a survey of John's situation in 1212–1213, see Cheney, *Innocent III and England*, pp. 326–337.

ation, had personally gone to Rome to plead his case with Innocent.[33] Some of John's high-placed subjects had reason to act on those rumors, quite apart from the fact that the monarch was excommunicate. For many years, the power of the monarchy had been increasing at the expense of the great barons. No better symbol of that tendency can be found than this: in 1154, there had been five baronial castles for every royal castle in England, and by 1214, there were only two. This shift represented not only military strength, but the financial resources that made possible such a royal program of building new castles and confiscating others. Moreover, those barons who declined to spend much time in the royal court rightly saw that court as assuming governmental responsibilities that had once been the prerogative of local barons.[34]

In addition to the unraveling in England and Wales, John faced a new threat from the continent. He had lost Normandy to Philip Augustus in 1204, and in the spring of 1213, a naval and military force began to gather there for an invasion of England. Philip Augustus commissioned his son Louis to lead the invasion and to claim the English crown.

These dangers were concrete and readily identified. But John and his familiars may also have had in the backs of their minds the fates of various rulers who had been at odds with Pope Innocent. The schismatic rulers of Constantinople had been replaced entirely by a crusading force and their city had been sacked. Philip of Swabia had been assassinated (though he had by then returned to the pope's good graces). Raymond VI of Toulouse had seen his lands overrun and devastated. Otto of Brunswick was about to be displaced by King Frederick of Sicily. The modern historian can see that Innocent exercised only the loosest control over forces he set in motion, but contemporaries may have focused rather on the remarkable outcomes of the pope's initiatives. It seemed clear that it was better to be the pope's friend than his enemy.

In April 1212 Innocent had warned John that unless he made amends for his offenses against the church, Innocent would "make heavy our hands against you, so that one who is unmoved by kindness may at least be changed by tribulation—although you might

---

[33] Reg. 14:163 = PL 216:524–525.
[34] Turner, *King John*, 180.

well fear that penitence will be too late after your downfall."[35] It
was a strong warning, but the letter was brief, with a tone more of
sorrow than anger. But in the letter he sent in February, 1213, the
reinvigorated pope wrote in great detail exactly what conditions the
king must meet—the documents to be delivered and the compen-
satory payments to be made to English prelates—and set a deadline
of 1 June for the king to comply.

> Otherwise, by the example of him who with a strong hand freed his
> people from the bondage of the Pharaoh, we intend with a mighty
> arm to free the English church from your bondage: and we now truth-
> fully and firmly forewarn you that, if you will not accept peace when
> you may, you may not when you will, and repentance will be useless
> after your downfall—as you may learn from the instances of those who
> in your own time have acted with a similar presumption.[36]

Faced with this allusion to the fates of other princes, John accomplished a complete reversal of the entire situation with a bold and
astonishing act. At Dover on 13 May 1213, he agreed to all the
pope's terms for the settlement of the Canterbury affair. Two days
later, in the presence of the pope's legate Pandulf, he surrendered
the kingdoms of England and Ireland to the pope, to be held by
John as fiefs of the papacy.

> Inspired by the grace of the Holy Spirit, not led by force, nor forced
> by fear, but acting out of our own good and free will and with the
> common counsel of our barons, we offer and freely concede to God
> and his holy apostles Peter and Paul and to the holy Roman church
> our mother and to our lord Pope Innocent and his Catholic succes-
> sors the entire kingdom of England and the entire kingdom of Ireland,
> with all right and their appurtenances for the remission of our sins
> and those of all our family, both living and dead.[37]

The feudal obligation was to be discharged through annual payments
of seven hundred marks sterling for England, three hundred for
Ireland. In July, John's excommunication was removed. The interdict was to remain for another year, until John had proven his good

---

[35] Text and trans. in Cheney and Semple, pp. 128–9, no. 43. The letter is not
in the papal register.
[36] Reg. 15:234 = PL 216:772–773; text and trans. Cheney and Semple, pp.
130–136, no. 45.
[37] The two letters of John were entered in the papal registers in June: Reg.
16:76–77 = PL 216:876–880.

faith by beginning to make reparation payments to the despoiled clergy, but the crisis between pope and king was clearly over.

The wisdom of John's action has been much debated from that day to this. Many modern scholars have come to agree with a thirteenth-century chronicler who wrote:

> The king provided wisely for himself and his people by this deed, although to many it seemed ignominious and a monstrous yoke of servitude. For matters were in such extremity and so great was the fear on all hands that there was no shorter way—perhaps no other way—of evading the impending danger. For from the moment he put himself under apostolic protection and made his kingdoms part of St. Peter's Patrimony, there was no prince in the Roman world who would dare attack him or invade his lands to the damage of the Apostolic See, since everyone stood in greater awe of Pope Innocent than of his predecessors for many years past.[38]

The news reached Innocent at the Lateran in late June or early July 1213, and Innocent immediately dispatched Cardinal Nicholas de Romanis, bishop of Tusculum, to England with full power "to root up and pull down and build and plant." And that included the authority to punish those rebelling against the king, who was now a papal vassal.[39] His main task, though, was to negotiate the terms under which the interdict would be lifted, since John's exploitation of church lands during the interdict required that he pay reparations. Across the channel, however, the French force that was ready to take the crown from the excommunicate king of England was now faced with a vassal of the pope, and Innocent's agents immediately took up the defense of the new papal vassal against all his enemies, domestic and foreign.[40] As the English allies of Philip Augustus began to return their support to John, the plans for the invasion of England were perforce abandoned, at least for the time being.

* . * . *

The pope's support for his vassal, however, did not extend to the vassal's nephew in Germany. Otto was still excommunicate and his

---

[38] *Barnwell Chronicle of Coventry*, quoted and trans. by Cheney, *Innocent III and England*, p. 333.

[39] Reg. 16:79–83 = PL 216:881–885; text and translation of 79, 81–82, in Cheney and Semple, pp. 149–154, nos. 53–55.

[40] Cheney, *Innocent III and England*, pp. 237–8.

opponent Frederick Hohenstaufen was enjoying great success in recruiting supporters.[41] Unlike the sour and tight-fisted Otto, Frederick moved through Germany offering money and property—and promises of much more to come. Philip Augustus sent envoys to meet with Frederick, and they provided him with substantial funds to continue his largesse. The enthusiasm he generated can be gauged by this line from one grateful recipient, the poet Walther von der Vogelweide: "I have my fief! O all the world, I have my fief! . . . The noble King, the generous King, has cared for me. . . ."[42]

After Frederick's difficult passage through Italy and his close call at Constance in late summer 1212, his support in Germany increased rapidly. On 5 December 1212, an assembly of German princes at Frankfurt elected him king of the Romans and on 9 December, in Mainz, Siegfried (II) von Eppstein, the archbishop of Mainz (and also papal legate), crowned and anointed him. As he continued to move from city to city, his support grew. And in July of 1213, at Eger, he swore to honor all the rights claimed by the pope, basically using the same words that papal agents had dictated to Otto in 1209. He promised to respect the papal claims to the Papal State and to help recover any lands the pope claimed but had not yet recovered. He promised that ecclesiastical elections would be left to the clergy, without any secular interference. He would not interfere with appeals to Rome and he would not occupy the lands of any bishopric while the office was vacant. And he would support the war against heresy.[43] All these promises had proved worthless in the case of Otto, but they represented the only hope of Innocent for procuring a secure and independent Papal State.

In the year that followed, Europe-wide alliances developed that reflected both old political and new economic realities. Northern Germany, traditionally loyal to Welf interests, continued to support Otto, and German and Flemish cities—Cologne, Ghent, Bruges, Ypres—needed English markets too much to ally with anyone hostile to John. And because John and his German and Flemish allies were a threat to

---

[41] The following is based on Van Cleve, *Emperor Frederick*, pp. 84–86.

[42] Ibid., p. 84.

[43] MGH, *Constitutiones*, 2 (Hanover, 1896), ed. Ludewicus Weiland. pp. 57–63, nos. 46–51, especially 46/47; PL 217:301–303. For an English translation of the document, see Oliver J. Thatcher and Edgar Holmes McNeal, eds., *A Source Book for Mediaeval History*, (New York, 1905), p. 231.

Philip Augustus in almost every part of his kingdom, Philip would inevitably support their enemy, now Frederick Hohenstaufen.[44] In the south of France, John, as duke of Aquitaine, gave covert assistance to his vassal and former brother-in-law Count Raymond VI of Toulouse against the Albigensian crusade.[45] Allied with them was King Pedro of Aragon, who also had interests in the south that were threatened by the crusade. Meanwhile, Philip Augustus stood by to see whether the crusaders would bring the county of Toulouse under his own lordship. That result came a step closer when the crusaders defeated John's allies at the battle of Muret in September of 1213, even killing King Pedro of Aragon.

Meanwhile, the curia continued its usual routine of business. In the fall of 1213, while still in Segni, Innocent dispatched the Spanish Cardinal Pelagius to Constantinople, along with letters to the emperor and clergy telling them that they should treat the cardinal as they would the pope and that the cardinal was coming "to root up and destroy, to build and to plant."[46] Divisions among Christians in the east were abundant, including that between Latins and Greeks (some of whom had set up a rival imperial court in Nicaea), and Pelagius was not to enjoy much success.[47] Innocent also sent a batch of letters to another frontier of Christendom. Further north, the Livonian Brothers of the Sword (here called the Militia of Christ in Livonia) and the bishop of Riga were quarreling about authority over the recently conquered and converted Livonians. These letters were intended to settle the disputes, protect the knights of Livonia and their new converts, and to establish a new bishopric in Livonia.[48] At the same time, he warned the knights themselves about being too grasping. The kingdom of God, he said, lay not in possessions and manors but in peace and justice.[49] Innocent had to know, however, that the success in Livonia had been driven by more than religious zeal. German clergy, knights, and merchants had profited greatly from the enterprise.[50]

---

[44] Holzapfel, *Papst Innozenz III*, pp. 189–269.

[45] See Claire Taylor, "Innocent III, John of England and the Albigensians Crusade," in *Pope Innocent III and his World*, pp. 205–228.

[46] Reg. 15:104, 105 = PL 216:901–903.

[47] Maleczek, *Papst und kardinalskolleg*, p. 167.

[48] Reg. 16:119–124 = PL 216:916–920.

[49] Reg. 16:123 = PL 216:921–2. On the Livonian crusades, see Christiansen, *The Northern Crusades*, pp. 93–94, 122–124.

[50] The bishop of Riga and the Livonian Knights of the Sword were the secular

Innocent continued to urge John and Philip to make peace,[51] but both ignored him. John's submission to the pope had delivered him from the threat of a French invasion, and in 1214, he led his forces from England to Poitou. From there, he would move against Philip from the west while Otto and the count of Flanders came east to meet him. But Philip's son Prince Louis blunted John's thrust from the west and Philip himself led a force to meet Otto. The armies finally met in northeastern France, near Bouvines, on a hot Sunday afternoon, 27 July 1214. It was against the better judgments of many on both sides to fight a battle on the Lord's day, but the French could at least draw comfort from the fact that the battle was being forced upon them by the other side, many of whose leaders were excommunicate. A modern estimate puts the total number of horsemen involved in the battle at about four thousand, supported by about twelve thousand foot soldiers.[52] A chronicler gives the French view of the battle:

> In this place, on one side, Philip, the noble king of the Franks, had gathered a part of his kingdom. On the other side was Otto with the accomplices in his wickedness (having persisted in the obstinacy of his wickedness, Otto had been deprived of the imperial dignity through the decree of the Holy Church). With him, Ferrand count of Flanders, Renaud count of Boulogne, many other barons, and also those receiving a stipend from John the king of England, had assembled in order, to fight against the French, as the events were to show.... As soon as the order of the [French] royal power was heard in the army, the knights and the auxiliaries, armed and arranged into ordered echelons, prepared in all haste for the battle. The trappings of the horses were eagerly and vigorously secured by the auxiliaries. The armor shone in the splendor of the sun and it seemed that the light of day was doubled. The banners unfolded in the winds and offered themselves to the currents, presenting a delightful spectacle to the eyes. What then? The armies, thus ordered for battle on each side, entered into combat, full of ardor and desire to fight. But very quickly the dust rose toward the sky in such quantities that it became hard to see and to recognize one another. The first French echelon launched a

---

as well as the religious rulers of the area, and Christensen says, "... the Lübeck-Livonia run became a steady source of profit and absolution for skippers, knights, burghers and princes" (*Northern Crusades*, p. 94).

[51] Cheney and Semple, p. 184, no. 68 = PL 217:227.

[52] Georges Duby, *The Legend of Bouvines: War, Religion and Culture in the Middle Ages*, trans. Catherine Tihanyi (Berkeley, 1990), p. 19.

manly attack against the Flemings, breaking their echelons by nobly cutting across them, and penetrated their army with a strong attack and tenacious perseverance. The Flemings, seeing this and defeated in the space of an hour, turned their backs and quickly took to flight. At this perilous moment, dependants abandoned to distress their lords, their fathers, their sons, and their nephews. However, Ferrand count of Flanders and Renaud count of Boulogne remained in the battle and resisted the onslaught of the French with manly fighting. In the end, they were wounded and taken by the French, along with innumerable nobles whose names we will not give. They were imprisoned in a number of castles in Gaul. As for Otto (who, by the authority of the pope, we refrain from calling emperor), deprived of everyone's help, thrown three times to the ground from his horse, or rather his horses as some claim, almost alone except for a single count, he rushed to take flight. Thus, surreptitiously fleeing from the hand of the king of France, he escaped, vanquished in battle. In this manner, the providence of divine mercy ended this battle which had been fought, as we have said, near the bridge of Bouvines, for the praise and glory of his majesty, and for the honor of the holy church. May its honor, its virtue, and its power remain through the infinity of centuries to come.[53]

After Bouvines, Otto's chances of regaining the empire and John's chances of recovering Normandy were dead.

* * *

Among those agents commissioned in April 1213, to preach the crusade and prepare for the Lateran Council was Cardinal Robert Courson. Innocent was constantly complaining about ineffectual clergy, calling them "dogs who do not bark." In Robert, he had a dog who barked.

Robert Courson had superb credentials to serve the pope in France.[54] An Englishman, he had, like Innocent, studied at Paris (probably after Innocent had moved on) and, like Innocent, had been much influenced by the master there Peter the Chanter. He shared the pope's enthusiasm for the crusade and for preaching. In the late 1190s, he had traveled with the famous preacher Fulk of Neuilly, also a student of Peter the Chanter, and if he had not

---

[53] *Relatio Marchianensis*, MGH SS 26:390–391, translation adapted from that of Tihanyi in Duby, *Legend*, pp. 192–193.

[54] The following account of the career of Robert Courson is based on Marcel and Christiane Dickson, "Le Cardinal Robert de Courson: sa vie," *Archives d'histoire doctrinale et littéraire du moyen âge*, 9 (1934): 53–142, and Maleczek, *Papst und Kardinalskolleg*, pp. 175–9.

actually joined Fulk in the preaching, he had at least had the chance to see a master preacher at work. Shortly thereafter, Robert was teaching theology at Paris, drawing his income first from a canonry at Noyon and then later as a canon at Paris. As a master at Paris, he maintained the tradition of Peter the Chanter, showing a strong concern for the spiritual and pastoral aspects of learning, offering his erudition as an instrument of reform.

Although his stern moral outlook led him sometimes to disparage secular learning, he had over the years acquired a thorough grounding in the liberal arts as well as an expertise in both canon and civil law. During the first decade of the century, his academic experience was buttressed with experience in the world of practical affairs. He was frequently called upon by the pope to serve as papal judge delegate in France, serving with many other French prelates and becoming well known throughout the kingdom. He handled cases of major importance, including disputed episcopal elections in Rheims, Amiens, Troyes, and Thérouanne and the delicate matter of whether or not the marriage of the king to Ingeborg had in fact been consummated. By the time he was appointed cardinal in 1212, he was both an experienced papal agent and the author of a *summa*, a work that was at once a theological treatise and an inventory of abuses in the French church that needed reform. His reputation was such that in 1211, he was one of the nominees for the office of patriarch of Constantinople.

By June 1213, Robert was in Paris, where he summoned a council of prelates of the area. The program of the Paris reformers had been the basis of the legislation issued in Paris in 1208 by Cardinal Guala,[55] and it was now the basis of the council's legislation. The constitutions of the council condemned priests who had women in their homes and those who demanded pay for spiritual services. They set standards regulating the dress and behavior of clergy so as to eliminate scandalous example. Bishop William of Paris had added his own more stringent requirements. They called for both priests and laity to confess their sins, and parish priests were to keep the bishop informed about parishioners who were failing to confess, to attend mass, or to give alms.[56] Robert's council issued a lengthy set

---

[55] See Maleczek, *Papst und Kardinalskolleg*, p. 142.
[56] Joannes Dominicus Mansi, *Sacrorum Conciliorum nova et amplissima collectio*, 22 (Graz, 1961 repr. of 1767 ed.), cols. 763–766.

of regulations organized into five parts: secular clergy, monks and other men belonging to religious orders, nuns, archbishops and bishops, and finally usurers and bandits.[57] In general, the acts of the council were intended to stop the corrupting influence of money among the clergy, to enforce clerical celibacy, and to institute organizational changes to effect these reforms. The legislation at Paris became the model for the other councils called by Robert and then for the great ecumenical council itself.

After the council at Paris, Robert moved on to the vicinity of Champagne, where he took up a quite different matter, the fortunes of Blanche of Navarre, countess of Champagne, and her young son, Thibaut.[58] Champagne was a land of crusaders. Count Henry had died in the Holy Land, having first left word that should he die, his vassals should accept his brother Thibaut as count. So in 1198, the eighteen-year old brother became Count Thibaut III. But in 1201, after committing himself to the Fourth Crusade, Thibaut died, leaving Blanche pregnant. The future count Thibaut IV was born 31 May 1201, a few days after his father's death. In the ensuing years, Blanche made great efforts to buttress her position and that of her son, paying dearly for various guarantees from the king. But in 1213, a new threat appeared in the person of Erard of Brienne.

While Count Henry was in the Holy Land, he had sired two daughters in an invalid marriage. Erard conceived the plan of going to the Holy Land to marry one of the daughters. He hoped then to lay claim to the county of Champagne on the grounds that the county should be inherited by direct heirs (the daughter), not by Henry's brother and his descendants. Blanche immediately appealed to Robert and to Rome to declare, first, that the girls were illegitimate and therefore lacking right of inheritance and, second, that Erard was too closely related to them to marry them. Her emissaries were very successful in mobilizing papal authority. Both Robert and Innocent authorized investigations, the purpose of which was to produce documents that affirmed the arguments of Blanche regarding Henry's testament and the marriages in question. Innocent took the matter a step further by dispatching messages to the Holy Land

---

[57] Ibid., cols. 817–854.

[58] The following account is based mainly on Moore, *Pope Innocent III and His Relations with the French Princes* (Ph.D. diss., Johns Hopkins, 1960), pp. 140–63. For various documents on the matter, see PL 216:967–92.

requiring the prelates there to prevent any marriage between Erard and the girls[59] and he even sent Blanche copies of his own registers to support her cause.[60]

Despite the best efforts of pope and legate, Erard reached the Holy Land, married one of Henry's daughters, and made his way back to Champagne to lead a rebellion against Blanche and Theobald. Innocent's successor was to continue the support of Blanche, but the mountain of documents generated by papal judges was not enough to stop Erard. Apparently Blanche and her ministers had so antagonized various people in the area, including many prelates, that the letters inspired little local support for Blanche. Theobald's title was ultimately made secure, but only by buying off Erard with generous grants of land and money from Blanche and Theobald.[61]

But that lay well into the future. In the meantime, Robert dealt with miscellaneous problems in the areas he visited, including being present for the final settlement of a long-standing dispute between the count of Nevers and the abbey of Vézelay. In early 1214, he was in Brittany and Normandy, and he held a council at Rouen that adopted measures similar to those approved at the council of Paris.[62]

Robert's commission was to prepare for the council and the crusade, but he interpreted that commission broadly. Innocent had responded to the flourishing heresy in the south of France with a domestic crusade, and in the spring of 1214 Robert went south to participate. His interest in rooting out heresy had been shown while still a master at Paris when he had joined with others in ferreting out those advancing the heretical ideas of one Amaury.[63] Now he joined the crusading forces in southern France and took an active role in directing the warfare and in prosecuting heretics. There Simon de Montfort seemed invincible. At the battle of Muret, the previous

---

[59] Reg. 16:149–151 = PL 216:940–942.
[60] Pott. 4940.
[61] *Layettes*, 1:532–33, no. 1479, dated November 1221.
[62] Mansi, 22, cols. 904–924. See also Foreville, *Le Pape Innocent III et la France*, pp. 320–325; Odette Pontal, ed. and trans. into French, *Les statuts synodaux français du XIIIe siècle*, tome 1: *Les statuts de Paris et le synodal de l'ouest (XIIIe siècle)*, (Paris, 1971), p. 105.
[63] Dickson, "Cardinal Robert de Courson," pp. 80–81.

September, he had defeated even an alliance led by Pedro of Aragon, the hero of Las Navas de Tolosa.

Robert was definitely a dog who barked, but there were a number of other dogs in France who barked back. The prior of Grandmont complained to the pope that Robert had rendered a judgment against him despite the prior's appeal to Rome. The prior sent with his complaint copies of Robert's letters—presumably accurate transcriptions—that urged the underlings of the prior to withdraw their obedience. In March of 1214, Innocent wrote to Robert with unusual severity and sarcasm:

> We are forced to be astonished and disturbed concerning your good judgment [*prudentia*], since, as we have learned from copies of your letters, you are known to have created the cause of dissension and scandal—you, who ought to be a model for others of how to live and an exemplar of religion and honesty.

In supporting the prior's rebel underlings (the *conversi*), Robert had "gone beyond the limits of his legation." When the prior continued to resist Robert's actions, Robert had partially suspended him, although the prior was not "cited, convicted, confessed, nor guilty of any known fault." When the prior appealed to Rome, Robert declared the appeal annulled.

> What therefore should we say about these things, when we are to some degree openly embarrassed [*confundamur*] by you, when we hear that you have done things we never thought we would hear, things any ignoramus [*idiota*] would not dare to do?
>
> For who has constituted you to be judge over our appeals . . .? What wise and discreet man would dare to issue a sentence of suspension against such a man [as the prior] after an appeal to us had been legitimately lodged and announced—removing by your own authority rebellious underlings from obedience to their superiors?

God himself, Innocent continued, took the trouble to investigate the charges against Sodom before giving a judgment against it. Christ himself had not removed the people from obedience to the scribes and pharisees, telling them rather to obey their precepts.

Innocent annulled all of Robert's actions in the matter and suggested that Robert should be glad that he had been so sternly censured. He said that he had not spared the rod, but his actions were those of a father who disciplines the son he loves. He urged him to so work with others that he could return to the pope "with exultation, without your vestments' [*manipulos*] being singed by any blight or darkened by any noxious stain."[64]

Similarly, Robert's actions against usury provoked a reaction from no less than the king and several unnamed barons. They complained that Robert's mandate from the pope pertained only to the council and the crusade, not to usury. Innocent responded that although usury was not explicitly part of the mandate, it was so consuming the resources of Christians that it was impeding the crusade—which was Robert's mandate. Usury also fell under Robert's responsibility to call councils to reform those spiritual matters in need of reform. But while urging the king not to obstruct Robert in his efforts, Innocent also said that he would tell Robert to show moderation, to respect "honest customs and rational practices," and to leave difficult matters for the general council.[65] Robert created even more enemies when he tried to replace the aged abbot of Saint Martial of Limoges with his own candidate. The monks appealed to Rome, and by the time the matter was settled—after Innocent's death—Robert's candidate lost out.[66]

Innocent's scolding had been severe, but it had ended on an encouraging note, and Robert continued to pursue his duty. His mission to organize the crusade could only be carried out if he could end the warfare in France. A clear victory for Simon de Montfort in the south would have that effect, hence Robert's diversion to the south to support Simon. He also tried to effect a truce between King John and Philip Augustus. Robert seemed to have had very good relations with John. Perhaps Robert's origins helped here, although the English birth of Stephen Langton, another Paris master, had not made him any more palatable to the English king. As papal vassal, however, John may well have seen the English papal legate as a natural ally. John provided Robert with letters of introduction when Robert traveled in John's French possessions. After John's forces were defeated at Bouvines, he turned to Robert to help him make a truce

---

[64] "Ad quod obtinendum cum Dei adjutorio debes totis viribus laborare, ut cum exultatione ad nos rediens manipulos tuos portes nulla ambustos uredine vel nociva nebula obfuscatos." *Recueil des historiens des Gaules et de la France*, vol. 19, ed. Michel-Jean-Joseph Brial, new ed. Léopold Delisle (Paris, 1880), pp. 593–4; Pott. 4903. The letter is dated 7 March 1214.

[65] PL 217:229–30.

[66] Dickson, "Cardinal Robert de Courson," pp. 103–5.

with Philip Augustus and to include in that truce John's ally (and Philip's disloyal subject) Hervé count of Nevers. Robert apparently played a significant role in effecting the truce established in September 1214, a truce fairly generous to John.[67]

Robert summoned additional councils, one to meet in Montpellier without him in January 1215, under the presidency of Cardinal Peter Beneventano. The decrees of that council repeated the reforming measures Robert had instituted at Paris and Rouen, but also stated that all the lands of Raymond VI should be forfeited to Simon de Montfort.[68] With that assertion, the council went well beyond the pope's intentions, since in April 1215, Innocent placed all of Raymond's lands under the protection of a papal legate and warned Simon and the other crusaders not to bother them until the Lateran Council could see to their disposition.[69] Robert summoned other councils to meet at Clermont-Dessous and Bordeaux.

In early 1215, Robert was in northern France and Flanders, promoting the crusade and preaching against heresy and usury. From there, he sent notice of a council to be held at Bourges in May, but by this time, he had rubbed too many people the wrong way. The prelates summoned to Bourges refused to come and appealed to the pope against the actions of his legate. Innocent's response is lost, but he evidently yielded to the bishops' resistance and agreed to put the matter off until the general council, where he annulled some of Robert's punitive actions.[70]

The chroniclers of the period said that Robert had indeed antagonized nearly every one in France.[71] William the Breton wrote,

> Robert Courson, legate of the Apostolic See, and many others under his authority were continually preaching throughout the kingdom of France. They bestowed the cross on many people without distinction: children, the elderly, women, the lame, the blind, the deaf, lepers. For this reason, many of the wealthy were very reluctant to take the cross because this sort of mixing seemed more likely to impede the crusade

---

[67] *Layettes* 1:405.

[68] Dickson, "Cardinal Robert de Courson," pp. 101, 110.

[69] Pott. 4966–69. For Pott. 4966, 4967, 4968, and 4969, see *Layettes*, 1:413, no. 1113; 1:414, no. 1114; 1:416, no. 1116; 1:415, no. 1115.

[70] Brenda Bolton, "Faithful to Whom? Jacques de Vitry and the French Bishops," *Revue Mabillon*, n. s. 9 (t. 70) (1998): 53–72 at 63, n. 89, quoting a document from Baldwin, *Masters, Princes, and Merchants*, 2:13, n. 55.

[71] Dickson, "Cardinal Robert de Courson," pp. 112–3.

than to bring help to the Holy Land. But in their preaching, in which they seemed to want to please the people more than was necessary, they defamed the clergy before the people, saying shameful things and inventing things about their lives. And thus they were sowing seeds of scandal and schism between the clergy and the people. Because of this and because of other serious matters, both the king and the entire clergy appealed to the Apostolic See against this legate.[72]

But despite his real or alleged excesses, Robert's two-year legation in France seems to have been quite successful. A large number of French aristocrats did in fact take the cross, including the duke of Burgundy, who had serious misgivings about papal policy regarding the crusade.[73] Some of the controversy regarding privileges granted to crusaders as they affected the rights of the king and other secular lords was settled when Philip Augustus set up a commission consisting of two French bishops and Robert Courson.[74] The decrees of Robert's councils in France were later incorporated into those of the Lateran Council, giving dramatic evidence for the influence of Robert—or better, of the school of Paris masters of which Robert was a part.[75] And although Innocent frequently reined in Robert, he never removed his legation, which was to expire once the council met. After Robert's summons to Bourges was rejected, he moved on to Paris to legislate for the university there.[76] The resulting rule, established, he said, "by special mandate of the pope," set out in considerable detail, how the masters and students were to live and conduct their studies. Lecturers in the liberal arts had to be at least twenty-one years old and they had to have completed six years of study. Lecturers in theology had to be thirty-five and have completed eight years of study. All were to be of good character and were to be licensed to teach by the chancellor after an examination. The curriculum was to include the logic of Aristotle, but not his metaphysics or natural philosophy (a restriction that was soon ignored). Masters and scholars were authorized to form their own constitutions or rules, and provisions were included for funerals of scholars.[77]

---

[72] *Gesta Philippi Augusti*, in *Oeuvres de Rigord et de Guillaume le Breton*, 1:303.
[73] Powell, *Anatomy*, 39–40.
[74] PL 217:239–41.
[75] Dickson, "Cardinal Robert de Courson," pp. 124–27.
[76] Ibid., pp. 117–24.
[77] Thorndike, *University Records*, pp. 15–17.

Robert was one of many cardinals who served the pope well, and he was able to see close-up the results of his labors. He attended Lateran IV, and ultimately he was to die in Egypt among the crusaders he had recruited.

* * *

Innocent had asked the Lord for a sign of his favor, and from the time of Las Navas de Tolosa, the signs seemed to multiply. The spring and early summer of 1213 had been a time of breath-taking, unforseen developments: Philip Augustus accepted Ingeborg as his queen, after years of resisting; John completely capitulated to the pope and gave him the kingdoms of England and Ireland, thus becoming the pope's vassal. The boy-king Frederick, having barely made it into Germany through the pickets of his enemies, won the loyalty of most of Germany, was elected and crowned king of the Romans (the next step to being crowned emperor by the pope), and now seemed on the verge of complete victory over Otto. In July, Frederick would issue the "Golden Bull" of Eger, guaranteeing to the pope everything that Innocent required. These unexpected and fortuitous developments, together with the victory at Las Navas de Tolosa, seemed a sure sign of divine approval for the plans of Innocent. He had launched a flotilla of papal letters that were to produce a great ecumenical council to meet in Rome and a great crusade to recapture, once and for all, the Holy Land and the city of Jerusalem. Whereas in the summer of 1212, Innocent set out for Segni deeply discouraged, it was a renewed and optimistic pope who led his curia back to Segni in mid-July of 1213. So far as we know, nothing happened during the next two years to dampen that enthusiasm. After Bouvines, war among the major princes was suspended, and Robert Courson and the other papal agents effectively carried out the preparations for council and crusade.

CHAPTER NINE

COUNCIL AND CRUSADE (1215)

Innocent seems to have been the first pope to establish the systematic preservation of papal records, and the registers into which his clerks copied many of his letters have been long lasting and well traveled. As years passed, the papal archives proved sufficiently useful that they began to follow the popes in their excursions. At one time or another, the papal registers spent time in Lyons, Cluny, Perugia, Assisi, Avignon, Florence, Bologna, and Ferrara. Their most remarkable adventure, however, was not the work of a pope. Part of the humiliation Napoleon inflicted on the papacy was the transport of over three thousand chests full of archival material from Italy to Paris. The archives made their way back to Rome only after his final defeat. In the process of all this moving, many things were lost, including some things sent to the bottom of the Lago di Garda.[1] Unfortunately, among the missing items are Innocent's registers for the years 1214, 1215, and 1216 as well as most of those for 1203 and 1204. So there are great holes in our records. Still, from the many other sources that have survived, we are certain that council and crusade dominated his last years.

In the fall of 1215, Robert Courson returned to Rome. The curia, having summered in Ferentino and Anagni, also returned to the Lateran about the same time, and soon the prelates of Christendom began to arrive for the council. For many of the participants, this was probably a first visit to Rome. Modern tourists at least have been prepared beforehand by the depictions of the city in various visual forms, but for many of the visitors of 1215, the sights were all new. The remnants of pagan antiquity were impressive enough— no one can forget the coliseum, once seen—but for these pilgrims, Rome was a sacred city second only to Jerusalem. They walked the sacred ground that had been trod by the apostles Peter and Paul.

---

[1] Leonard E. Boyle, O.P., *A Survey of the Vatican Archives and of Its Medieval Holdings* (Toronto, 1972), pp. 7–10.

They visited the tombs of dozens of martyrs. Everywhere, they saw evidence of the triumph of Christianity over paganism, pagan buildings converted or dismantled to create splendid Christian churches.[2]

The fathers who wandered through the Lateran palace found on the walls there graphic representations of more particular triumphs, the triumphs of popes.[3] There they saw pictures of Christ commissioning the apostles to preach to all nations, they saw St. Peter investing Pope Leo III with the symbols of his office. In the audience hall decorated under Pope Calixtus II, they saw four different popes who had been challenged by anti-popes. The pictures showed the anti-popes serving as footstools for the legitimate popes (Psalm 110: "Sit at my right hand, till I make your enemies your footstool"). The image of the enthroned Calixtus himself portrayed the emperor Henry V standing nearby while they both held the Concordat of Worms. Another wall bore the entire text of the Concordat. In another room, pictures dating from the time of Innocent's name-sake Innocent II showed the pope standing above the emperor Lotarius II placing a crown on his head. In the portico to the Lateran basilica, they saw Constantine making his famous (but fictitious) donation of the western empire to the pope.

It was surely the largest peaceful invasion that Christian Rome had ever seen.[4] In addition to the multitude of representatives of the cathedral chapters and monasteries, there were over four hundred bishops, archbishops, patriarchs, and cardinals, representing over eighty ecclesiastical provinces. The kings of France, Hungary, Jerusalem, Cyprus, and Aragon sent representatives, as did Frederick the emperor-elect of the west, and Henry the emperor of Constantinople. Other princes came in person, especially those concerned with the disposition of lands conquered by the Albigensian crusade: Raymond of

---

[2] For the pilgrimage attractions in Rome, see Debra J. Birch, *Pilgrimage to Rome in the Middle Ages: Continuity and Change* (Woodbridge, 1998), pp. 89–122.

[3] The following description is based on Christopher Walter, "Papal Political Imagery in the Medieval Lateran Palace," *Cahiers archéologiques*, 20 (1970) 155–176 and 21 (1971 [1972]): 109–136.

[4] For the following, see Raymonde Foreville, *Latran I, II, III et Latran IV* (Paris, 1965), pp. 251–306; Stephan Kuttner and Antonio García y García. "A New Eyewitness Account of the Fourth Lateran Council," *Traditio*, 20 (1964) 115–178, hereafter cited as "New Eyewitness"; and Brenda Bolton, "A Show with a Meaning: Innocent III's Approach to the Fourth Lateran Council, 1215," *Medieval History*, 1 (1991): 53–67, repr. in *Innocent III: Studies*. The latter article also contains a diagram of the Lateran complex (p. 54).

Toulouse and his wife and son, the counts of Foix, Béarn, and
Comminges. Princes who were not there in person or through delegates certainly expected the clerics from their areas to keep an eye
out for princely concerns. Although all five ancient patriarchs were
represented—Jerusalem, Antioch, Alexandria, Constantinople, and
Rome—the eastern representatives were in fact almost entirely from
the Latin church. The other eastern rites were scarcely present, a
clear indication that the "union" between Latin and Greek churches
was hardly skin deep.

Among the prelates arriving in Rome was the unfortunate Stephen
Langton. The man for whom all of England had been placed under
interdict had been severely scolded by Innocent the previous March
for not supporting King John against the rebel barons.[5] John was
now a papal vassal and a crusader, so the baronial rebellion was a
double affront to Innocent. After John had accepted Magna Carta
in June 1215 (which Innocent immediately declared null and void),[6]
the papal legates in England suspended Stephen from the office of
archbishop because of his sympathies for the rebels. Stephen's reception in Rome was surely not a warm one, since the pope had just
confirmed the suspension.[7] Although Innocent soon removed the suspension, Stephen was forbidden to return to England until the civil
war was ended.[8] Stephen was in exile once again, but this time it
was an exile imposed by the pope instead of the king, and it was
to last until after both Innocent and John were dead.

The council was scheduled to begin 1 November 1215, and perhaps small informal sessions began about that time, but the first formal session was held on Wednesday, 11 November. At dawn, Innocent
said mass in the Lateran basilica for only the upper prelates. After
they had then taken their proper places, the doors were opened and
a great crowd of clergy and laity was admitted, nearly filling the
great basilica. Innocent led them in the hymn "Veni Creator," and
as the sound reverberated from the high wooden ceiling in the great

---

[5] Cheney and Semple, p. 196, no. 75.

[6] Cheney and Semple, pp. 212–16, no. 82. Shortly after the deaths of Innocent
and King John, the papal legate Guala would join the royal government in approving a revised version of the Charter.

[7] Cheney and Semple, p. 220, no. 84.

[8] Cheney and Semple, pp. 196–197, no. 75; Cheney, *Pope Innocent III and England*,
pp. 389–390.

hall, not a few were moved to tears. He added a prayer, though only a few could hear it because of the crush of people. Innocent's sermon that followed was also inaudible in the far reaches of the basilica, but written copies were soon made available to be copied by the attendees.[9]

Innocent took as his theme the quotation from Jesus at the last supper, "With desire I have desired to eat this pascal meal with you, before I suffer" (Luke 22:15), and he added, by way of explanation, (ominously?) "that is, before I die." He began,

> Since "For to me, to live is Christ: and to die is gain" (Phil. 1:21), I do not refuse, if it is God's will, to drink from the cup of suffering, whether it be for the defense of the Catholic faith, for aid to the Holy Land, or for the sake of ecclesiastical liberty, although I do want to remain in the flesh until the work begun is consummated. But God's will, not mine, be done.

He then proceeded in the style of his time to analyze the scriptural passage, examining the meanings of *desire* and of *pascal* (giving the Hebrew and Greek versions of the latter as well as the Latin, to show that it meant "passing-over"). His was, he said, a spiritual not a corporeal desire:

> Not for the sake of earthly convenience or temporal glory, but for the sake of the reform of the universal church and the complete liberation of the Holy Land—it is for these two causes that I have principally and especially convoked this holy council.

He noted that in the Old Testament, the people ate joyfully because it was the pass-over of the Lord and that a pascal meal was celebrated in the eighteenth year of the reign of King Josiah when the temple was restored (2 Kings 23). He continued:

> Would that this history may be a parable of the present time, so that in the eighteenth year of our pontificate, the temple of the Lord (that is, the church) may be restored, and the pascal meal may be celebrated (that is, this solemn council), through which there may be within the Christian people, seeing God through faith, a pass-over from vices to virtues such as has not truly taken place in Israel since the days of the judges and kings (that is, since the times of the holy fathers and Catholic princes).

---

[9] "New Eyewitness," pp. 124, 132.

It was a triple passing-over that Innocent sought: corporeal, spiritual, and eternal: corporeal, in the sense of a passing-over to liberate Jerusalem, spiritual in the sense of a passing-over from one condition to another in the reform of the universal church, and eternal in the sense of passing-over from this life to the life of celestial glory. He then discussed each of these in turn. The Muslim occupation of Jerusalem meant, he said, shame, confusion, and opprobrium.

> Behold, dear brothers, I commit myself totally to you, I present myself completely prepared, according to your counsel if you find it expedient, to undergo the personal labor, to pass-over to kings and princes and peoples and nations, to do this and more, if I can excite them with forceful cries so that they rise up to fight the Lord's fight and vindicate the injury done to the Crucified, who, because of our sins has been cast out from his land and his seat, which he made ready with his blood and in which he accomplished the complete sacraments of our salvation.

Innocent told the clergy that they in particular should be willing to offer their persons and their possessions for the needs of the Holy Land.

Regarding the spiritual pass-over, Innocent used the text of Ezechiel, ch. 9. There is described God's order to a man clothed in white linen to go through the city of Jerusalem and mark with the letter Tau (T) the foreheads of those men "who sigh and mourn for all the abominations that are committed in the midst thereof." Then six men carrying weapons of destruction were to go through the city and kill all those not so marked. The supreme pontiff, who is constituted over the house of Israel, Innocent said, should go through the universal church and inquire as to the morals of each person, and mark those who mourn the abominations in the church. Then: "You should be the six men, each with a weapon of destruction in his hand." They should follow the chief priest though the middle of the city and strike with interdict, suspension, excommunication, and deposition, as the gravity of the fault requires. Their blows, though, are not to be lethal. "Strike in such a way that you heal, kill in such a way that you give life."

Innocent then turned to one of his favorite themes, the need for good example from the clergy:

> For every corruption in the people proceeds principally from the clergy, since "if the priest, who is anointed, sins, he makes the people offend" (Lev. 4:3). Indeed, when the laity see [the clergy] indulging in foul

and outrageous excess, they are led by their example into iniquity and crime.

And from this, all sorts of evil afflict Christendom, including the triumphs of Muslims.

Finally, Innocent said that more than the other two pass-overs, he desired to eat with them the eternal pass-over, from this life to eternal glory:

> It is in this final meal that I especially desire to eat this pascal meal with you, so that we may pass-over from labor to rest, from sorrow to joy, from unhappiness to glory, from death to life, from corruption to eternity—through the gift of our Lord Jesus Christ, to whom is honor and glory, for ever and ever. Amen.[10]

Filled with biblical quotations and allusions, the sermon lasted for nearly an hour. The council then passed from thoughts of eternal glory to the more earth-bound problems of Christendom. The patriarch of Jerusalem addressed the assembly on the need to aid the Holy Land, and the bishop of Agde spoke on the state of heresy in Christendom. The themes of the council had been sounded, and the pope dismissed them for the day.

The next two days were spent on painfully mundane topics. On the first day, there was an extended discussion of the open and contested office of patriarch of Constantinople, and the second day was given to the longstanding dispute between the archbishop of Toledo, who claimed to have the right to exercise primacy over the other archbishops of Spain, and those archbishops, who resisted that claim. The time-consuming debate about primacy hardly concerned the major issues of the day, and the only agreement reached was that the litigation would continue into the following year.

On Saturday, 14 November, or shortly thereafter, the council then turned to the situation in southern France. Innocent had persuaded all parties to leave to the council how the conquered lands in southern France would be allotted. Count Raymond VI of Toulouse and Count Raymond-Roger of Foix were permitted to present their own cases to the council. They knelt at Innocent's feet and begged the

---

[10] PL 217:675–680. An almost identical text is found in Richard of San Germano. The sermon is analyzed by Wilhelm Imkamp in "Sermo ultimus, quem fecit Dominus Innocentius papa tercius in Lateranensi concilio generali," *Römische Quartalschrift für christliche Altertumskunde und Kirkengeschichte*, 70 (1975): 149–179.

pope to restore their confiscated lands—a sight not easily forgotten
by those who saw it or later heard of it. Innocent was well disposed
to both counts. In the months before the council, he had found himself in the odd position of trying to protect Raymond and his lands
and to restrain the crusading force he himself had sent to southern
France.[11] Both Raymond and Raymond-Roger now had promised
to adhere to papal policies if restored, but the new reforming bishops of the Languedoc were relentless in their prosecution of the
counts as men who supported heresy. Three hundred bishops, well
over two-thirds, voted to give the county of Toulouse to Simon de
Montfort. All that Raymond and his supporters achieved was that
he would receive an annual pension of four hundred marks for the
rest of his life, his wife could keep her dowry, and his young son
would get the unconquered lands when he reached his majority.
Raymond-Roger's lands were to await further adjudication.[12] Innocent
had for some time been saying that disposition of the conquered
lands should be left to the council, and although it was not a judgment that he liked, he bowed to the will of the majority. Raymond
left and immediately began to look for ways to overcome the judgment.

The next day, Sunday, 15 November, was given to a splendid
ceremony surrounding the reconsecration of the church of Santa
Maria in Trastevere. Innocent was led across the city by a great
procession including Roman nobles in festive attire, ordinary people
carrying olive branches, and all those attending the council who did
not want to miss such a spectacle. Drums and trumpets competed
with the people chanting "Kyrie eleison, Christe eleison." Houses
and high towers were adorned with banners and decorations, and
when those in the procession crossed the Tiber into Trastevere, they
found the houses decorated with bright lanterns. By the time the
ceremonies in the church were completed, it was late in the day,
and the procession led the pope back through the city to the Lateran.[13]

A few days later, a similar procession made its way from the
Lateran across the city and the river to St. Peter's basilica on the
Vatican hill. The crowds were such that the pope could scarcely get
into the church.

---

[11] Pott. 4950, 4966, 4967.
[12] Pott. 5009–5011, 5014; Costen, *The Cathars*, pp. 144–5.
[13] "New Eyewitness," p. 125. See also Brentano, *Rome before Avignon*, pp. 57–58.

The second full session took place on Friday, 20 November, and this one was occupied with another major political matter, the office of emperor of the Romans. Frederick's position had grown even more secure since Bouvines. In the summer of 1215, both Aachen and Cologne had submitted to him, and he had been crowned king of the Romans once again, this time as tradition required, in the city of Aachen. He had taken the cross, thereby acquiring the right of papal protection as owed to all crusaders.[14] He had promised that, once crowned emperor, he would relinquish the kingdom of Sicily to his son and acknowledge that it recognized no overlord but the pope.[15] But Otto of Brunswick had not given up, despite the loss of virtually all real support in Germany, and his representatives were in Rome to make his case.

First, the archbishop of Palermo spoke for Frederick II, urging the pope and council to confirm Frederick's election. Then Milanese representatives of Otto asked to read a letter from Otto, at which point the audience tried to shout them down, opposing any presentation from Otto. Marquis William of Montferrat had come well prepared, and he rose to make a series of legal objections to any representation from Otto. The two parties almost came to blows before Innocent intervened. He reined in the opposition to Otto, saying that the council was instituted to hear both the guilty and the innocent, the rich and the poor, and if the devil himself were able to repent, even he would certainly be admitted. He also displayed his legal erudition by explaining to the assembly each of the legal objections raised by the marquis.

The Milanese emissary read the letter, in which Otto asked forgiveness for past offenses and promised to reform. The emissary also sought to rebut the charges of the marquis of Montferrat. Since everyone knew, and the Milanese legate conceded, that Otto had flagrantly violated his promises to the pope when he invaded the Papal State, and since everyone knew that since the defeat of his forces at Bouvines Otto's candidacy was dead, all of this was in one sense an empty exercise. But for Innocent, it must have been extremely gratifying. To have the two candidates for the Roman empire making their cases in a grand council of all of Christendom, presided

---

[14] Van Cleve, *Emperor Frederick*, pp. 96–98.
[15] PL 217:305–306 = MGH LL 2:228.

over by the pope, must have fulfilled his highest hope for a peaceful and well-ordered society, working under clerical and papal direction. It was like his councils in Viterbo in 1207 and in San Germano in 1208, only this time writ large.

At some point, the council was treated to one of the great success stories of their day. The archbishop of Riga and the bishop of Estonia had traveled to Rome, and they reported to an enthusiastic audience about the battles won and the heathen converted.[16]

The third and final formal session came on Monday, 30 November. Innocent celebrated mass and preached on the Trinity in a sermon now lost.[17] He and the fathers then took their places for council business, and he had the first canon read, the declaration of the faith. Innocent called in a loud voice, "Do you believe all these?" and the fathers responded "We believe." Likewise, they condemned the heresies mentioned in the second canon. Plans for the crusade were then presented, probably in the form of a draft of the papal letter to be issued in December as *Ad liberandam*. To prepare further for the crusade, Innocent gave judgments on major political issues. First, he renewed the excommunication of all those rebelling against King John of England, papal vassal and crusader. (Innocent had earlier offered to the rebels to have their grievances addressed at the council,[18] but they had ignored the offer.) He stressed the support John had promised for the crusade. Innocent also condemned anyone aiding the rebels, an oblique warning to Philip Augustus and to his son Prince Louis, whom the rebels had invited to England to claim the crown.[19] At this point, Siegfried, archbishop of Mainz, leapt to his feet to assert that England was legally subject to the emperor of the Romans and the German princes. It was an interruption termed by two distinguished scholars as "inconsiderate, not to say stupid,"[20] inasmuch as Innocent had in fact accepted England as a fief held of the papacy. Innocent raised his hand to silence the archbishop saying, "Just hear me now; I will hear you afterwards."[21] The bold but impetuous archbishop had to be silenced two more

---

[16] *Chronicle of Henry of Livonia*, p. 152.
[17] "New Eyewitness," p. 154.
[18] Cheney and Semple, p. 219, no. 83.
[19] Cheney, *Innocent III and England*, pp. 390–393.
[20] "New Eyewitness," p. 160.
[21] Ibid., p. 128.

times before the pope finished his remarks about England. Innocent then confirmed the election of Frederick as emperor of the Romans and, in effect, promised to crown him.

At this point, the many remaining canons were read to the assembly. It is tempting to see the entire council as a rubber stamp, but the fathers did override the pope's preferences regarding Raymond of Toulouse, and according to Gerald of Wales, Innocent's old acquaintance, they rejected his proposal to impose a permanent ten percent tax on all cathedral churches in order to support papal government.[22] We have no record of the working sessions in between the formal sessions, but presumably the fathers had been made acquainted with the formidable list of doctrinal and disciplinary canons that they heard at this last session. The content of the canons was, moreover, not especially new. Some repeated provisions of earlier Lateran councils, and others were modeled on the canons of earlier French councils, those called by Robert Courson, but also those called earlier by local prelates.[23] So it is possible that at one time or another, council participants played some role in the shaping of the canons. But given the fact that most of the canons were read aloud only on the last day and that there is no record of any discussion of their content, it is extremely likely that they had been prepared ahead of time in the papal curia[24] and that the fathers did little more at the council than accept them passively. By the time they had been read at the end of a long day at the very last session, no one was in the mood to quibble about wording.

The following list of canon titles indicates the wide range of their subject matter:

1. On the Catholic faith
2. On the error of abbot Joachim
3. On heretics
4. On the pride of Greeks toward Latins
5. On the dignity of patriarchs
6. On provincial councils
7. On the correction of offences

---

[22] Cheney, *Innocent III and England*, p. 396.

[23] Pontal, *Les statuts de Paris*, pp. 47–48, 54–93.

[24] Antonius García y García, *Constitutiones Concilii quarti Lateranensis una cum Commentariis glossatorum*, (Vatican, 1981), Monumenta iuris canonici, Series A: *Corpus Glossatorum*, 2:5–8.

8. On inquests
9. On different rites within the same faith
10. On appointing preachers
11. On schoolmasters
12. On general chapters of monks
13. On the prohibition against new religious orders
14. On punishing clerical incontinents
15. On preventing drunkenness among the clergy
16. On the dress of clerics
17. On prelates' feasts and their negligence at divine services
18. On sentences involving either the shedding of blood or a duel being forbidden to clerics
19. That profane objects may not be introduced into churches
20. On keeping the charism and the eucharist under lock and key
21. On confession being made, and not revealed by the priest, and on communicating at least at Easter
22. That the sick should provide for the soul before the body
23. That a cathedral church or a church of the regular clergy is not to remain vacant for more than three months
24. On making an election by ballot or by agreement
25. That an election made by a secular power is not valid
26. On the penalty for improperly confirming an election
27. On the instruction of ordinands
28. That those who have asked for permission to resign are to be compelled to do so
29. That nobody may hold two benefices with the cure of souls attached
30. On the suitability of those instituted to churches
31. On not instituting the sons of canons with their fathers
32. That patrons shall leave a suitable portion to clerics
33. On not receiving procurations without a visitation being made
34. On not burdening subjects under the pretext of some service
35. On stating the grounds for an appeal
36. That a judge can revoke an interlocutory and a comminatory sentence
37. On not procuring letters which entail more than two days' journey and are without special mandate
38. On writing acts so that they can be proved
39. On granting restitution against a person in possession who was not the robber
40. On true possession
41. On continuing good faith in every prescription
42. On secular justice
43. On a cleric not doing fealty to a layman without good reason
44. That the ordinances of princes should not be prejudicial to churches
45. A patron who kills or mutilates a cleric of a church loses his right of patronage
46. On not exacting taxes from clerics

47. On the form of excommunication
48. On how to challenge a judge
49. On the punishment for excommunicating someone unjustly
50. On the restriction of prohibitions to matrimony
51. On the punishment of those who contract clandestine marriages
52. On rejecting evidence from hearsay in a matrimonial suit
53. On those who give their fields to others to be cultivated to avoid paying tithes
54. That tithes should be paid before taxes
55. That tithes are to be paid on lands that are acquired, notwithstanding privileges
56. That a parish priest shall not lose tithes on account of some people making a pact
57. On interpreting the words of privileges
58. On the same in favour of bishops
59. No religious may give surety without the permission of his abbot and convent
60. That abbots should not encroach on the episcopal office
61. That religious may not receive tithes from lay hands
62. That saints' relics may not be exhibited outside reliquaries, nor may newly discovered relics be venerated without authorization from the Roman church
63. On simony
64. On the same with regard to monks and nuns
65. On the same with regard to the illegal extortion of money
66. On the same with regard to the avarice of clerics
67. On the usury of Jews
68. That Jews should be distinguished from Christians in their dress
69. That Jews are not to hold public office
70. That converts to the faith among the Jews may not retain their old rite

The seventy canons of the council can be grouped—to be sure, without great precision—under these headings: heretics and Jews, organizational and judicial reforms, marriage law, clerical appointments and support, reforms of the clergy, and reforms of the laity.[25]

The first three canons of the council addressed the problem of heresy. The first is the formal credo to which the council assented, asserting the basic doctrines of Christianity so as to reject the doctrines of the major heresies of the day. Against the Cathar doctrine of a good God and an evil God, the council asserted "there is only

---

[25] For the text of these canons with English translation, see Tanner, 1:230–271. The translations in the following section are from that edition.

one true God, eternal and immeasurable, almighty, unchangeable, incomprehensible and ineffable, Father, Son, and holy Spirit, three persons but one absolutely simple essence, substance or nature." Against the Cathar doctrine that the material world was evil and the work of the evil God, it stated that God was the "creator of all things invisible and visible, spiritual and corporeal. . . ." As for the evil power, it stated, "The devil and other demons were created by God naturally good, but they became evil by their own doing." In rebuttal of the idea that Jesus was only a spirit who did not actually die, the council referred to "the only begotten Son of God, Jesus Christ, who became incarnate by the action of the whole Trinity in common and was conceived from the ever virgin Mary through the cooperation of the holy Spirit, having become true man, composed of a rational soul and human flesh. . . ." It continued, "Although he is immortal and unable to suffer according to his divinity, he was made capable of suffering and dying according to his humanity." Jesus rose in the body, and all humans "will rise with their own bodies, which they now wear, so as to receive according to their deserts, whether these be good or bad. . . ."

Against those heretics who challenged the existing church, its clergy, and its sacraments, the canon declared,

> There is indeed one universal church of the faithful, outside of which nobody at all is saved, in which Jesus Christ is both priest and sacrifice. His body and blood are truly contained in the sacrament of the altar under the forms of bread and wine, the bread and wine having been changed in substance (*transsubstantiatis*), by God's power, into his body and blood. . . . Nobody can effect this sacrament except a priest who has been properly ordained . . . . . . the sacrament of baptism . . . brings salvation to both children and adults when it is correctly carried out by anyone in the form laid down by the church. If someone falls into sin after having received baptism, he or she can always be restored through true penitence.

And in defense of marriage against the Cathars, it added, "For not only virgins and the continent but also married persons find favour with God by right faith and good actions and deserve to attain to eternal blessedness."

The second canon, also approved vocally by the fathers, rejected the trinitarian ideas of Abbot Joachim of Fiore and the doctrines of Almaric of Bène, matters of interest only to the well educated. But the third canon presented in detail all the measures to be taken

against heretics and their supporters, basically affirming the poli
that Innocent had been applying elsewhere. Spiritual and secular
authorities were to use all their powers against heretics; accused
heretics who did not prove their innocence through oaths were to
lose their property and all their rights to hold office at any level or
to act in a court of law. Similar penalties, short of the loss of property,
were set forth for those who defended or sheltered heretics. The
canon, like Innocent's earlier decretal *Vergentis in senium*,[26] did not call
for the death penalty either for heretics or for their supporters.

Canons 67–70 dealt with Jews. In hostile tones, the council required
Jews (and Saracens) in Christian provinces to wear distinctive dress
so as to prevent intermarriage with Christians. It condemned any
instances of Jewish mocking of Christian belief or practice (probably based on reports of Jewish celebration of the feast of Purim
which often coincided with Holy Week), and condemned the Christian
practice of placing Jews in offices over Christians. Jews who had
become Christians were not to continue any of their former Jewish
forms of worship.

The canon on Jewish money lending complained that Christians
were being impoverished by "the perfidy of the Jews," but the council did not condemn all money lending. Rather, it ordained that
Jews would be required to make satisfaction only for "oppressive and
immoderate interest" (*graves et immoderatas usuras*) taken from Christians.
It also required Jews to pay tithes to churches for any land which
Christians had forfeited in default of debts. The reference to "immoderate interest" suggests that there was such a thing as "moderate
interest," a subject to be returned to below.

A number of canons were aimed at increasing the centralization
of the church, already well advanced, as a means of improving the
discipline and the quality of the clergy. Taking a very broad view
of the Christian world, canon 5 (On the dignity of patriarchs) presented this ordering of honor among the ancient patriarchs: The
Roman church ("the mother and teacher of all Christ's faithful"),
then in descending order, the church of Constantinople, the church
of Alexandria, the church of Antioch, and the church of Jerusalem.
Canon 9 insisted that there be only one bishop in each diocese,
regardless of the variety of rites (such as Latin and Greek), but the

---

[26] Reg. 2:1.

council did allow that bishop to appoint a vicar bishop for a different rite within his diocese. The arrangement was a skillful way to maintain a unified authority while recognizing the diversity in areas like Constantinople and southern Italy. Canon 4 indicated that the union with the Greek church was still not going smoothly, since the council castigated the "pride of Greeks toward Latins," mentioning that Greeks were reported to be washing their altars after Latin clergy used them and that some Greeks were even re-baptizing people baptized by Latins.

The most ambitious organizational canon was that (6) which required all metropolitans (archbishops) to call a council of their suffragans every year, to consider "the correction of excesses and the reform of morals, especially among the clergy." The requirement that these provincial councils be held was not a new one, but it was now renewed, with the additional requirement that each metropolitan appoint a person to spend the year investigating the province and then report to the council what needed to be reformed. The provincial council was, then, to be a regional version of the Lateran council itself.

Even the most conscientious provincial council, however, could not do much to reform the monastic orders within their territories, since those orders were often exempt from episcopal authority. In canon 12, the council addressed that problem by introducing for all monastic orders the practice already employed by the Cistercians, the general chapter. Every three years, the abbots and priors were to meet in a fashion analogous to the provincial councils of bishops so as to "treat carefully of the reform of the order and the observance of the rule." And just as the metropolitan was to appoint an investigator to visit the entire province, the general chapter of each order was to appoint a similar person to visit all the houses of nuns or monks throughout "the kingdom or province." To make sure that all religious orders fell under one or the other of these provisions, canon 13 forbad the establishment of any new religious orders. The relationship between bishops and the monasteries in their dioceses was further regulated by canons 57, 58, and 60, all aimed at preventing conflicts of jursidiction and authority.

By 1215, Innocent had acquired a great deal of legal and judicial expertise and had become the most active legislator in all of Christendom. The council reflected the experience he and the other prelates had acquired in the burgeoning business of ecclesiastical courts. Twelve of the canons were directly concerned with legal procedure and principles. Canons 39, 40, and 41 dealt with a relatively minor matter, namely the wrongful possession of goods. Several canons were intended to regulate the large number of appeals going to Rome, discouraging unfounded appeals (canon 35) and trying to prevent appeals from frustrating legitimate justice (36, 37, 48). The rest, however, were of much greater import.

Having called for investigations by provincial councils and general chapters, the council laid down in canon 8 the rules for conducting such investigations (*inquisitiones*), especially when a prelate was accused. "The person about whom the inquiry is being made ought to be present, unless he absents himself out of contumacy. The articles of the inquiry should be shown to him so that he may be able to defend himself. The names of witnesses as well as their depositions are to be made known to him so that both what has been said and by whom will be apparent; and legitimate exceptions and responses are to be admitted. . . ." (These admirable principles, like some of those listed below, were later to be denied to those accused of heresy.) Canons 47 and 49 laid down rules intended to prevent the unjust use of excommunication.

The growing sophistication of legal procedures was evidenced in a number of canons. Canon 38 required that the business of all judicial proceedings in church courts be put in writing and copies provided for all parties involved. It began, "An innocent litigant can never prove the truth of his denial of a false assertion made by an unjust judge, since a denial by the nature of things does not constitute a direct proof."

Two canons regarding the relationship between secular and ecclesiastical justice were of enormous import. Canon 42 stated:

> Just as we desire lay people not to usurp the rights of clerics, so we ought to wish clerics not to lay claim to the rights of the laity. We therefore forbid every cleric henceforth to extend his jurisdiction, under pretext of ecclesiastical freedom, to the prejudice of secular justice. Rather, let him be satisifed with the written constitutions and customs hitherto approved, so that *the things of Caesar* may be rendered *unto Caesar, and the things of God* may be rendered *unto God* by a right distribution. [Italics indicating scriptural passages.]

That canon was not to end jurisdictional disputes, but it affirmed unequivocally that secular jurisdiction had its own legitimate sphere and that there were limits to ecclesiastical jurisdiction.

The other canon, canon 18, was of equal weight;

> No cleric may decree or pronounce a sentence involving the shedding
> of blood, or carry out a punishment involving the same, or be pre-
> sent when such punishment is carried out. If anyone, however, under
> cover of this statute, dares to inflict injury on churches or ecclesiasti-
> cal persons, let him be restrained by ecclesiastical censure. A cleric
> may not write or dictate letters which require punishments involving
> the shedding of blood; in the courts of princes this responsibility should
> be entrusted to laymen and not to clerics. Moreover no cleric may be
> put in command of mercenaries or crossbowmen or suchlike men of
> blood; nor may a subdeacon, deacon or priest practise the art of
> surgery, which involves cauterizing and making incisions; nor may any-
> one confer a rite or blessing or consecration on a purgation by ordeal
> of boiling or cold water or of the red-hot iron, saving nevertheless the
> previously promulgated prohibitions regarding single combats and duels.

Under Innocent III, the march toward "the imperial papacy" begun
in the eleventh century continued, to be culminated under Innocent
IV and Boniface VIII. But this canon, like 42, clearly defined limits of clerical competence. Although the world was still to see clerical soldiers, and although inquisitors were to circumvent the restrictions
on blood sentences by turning their prisoners over to secular exe-
cutioners, this canon would remain as a permanent obstacle to any
clerical vision of Christian society as a one-party state ruled and
policed entirely by clergy.

The final provision of canon 18 was also to have long-range consequences for secular justice. In most of Latin Christendom in 1215,
trial by ordeal was still the preferred procedure of secular justice
when purgation (oath-taking) did not settle a matter. Trial by ordeal
required the participation of the priest, who blessed the hot iron or
hot water or the pond into which the accused was immersed. The
masters at Paris had long been arguing that trial by ordeal was irra-
tional and was, even worse, a "test of God" in that it presumed to
demand God's pariticpation in a judicial decision. Now, by forbidding the clergy to participate, the council accelerated the movement
toward more rational forms of justice already developing in Europe.[27]
The English, for example, turned gradually and reluctantly to trial
by jury as an alternative to trial by ordeal.

---

[27] John W. Baldwin, "The Intellectual Preparation for the Canon of 1215 against
Ordeals," *Speculum*, 36 (1961): 613–636.

It has occasionally been suggested that much of the canon law of the middle ages was designed to increase the income of the clergy. Although the continued insistence that marital matters should be governed by canon law can be seen in that light, Innocent III and Lateran IV provide instances where the clergy diminished their opportunities to profit from laws governing marriage. Innocent's persistent refusal to accept the authority to grant divorces is one such example. He did claim the authority to move a bishop from one diocese to another, thus breaking what he frequently referred to as the spiritual marriage between the bishop and his see. It would have been a theory characteristic of him to say that if he could dissolve a spiritual marriage, all the more could he dissolve a corporeal marriage. In fact, though, he consistently stated that dissolving a valid marriage was beyond his authority, no matter how useful it might be politically or financially.[28]

Similarly, canon 50 relaxed the laws governing marriages between relatives, notably permitting previously forbidden marriages between people related within the fourth, fifth, and sixth degrees. The earlier prohibition had extended so far that many marriages were of doubtful legitimacy, and the uncertainty thereby generated created opportunities for all sorts of mischief. Enemies could be harassed and inheritances could be claimed by challenging the validity of a marriage; clergy could enrich themselves by granting dispensations. Canon 50 very much reduced the danger of these abuses, and canon 52 also made it more difficult to challenge existing marriages on the basis of consanguinity and affinity, "For it is preferable to leave alone some people who have been united contrary to human decrees than to separate, contrary to the Lord's decrees, persons who have been joined together legitimately."

Canon 51 further developed the law concerning marriage. By 1215, canon lawyers and theologians had come to the remarkable conclusion that the presence of a clergyman was not necessary for a valid marriage, that all that was required was the commitment made to each other by a man and woman otherwise eligible for a valid marriage. This canon, however, forbad such marriages entered

---

[28] See Reg. 1:326, 530, and Michele Maccarronne, "Sacramentalitá e indissolubilitá del matrimonio nella dottrina di Innocenzo III," *Lateranum* 44 (1978): 449–514, at 507–512.

secretly. Marriages were to be publicly announced so that any possible impediments could be brought to light beforehand. Further provisions were added to make "clandestine marriages" forbidden and
disadvantageous, but they were still valid marriages.[29]

* * *

Since the eleventh century, the role of laymen in the appointment
of clergy had been bitterly disputed, even costing the lives of men
like Thomas Becket. Canons 23 through 31 and canons 43 and 61
were intended to clarify the law, although everyone probably knew
that the disputes would not end. Generally, the canons provided that
ecclesiastical offices were not to be left vacant for more than three
months, that elections should be conducted and confirmed properly,
that no one should be elected "through abuse of the secular power,"
that only those truly qualified should be selected, that no one should
hold simultaneously more than one office with pastoral responsibilities attached. Canon 43 forbad lay lords to require loyalty oaths
from clergy unless the clergy held secular possessions from the lords.
Canon 28 added the curious requirement, reflecting Innocent's experience, that those clerics who had requested the right to resign from
office and had obtained it could not then change their minds.

Closely related to the appointment of clergy was the need to provide for their income. Canons 32 and 53 through 56 were intended
to make sure that parish priests actually received an appropriate
share of the tithes given by the people, although no attempt was
made to define that share. Neither lay nor religious patrons of parishes
were to violate this rule. Canon 59 forbad members of monastic
orders to enter into any kind of borrowing or lending without the
approval of the proper monastic authorities.

The selection and financial support of the clergy was only the
beginning. The subject of most of the canons was the reform of
the clergy. After a general canon (7) requiring prelates to "attend to
the correction of their subjects' offences," the council adopted canons
on clerical incontinence (14), drunkenness (15), extravagant dress (16),
and extravagant feasting and neglect of the liturgy (17, 19, 20).
Various clerical officials visited churches and while there received

---

[29] For the development of the law of marriage in the late twelfth century, see
Brundage, *Law, Sex, and Christian Society in Medieval Europe*, pp. 331–341.

"procurations" for their support. Canon 33 said that procu
should only be collected when an actual visit had been made. __ _
reflected discontent that had evidently been voiced concerning the
procurations demanded by papal officials when they traveled. The
canon advised moderation, but actually broadened the right of those
officials to demand procurations from churches in the area that were
not actually visited but were nevertheless now expected to share the
burden with those that were. Canon 34 condemned those prelates
who acted as middlemen, collecting procurations on behalf of a vis-
itor but then keeping part for themselves.

Canon 62 addressed problems that were to haunt Catholic Christianity for centuries to come: the veneration of relics, the collection of
alms for charitable purposes, and the granting of indulgences.

Since the early years of Christianity, when Christians had begun
to build churches over the graves of martyrs, the faithful had placed
a high value on bodies of the saints—or pieces thereof—and other
items closely associated with Jesus or the saints (like the wood of the
true cross). The sack of Constantinople had brought a flood of relics
to the West and had provided new opportunities for charlatans to
defraud believers. Now the whole process was to be brought under
papal or episcopal licensing. Canon 62 stated:

> The christian religion is frequently disparaged because certain people
> put saints' relics up for sale and display them indiscriminately. In order
> that it may not be disparaged in the future, we ordain by this pre-
> sent decree that henceforth ancient relics shall not be displayed out-
> side a reliquary or be put up for sale. As for newly discovered relics,
> let no one presume to venerate them publicly unless they have previ-
> ously been approved by the authority of the Roman pontiff.

Alms-collectors were to carry letters of authorization, either from the
pope or from the local bishop, and limits were placed on indulgences granted by bishops so as to avoid "indiscriminate and exces-
sive indulgence." That these provisions did not end the abuses is
well known from Chaucer's "Pardoner's Tale" and from the experience of Martin Luther.

The corrupting influence of money was further addressed in canons
63–66. Too often money changed hands when bishops were consecrated, when abbots were installed, when clerics were ordained, when
men and women were admitted into convents, and even when funerals or weddings were sought by the faithful. On this last point, however, the canon presented a studied ambiguity rather than a flat

prohibition, forbidding "wicked exactions" on the one hand, but permitting "a praiseworthy custom of holy church, introduced by the pious devotion of the faithful,"—evidently voluntary donations made on the occasion of funerals or weddings.

Finally, there were the canons aimed at reforming the laity. Canons 44 and 45 forbad lay authorities to seize clerical properties or jurisdiction (since in ecclesiastical matters the lot of lay people is "to obey, not to be in command") or to lay violent hands on clerics. Canon 46 asserted a right that was to prove to be intolerable to European rulers: lay authorities were not to tax ecclesiastical persons or property. The canon did provide that "If at some time, however, a bishop together with his clergy foresee so great a need or advantage that they consider, without any compulsion, that subsidies should be given by the churches, for the common good or the common need, when the resources of the laity are not sufficient, then the above-mentioned laymen may receive them humbly and devoutly and with thanks." Greater foresight would have enabled the pope and the fathers to see that the continuing accumulation of ecclesiastical property would inevitably make this provision untenable. Something would have to give way, as Boniface VIII was to discover at the end of the century.

Canon 22 required physicians visiting the sick to advise their patients to look to the health of their souls. The canon acknowledged that sometimes such advice, by suggesting that the condition was terminal, caused the patient to fall into despair and become more vulnerable to the illness, but it countered with the theory that spiritual health would better enable the patient to profit from medical treatment. Modern medical practitioners would probably acknowledge the validity of each of these conflicting theories.

The last canon directly concerning the laity was one of the few in this group that we know was certainly implemented, at least in the long run. It required every lay person who had reached the "age of discernment" to confess his or her sins to the parish priest at least once a year and to receive the eucharist at Easter time. The latter requirement is still in effect today and is observed by millions of Catholics throughout the world as their "Easter Duty."

Throughout his pontificate, Innocent had promoted the value of individual confession of sins. When he offered the crusading indulgence, it was always conditional on "repentance of heart and confession of mouth." In this canon, his favorite metaphor for spiritual healing was used again: the confessor as skilled physician:

The priest shall be discerning and prudent, so that like a skilled doctor he may pour wine and oil over the wounds of the injured one. Let him carefully inquire about the circumstances of both the sinner and the sin, so that he may prudently discern what sort of advice he ought to give and what remedy to apply, using various means to heal the sick person. Let him take the utmost care, however, not to betray the sinner at all by word or sign or in any other way. If the priest needs wise advice, let him seek it cautiously without any mention of the person concerned.

The canon continues to provide severe punishment for any priest who betrays the confidence of the confessional.

This canon can be seen in many ways. It was, first of all, certainly not a product of Innocent's unique religious outlook. Provincial councils held in Paris well before Lateran IV had given similar extended attention to the sacrament of confession.[30] As to its impact on contemporary society, its religious value can be left for another forum, but one can argue that it probably contributed to the mental and emotional health of many Christians. The priest was likely to be the best educated person in most communities, and the confessional gave the individual an opportunity to receive guidance on moral matters and to be relieved of the guilt that inevitably afflicts anyone with an active conscience. To be sure, many moderns would challenge the notion that at the time, priestly advice in sexual and economic matters was likely to be conducive to mental health, but in any case, the canon stands as a monument in the development of inner awareness among Europeans.[31]

It may also stand as a monument in the development of oppressive institutions in European life. The canon rests on the assumption that parish priests could be expected to be wise physicians, although the other canons of the council demonstrate that Innocent and his contemporaries knew perfectly well that the assumption was unrealistic. By making confession mandatory, the canon placed enormous power in the hands of parish priests, and although many priests no doubt used the power well, it is certain that many others abused it. The exploitive and deceitful confessor become a fixture in European

---

[30] Pontal, *Les statuts de Paris et le synodal de l'ouest (XIIIᵉ siècle)*, pp. 62–67.

[31] In *Handling Sin: Confession in the Middle Ages*, ed. Peter Biller and A. J. Minnis (Woodbridge, 1998), see especially Peter Biller, "Confession in the Middle Ages: Introduction" (pp. 1–33) and John Baldwin, "From the Ordeal to Confession: In Search of Lay Religion in Early Thirteenth Century France" (pp. 191–209).

literature. Even the conscientious confessor—*especially* the conscientious confessor—represented a grave danger for the parishioner whose faith strayed from strict orthodoxy.

Finally, it should be noted that the often-repeated notion that the council set the number of sacraments at seven is an error. Although the number seven was commonly used for this purpose in the thirteenth century, it was not formally defined until the Council of Trent in the sixteenth century.[32]

What was in the minds of the representatives at the council who heard all these canons read on a Monday afternoon in late November, it is difficult to say. Some no doubt were enthusiastic in their approval, others may have felt sullen resignation, and some probably dozed off in indifference. Those with little idealism and ample experience may have recognized immediately that most of the canons would soon be ignored, as much because of human inertia as from active opposition. In any case, when the reading was completed, the pope intoned the *Te Deum*, said a closing prayer, and blessed the assembly with a relic of the cross. The council was completed. Some bishops, with the pope's permission, left Rome immediately; others stayed to conduct other business with the curia.

With all these supplicants still in Rome and with the need to issue papal letters communicating and implementing the decisions made at the council, the clerks of the curia must have had a busy Christmas season. The most important task at hand was seeing that the letter *Ad liberandam*[33] was sent to all parts of Christendom. A long and detailed exposition of the preparations to be made, it summoned all crusaders planning to go by sea to meet in the kingdom of Sicily in June 1217, at Brindisi, Messina, and neighboring places. Innocent himself would be there. Besides providing a substantial subsidy himself, Innocent was also taxing himself and the cardinals ten percent of their income, and he required all other clerics who were not going on the crusade—he said the council had approved this—to pay five percent of their incomes for the next three years. Crusaders were to be exempt from taxation and from interest on their debts. Christians were forbidden not only to sell war or naval materials to Muslims,

---

[32] Tanner, 2:684, session 7, canon 1. The error was repeated, for example, by myself in "Sermons," p. 86.

[33] The text is included in Tanner, 1:267–271.

but they were forbidden even to send their ships to Muslim territories in the East, a prohibition intended to make ships available to transport crusaders. Tournaments were strictly forbidden (in such a way as to acknowledge that earlier prohibitions of tournaments had been widely ignored).

* * *

In January of 1216, Innocent took time from all the great issues to present a gift to the monks of St. Denis in Paris. There had long been a controversy, he said, whether the St. Denis (Dionysius) who preached in France was St. Denis the Areopagite, a convert of St. Paul in Greece. The body of the former rested in the church of St. Denis, but it was uncertain whether it was also a relic of the latter. Now Innocent sent with the monks returning home from the council relics of the Areopagite which the late Cardinal Peter Capuano had brought from Greece to Rome. St. Denis would now unquestionably have a relic of the Areopagite. He said, "Receive these relics reverently, and then give this to us in return, that in your prayers, there may always be a special remembrance of us to God, and that in accordance with the offer of the monks already mentioned, our memory will be solemnly celebrated on the anniversary of our death."[34] It was a generous and thoughtful act, but it reflected the moral ambiguity of much of Innocent's pontificate. In accepting the relic from Cardinal Peter, he was sharing in the looting of Constantinople.

In December of 1215, Innocent excommunicated by name a number of the leading rebels in England, declaring them to be "worse than the Saracens."[35] At the same time, he named a new legate for England, Cardinal Guala Bicchieri, a man who was to have enormous influence in England in the following years. The English rebels were not fazed by Innocent's condemnations. What is more surprising, Philip Augustus and his son Prince Louis decided to brave the threat of excommunication and respond to the rebels' plea for help. In the following months, Prince Louis began again to prepare for an invasion of England so that he could claim the English crown that had been offered him. The plans not only occupied French and English knights who might have joined the crusade, it even took

---

[34] PL 214:241.
[35] Cheney and Semple, p. 221, no. 85.

ships from as far away as Genoa, ships that might have been used to transport crusaders.[36]

Prince Louis sent envoys to the pope in the spring to justify his actions, and according to one report they found him deeply disturbed by the prospect of war between John and Louis.

> Woe is me, in this matter God's Church cannot fail to be confounded. For if the king of England is defeated we are confounded with him, since he is our vassal and we are bound to defend him. If the lord Louis is defeated the Roman church is injured by his injury and his injury is ours. We always hoped, and still hope, that he would be an arm of the Roman church in all its needs, a solace in oppression, and a refuge against persecution.[37]

Louis landed at Dover on 21 May 1216, on a fruitless adventure that lasted two years.

But the preparations for the crusade proceeded. In previous calls for crusaders, more often than not ignored, Innocent had made general appeals and perhaps relied on a cardinal or two to recruit. But this time, in 1213, in addition to cardinal legates, he had appointed papal commissioners for each region and at the same time he had announced the general council for 1215. The commissioners—bishops, abbots, academics—were generally men who were from the region in question, who had worked with the papacy before, and who were considered reliable. They were required to submit annual reports on recruiting and fund raising, and they (and all the prelates of Europe) knew that in two years they would be meeting the pope face to face in Rome. Two years of temporizing would be difficult to explain. By 1213 they also knew the price paid by those who antagonized the pope. Quite apart from the catastrophes that had struck the people of Constantinople and of southern France, there were the dozens of bishops who had been removed from their posts as dogs that did not bark. So despite the diversions of regional wars, the business of the crusade progressed.[38]

---

[36] Cheney, *Innocent III and England*, pp. 391–393.

[37] Translated from Roger Wendover's chronicle by Cheney, who says the account "has an authentic air" (*Innocent III and England*, p. 392, and n. 21). See also Brenda Bolton, "Philip Augustus and John: Two Sons in Innocent III's Vineyard?" in *The Church and Sovereignty c. 590–1918: Essays in Honour of Michael Wilks*, ed. D. Wood (Oxford, 1991), pp. 113–134, at 132–134, repr. Bolton, *Innocent III: Studies*.

[38] Powell, *Anatomy*, pp. 21–26 et passim.

CHAPTER TEN

THE END (1215–1216)

Pope Innocent III, son of Trasmondo of the counts of Segni, and of Clarina of the noble families of the City, was a man of acute intelligence and tenacious memory, learned in divine and human literature, eloquent in speech, both in Latin and the vernacular, well trained in chant and psalmody. He was of medium stature and handsome appearance. He avoided both prodigality and avarice, though he was more generous in providing alms and food, less so in other things except when necessity required it. He was severe against the rebellious and the contumacious, but kind toward the humble and the devout. He was strong and consistent, magnanimous and astute, a defender of the faith and a foe of heresy. In matters of justice he was unbending but in mercy he was compassionate. He was humble in prosperity and patient in adversity, by nature somewhat impatient, but easily forgiving.[1]

So wrote the anonymous Biographer of Innocent, about half way through the pontificate. It was a remarkably fair and thorough assessment, though suffering from one omission: Innocent was obsessed with recapturing the Holy Land. It was an omission the Biographer corrected in a later chapter, when he wrote that among Innocent's many concerns, "he aspired most fervently to the support and recovery of the Holy Land."[2]

Religious believers have always been inclined to see divine judgments in historical events, especially events that are particularly striking. Nearly everything in the Judaeo-Christian Bible encouraged believers to do so. Several centuries before Innocent, an English poet had Beowulf say before he went to fight Grendel, "Whichever one death fells must deem it a just judgement by God."[3] Several centuries later, when the English destroyed the Spanish Armada, both Protestant English and Catholic Spanish saw in the defeat the hand of God. Protestants welcomed the confirmation that God was on their side, Catholics, faced with God's punishment for their sins,

---

[1] *Gesta*, PL 214:xvii = Gress-Wright, p. 1.
[2] *Gesta*, PL 214:lxxxix = Gress-Wright, p. 67.
[3] *Beowulf*, trans. Seamus Heaney (New York, 2000), p. 31.

could resolve to reform their lives in the hope of conquering another day.[4]

Although Innocent forbad clergy to participate in trial by ordeal or battle because it "tempted God.,"[5] that is, it required God to give judgment in a judicial procedure, he remained very much in the tradition of looking after the fact for divine judgments in human affairs. His motto was, after all, "Show me, Lord, a sign of thy favor." Innocent began his career in the papal curia at a time when Pope Gregory VIII and his advisers saw the fall of Jerusalem as a sign of divine wrath because of the sins of Christian princes, and Innocent carried that conviction throughout his lifetime. He longed for the ultimate sign of God's blessing on Christendom, the recovery of Jerusalem. In the meantime, he had probably seen his election as such a sign and he threw himself into the reform, organization, defense, and expansion of Christendom. He found another such sign, at least for a while, in the unexpected reunion of Greek and Latin Christendom. The parliaments within the Papal State and the Regno in 1207 and 1208 were surely seen as welcome signs of the Lord's favor, but the most invigorating sign had been the Christian victory at Las Navas de Tolosa, which moved Innocent to the great effort that resulted in Lateran IV and the Fifth Crusade. The letter of 1213 that announced the crusade and the council said that the time was right, "since the Lord is showing a sign of his favor."[6]

During the months that followed that letter, the signs had multiplied: Philip's acceptance of Ingeborg, the submission of John, the success of Frederick of Sicily in Germany and his submission to papal expectations. Lateran IV itself was an extraordinary achievement, a parliament of all Christendom that Innocent had to see as God's blessing on his efforts. The previous century had been full of talk about the coming of the anti-Christ and the end of time. Before his death in 1202, Joachim of Fiore had predicted the imminent beginning of a new age, accompanied by the conversion of Jews and Gentiles. Innocent was aware of those predictions, drew on them, and hoped to play his part in their fulfillment.[7]

---

[4] Garrett Mattingly, *The Defeat of the Spanish Armada*, 2nd ed. (London, 1983), p. 349.

[5] Reg. 14:138 = PL 216:502.

[6] Reg. 16:30 = PL 216:823. Text and translation of this letter, *Vineam domini*, can be found in Cheney and Semple, pp. 144–147, no. 51.

[7] Egger, "Joachim von Fiore, Rainer von Ponza and die römische Kurie," pp.

As he set out in the spring of 1216 to visit the northern part of the Patrimonium—Viterbo, Orvieto, Todi, Perugia—it was another triumphant tour into a region he had not visited since the first year of his pontificate. Orvieto sits on a pillar of tuff that seems thrust up like a mushroom from the surrounding countryside. This was the city that at the beginning of Innocent's pontificate had resisted his authority and murdered the young rector that he sent as his vicar.[8] Innocent arrived on 28 April, and the following Sunday he said mass and preached to the people, calling on them to take the cross. He bestowed the cross on a clamoring throng until he had to retire for a while to rest. Later in the day, despite a falling rain, an even larger crowd gathered in an open field, overflowing into the surrounding houses and trees to hear the pope preach. He stood under a portico, but soon the downpour came in such torrents that the people avidly seeking his word were thoroughly soaked. Innocent himself was overwhelmed with joy at their enthusiasm and again worked himself to exhaustion, affixing crosses to all the would-be crusaders. The rains would cause flooding and considerable destruction to people and property, but if Innocent saw a sign, it was in the wondrous fervor of the people, not in the hostile elements.[9] The signs of God's favor continued to multiply. This time, unlike the other periods of optimism, he would not live to see his hopes disappointed.

* * *

For the eighteen years he was pope, Innocent carried with him, along with his official titles, two conceptions of his office that were not easily reconciled, the one stressing service, the other dominion. Both were powerful ideas in his mind. Every letter that left his curia began by identifying him as "Innocent, bishop, servant of the servants of God." It was a formula that popes had used since Gregory the Great, and Innocent took it as the theme for his sermon when

---

129–162; Elizabeth Siberry, *Criticism of Crusading: 1095–1274* (Oxford, 1985), pp. 199–204; Robert E. Lerner, *The Feast of Saint Abraham: Medieval Millenarians and the Jews* (Philadelphia, 2001), pp. 1–37.

[8] Carol Lansing, *Power and Purity: Cathar Heresy in Medieval Europe*, (New York, 1998), pp. 3, 29–37.

[9] This account is based on two local accounts published in Michele Maccarrone, "La Notizia della visita di Innocenzo III ad Orvieto nel cod. M 465 della Morgan Library di New York," *Studi su Innocenzo III* (Padua, 1972), pp. 3–9 at 8–9.

consecrated pope.[10] It was a theme of his letter to the Latin clergy of Constantinople when he finally accepted the fall of the city as God's will. The notion that the pope was called to service was further stressed by Innocent's frequent use of Romans 1:14, "To the Greeks and to the barbarians, to the wise and to the unwise, I am a debtor."[11] It was not easy to imagine how a "servant of servants" should behave. Francis of Assisi may have been a rare model, though even he was strict in disciplining his own followers. It may be that the only pope ever truly to act like a servant of the servants of God came later in the century, Celestine V. His pontificate was a chaotic disaster and he finally resigned. Nevertheless, Innocent took these texts seriously. His letters are full of evidence that he would try to respond generously to anyone who humbly and persistently sought his help. It seems likely that he saw all of his actions as being in the long-range interests of the people he served. As anomalous as it may seem for a man with such authority to call himself the 'servant of the servants of God,'—an irony commented on by Innocent's contemporaries[12]—the idea survives in secular democracies when heads of state are called "public servants." The idea was echoed when President Harry Truman told the American people, "The responsibility of a great state is to serve and not to dominate the world."[13]

Competing with the conception of service, however, was that of dominion or lordship. Perhaps Innocent's favorite biblical text was: "See, I have set you this day over nations and over kingdoms, to root up and to pull down, to destroy and to overthrow, to build and to plant" (Jeremiah, 1:10). Whereas models of service at high levels were rare, models of lordship were everywhere in Innocent's society, in both ecclesiastical and secular positions. Although Innocent genuinely believed he was the servant of the servants of God and that he was a debtor to all, his actual behavior flowed more from "I have set you this day over nations and over kingdoms. . . ." Innocent frequently protested his unworthiness, but he nevertheless believed that these words of Jeremiah referred to Christ and to the pope as Christ's vicar.

---

[10] Stephan Kuttner, "Universal Pope or Servant of God's Servants: The canonists, papal titles, and Innocent III," *Revue de droit canonique* 31 (1981): 109–150; repr. in Kuttner, *Studies in the History of Medieval Canon Law* (Hampshire, 1990).

[11] E.g., Reg. 15:59 = PL 216:860.

[12] Kuttner, "Universal Pope," pp. 128–130.

[13] David McCullough, *Truman* (New York, 1992), p. 360.

Over the course of a papacy of eighteen and a half years, Innocent gave many expressions to his ideas about the pontifical office, its place in society, and its relationship with secular power. His frequent claim to *plenitudo potestatis*, the plenitude of power, might give the impression that he set no limits on his authority, but that is not the case. Innocent never intended to replace the various temporal or secular governments of Christendom, and he was sincere when he asserted his intent to respect the rights of secular rulers. He quoted the gospel on the distinction between what is God's and what is Caesar's, and with canon 42 of Lateran IV, he cautioned clergy against infringing on the legitimate sphere of secular rulers. One sign that Innocent recognized some limitations on his temporal power is the fact that in calling for secular crusaders, he always asked for volunteers. When city-states and princes called for military service, they did not recognize the right of their subjects simply to refuse. Innocent did. He exerted pressure, he offered incentives, he tried to shame those who might be reluctant, but he did not command, as he did in matters where he was sure of his authority. Similarly, to support the crusade, he levied a tax on the clergy, but the laity were asked for voluntary contributions.

Innocent even acknowledged limits on his spiritual powers. He claimed the exclusive right, as vicar of Christ, to dissolve the spiritual marriage between a bishop and his diocese,[14] and he would grant dispensations to permit otherwise illegal marriages if required by "urgent necessity and evident utility."[15] Had he used similar arguments to justify the dissolution of a valid marriage he would have acquired an extremely useful (and, for a corrupt pope, profitable) weapon, but he did not. On the contrary, he and his curia agreed that he did not have the authority to dissolve a valid marriage, however much he might want to do so.[16]

Still, his most basic principle was that as vicar of Christ, he was responsible for the whole human race and that the whole human race should be subject to his religious authority. Everyone was in some sense subject to the pope and the pope was subject to no one.

---

[14] Reg. 1:326.

[15] RNI, no. 181, cited by Constance M. Rousseau, "A Papal Matchmaker: Principle and Pragmatism during Innocent III's Pontificate," *Journal of Medieval History*, 24 (1998): 259–271 at p. 263.

[16] Reg. 15:106 = 216:617–618.

As he wrote to the patriarch of Constantinople, Jesus had bestowed on Peter (whose place the pope occupied) the whole world to govern.[17]

Papal independence was to be guaranteed by papal rule of the Papal State, where the pope was temporal as well as spiritual ruler. The Papal State was an anomaly. On the one hand, it seemed obvious that the man who held the title emperor of the Romans should in fact rule Rome. It certainly seemed obvious to the Hohenstaufen emperors. On the other hand, the popes had reasonable legal claims that central Italy had been conceded to them by the emperors (Innocent did not use the specious Donation of Constantine in this regard).[18] Whatever flaws there were in the legal argument were remedied when Innocent obtained in addition the written concessions of Otto IV and Frederick II.[19] The fundamental motive for this papal policy was the experience of all Christendom that when princes ruled the lands of a bishop, they were also likely to exercise undue influence on the selection and the behavior of that bishop. Some modern authors have argued that the experience of twentieth-century popes has shown that they have not needed an independent state to act as independent religious leaders, but the controversies over Pius XII's policies toward the Jews indicate that the pope might have acted differently had he been the secure ruler of his own principality. The experience of the patriarchs of Moscow under the Soviet regime also serves to confirm the fears of the medieval popes. In any case, Innocent was determined to shape an independent papal state.

He also clearly welcomed any opportunity to extend his secular authority elsewhere as a buttress to his spiritual authority. Innocent never turned down any offer to make him the secular lord of some principality, welcoming the submission of Aragon in 1204 and England and Ireland in 1214. Accepting John's submission in 1214, he wrote:

> Jesus Christ ... has so established in the Church His kingdom and His priesthood that the one is a kingdom of priests and the other a royal priesthood, as is testified by Moses in the Law and by Peter in

---

[17] Reg. 2:200 (209).

[18] Innocent referred to the Donation only once in his writings. See O. Hageneder, "Das Sonne-Mond-Gleichnis bei Innocenz III," *Mitteilungen des Instituts für Österreichische Geschichtsforschung* 65 (1957): 356, referring to a sermon for the feast of St. Silvester (PL 481–484), and Domenico Maffei, *La Donazione di Costantino nei Giuristi Medievali* (Milan, 1964), pp. 46–69, 293–4. Concerning the claims to central Italy, see Moore, "Pope Innocent III, Sardinia," pp. 85–87, and the works cited there.

[19] Manfred Laufs, *Politik und Recht bei Innozenz III.* (Cologne, 1980), pp. 308–309.

his Epistle; and over all He has set one whom He has appointed as His Vicar on earth, so that, as every knee is bowed to Jesus, of things in heaven, and things in earth, and things under the earth, so all men should obey His Vicar and strive that there may be one fold and one shepherd. All secular kings for the sake of God so venerate this Vicar, that unless they seek to serve him devotedly they doubt if they are reigning properly. To this, dearly beloved son, you have paid wise attention; and by the merciful inspiration of Him in whose hands are the hearts of kings which He turns whithersoever He wills, you have decided to submit in a temporal sense yourself and your kingdom to whom you knew them to be spiritually subject, so that kingdom and priesthood, like body and soul, for the great good and profit of each, might be united in the single person of Christ's Vicar. He has deigned to work this wonder, who being alpha and omega has caused the end to fulfill the beginning and the beginning to anticipate the end, so that those provinces which from of old have had the Holy Roman Church as their proper teacher in spiritual matters should now in temporal things also have her as their special lord.[20]

Innocent's parliaments at Viterbo and San Germano and then the great Lateran Council anticipated the Christendom he envisaged, a kind of federation of principalities and city-states, all acknowledging his expansive spiritual authority and all recognizing his right to call their representatives to deal with matters, temporal and spiritual, that bore on the spiritual health of Christendom. In the best of all worlds, they would also offer temporal submission as well, so that the pope could more readily provide orderly government leading to peace and justice for all subjects, benefits he was in fact providing in central Italy.[21] Latin Christianity and the authority of the papacy were the principal sources of what cultural and institutional unity there was in Europe,[22] and Innocent certainly wanted to enhance that unity so as to deal more effectively with internal and external threats. His confidence that papal authority overrode secular authority when necessary is clearly manifested in the privileges awarded to crusaders, exempting them from secular courts and from secular debt obligations.[23]

---

[20] Trans. Cheney and Semple, pp. 177–178, no. 67. Where I have "special lord" at the end, for "dominam . . . specialem," they have "peculiar sovereign."

[21] Lackner, "Studien zur Verwaltung des Kirchenstaates," pp. 185–186.

[22] Robert Bartlett, *The Making of Europe: Conquest, Colonization and Cultural Change, 950–1350* (Princeton, 1993), p. 250; William Daly, "Christian Fraternity, the Crusaders, and the Security of Constantinople, 1097–1204: The Precarious Survival of an Ideal," *Medieval Studies*, 23 (1960) 43–91.

[23] James A. Brundage, *Medieval Canon Law and the Crusader* (Madison, 1969), pp. 170–177.

Similarly, he did not hesitate to annul oaths of political allegiance when he thought circumstances warranted his doing do. In his understanding of his authority, he did not go as far as did canon lawyers and popes later in the thirteenth century, many of whom recognized no limits to the authority of the pope,[24] but in practice, Innocent would find justification for just about any action he thought necessary for the good of Christendom.

It was a political vision, but it was also a pastoral vision. Innocent accepted the image of the pope as shepherd (*pastor*), but the shepherd's role as he saw it was not passive or even pacific. The shepherd's staff, he said in a sermon, is sharp at the end so that the shepherd can poke the slow and fat sheep, it is straight in the middle so that he can support the sick and infirm sheep; it is curved at the top so that he can gather in the sheep who stray.[25] Innocent was a shepherd, but a decidedly lordly sort of shepherd.

Many critics of Innocent's political and pastoral vision have implicitly applied two basic principles: (1) that the secular national state was the natural and proper product of the historical development of Europe, and (2) that ecclesiastical authorities should play no role in the formation or policies of those secular states. By those standards, Innocent's use of his office frequently constituted "interference" deserving of condemnation. His "interference" has been especially galling for German historians, who have seen his policies in the empire as promoting civil war and ultimately preventing the national unification of Germany. Even Helene Tillmann, whose judgment of Innocent is generally quite favorable, finds Innocent guilty of indefensible interference in the affairs of Germany and the Holy Roman Empire.[26] The charge is not anachronistic, since Innocent's contemporaries made the same complaints, but it should be noted that the princes who complained bitterly of papal "interference" when papal policies went against their own interests were often the same princes who

---

[24] See Brian Tierney, *Foundations of the Conciliar Theory: The Contribution of the Medieval Canonists from Gratian to the Great Schism* (Cambridge, 1955), pp. 87–95; Pennington, *Pope and Bishops*, pp. 13–74; and Othmar Hageneder, "Anmerkungen zur Dekretale *Per venerabilem* Innocenz' III. (X 4.17.13)," *Studien zur Geschichte des Mittelalters: Jürgen Petersohn zum 65. Geburtstag*, ed. Matthias Thumser, A. Wenz-Haubfleisch, and P. Wiegand (Stuttgart, 2000), pp. 159–173.

[25] PL 217:410.

[26] *Pope Innocent III*, pp. 26, 120–121.

routinely sought papal "interference" on their own behalf. King Richard had little tolerance for papal actions in his territories, but he urged the pope to use spiritual censures against the supporters of Philip Augustus.[27] Philip Augustus objected to Innocent's interventions in the kingdom of France, but he routinely inserted into the loyalty oaths he extracted from subordinates a provision that they would suffer ecclesiastical censure if they failed to keep their vows. In his opposition to Otto IV, Philip Augustus also urged Innocent to release all of Otto's supporters from their oaths of fealty.[28] Count Albert of Dagsburg and Metz, Duke Henry of Lotharingia and Brabant, and Count Henry of Kuik joined ecclesiastical prelates in urging the pope to use ecclesiastical censures on behalf of Otto and against the supporters of Philip of Swabia.[29] Even the Venetians wanted to use papal excommunication as a weapon to fortify their agreements.[30] In any case, if one begins by believing that papal action in secular matters was inherently wrong, then Innocent's pursuit of his vision was certainly disruptive and improper.

But one could begin with principles like these: (1) a European federation under a papal presidency, had it succeeded, would have had a claim to historical legitimacy equal to that of the sovereign national states that did in fact emerge, (2) a unified Europe might have been better for the people of Europe, offering greater peace and prosperity than did Europe fragmented into rival and pugnacious sovereign states. To be sure, it is not easy for most twentieth-century historians to accept the historical legitimacy of a theocracy, especially one headed by a government that showed little respect for the civil liberties treasured by modern democratic societies, especially freedom of thought, speech, and religion. On the other hand, these civil liberties were not highly regarded by most of the European states that evolved in the wake of the papal failure to unite them (consider Spanish treatment of Muslims and Jews). Those liberties have also been deliberately and systematically suppressed by many secular societies of twentieth-century Europe—at home and in their imperial possessions. It is entirely possible that a European commonwealth

[27] RNI, no. 5.

[28] Van Cleve, *Emperor Frederick*, pp. 74–5, citing L. Delisle, *Catalogue des actes de Philippe-Auguste*, no. 1251.

[29] RNI, nos. 8, 10.

[30] *Gesta*, PL 214:cxliii = Gress-Wright, p. 229.

under a papal presidency might have developed over time a more tolerant attitude toward religious and intellectual diversity than what Europe was to experience in the heat of religious and political conflict, although it must be admitted that no secular government had the single-minded and long-term commitment to religious conformity that the papacy displayed, right into the second half of the twentieth century.

One might argue that even though a European federation could have given more domestic peace to Europeans it would have been even more dangerous to its non-Christian neighbors than were the separate European states. Spanish Islam survived as long as it did largely because of divisions among the Christians powers of Spain, and it is certainly true that Innocent wanted to unite Latin Christendom precisely so that he could attack Islam in Spain and the eastern Mediterranean. The crusades were, from the popes' point of view, a legitimate attempt to regain for Christianity what Muslims had wrongly taken by force in the seventh and eighth centuries. On the other hand, later European expansion was fueled at least in part by competition among European states, competition manifested in destructive wars throughout the world. However presumptuous it may seem for a pope to have divided the world between Portugal and Spain with the Line of Demarcation in 1493, doing so probably saved many European and non-European lives. A congress of Latin Christendom, similar to the one that met at the Lateran complex in 1215, meeting regularly to resolve differences, might have made European expansion somewhat less destructive than it proved to be, just as the Berlin Conference of 1884–1886 prevented bloodshed through its outrageous but cooperative arrangements for the partitioning of Africa.

All this is not to claim superiority for the political/pastoral vision that enlivened Innocent's conception of his office. It is rather to assert a historical neutrality, to say that his aspiration to expand papal authority throughout all Christendom and the world had as much inherent legitimacy as did the aspiration of secular princes to expand theirs. It is also to note that the program of Innocent III had a moral vision loftier than that of any of the secular princes— a society based on the rule of law and the peaceful resolution of conflict. Moreover, Innocent was less moved by the desire to enhance personal and familial wealth than any secular prince of his day and he was more humane than most.

Those secular princes were, after all, a brutal bunch, and the clergy often suffered from their brutality. Although Innocent III was not personally the victim of that raw military power, the danger was always before him. He had visited the shrine of Thomas Becket, the best known victim of the secular sword. Among those prelates murdered during his pontificate were the bishop of Würzburg,[31] the bishop of Ploaghe and two monastic officials in Sardinia,[32] the bishop of Liège (Lüttich),[33] the patriarch of Antioch,[34] and the papal legate Cardinal Peter of Castelnau. The young Roman citizen whom Innocent sent to Orvieto as papal rector was kidnaped and murdered.[35] The archbishop of Salerno was carried off to prison in Germany, and the papal legate Peter cardinal-deacon of St. Maria in Vialata was beaten and robbed in Lombardy.[36] Innocent tried to rein in the violence of princes, but he expected every prelate to be willing to suffer exile or martyrdom, and he stated his own willingness to give up his life for his sheep.[37]

In pursuit of his vision, however, Innocent himself was certainly not reluctant to use force. The violence of the Christian middle ages has been seen as an anomaly, seemingly in glaring contrast to "Thou shalt not kill," and "Turn the other cheek." But those pacific passages are not the only kind found in the Bible. The minds of the educated were shaped by the Old Testament/Hebrew Scripture, and those texts were full of violence exercised with divine approval. Every week, the monks of Europe read all one hundred fifty psalms, where passages like these abound: "Ask of me, and I will make the nations your heritage, and the ends of the earth your possession. You shall break them with a rod of iron, and dash them in pieces like a potter's vessel" (Ps. 2); "You made my enemies turn their backs to me and those who hated me I destroyed. They cried for help, but there was no one to save them: they cried to the Lord but he did not answer them" (Ps. 18); "Gird your sword on your thigh, O mighty one, in your glory and majesty. In your majesty ride on victoriously for the cause of truth and to defend the right; let your right hand

---

[31] Reg. 5:154 (155).
[32] Moore, "Pope Innocent III, Sardinia," p. 89.
[33] RNI, no. 56, p. 153; RNI, no. 80, p. 219.
[34] Moore, "Peter of Lucedio," p. 234.
[35] See Lansing, *Power and Purity*, pp. 3, 29–37.
[36] Reg. 1:3, 1:121–123.
[37] Reg. 8:141 = PL 216:1455.

teach your dread deeds. Your arrows are sharp in the heart of the
king's enemies; the peoples fall under you" (Ps. 45); "The righteous
will rejoice when they see vengeance done; they will bathe their feet
in the blood of the wicked" (Ps. 58); "But God will shatter the heads
of his enemies, the hairy crown of those who walk in their guilty
ways" (Ps. 68). Victory in combat was a sign of God's favor: "By
this I know that you are pleased with me; because my enemy has
not triumphed over me" (Ps. 41). Innocent knew his Bible extremely
well.

* * *

The first part of Jeremiah's prophecy placed Innocent over nations
and kingdoms, the second part called on him "to root up and to
pull down, to destroy and to overthrow, to build and to plant." In
his implementation of his office, Innocent understood this prophecy
in the broadest sense, to do whatever was necessary to bring about
the world he imagined. He was part of a growing tendency among
the educated to see the active life (Martha's role) in the world as
equal if not superior to the contemplative life of prayer in the
monastery (Mary's role).[38] His preference for the active life can be
seen not only in his own life but in his common practice of calling
monks from their monasteries to be agents of his policies. The over-
all consequence of Innocent's rooting up and planting will probably
always be a matter of dispute.

Innocent rooted up a great deal. To reform the clergy, he chastised and if necessary removed ineffective or insubordinate prelates.
The Biographer lists the following episcopal sees in which men had
been removed or their appointments thwarted: Cologne, Worms,
Mainz, Hildesheim, Würzburg, Gurk, Salzburg, Nuremberg, Milan,
Asti, Ivrea, Toulouse, Béziers, Vence, Viviers, Langres, Palermo,
together with a number of abbots throughout Christendom.[39] Since
the Gesta does not carry the story beyond 1208, the list needs to be
expanded to include, among others, the bishop of Melfi[40] and those
removed during the Albigensian Crusade: the archbishops of Auch
and Narbonne, and the bishops of Carcasonne, Rodez, and Vienne.[41]

---

[38] Giles Constable, *Three Studies in Medieval Religious and Social Thought* (Cambridge.
1995), pp. 87–111.
[39] *Gesta*, PL 214:clxxii–clxxiii = Gress-Wright, pp. 319–320.
[40] Reg. 15:115 = PL 216:625.
[41] Reg. 14:32–34.

Many other prelates, like Stephen Langton, were suspended. A conviction of simony (the payment of money for ecclesiastical office) would cost a prelate his office. It seems very likely that this record must have influenced the behavior of prelates in ways Innocent thought desirable, but it is difficult to prove.

His reforms in the curia in 1208 had a similar purpose, but he did not end the ambiguous moral tone of the curia. It seems true that much of the criticism of the curia in the following century arose from the resentment of people who did not want to pay taxes for the services they received,[42] but Innocent still might have done more to root up questionable curial practices. He showed an awareness of the corrupting power of gifts when, after accepting the gift from the repentant bishop of Hildesheim, he countered with his own gift of greater value.[43] The Biographer says that he hated venality and set out to eliminate it from the Roman church. No one in the curia was to demand anything except those who prepared documents, and they were put on fixed fees. But at the same time, he permitted the officials to receive gifts "freely given,"[44] and in fact, those visiting the curia were routinely expected to give gifts. Under Innocent, the curial officials apparently made a distinction between visitation gifts from those visiting the curia, which were accepted, and gifts offered by those who had a case before them—an overly subtle distinction, since visitors were nearly always about to become petitioners. And petitioners were expected to present gifts when they departed for home.[45] The Biographer considers it high praise when he says that Innocent, as cardinal, never demanded anything from anyone and never accepted any gift "before the business had been terminated."[46] But if it had been Innocent's highest priority to root up venality, he might have forbidden his officials to accept any gifts at all and established a strict system of fixed fees for services. He also could have

---

[42] John A. Yunck, *The Lineage of Lady Meed. The Development of Mediaeval Venality Satire* (Notre Dame, 1963), pp. 112–117 *et passim*.

[43] *Gesta*, PL 214:lxxxviii = Gress-Wright, pp. 65–66.

[44] *Gesta*, PL 214:lxxx = Gress-Wright, p. 60.

[45] Thomas of Marlborough reported that the cardinals of the curia would not accept the visitation gift of one hundred marks until they had been persuaded that Thomas and his fellow monks did not have a case in the curia at the moment. But they certainly knew that Thomas was there on legal business. Thomas left Rome surreptitiously in 1206 because he had no money for the customary gifts. *Chronicon abbatiae de Evesham*, pp. 146, 200.

[46] *Gesta*, PL 214:xix = Gress-Wright, p. 2.

found the money to put all curial officials on salaries. He certainly found the money for many other things, for elaborate building programs on behalf of churches, for the wars in southern Italy, and especially for the crusades.[47] But there is no record of his trying to eliminate gift giving at all levels of the papal government, and Rome's reputation for avarice was to endure, fairly or not.

The tone of moral ambiguity remained, despite Innocent's reforms. Jacques de Vitry was with the curia immediately after Innocent's death and was depressed by all the secular business that seemed to occupy the papal court, "so that scarcely anything could be said about spiritual matters." On the other hand, Jacques found the new pope, Honorius III, to be "a good and religious old man, very open and kind," who gave generously to the poor, and he was encouraged to see the evangelical lives of the friars and sisters minor (the followers of Francis of Assisi). They led exemplary Christian lives and influenced others to greater virtue. The fact that these holy people were revered and supported by the pope and the cardinals was a sign that the curia did in fact value spiritual matters.[48]

* * *

Innocent has been accused of destroying the Holy Roman Empire and depriving the German people of the chance for a unified nation. The gist of the accusation is that Innocent should have accepted and crowned Philip, the man most able to unify the empire. But it is difficult to see why he should have, considering the danger to the papacy and to the church that Philip represented. Innocent pointed out more than once that Philip was excommunicate, that he had occupied and ravaged papal territory as duke of Tuscany, that he had imprisoned the archbishop of Salerno, and that he continued to support the depredations of Markward of Anweiler in the Regno. Innocent argued (1) that Philip had accepted his election despite his

---

[47] For southern Italy, see *Gesta*, PL 214:xlii, lii–liii, lvii–lviii = Gress-Wright, pp. 21, 36–37, 43; and for his subsidies of many churches and monasteries, see *Gesta*, PL 214:ccxxvii = Gress-Wright, pp. 353–354. For Innocent's tentative proposal to impose a ten percent income tax on cathedrals in order to cover curial expenses, see Richard Kay, "Gerald of Wales and the Fourth Lateran Council," *Viator* 29 (1998) 79–93, especially pp. 79, 84. For a survey of Innocent's finances, see Sayers, *Innocent III*, pp. 71–76.

[48] Jacques de Vitry (Jacobus de Vitriaco), *Lettres de Jacques de Vitry*, ed. R. B. C. Huygens (Leiden, 1960), pp. 74–76.

oath to support the young Frederick, (2) that Otto, not Philip, had been crowned king of the Germans by the proper archbishop and at the proper place, (3) that the pope, as the creator of the empire in the west, was not bound to crown just any candidate presented, regardless of worth, (4) that Philip gave every indication that he would continue the anti-papal tradition of the Hohenstaufens, who had encouraged schismatic popes and confiscated papal territories in Italy. He made the additional point that the approval of Philip would make a hereditary monarchy more likely, to the disadvantage of the electors.[49] Whether or not these arguments were more persuasive than those of the Hohenstaufen party, they do not seem dishonest or deceptive, and they gave Innocent a moral and legal alternative to the supine acceptance of Hohenstaufen domination of all Italy and of the papacy. It is also difficult to see why Innocent should be blamed for the fact that the German princes refused to follow his advice to stop fighting among themselves and seek a peaceful resolution.[50] They might even have decided, as Napoleon was to do, that papal coronation would no longer be a part of the process of selecting and installing an emperor. We might add that in the long run, the German nation probably would have been better off if the German kings had left Italy to the Italians, as Innocent wanted them to do. The German nation should not be listed among the things that Innocent destroyed.

In rooting up and destroying, Innocent's deliberate use of violence was not especially destructive by the standards of the day. He valued peace and knew the suffering caused by war. He knew that the civil war in Germany brought about the "despoiling of churches, the slaughter of bodies, and the endangerment of souls."[51] He condemned the shedding of blood at Zara[52] and he was appalled at the atrocities committed in the sack of Constantinople.[53] But lordship was the stronger model than that of servant in Innocent's actions. He was still the product of an aristocratic culture that took for granted the suffering of warfare, especially suffering among the lower orders, and embraced the heroic killing celebrated in epics like *The Song of Roland*.

---

[49] RNI, nos. 15, 18, 21, 29, 33, 62, 79.
[50] RNI, no. 79.
[51] RNI, no. 1.
[52] Reg. 5:160 (161).
[53] Reg. 8:126 = PL 215:701.

Besides the authority of the Old Testament, he had the authority of
the great Cistercian St. Bernard and of the great canon lawyer
Gratian to reassure him that warfare on behalf of the faith was
praiseworthy.[54] He chided the men of Sicily for failing to resist the
Germans, saying that they had grown effeminate from "too much
peace."[55]

Some things Innocent destroyed inadvertently. He certainly did
not intend the conquest of Constantinople, and he did not intend
the extended destruction that came with the Albigensian Crusade,
but he accepted both. The bombs that he threw were not well aimed
and had unintended consequences, but they exploded and destroyed,
nonetheless, and they impressed upon the Christian world the destructive power of the papacy. He continued to promote military crusades
throughout his life, despite what he had heard about Zara and
Constantinople. He may or may not have been horrified (we have no
evidence, one way or the other) when his legates in France reported that
the crusaders had "fed into the mouth of the sword nearly twenty
thousand people, without regard to status, sex, or age," but his legates
did not seem to think that expressions of regret were called for in
their report.[56] In another context, Innocent referred to the way God
punished innocent Israelites for the sins of King David (2 Sam. 24)
and told the Venetians that "it is neither new nor absurd when subjects are punished for rulers."[57] His sporadic and half-hearted defense
of the rights of Count Raymond VI of Toulouse showed that he
sensed that the results of the crusade had been less than just, but
he accepted Simon de Montfort's confiscation of Raymond's land,
just as he accepted the Latin conquest of Constantinople.

There were some things that Innocent left untouched that he might
well have tried to root out. The system he inherited provided that
property once acquired by clergy could never be alienated. The rule
was not always observed, but the amount of property controlled by
clergy was enormous throughout most of European history. It was
inevitable that secular princes would expect to turn that clerical
wealth to their own purposes by controlling the appointment of eccle-

---

[54] Siberry, *Criticism*, pp. 209–210.
[55] Reg. 1:26.
[56] Reg. 12:108 = PL 216:137–141.
[57] Reg. 9:139 = Gress-Wright, p. 257 (*Gesta*, ch. 104).

siastical officers. Even though the great wealth of the upper (
was a major source of humanitarian and educational benefits,⁵⁸ it
continued to be an irresistible temptation to princes and worldly clerics and it continued to undermine the credibility of clerics as Christian
ministers. If Innocent considered this to be a problem at all, he evidently did not think it one he could solve. Ultimately there would
be violent and unilateral confiscation of clerical property during the
Protestant Reformation and during the "democratic" revolutions of
more recent centuries.

Secular princes were not the only ones seeking to tap clerical
wealth; so also did the popes. Innocent himself expanded a practice
that was to grow after him: papal provisions and reservations. The
pope would claim a particular office in some outlying region, usually that of a cathedral priest called a canon, and claim the exclusive right to appoint its holder. There are many examples of Innocent
rewarding papal clerks with such prebends in distant places. Later
popes would anticipate future openings by using a "papal reserva-
tion," reserving the position for a future papal appointment when
its present occupant moved on. In fact, within a century, the right
of appointment was even being applied routinely to bishoprics, offices
that in Innocent's day were still elective (though often controlled by
local princes).⁵⁹ This system of papal patronage did not even deliver
clerical offices from secular control, since the popes usually appointed
important prelates only with the approval of the local secular prince.
Innocent had been moving in that direction as his pontificate wore
on.⁶⁰ He advised the bishops of Auxerre and Orléans to try to accommodate the king, saying that "sometimes kings and princes are better overcome with kindness than with rigor."⁶¹ He accepted King
John's preferences for bishops in England, once the Canterbury affair
was settled.⁶²

* * *

---

[58] See for example, Michel Mollat, *The Poor in the Middle Ages*, pp. 87–90.

[59] Geoffrey Barraclough, *Papal Provisions: Aspects of Church History Constitutional, Legal and Administrative in the Later Middle Ages* (Oxford, 1935, repr. Westport CT, 1971), passim; Pennington, *Pope and Bishops*, pp. 115–153; Agostino Paravicini Bagliani, *Il Trono di Pietro* (Rome, 1996), pp. 104–106.

[60] Cheney, *Innocent III and England*, pp. 343–345, 394.

[61] Reg. 15:109 = PL 216:620.

[62] Cheney, *Innocent III and England*, p. 177.

But what did Innocent build and plant? A harder question to answer, since planters and plants are usually separated in time, and building is usually not as spectacular and noisy as destroying. Medieval farmers enjoyed remarkable successes in their planting. The agricultural revolution of the centuries before Innocent's reign witnessed unprecedented increases in the food supply. The essential ingredients were the application of new technology, such as the yoke collar for draft animals and the "heavy" plow with iron edges, expansion of the arable, and the introduction of new crops. Innocent's "planting" followed a similar pattern. But although the agricultural revolution of the eleventh and twelfth centuries certainly increased the productivity of Europe, by modern standards, the results were modest. One estimate is that with all the improvements, the yield was about three times the seed planted, a yield that is only about one tenth of modern yields.[63] How successful was Innocent's planting and what kind of yield constitutes success or failure?

Throughout his pontificate, Innocent saw the reform of the clergy as the necessary step toward the reform of the laity. That two-fold reform was necessary for the recovery of the Holy Land. His letters and the canons of the council reaffirm old requirements of the clergy, requirements that would be repeated centuries thereafter, since a perfect clergy would never be realized. The clergy should be educated, they should be celibate, they should avoid dishonesty and drunkenness, and so forth. Besides simple exhortation, though, Innocent introduced what might be called "new technology,"[64] that is, more centralized institutions intended to bring the behavior of clergy into closer harmony with their stated beliefs and with the rules they lived under. Innocent himself was a formidable organizer, who learned from his mistakes, at least on the practical level. The preparations for Lateran IV and for the fifth crusade were extremely well designed for the purposes at hand, and Lateran IV itself was largely addressed to organizational matters. With canon 13, Innocent sought to control the proliferation of religious fraternities by requiring all new ones to live under either the Benedictine rule (*vita monastica*) or the Augustinian rule (*vita apostolica*). His plan for reform through cen-

---

[63] Hans-Werner Goetz, *Life in the Middle Ages from the Seventh to the Thirteenth Century*, trans. Albert Wimmer (Notre Dame, 1993), p. 157.

[64] James B. Given speaks of the "technology of power" in *Inquisition and Medieval Society: Power, Discipline, and Resistance in Languedoc*, (Ithaca, 1997), passim.

tralization required archbishops to hold annual councils and regular clergy (men and women living under a rule) to hold general chapters every three years. What effect these new requirements had on the spiritual yield is difficult to say. It is certain that they were applied only sporadically throughout Europe, partly because of resistance to the ideas, partly because of sheer inertia. On the other hand, even sporadic application meant some changes along the lines Innocent intended,[65] and the ideas were to be invoked and applied into the twentieth century. Whether the "yield" can be seen as an improvement or a disappointment is a fairly subjective thing. It probably would have been disappointing to Innocent, but he had high expectations. He expected to bring Romagna and Tuscany under papal control and was disappointed in both, but he still left his successors a better defined and more secure Papal State than the one he inherited.[66] Perhaps something similar can be said about his organizational reforms.

Just as farmers brought new lands under cultivation, Innocent supervised and supported the expansion of Latin Christendom. The most dramatic expansion was the new Latin Empire of Constantinople. He did not plant it deliberately, but he was willing to see its establishment as a sign of God's favor and he did his best to cultivate it. This new field, however, soon returned to its previous owners. The Greeks regained Constantinople in 1261, and the most enduring legacy of the whole venture was the deep resentment and distrust that Greek Christians would feel toward Latin Christians, a legacy that survives to this day. On the other hand, the expansion of Latin Christendom along the southern Baltic coast and in southern Spain, although a violent business, was permanent.

As for new crops, Innocent introduced some himself and allowed

---

[65] See M. Maccarrone, "Le costituzioni del IV concilio Lateranense sui religiosi," *Dizionario degli istituti di perfezione*, 5 (Rome, 1975): 474–495, repr. in Maccarroni, *Nuovi studi su Innocenzo III*, pp. 1–45; Marion Gibbs and Jane Lang, *Bishops and Reform, 1215–1272, with special reference to the Lateran council of 1215* (Oxford, 1934); Peter Linehan, *The Spanish Church and the Papacy in the Thirteenth Century* (Cambridge, 1971); Pixton, *The German Episcopacy*; R. N. Swanson, *Religion and Devotion in Europe, c. 1215–c. 1515* (Cambridge, 1995), p. 99; Richard Kay, *The Council of Bourges 1225: A documentary history*, forthcoming. I am indebted to professor Kay for sending me a typescript of chapter eight of this book.

[66] For Tuscany, see Moore, "Pope Innocent III, Sardinia," pp. 85–87; for Romagna, see Glauco Maria Cantarella, "Innocenzo III e la Romagna," *Rivista di Storia della Chiesa in Italia* 52 (1998): 33–72, at 67–68.

others to flourish that he might have rooted up as weeds. He had little to do with the establishment of the Franciscans and the Dominicans, but both received his blessing. Their acceptance can be credited to the openness with which Innocent generally viewed new religious movements, as long as they submitted to ecclesiastical authority. Those two orders of friars are commonly credited with making Roman Catholic Christianity meaningful and palatable to the new urban classes of Europe. Giotto's fresco at Assisi that shows St. Francis holding up the collapsing church of Innocent has some historical justification. But there is no evidence that Innocent's approval meant that he had any great hopes for them. Other groups must have seemed more promising to him, such as the *Humiliati*, with their many congregations of pious clergy and lay people throughout northern Italy, and perhaps also the inspiring Trinitarians. The latter had been founded by a Paris theologian John of Matha for the mission of ransoming Christians held captive by the infidel, with one third of all their income reserved for that specific purpose. In his first year, Innocent approved their rule and shortly thereafter gave them a letter of introduction to present to the Muslim "king of Morocco" when they went to free Christian prisoners.[67]

The planting that can be attributed directly to Innocent falls mainly into three categories: his letters, the decrees of the council, and his personal writing. Innocent's letters of admonition and encouragement no doubt had their effect, but it is impossible to estimate. Many letters, however, were incorporated into three widely circulated legal collections during and immediately after his pontificate, and then were carried by the dozens into the official canon law collection approved by Pope Gregory IX in 1234. Generally speaking, those decretals embodied rational and useful principles, shaped by the best canonistic thought of the day and well designed for orderly church government. Innocent's treatment of canonization of saints provides an example of the rationalization of procedure: reports of miracles were no longer adequate; the life of the candidate for sainthood had now to be investigated carefully to make sure that canonization was appropriate.[68] He also authorized the use of medical opinion to

---

[67] Giulio Cipollone, *Cristianità-Islam. Cattività e Liberazione in Nome di Dio. Il tempo di Innocenzo III dopo 'il 1187'*, Miscellanea Historiae Pontificiae 60 (Rome, 1992): 394–404; Reg. 1:252, 481, and 549 (552); Reg. 2:9.

[68] Cheney, *Innocent III and England*, pp. 51–59; Paravicini Bagliani, *Il Trono*, pp. 107–108.

determine the cause of death in two cases of purported murder.[69]

Of course, what was rational and useful did not always work for the best. In general, the papal office and the church itself came to be seen more in legalistic terms than had been the case in the past, a process Innocent did not begin but certainly accelerated. On a more particular level, the ambiguous character of some of Innocent's legal contributions can be seen in his introduction of the inquisitorial method of prosecution. It replaced outmoded and awkward kinds of judicial procedure, but it also put great power into the hands of the "investigator/prosecutor/judge." Innocent cannot be blamed for every abuse that developed later in ecclesiastical courts, but the procedure lent itself to abuse.[70] Another of his decretals was also an invitation to abuse. Before Innocent, there was a strong doctrinal tradition forbidding forced baptism. He preserved that prohibition, but he also introduced the distinction between a baptism imposed on a subject refusing consent (invalid) and one imposed on a subject consenting out of fear (forbidden, but valid nonetheless).[71] It placed Jews and other non-Christians further in jeopardy.

Innocent did not set out to expand the legal business of the papacy. The vast majority of legal cases that came to Innocent's court and prompted the outflow of letters resulted from the initiative of others. On the other hand, it was extremely rare for Innocent to refuse to consider a case or declare it outside of his competence, although that did happen sometimes. He refused to make legitimate the bastard children of William of Montpellier, saying the jurisdiction belonged to William's secular superior. Occasionally he would admit that he was too ill-informed to act in a particular instance. But most times, the case would be assigned to judges delegate in the area of the case, where it might or might not be settled. On the plus side, appeals to the papal court often gave a good alternative to people stymied by local injustice. On the minus side, appeals tended to

---

[69] Ynez Violé O'Neill, "Innocent III and the Evolution of Anatomy," *Medical History* 20 (1976): 429–433, citing PL 216:64–66, and 161 (both in 1209).

[70] Brundage, *Medieval Canon Law*, pp. 94–96, 147–149; Richard M. Fraher, "IV Lateran's Revolution in Criminal Procedure: The Birth of *Inquisitio*, the End of Ordeals, and Innocent III's Vision of Ecclesiastical Politics," in *Studia in honorem eminentissimi Cardinalis Alphonsi M. Stickler* (Rome, 1992) pp. 97–111.

[71] Benjamin Z. Kedar, *Crusade and Mission: European Approaches toward the Muslims* (Princeton, 1984) p. 73 and n. 89, citing X 3.42.3; trans. in Grayzel, *The Church and the Jews*, 100–103, no. 12.

undercut the authority of local bishops by removing cases from their jurisdiction and appeals frequently prevented fair settlements by enabling dissatisfied litigants to make appeal after appeal for years.[72]

When Innocent's letters (and his preachers) encouraged all to take the cross with the understanding that those unfit for warfare could still participate with financial donations, it was perhaps a reasonable, even egalitarian, step. Why deny to the ordinary Christian the chance to participate in a military pilgrimage, with all of its spiritual benefits? But the practice of receiving spiritual benefits for money donated was almost inevitably to be abused. The abuses multiplied until they started Martin Luther down the road to revolution.

Innocent was not a great innovator in his treatment of marriage.[73] As in other areas, he preserved and cultivated. Alexander III had established that consent of the two parties was what made a marriage (not a ceremony, the participation of a priest, or the consent of the families), and Innocent enforced that decision with vigor. In standing firm in the matter of the marriage between Ingeborg and Philip Augustus, he reinforced the notion that the validity or invalidity of marriages could only be established in an ecclesiastical court. He showed some flexibility in permitting questionable marriages to stand when they had gone unchallenged for years,[74] and he followed contemporary theory in affirming that husband and wife had equal rights to the marital debt, that is, to sexual intercourse. Although some of his applications of marital law seem harsh, he was generally a fairly humane interpreter of the canons, requiring husbands to respect the rights of their spouses and to extend to them "marital affection."[75]

In any case, the decisions rendered in Innocent's court and the instructions sent to outlying judges remained major ingredients in

---

[72] For a favorable view of the system, see James Ross Sweeney, "Innocent III, Canon Law, and Papal Judges Delegate in Hungary," in *Popes, Teachers, and Canon Law in the Middle Ages*, ed. James Ross Sweeney and Stanley Chodorow (Ithaca, 1989), pp. 26–52 and Foreville, *Le pape Innocent III et la France*, p. 353 et passim. For a less favorable view, see John C. Moore, "Papal Justice in France Around the Time of Pope Innocent III," *Church History*, 41 (1972): 295–306.

[73] For much of what follows, see Constance M. Rousseau, "The Spousal Relationship: Marital Society and Sexuality in the Letters of Pope Innocent III," *Mediaeval Studies* 56 (1994): 89–109; Maccarrone, "Sacramentalità e Indissolubilità," repr. *Nuovi Studi su Innocenzo III*, pp. 47–110, especially p. 66.

[74] Reg. 9:61 = PL 215:873.

[75] Constance M. Rousseau, "A Papal Matchmaker," pp. 259–271.

the canon law of the Roman Catholic Church into the twentieth century. This record may justify the fact that he is one of twenty-three lawgivers whose relief portraits adorn the Chamber of the House of Representatives of the Congress of the United States.

Innocent's letters were usually written with an eye to the immediate problem, although many ended up in decretal collections. The canons of Lateran IV were another matter, definitely intended to have long lasting effects. The first canon was a thorough and concise statement of basic beliefs, approved by the assembled bishops of Christendom. It was the most authoritative statement of its kind since the fifth century and until the Council of Trent in the sixteenth century. Canon 50 changed the rules of consanguinity so that marriages were henceforth valid even if the couple was related in the fourth, fifth, and sixth degree. That brought the law more in line with practice, a sensible accommodation. Canon 21 required all the faithful to confess their sins to a priest and to receive communion at least once a year, and that was a remarkably fruitful planting. In a modified form, it has lasted to the present, thereby affecting the lives of millions. When canon 18 forbad clerical participation in trials by ordeal and battle, it forced all of Latin Christendom to develop more rational and less arbitrary forms of proof. And generally, Lateran IV gave official recognition to the growing movement that stressed the parish priest, in his preaching and administration of the sacraments, as the foundation of pastoral care.[76]

Innocent will always be remembered for his political and legal legacy, but for many centuries, his personal writings were among his most fruitful plantings, inspiring even the twentieth-century pope John XXIII.[77] Innocent's sermons were widely read and were admired and annotated by Petrarch.[78] *On the Misery of the Human Condition*, with its three sections on "the miserable entrance upon the human condition," "the guilty progress of the human condition," and "the damnable exit from the human condition," seems dreadfully morbid to most modern readers, but it was remarkably popular in the centuries following Innocent's death. It survives in nearly seven-hundred

---

[76] Joseph Goering, *William de Montibus (c. 1140–1213) The Schools and the Literature of Pastoral Care* (Toronto, 1992), pp. 60, 79.

[77] John XXIII, *Journal of a Soul*, trans. Dorothy White (New York, 1965), p. 319.

[78] Wilhelm Imkamp, "'Virginitas quam ornavit humilitas'. Die Verehrung der Gottesmutter in den Sermones Papst Innocenz' III.," *Lateranum*, n.s. 46 (1980): 345.

manuscript copies and underwent more than fifty printed editions
by 1700. It was translated into nearly every European language,
including a translation by Chaucer that has not survived. If happiness lies in adjusting expectations to what can be realized, the work
must have provided comfort to many by reminding them of the
inevitability of suffering and the inherent limitations of human life.
It is clear, succinct, full of pithy quotations from scripture and other
writers, and it is well-seasoned with engaging word-play. And it is
radically egalitarian. Everyone suffers the human condition, rich and
poor, master and serf; everyone feels the assaults of lust, young and
old, men and women, wise and foolish. His castigation of the vices
of the rich and powerful—especially those he had observed in the
papal court—must also have been soothing to the victims of those
vices. This work should not, however, be misinterpreted so as to
make Innocent an otherworldly ascetic who underestimated the human
capacity to change the world. Innocent never wrote the comple-
mentary work he intended, which was to be on the dignity of man,
"so that, as in the present work the proud man is brought low, in
that [work] the humble man will be exalted,"[79] but his life showed
how a human being could be exalted through a whole-hearted engage-
ment with the world.

The course of papal development from the Gregorian reformers
to the end of the thirteenth century had many detours, but there is
a continuity of direction in which Innocent's pursuit of his vision
plays a major role. He expanded the theoretical rights and the actual
power of the papacy as he inherited it, and he passed it on to his
successors to expand even further. He moved the papacy closer to
the papal monarchy as it was to be set forth, in theory and in practice, in mid-century by canon lawyers, especially by Pope Innocent
IV.[80] Innocent III's determination to rule central Italy without impe-

---

[79] See Moore, "Innocent III's *De Miseria*," passim, as well as the translations and
editorial material in *De Miseria Condicionis Humane*, ed. and trans. Robert E. Lewis
(Athens, Georgia, 1978) and *On the Misery of the Human Condition*, ed. Donald Howard,
trans. Margaret Mary Dietz (Indianapolis, 1969). The quotation is from the latter,
p. 3.
[80] See Tierney, *Foundations of the Conciliar Theory*, pp. 87–95; Alberto Melloni,
Innocenzo IV: La concezione e l'esperienza della cristianità come regimen unius personae
(Genoa, 1990), p. 48 et passim; Kenneth Pennington, "Pope Innocent III's Views
on Church and State: A Gloss to *Per Venerabilem*," in *Law, Church and Society: Essays
in Honour of Stephan Kuttner* (Philadelphia, 1977), pp. 1–25, repr. in *Popes, Canonists
and Texts, 1150–1550* (Aldershot: 1993).

rial interference led to the battle-to-the-death between Innocent IV and Innocent's one-time protégé Frederick II, but it also led to the survival of that Papal State into the nineteenth century and, in the Vatican remnant, even to the present. It was Innocent III's understanding of the church and of the papacy that was disrupted in the schism from 1378 to 1415, in the Protestant Reformation, and then later in the democratic revolutions of modern times. It is largely his papal program, minus the crusade, that survives today in the papal rule of the Roman Catholic Church.

* * *

Before he became pope, Innocent had written, "These three things are especially necessary for those who rule, that they be truthful in speech, gentle in heart, and just in deed."[81] He did reasonably well in meeting those standards. In his many letters, some have found examples of dishonesty or duplicity, but I find none, with the possible exception of the self-deception that he practiced after the fall of Constantinople.[82] His decisions as judge were never influenced by bribes, though political advantage may have caused him to prefer one reasonable conclusion over another.[83]

Even "gentle in heart" can be applied to Innocent. He was a man of genuine compassion. His quick temper and ready wit might occasionally embarrass a suitor in his court, and his righteous anger could produce rhetorical onslaughts, but he ordered the death of no one and he did not call for the death penalty for any crime.[84] The severest

---

[81] PL 217:954–955.

[82] See Andrea and Moore, "A Question of Character," (forthcoming). In another matter, Bernd Ulrich Hucker asserts that in a letter to Otto, Innocent falsely claimed to be supporting Otto's candidacy for the imperial title when he had in fact switched his support to Philip (*Kaiser Otto IV.* [Hannover, 1990], p. 111). But the letter in question (RNI 153, p. 350) can be read to mean that Innocent was claiming to be looking out for Otto's interest, a factual claim, even though he was accepting the likelihood of Philip's success in the contest for the imperial crown.

[83] This is essentially the criticism Friedrich Kempf makes of Innocent's adjudication of the contest between Otto of Brunswick and Philip of Swabia. See "Innocenz III. und der deutsche Thronstreit," *Archivum Historiae Pontificiae* 23 (1985): 63–91 at 77–78.

[84] His decretal on heresy, *Vergentis in senium*, was harsh, but did not call for the death of convicted heretics. See Peter D. Clarke, "Innocent III, Canon Law and the Punishment of the Guiltless," in *Pope Innocent III and His World*, pp. 271–285, especially 272–278. Clarke rightly points out that Innocent's actions punished the innocent along with the guilty, though it is worth noting that it is very difficult to

penalty he prescribed, for imposters who passed themselves off as
bishops, was life imprisonment with a diet of "the bread of sorrow
and the water of anguish."[85] His readiness to sympathize with petitioners made him, if anything, too ready to believe one-sided stories
presented in his court, sometimes being deceived in monumental
fashion.[86] There are many expressions of compassion in his letters.
The patriarch of Alexandria lived in the very heart of Muslim territory and ministered to the Christians held captive there. Innocent's
letter summoning him to the Lateran Council was full of sympathy
and encouragement.[87] Similarly, he gave his approval and support
to men who wanted to establish orders for charitable purposes: Guy
of Montpellier founded the order of the Holy Spirit to staff hospi-
tals and John of Matha (a Paris alumnus) founded the Trinitarians,
dedicated to the ministry of ransoming Christian captives from Muslim
hands.[88]

On more than one occasion, Innocent showed concern for the
well-being of women.[89] He did not abandon the aristocratic women
who sought his help when their husbands wanted to be rid of them:
Queen Ingeborg of France and Queen Marie of Aragon. Blanche
countess of Champagne, the widow of a crusader, found in Innocent
a persistent and important champion against anyone who would
deprive her son of his inheritance. His support for these women and
their children was not dictated by expediency or political advantage,
quite the contrary. He could also show a sympathetic understanding of women of lower ranks. He told the archbishop of Armagh
that on the one hand, women need not go through an extended
purification after childbirth, but on the other, if it gave comfort to
the women, they should be permitted the practice. His endowment
of the Hospital of Santo Spirito provided for the sick and even

---

deprive the guilty of freedom or property without adverse effect upon the guilty's
family. It is also worth noting that the modern use of economic embargoes is similar in this regard to the medieval use of interdict.

[85] Reg. 15:118 = PL 216:630; Reg. 16:10 = PL 216:794.

[86] Flanders seems to have been an especially fertile source of frauds perpetrated
on Innocent. See Moore, "Count Baldwin IX," pp. 82–87, and Ch. Duvivier, *Les
influences françaises et germaniques en Belgique au XIIIe siècle. La Querelle des d'Avesnes et des
Dampierres jusqu'à la mort de Jean d'Avesnes (1257)*, 2 vols. (Brussels, 1894), 1:44–66.

[87] Reg. 16:34 = PL 216:828–830.

[88] Foreville, *Le pape Innocent III et la France*, pp. 87–90; Brentano, *Rome Before
Avignon*, pp. 14–15.

[89] See Rousseau, "The Spousal Relationship," 89–109.

offered a haven for prostitutes who wanted to be chaste during the Lenten and Easter season. The hospital also had a "baby box," a turntable set into the wall, so that mothers who did not want to keep their babies could anonymously leave them to the care of the hospital. The alternative before had often been the Tiber River.[90]

When, in 1210, Innocent learned that Spanish abbesses were hearing the confessions of their nuns and preaching to them as well, he ordered that the practice cease immediately. On the other hand, he did not prescribe any punishment or make derogatory remarks about the women. Rather, he noted that "although the most blessed Virgin Mary was of greater dignity and excellence than all the apostles, the Lord, nevertheless, committed the keys of the kingdom to them, not to her."[91]

Still, it must be acknowledged that his compassion did not show itself in any special or extended concern for women or for the lower orders. His passion for the crusade led him to remove one right that women had previously enjoyed. An earlier legal principle provided that no man could take the cross without his wife's consent, because to do so would be to deprive her unjustly of the conjugal debt. Innocent decided that just as terrestrial kings summon their men without the wives' consent, so could the celestial king.[92] His sermons show a man at home in his own clerical, academic culture with little awareness of the concerns of the laity. His effort to mobilize the spiritual resources of all the laity in support of the crusade had as its main goal the recovery of the Holy Land rather than the spiritual enrichment of their lives. Apart from expanding the independence of the clergy, he showed no interest in structural changes in society that might have benefitted the lower orders. Men and women of every level could expect a fair hearing in his court, but his conception of how to promote their general well being came down to the maintenance of law and order, the elimination of heresy, the

[90] Bolton, "Qui fidelis," pp. 113–140; Bolton, "'Received in His Name'" pp. 152–167; Constance M. Rousseau, "Innocent III, Defender of the Innocents and the Law: Children and Papal Policy (1198–1216)," *Archivum Historiae Pontificiae* 32 (1994): 31–42; Brentano, *Rome Before Avignon*, pp. 19–20. For the founding document of Santo Spirito, see PL 215:376–380, and for Innocent's rule governing the hospital and its staff, see PL 217:1129–1156.

[91] Reg. 13:187 = PL 216:356.

[92] Rousseau, "Spousal Relationship," pp. 101–3, citing James A. Brundage, "The Crusader's Wife: A Canonistic Quandary," *Studia Gratiana* 12 (1967): 428–441.

moral reform of the laity through required participation in the sacraments and through better preaching from the clergy.

Innocent's treatment of Jews and heretics may be the most difficult to reconcile with gentleness of heart, especially his persecution of heretics. Although he showed some flexibility in making room within the church for the *Humiliati*, for the followers of Durand, and for the new forms of religious life represented by Francis of Assisi and Dominic of Osma, he concluded, as did most of his peers, that Waldensianism and especially Catharism were simply too dangerous for individual souls and for social harmony to be allowed to exist undisturbed. It was in fact true that only religion could provide a basis for unity in Christendom when there was no unifying ideological or ethnic identity. A modicum of religious pluralism was tolerable, since both Jews and Muslims were allowed a legitimate if disadvantaged place within Christendom, but the baptized Christian who denied the legitimacy of clerical authority, who denied the value of the Christian sacraments, or who rejected absolutely the social cement represented by oaths, that heretic could not be allowed to endanger souls and social harmony and was to be driven out. Ideally, Innocent might have been sufficiently clairvoyant to anticipate the possibility of religious liberty as it developed in modern times. But the value of religious liberty has proved to be a hard-won insight, still opposed in much of the modern world, and it is not surprising that it did not occur to Innocent.

Innocent had many virtues and few vices. He was sincere when he constantly referred to himself as "unworthy" of his position, but like most humans who genuinely value humility, he found it a most elusive virtue. Especially in the early years of his papacy, he strove to show what his own youth and vigor could do for the papacy, and it was at that time he made the most expansive claims for his authority. He loved to display his skill in disentangling complicated cases and, in the normal human way, forgot for awhile his own "unworthiness" while savoring his personal abilities and the recognition they won from others. He held back from claiming credit for the expansion of Latin Christendom in eastern Europe and in the Greek East, but he had little doubt about the judgment of others when he wrote Emperor Baldwin, "As to whether during these days the boat has been put out into the deep, I prefer to remain silent, lest I seem to commend myself, but I do boldly affirm this one thing, that I have let down the nets for a catch."[93] Still, while occupying an exalted office and being proud by nature, he tried mightily to be humble and he often succeeded.

Innocent was neither greedy nor ostentatious. The sobering experiences that began with news of the rape of Constantinople moved him to greater simplicity, and he tried to remove luxury from his own court in early 1207. He urged greater simplicity upon preachers and prelates who traveled in elaborate entourages because he knew that their ostentation compared unfavorably to the simplicity of the heresiarchs they opposed. He warned those preaching the crusade to accept no gift beyond their immediate needs and not to travel with large retinues.[94] But there were limits that neither they nor he could cross if they were to maintain their lordship. If he aspired to be a great prince—and that is precisely what he sought in the Papal State—he could not expect to hold the loyalty and respect of subordinate princes and cities in central Italy without suitable display and majesty, the sort of thing surrounding the papal court in Viterbo in 1207 and San Germano in 1208.

Innocent generally presented himself as a confident and powerful authority, but he was not without uncertainty and ambivalence. His faith was not held blindly, without reflection. On the deepest level of faith, he gave no sign of doubt or uncertainty, but he was capable of offering a very pragmatic argument in favor of belief, a version of what was later known as Pascal's wager: To believe in a final resurrection and judgment is harmless if it is not true, but very beneficial if it is true; disbelief is harmless if the doctrine is not true, but disbelief can do great harm if the doctrine is true.[95] Innocent did not share the contemporary enthusiasm for the cult of the Virgin Mary. He rarely mentioned her in sermons or letters, and he did not accept the doctrine later called the Immaculate Conception, that Mary was conceived without the blemish of original sin.[96] He also believed that a pope could fall into heresy and be deposed, though he thought it unlikely.[97]

---

[93] Reg. 7:203.
[94] Reg. 16:29 = PL 216:822-823.
[95] PL 217:632-633.
[96] Wilhelm Imkamp, "'Virginitas quam ornavit humilitas,'" pp. 344-378, especially 355-359.
[97] PL 217:665, 670.

Regarding some contemporary Christian moral doctrines, Innocent may have been less committed than some of his predecessors. Tournaments, for example, had been strongly condemned by clerical authorities, including condemnations at Lateran II (1139) and Lateran III (1179). Although Innocent would never feel free simply to reverse those prohibitions, he was faced with the fact that European knights would not give them up,[98] and that if he was to obtain their cooperation for crusades, some accommodation must be made. It was an embarrassing fact that the real beginning of the Fourth Crusade took place at a tournament in Champagne. In 1206 and 1207, when the bishop of Soissons had taken a hard line on tournaments, he discovered the nobles he had excommunicated for the offense showed no interest in crusading. Innocent said he did not want to permit tournaments, but that he would permit the bishop (and others) to remove the excommunication "as it seems useful to you."[99] Similarly, in 1213, he apparently permitted Robert Courson to go easy on tournaments when he gave him this rather opaque advice, "Regarding tournaments, we have granted to you that, with the counsel of prudent men, you may make what wholesome arrangements seem to you to be useful to the Holy Land."[100] In his triumphant tour of the southern borders of the papal state in 1208, part of the celebration was a tournament staged in his presence by the count of Ceccano and his knights and Innocent seems to have raised no objection.[101] And even at Lateran IV, Innocent and the council seemed to accept the general inevitability of tournaments, hoping only to suspend them while the crusade was in progress:

> Although tournaments have been forbidden in a general way on pain of a fixed penalty at various councils, we strictly forbid them to be held for three years, under pain of excommunication, because the business of the crusade is much hindered by them at this present time.[102]

That prohibition was a far cry from the language of Lateran II:

---

[98] Keen, *Chivalry*, pp. 96–98, 99–100.

[99] Reg. 9:197 = PL 215:1035, Reg. 10:74 = PL 215:1174.

[100] Reg. 16:32 = PL 216:827.

[101] *Annales Ceccanenses*, MGH SS 19:296–297. "Post nonam usque in hora coenae cum suis militibus domnus Iohannes de Ceccano in presentia domni papae iocavit burbudando."

[102] Tanner, 1:270, canon [71].

We entirely forbid, moreover, those abominable jousts and tournaments in which knights come together by agreement and rashly engage
in showing off their physical prowess and daring, and which often
result in human deaths and danger to souls.[103]

It is even possible that Innocent was less convinced than his learned
contemporaries that all forms of interest were evil. Generally, scholars of his day had not yet learned to distinguish between exorbitant
interest charged to those trying to survive and moderate interest
charged for business or other institutional purposes. Interest rates for
the latter were likely to run from five percent to thirty-five percent.[104]
In the region of Toulouse, money could be borrowed at twenty percent in the 1190s and at three to twenty-three percent in the 1180s,
"with an average of around fifteen percent, the interest being higher
the smaller the capital invested."[105] But short-term consumer loans
were commonly going at two pennies on the pound per week, that
is, at forty-three and 1/3 percent per year,[106] a rate that could be
deadly for the poor, especially at times of food-shortages. Neither
scripture nor tradition made any distinction regarding different kinds
of interest, and canon lawyers and theological moralists were unanimous in condemning all interest-taking.[107] But clergy in the practical world did not see things in quite the same way. In 1139, Lateran
II had condemned all usurers in strong terms.[108] At Lateran III in
1179, however, while decrying the ubiquity of usury, the prelates
backed away a fraction by calling for the punishment only of "manifest" or notorious usurers.[109]

Innocent himself did not seem especially concerned about usury,
except when it violated the exemption from usury he had granted
crusaders or when it was associated with other sins, such as clerical

---

[103] Tanner, 1:200, canon 14.

[104] Jacques le Goff, *Your Money or Your Life: Economy and Religion in the Middle Ages*
(New York, 1988), pp. 71–72.

[105] Mundy, *Society and Government at Toulouse*, pp. 216–217.

[106] Jean Ibanès, *La doctrine de l'église et les réalités économique au xiiiᵉ siècle: L'intérêt, les
prix et la monnaie* (Paris, 1967), pp. 90–91.

[107] Le Goff, *Your Money or Your Life*, pp. 13–27; Lester K. Little, *Religious Poverty
and the Profit Economy in Medieval Europe* (Ithaca, 1978), pp. 179–183; Ibanès, *La
Doctrine de l'église*, pp. 16–22 et passim; T. P. McLaughlin, "The Teaching of the
Canonists on Usury (XII, XIII, and XIV Centuries," *Mediaeval Studies* 1 (1939):
81–147, 2 (1940): 1–22.

[108] Tanner, 1:200, canon 13.

[109] Ibid., 1:223, canon 25.

vice or heresy.[110] When called upon, he enforced the laws against usury,[111] although he acknowledged to the bishop of Arras in 1208 that if the laws were strictly enforced in that city, all the churches would be closed (he suggested selective enforcement).[112] In a case in which one Bolognese money lender was charging another with usury, Innocent said that the suit could not move forward unless the complainant first returned all the interest that he had himself collected. That judgment was to become the official law of the church,[113] thereby rendering most business people immune from the charge by other business people. Even the exemption from interest that Innocent granted to crusaders shows that interest-taking was a practice otherwise tolerated most of the time.

He himself bent before the necessity of interest-paying. When he levied an income tax on the clergy in 1199, he allowed them to deduct unavoidable interest.[114] To support Walter of Brienne's war against Markward in the Regno, Innocent offered to guarantee any loans made to Walter, "even with usury."[115] He knew that suitors at the papal court, like Gerald of Wales, were routinely borrowing at interest, and in a letter to some nuns in England who owed money to some Roman merchants, he referred to the fact that the merchants had agreed to forego interest as an act of extraordinary generosity.[116] Although Lateran IV did not reverse the condemnations of usury enacted by earlier councils, neither did it repeat them, and the canon that forbad Jews to charge "heavy and immoderate usury" may reflect an unspoken opinion that perhaps there was such a thing as moderate interest, which might be tolerated even when practiced by Christians.[117] It would take a few more generations before scholars found arguments to legitimate interest-taking, but Innocent and some of his fellow-prelates may have had an adumbration that the arguments were needed.

A man of many virtues and few vices, Innocent was also a man

[110] E. g., Reg. 5:32 (33), 33 (34), 35 (36), Reg. 7:213.
[111] E.g., Reg. 6:15, Reg. 10:61, 92. 204.
[112] Reg. 11:62 = PL 215:1380.
[113] Pott. 5039; X 5.19.16.
[114] Reg. 2:258(270).
[115] PL 214:1072–1073.
[116] Cheney and Semple, pp. 100–101, no. 33.
[117] Tanner, 1:265, canon 67. Canon lawyers rejected this interpretation of the canon, however. See Ibanès, La Doctrine de l'église, p. 16.

of extraordinary talent. He was learned in literature in general and in Scripture in particular, and he was an able writer. If not an especially original theologian, he was well versed in the discipline and was comfortable addressing major theological issues of the day. At Lateran IV, his use of the term *transubstantiation* to describe the Eucharistic change from bread and wine into the body and blood of Christ reflected his participation in a growing interest in natural processes, an interest stimulated by increasing knowledge of the works of Aristotle.[118] He was an administrator of great skill and a man who could attract men of the highest character and ability to his service. Few people in European history have had as much impact on their world with as few material resources as have able popes, and Innocent III was among the ablest.

* * *

Lord Acton, speaking of the papacy, gave us the well know dictum, "Power tends to corrupt, absolute power corrupts absolutely." Whether or not that is true, power certainly magnifies personal attributes so that a minor vice that might easily be tolerated in an ordinary person can become an affliction for thousands when the person in question has great power. Conversely, an inconspicuous virtue in a private person can benefit thousands when manifested in someone powerful. Innocent's political and pastoral vision might have gone no further than parchment and ink, but the papal office projected it onto world history. Thousands benefitted from Innocent's compassion, his sense of justice, his generosity, his gift for orderly, rational government. Conversely, thousands suffered from his obsession with the crusade and his tendency to overestimate his ability to direct the flow of history.

Innocent longed to have divine approval of his own papal stewardship and perhaps even to be part of a great eschatological turning point that would witness the conversion of Jews and infidels. His promotion of the crusade therefore emphasized the recovery of Jerusalem rather than the crusade as a means to achieve and manifest personal virtue, as was the tradition established by St. Bernard.[119] His obsession with the recovery of the Holy Land made him incapable

---

[118] Egger, "Papst Innocenz II. als Theologe," pp. 55–123.
[119] Helmut Roscher, *Papst Innocenz III. und die Kreuzzüge* (Göttingen, 1969), pp. 269–272.

of even considering alternatives (except the unlikely one of a voluntary surrender of the city by the Muslims). He apparently never wavered from the notion that the recovery of the earthly Jerusalem was the only certain sign of God's approval of Christendom and of his own pontificate. He evidently never seriously considered negotiations as an alternative to war. They were at best a means to reach a truce, so that the war could continue later. At the same time, Innocent's overconfidence in his ability to shape the future kept him from anticipating realistically the unwanted consequences his actions might have. He launched two major crusades and immediately lost control of them, but the massacres and pillaging that resulted did not dissuade him from launching a third. Or perhaps he did anticipate the undesirable results but was willing to pay the price for the recovery of the Holy Land. In his world, it was widely accepted that the city that refused to surrender and was taken by storm could expect the worst, regardless of the religious issues involved.[120]

Innocent was unduly confident that he could maintain the delicate balance of tolerance and disapproval that represented official papal policy toward the Jews. The canons of Lateran IV were not intended to change that balance, but he discovered that they did. The registers for 1215 and 1216 have been lost, but letter headings from those registers have been preserved. Two of those headings are as follows:

> He commands the archbishops and bishops in the kingdom of France that they restrain all Christians, especially crusaders, lest they molest Jews and their familiars.
>
> He commands the archbishops and bishop in the kingdom of France that they should permit Jews to wear such attire as to enable them to be distinguished from Christians, but that they should not require such attire to be worn through which they could suffer the loss of life.[121]

It is impossible to identify with certainty the full implications of these titles or to offer any more than guesses as to who appeared in Rome to solicit the corresponding letters. But it does seem clear that Innocent had become aware of unintended damage being done to Jews and was trying to preserve their traditional if limited rights to live and function in Christian society. Belatedly, he was even willing to ameliorate the dress requirements prescribed at Lateran IV.

---

[120] Bradbury, *The Medieval Siege*, pp. 317–333.
[121] Pott. 5257, 5302; PL 216:994.

Innocent elevated the authority of the clergy over the laity in a number of ways, but apparently without considering the consequences if his reforms failed to make the clergy worthy of that authority. When Lateran IV required all the faithful to confess their sins to their parish priests, it gave those priests enormous power over their parishioners. The faithful might very well derive spiritual and psychological comfort from shedding guilt through confession, given a wise and understanding confessor. But Innocent did not seem to anticipate the abuses that might arise when the confessor was something less than that. Something similar can be said for a number of his policies: using indulgences to raise money for the crusades, appointing relatives to ecclesiastical offices, appointing clerical officials to distant prebends (papal provisions), granting papal dispensations from the very rules he supported as instruments of reform. All of these practices were going to be much more destructive to Christian society than Innocent anticipated.

* * *

After Innocent's visit to the rain-drenched Orvieto, he moved on to Todi and then to Perugia, where he stayed for several weeks. The bishop there was John of Casamari, who had earlier served Innocent extremely well as papal chaplain and legate in the Balkans and Constantinople. On 5 July 1216, the pope sent a letter to the city of Cahors. Through its proctors, the city sought papal forgiveness for momentarily failing to give full cooperation to Robert Courson and Simon de Montfort during the Albigensian Crusade. They had already paid heavy fines, but to be sure that they would suffer no other unpleasant consequences, they now asked to be held quit of all further penalties. Innocent wrote, "Since therefore we, however unworthy, hold the place on earth of that one to whom supplication is never made without hope of mercy, with the accustomed kindness of the Apostolic See, we forgive the stated offense and we release you from any penalty that may be owing to you."[122]

Among those following the curia to Perugia was Jacques de Vitry, alumnus of Paris and one of the most effective preachers for the crusade. Recently elected to be bishop of Acre, he traveled south through Italy on his way to the Holy Land, pausing in Milan to

---

[122] Pott. 5125; Bouquet, RHGF, 19:604.

preach. He called that city a "pit of heretics" where the only ones opposing heresy were the men and women called *Humiliati*. They lived in some 150 houses throughout the city, segregated by sex, plus many married couples who lived in their own homes. They all supported themselves through their own labor. Jacques noted that they had been authorized by the pope himself to preach and oppose heretics, despite the fact that their detractors accused them of being Patarines (and therefore heretics).

Jacques proceeded to Perugia where he no doubt would have praised to the pope the good work of the Humiliati, but he arrived too late. Innocent died on 16 July 1216.

Through some amazing oversight, Innocent's body was left unguarded in the cathedral of Perugia throughout the night and thieves slipped in and stripped it of all the precious vestments intended for the burial. When Jacques entered the church the next morning, he found the body "putrid and almost naked." He was moved to reflect on "how brief and how vain is the treacherous glory of this world"— a sentiment that Innocent himself had often expressed.[123] At the council, Innocent had said that he wanted "to remain in the flesh until the work begun is consummated," no doubt referring to the recovery of the Holy Land. It was just as well that he did not live to see the outcome of his crusade. The sign of God's favor was not forthcoming. In 1221, the formidable army Innocent had set in motion had become nearly as helpless and exposed in Egypt as the pope's body had been in Perugia. It withdrew in defeat.

*　*　*

An anonymous poet of his day provided one epitaph for Innocent III:

> Nox accede, quia cessit sol, lugeat Orbis,
>   In medio lucis lumen obisse suum.
> Lumen obit mundi, quia decessit pater Inno-
>   centius; iste pater Urbis et Orbis erat
> Nomen utrumque tenens versum, notat hoc quod habebat,
>   Quid mundo posset, reddere quidve Deo.
> Si speciem, si mentis opes, si munera lingue
>   Attendes, cedet lingua cadetque stilus.[124]

---

[123] *Lettres*, pp. 71–74.
[124] *Ryccardi de Sancto Germano Notarii Chronica*, MGH SS 19:338.

Come, night, since sunlight fails, earth mourns
   To lose its light midday.
The world's light passes, father Innocent
   Has died. Father of Rome and world, he bore
Each name in turn, took note of what he had,
   what he could give the world and what to God:
Beauty, wealth of mind, and gifted tongue.
   You see: the tongue will cease, the pen will fall.

But Innocent might have preferred for his epitaph the one he himself
wrote for the murdered bishop of Würzburg:

> By dying in what was mortal and in what could decay in corruption,
> this bishop has put on the immortal and the incorruptible. He has
> exchanged the temporal for the eternal, the terrestrial for the heav-
> enly, a roadway for a homeland, and an exile for an eternal home.
> There neither clamor nor mourning nor heartache will endure. They
> have passed away as he has passed over from the world to the father.
> He fought the good fight, he finished the race, he served the faith. . . .[125]

Or he might have said about his life what he said of one of his
treatises: I have done as well as I could, but not as well as I wished.[126]

* * *

What judgment will the modern student of history offer? Muslims
and Jews cannot be expected to speak kindly of Innocent. The secular cynic might very well see in Innocent's life the playing out of
the dictum that religion began when the first fool met the first fraud.
In this light, Innocent's efforts had one simple goal: to maintain and
expand clerical wealth and power. From this point of view, Innocent's
reign was a great success. The wealth, power, and freedom of the
clergy, and especially of the pope, were certainly expanded and
solidified through Innocent's efforts. He played his hand well.

Western historians more sympathetic to religious values are likely
to find themselves somewhere between two poles. At one pole, the
militant papalist can see Innocent's pontificate as an unswerving effort
to strengthen the doctrinal and organizational unity of Christendom
under the leadership of the pope and to reform the morals of both
clergy and laity. As a moral counter-balance to secular governments,
he staunchly resisted their tendency to subordinate everything to their

---

[125] Reg. 6:114.
[126] "Feci diligenter ut potui, non sufficienter ut volui" (SAM, PL 214:914).

own political ends. From this point of view, his pontificate was successful, with some setbacks.

At least until the sixteenth century, nearly every ruler in Europe was to acknowledge at least in theory that some matters lay outside their authority. Moreover, the distinction between ecclesiastical and secular competence was a prerequisite for the emergence of the idea of the separation of church and state. For the church itself, the community of believers, Innocent's council set forth clear standards of belief and behavior. Standards were certainly necessary, since there are inevitably limits to the amount of non-conformity any group can tolerate if the group is to survive, be it family, church, or political community. In enforcing those standards, Innocent's combination of reform and political suppression did in fact reduce the amount of heresy in Christendom and probably enhanced popular devotion. His support for St. Francis and St. Dominic produced in the success of the friars fruits far beyond what Innocent could have imagined. His support for crusaders and missionaries along the Baltic coast helped make Latvia and Lithuania a permanent part of Latin Christendom. Innocent's efforts to organize Christendom against Islam failed in their central goal, the re-conquest of Jerusalem and the Holy Land, but they did help regain Spain for Christianity, and they did unite Christians, especially Christian warriors, in projects that sometimes subordinated their own political and material well-being to the service of Christ the King and the Christian community. Finally, Innocent was a vigorous and effective champion of the notion that the Christian church must not become an agency or instrument of the civil authority.

As for the setbacks, Innocent's reunification of Greek and Latin churches was illusory, lasted less than sixty years, and left a permanent legacy of bitter resentment among Greek Christians. The reforms urged upon the clergy and laity certainly did not eliminate all abuses, since the same complaints about moral failings of clergy and laity were to be as recurring in the following centuries as the waves of the sea. Still, that is not to say that there was no effect. The commandment "Thou shalt not steal" continues to be violated by believers century after century, but the commandment's repetition has almost certainly affected behavior and reduced theft. In any case, from this point of view, the policies of Innocent III offered humankind the promise of peace in this world and salvation in the next, even if the promise was not completely realized.

At the other pole would be those religious opponents of the papacy who are part of a tradition dating at least from the fourteenth century. That tradition believes that the Christian Church took a disastrous turn when it permitted one of its ministers to elevate himself to the position of an emperor. From this point of view, Innocent III was one of the most successful practitioners of the imperial papacy and is for that reason all the more to be condemned. The elevation of the clergy to a dominant position over the laity, the use of massive, brutal force to destroy even the most peaceful opponents of the papal program, the elaborate machinery for turning alleged spiritual benefits into real financial profits—all these seem signs of the anti-Christ more than the vicar of Christ.

Between those two poles, there is room for many views of Pope Innocent III. My own fluctuates somewhere in between.

BIBLIOGRAPHY OF WORKS CITED

Primary Sources

Andrea, Alfred J. *Contemporary Sources for the Fourth Crusade*. Leiden, 2000.

Andrieu, Michel. *Le pontifical romain au moyen âge*, 2: *Le Pontifical de la Curie romaine au XIIIe siècle*. Vatican City, 1940.

Annales Ceccanenses. MGH SS 19:275–302.

Annales Stadensis auctore Alberto. MGH SS 16:271–379.

Beowulf. Trans. Seamus Heaney. New York, 2000.

Cartulaire du chapitre de la Cathédrale d'Amiens. Ed. J. Roux. 2 vols. Amiens and Paris, 1905–1912.

Chazan, Robert. *Church, State, and Jew in the Middle Ages*. New York, 1980.

Cheney, C. R. and W. H. Semple. Ed. and trans. *Selected Letters of Pope Innocent III concerning England (1198–1216)*. London, 1953.

Chronicon abbatiae de Evesham ad annum 1418. Ed. W. D. Macray. Rolls Series, no. 29. London, 1863.

Corpus iuris canonici. 2nd ed. by Emil Friedberg. 2 vols. Leipzig, 1879, repr. Graz, 1959.

Evergates, Theodore, trans. and ed. *Feudal Society in Medieval France: Documents form the County of Champagne*. Philadelphia, 1993.

García y García, Antonius, ed. *Constitutiones concilii quarti Lateranensis una cum commentariis glossatorum*. Monumenta Iuris Canonici, ser. A: *Corpus Glossatorum*. Vol. 2. Vatican City, 1981.

Gesta Innocentii III. PL 214:xvii–ccxxviii. Also in David Gress-Wright, ed. "The 'Gesta Innocentii III': Text, introduction and commentary." Bryn Mawr College dissertation, 1981.

"Gestorum Treveroum continuatio IV." MGH SS 24:390–404.

Giraldus Cambrensis. *Giraldi Cambrensis Opera*, ed. J. S. Brewer. Rolls Series, no. 21/1–3. London, 1861–1863.

———. *The Autobiography of Giraldus Cambrensis*, ed. and trans. H. E. Butler. London, 1937.

Grayzel, Solomon. *The Church and the Jews in the XIIIth Century*. Vol. 1, rev. ed. New York, 1966.

Hampe, Karl. "Eine Schilderung des Sommeraufenthaltes der römischen Kurie unter Innocenz III. in Subiaco 1202." *Historische Vierteljahrschrift* 8 (1905): 509–535.

Henry of Livonia. *The Chronicle of Henry of Livonia*. Trans. and introduction by James A. Brundage. Madison, 1961.

Horace. *Epistolae* or *Letters*. Book 1.

Innocent III, Pope. *De miseria humanae conditionis*. PL 217:701–746. Also in these three editions. Michele Maccarrone (ed.), Lotharii Cardinalis (Innocentii III), *De miseria humanae conditionis*. Lugano, 1955. Donald Howard (ed.), Lothario dei Segni (Pope Innocent III), *On the Misery of the Human Condition*, trans. Margaret Mary Dietz. Indianapolis and New York, 1969. Robert E. Lewis (ed. and trans.), Lotario dei Segni (Pope Innocent III), *De miseria Condicionis Humane*. Athens, Georgia, 1978.

———. *De quadripartita specie nuptiarum*. PL 217:921–968.

———. *De sacro altaris mysterio*. PL 217:773–916.

———. *Die Register Innocenz' III.* 7 vols. to date. Ed. Othmar Hageneder et al. Vienna, 1964–1997. Also in PL 214–217.

———. *Regestum Innocentii III papae super negotio Romani imperii.* Ed. Friedrich Kempf, S.J. Rome, 1947. Also in PL 216:995–1172.

Jacques de Vitry (Jacobus de Vitriaco). *Lettres de Jacques de Vitry,* ed. R. B. C. Huygens. Leiden, 1960.

Jaffé, P. (ed.). *Regesta Pontificum Romanorum ab condita ecclesia ad annum post Christum natum MCXCVIII.* 2nd ed. by S. Loewenfeld, F. Kaltenbrunner, and P. Ewald under the direction of W. Wattenbach. 2 vols. Leipzig, 1885–1888.

John of Salisbury. *Memoirs of the Papal Court.* Trans. Marjorie Chibnall. London, 1956.

Kuttner, Stephan, and Antonio García y García. "A New Eyewitness Account of the Fourth Lateran Council." *Traditio* 20 (1964): 115–178.

Layettes du trésor des chartes, ed. Alexander Teulet et al. 5 vols. Paris, 1863–1909.

Maccarrone, Michele. "La Notizia della visita di Innocenzo III ad Orvieto nel cod. M 465 della Morgan Library di New York." In Maccarone, *Studi su Innocenzo III,* pp. 3–9.

Mansi, Joannes Dominicus. *Sacrorum Conciliorum nova et amplissima collectio.* Vol. 22. 1961 repr. of 1767 ed. Graz, 1961.

Melloni, Alberto. *Vineam Domini*—10 April 1213: New Efforts and Traditional *Topoi*—Summoning Lateran IV." In *Pope Innocent III and His World,* pp. 63–73.

MGH, *Constitutiones,* 2 (Hanover, 1896) ed. Ludewicus Weiland.

Migne, J. P. *Patrologia latina [Patrologiae cursus completus . . . series Latina].* 221 vols. Paris, 1844–1864.

Oeuvres de Rigord et de Guillaume le Breton. 2 vols. Ed. François Delaborde. Paris, 1882–1885.

Peter of les Vaux-de-Cernay. *The History of the Albigensian Crusade.* Trans. W. A. and M. D. Sibly. Woodbridge, 1998.

Pontal, Odette, ed. and trans. into French. *Les statuts synodaux français du XIIIᵉ siècle.* Tome 1: *Les statuts de Paris et le synodal de l'ouest (XIIIᵉ siècle).* Paris, 1971.

Prevenier, W., ed. *De Oorkonden der graven van Vlanderen (1191–aanvang 1206).* 3 vols. Brussels, 1964.

Pullan, Brian, ed. and trans. *Sources for the History of Medieval Europe from the Mid-eighth to the Mid-thirteenth Century.* New York, 1966.

Recueil des actes de Philippe-Auguste. Ed. H. F. Delaborde et al. Vol. 2. Paris, 1943.

Recueil des historiens des Gaules et de la France. Vol. 19, ed. Michel-Jean-Joseph Brial, new ed. Léopold Delisle. Paris, 1880.

Relatio Marchianensis, MGH SS 26:390–391.

Richard of San Germano. *Ryccardi de Sancto Germano Notarii Chronica.* MGH SS 19:321–384.

Rigord. *Gesta Philippi Augusti.* In *Oeuvres de Rigord et de Guillaume le Breton,* 1:1–167.

Robert of Clari. *The Conquest of Constantinople.* Trans. Edgar Holmes McNeal. New York, 1979 repr. of 1936.

Roger de Wendover, *The Flowers of History.* Trans. J. A. Giles. 2 vols. New York, 1968, reprt of 1949.

———, *The Flowers of History.* Rolls Series, 84/1–3. London, 1886–1889.

Tanner, Norman P., S.J. (ed.). *Decrees of the Ecumenical Councils.* 2 vols. London, 1990.

Thatcher, Oliver J., and Edgar Holmes McNeal, eds. *A Source Book for Mediaeval History.* New York, 1905.

Van Dijk, S. J. P. *The Ordinal of the Papal Court from Innocent III to Boniface VIII and Related Documents.* Spicilegium Friburgense, 22. Fribourg, 1975.

Villehardouin, Geoffrey. *The Conquest of Constantinople.* In *Joinville & Villehardouin: Chronicles of the Crusades.* Trans. M. R. B. Shaw. Baltimore, 1963.

Wakefield, Walter L., and Austin P. Evans. Ed. and trans. *Heresies of the High Middle Ages: Selected Sources.* New York, 1969.

Willelmi Chronica Andrensis, MGH SS 24:684–773.

William the Breton. *Gesta Philippi Augusti.* In *Oeuvres de Rigord et de Guillaume le Breton,* 1:168–333.

Secondary Sources

Andrea, Alfred J. "Cistercian Accounts of the Fourth Crusade: Were they Anti-Venetian?" *Analecta Cisterciensia* 41 (1985): 3–41.

Andrea, Alfred J., and John C. Moore. "The Date of Reg. 6:102: Pope Innocent III's Letter of Advice to the Crusaders." In *Medieval and Renaissance Venice.* Ed. Ellen E. Kittel and Thomas F. Madden. Urbana, 1999. Pp. 109–123

———. "A Question of Character: Two Views on Innocent III and the Fourth Crusade." In *Innocentius Papa III: Urbis et Orbis.* 2 vols. Ed. Brenda Bolton and Werner Maleczek (in press).

Andrews, Frances. *The Early Humiliati.* Cambridge, 1999.

———. "Innocent III and Evangelical Enthusiasts: The Route to Approval." In *Pope Innocent III and His World*, pp. 229–241.

Baldwin, John W. "The Intellectual Preparation for the Canon of 1215 against Ordeals." *Speculum* 36 (1961): 613–636.

———. *Masters, Princes, and Merchants: The Social Views of Peter the Chanter and His Circle.* 2 vols. Princeton, 1970.

———. *The Government of Philip Augustus: Foundations of French Royal Power in the Middle Ages.* Berkeley, 1986.

———. "The Image of the Jongleur in Northern France around 1200." *Speculum* 72 (1997): 635–663.

———. "From the Ordeal to Confession: In Search of Lay Religion in Early Thirteenth Century France." In Biller, *Handling Sin*, pp. 191–209.

Barber, Malcolm. *The Cathars. Dualist Heretics in Languedoc in the High Middle Ages.* Harlow, 2000.

Barraclough, Geoffrey. *Papal Provisions: Aspects of Church History Constitutional, Legal and Administrative in the Later Middle Ages.* Oxford, 1935, repr. Westport CT, 1971.

Bartlett, Robert. *Gerald of Wales: 1146–1223.* Oxford, 1982.

———. *The Making of Europe: Conquest, Colonization and Cultural Change, 950–1350.* Princeton, 1993.

Bautier, Robert-Henri. "Philippe Auguste: la personnalité du roi." In Bautier, *La France de Philippe Auguste.*

———, ed. *La France de Philippe Auguste: Le Temps des Mutations.* Paris, 1982.

Benson, Robert L. *The Bishop-Elect: A Study in Medieval Ecclesiastical Office.* Princeton, 1968.

Berman, Harold J. *Law and Revolution: The Formation of the Western Legal Tradition.* Cambridge MA, 1983.

Biller, Peter. "Confession in the Middle Ages: Introduction." In Biller, *Handling Sin*, pp. 1–33.

Biller, Peter, and A. J. Minnis, eds. *Handling Sin: Confession in the Middle Ages.* Woodbridge, 1998.

Birch, Debra J. *Pilgrimage to Rome in the Middle Ages: Continuity and Change.* Woodbridge, 1998.

Bolton, Brenda M. "Innocent III's treatment of the *humiliati*." In *Popular Belief and Practice.* Ed. G. J. Cuming and Derek Baker. *Studies in Church History*, 8 (1972): 73–82.

———. "Philip Augustus and John: Two Sons in Innocent III's Vineyard?" In Wood, *Church and Sovereignty*, pp. 113–134.

———. "A Show with a Meaning: Innocent III's Approach to the Fourth Lateran

Council, 1215." *Medieval History* 1 (1991): 53–67. Repr. in Bolton, *Innocent III: Studies.*

——. "Hearts Not Purses? Pope Innocent III's Attitude to Social Welfare." In *Through the Eye of a Needle.* ed. Emily Alba-Hanawalt and Carter Lindberg. Columbia MO, 1994, pp. 123–145. Repr. in Bolton, *Innocent III: Studies.*

——. "'Received in His Name': Rome's Busy Baby Box." In *The Church and Childhood.* Ed. Diana Wood. *Studies in Church History,* 31 (1994): 152–167. Repr. in Bolton, *Innocent III: Studies.*

——. *Innocent III: Studies on Papal Authority and Pastoral Care.* Aldershot, 1995.

——. "Faithful to Whom? Jacques de Vitry and the French Bishops." *Revue Mabillon,* n.s. 9 (t. 70) (1998): 53–72.

——. "*Qui fidelis est in minimo*: The Importance of Innocent III's Gift List." In *Pope Innocent III and His World,* pp. 113–140.

Boureau, Alain. *La Papesse Jeanne.* Paris, 1988. (Now available as *The Myth of Pope Joan.* Tr. Lydia G. Cochrane. Chicago, 2001.)

Boyle, Leonard E., O.P. *A Survey of the Vatican Archives and of Its Medieval Holdings.* Toronto, 1972.

——. "Innocent III and Vernacular Versions of Scripture." In *The Bible in the Medieval World: Essays in Memory of Beryl Smalley.* Ed. Katherine Walsh and Diana Wood, pp. 97–107. Oxford, 1985.

Bradbury, Jim. *The Medieval Siege.* Woodbridge, 1992.

——. *Philip Augustus. King of France, 1180–1223.* London and New York, 1998.

Brand, Charles M. *Byzantium Confronts the West: 1180–1204.* Cambridge MA, 1968.

——. "The Fourth Crusade: Some Recent Interpretations." *Medievalia et Humanistica* 12 (1984): 33–45.

Brentano, Robert. *Rome Before Avignon: A Social History of Thirteenth-Century Rome.* New York, 1974.

Brundage, James A. *Medieval Canon Law and the Crusader.* Madison, 1969.

——. *Law, Sex, and Christian Society in Medieval Europe.* Chicago, 1987.

——. *Medieval Canon Law.* London, 1995.

Bynum, Caroline Walker. *Jesus as Mother.* Berkeley, 1982.

Cantarella, Glauco Maria. "Innocenzo III e la Romagna." *Rivista di Storia della Chiesa in Italia* 52 (1998): 33–72.

Chazan, Robert. *Medieval Jewry in Northern France: A Political and Social History.* Baltimore, 1973.

——. "Pope Innocent III and the Jews." In *Pope Innocent III and His World,* pp. 187–204.

Cheney, Christopher R. "The Letters of Pope Innocent III." *Bulletin of the John Rylands Library* 35 (1952–1953): 23–43. Repr. in idem, *Medieval Texts and Studies.* Oxford, 1973.

——. *Pope Innocent III and England.* Stuttgart, 1976.

Chenu, M. D. *Nature, Man, and Society in the Twelfth Century.* Ed. and trans. Jerome Taylor and Lester K. Little. Chicago, 1968, repr. 1983.

Christiansen, Eric. *The Northern Crusades: the Baltic and the Catholic Frontier, 1100–1525.* Minneapolis, 1980.

Cipollone, Giulio, *Cristianità-Islam. Cattività e liberazione in nome di Dio. Il tempo di Innocenzo III dopo 'il 1187'.* Miscellanea Historiae Pontificiae, 60. Rome, 1992.

Clanchy, M. T. *From Memory to Written Record: England, 1066–1307.* 2nd ed. Oxford, 1992.

Clarke, Peter D. "Innocent III, Canon Law and the Punishment of the Guiltless." In *Pope Innocent III and His World,* pp. 271–285.

Cohen, Jeremy. *The Friars and the Jews: The Evolution of Medieval Anti-Judaism.* Ithaca, 1982.

Cole, Penny J. *The Preaching of the Crusades to the Holy Land, 1095–1270.* Cambridge MA, 1991.

Constable, Giles. *Three Studies in Medieval Religious and Social Thought.* Cambridge, 1995.

Costen, Michael. *The Cathars and the Albigensian Crusade.* Manchester, 1997.

Daly, William M. "Christian Fraternity, the Crusaders, and the Security of Constantinople, 1097–1204: The Precarious Survival of an Ideal." *Medieval Studies* 23 (1960): 43–91.

Dickson, Gary. "La Genèse de la croisade des enfants (1212)." *Bibliothèque de l'École des chartres* 153 (1995): 53–103.

Dickson, Marcel and Christiane. "Le Cardinal Robert de Courson sa vie." *Archives d'histoire doctrinale et littéraire du moyen âge* 9 (1934): 53–142.

Dossat, Yves. "Le clergé méridional à la veille de la Croisade Albigeoise." *Revue historique et littéraire du Languedoc* 1 (1944): 263–278. Repr. in *Église et hérésie en France au XIIIᵉ siècle.* London, 1982.

Duby, Georges. *The Legend of Bouvines: War, Religion, and Culture in the Middle Ages.* Trans. Catherine Tihanyi. Berkeley, 1990.

Duggan, Charles. "Bishop John and Archdeacon Richard of Poitiers. Their Roles in the Becket Dispute and its Aftermath." In Duggan, *Canon Law in Medieval England. The Becket Dispute and Decretal Collections.* London, 1982.

Duvivier, Ch. *Les influences françaises et germaniques en Belgique au XIIIᵉ siècle. La Querelle des d'Avesnes et des Dampierres jusqu'à la mort de Jean d'Avesnes (1257).* 2 vols. Brussels, 1894.

Dykmans, Marc. "D'Innocent III à Boniface VIII. Histoire des Conti et des Annibaldi," *Bulletin de l'Institut Historique Belge de Rome* 45 (1975): 27–31.

Egger, Christoph. "Papst Innocenz III. als Theologe." *Archivum Historiae Pontificae* 30 (1992): 55–123.

——. "Joachim von Fiore, Rainer von Ponza and die römische Kurie." In *Gioacchino da Fiore tra Bernardo di Clairvaux e Innocenzo III.* Atti del 5o Congresso internazionale di studi gioachimiti San Giovanni in Fiore—16–21 settembre 1999. Ed. Roberto Rusconi. Pp. 129–162.

Evans, Austin P. "The Albigensian Crusade." In *A History of the Crusades*, ed. Kenneth M. Setton, vol. 2: *The Later Crusades: 1198–1311.* Madison, 1969.

Ferruolo, Stephen C. "*Parisius-Paradisus*: The City, Its Schools, and the Origins of the University of Paris," in *The University and the City from Medieval Origins to the Present*, ed. Thomas Bender. New York and Oxford, 1988, pp. 22–43.

Foreville, Raymonde. *Latran I, II, III et Latran IV.* Paris, 1965. *Histoire des conciles oecuméniques*, vol. 6.

——. *Le Pape Innocent III et la France.* Stuttgart, 1992.

Fine, John V. A. *The Late Medieval Balkans.* Ann Arbor, 1987.

Fraher, Richard M. "IV Lateran's Revolution in Criminal Procedure: The Birth of *Inquisitio*, the End of Ordeals, and Innocent III's Vision of Ecclesiastical Politics." In *Studia in honorem eminentissimi Cardinalis Alphonsi M. Stickler*, pp. 97–111. Rome, 1992.

Friedlaender, I. *Die päpstlichen Legaten in Deutschland und Italien am Ende des XII. Jahrhunderts (1181–1198).* Berlin, 1928

Fuhrmann, Horst. *Germany in the High Middle Ages, c. 1050–1200.* Trans. Timothy Reuter. Cambridge, 1986.

García y García, Antonio. "Innocent III and the Kingdom of Castile." In *Pope Innocent III and His World*, pp. 337–350.

Gibbs, Marion, and Jane Lang. *Bishops and Reform, 1215–1272, with special reference to the Lateran council of 1215.* Oxford, 1934.

Gillingham, John. *The Life and Times of Richard I.* London, 1973.

——. *Richard I.* New Haven, 1999.

Given, James B. *Inquisition and Medieval Society: Power, Discipline, and Resistance in Languedoc.* Ithaca, 1997.

Goering, Joseph. *William de Montibus (c. 1140–1213). The Schools and the Literature of Pastoral Care.* Toronto, 1992.

Goetz, Hans-Werner. *Life in the Middle Ages from the Seventh to the Thirteenth Century.* Trans. Albert Wimmer. Notre Dame, 1993.

Graboïs, A. "Les séjours des papes en France au XIIe siècle et leurs rapports avec le développement de la fiscalité pontificale." *Revue d'histoire de l'église de France* 49 (1963): 5–18.

Gregorovius, Ferdinand. *History of the City of Rome in the Middle Ages.* Trans. from the German 4th ed. by Annie Hamilton. 8 vols. in 13. Vol. 4/2. London, 1905.

Grundmann, Herbert. *Religious Movements in the Middle Ages.* Trans. Steven Rowan. Notre Dame, 1995.

Hageneder, Othmar. "Das Sonne-Mond-Gleichnis bei Innocenz III." *Mitteilungen des Instituts für Österreichische Geschichtsforschung* 65 (1957): 340–368.

———. "Innocenz III. und die Eroberung Zadars (1202): Eine Neuinterpretation des Br. V 160 (161)" *Mitteilungen des Instituts für Österreichische Geschichtesforschung,* 100 (1992): 197–213.

———. "Anmerkungen zur Dekretale *Per venerabilem* Innocenz' III. (X 4.17.13)." In *Studien zur Geschichte des Mittelalters: Jürgen Petersohn zum 65. Geburtstag,* ed. Matthias Thumser, A. Wenz-Haubfleisch, and P. Wiegand, pp. 159–173. Stuttgart, 2000.

———. "Die Register Innozenz' III." In *Papst Innozenz III.: Weichensteller Der Geschichte Europas.,* ed. Thomas Frenz, pp. 91–101. Stuttgart, 2000.

Hampe, Karl. *Germany under the Salian and Hohenstaufen Emperors.* Trans. Ralph Bennet. Totawa, 1973.

Harris, Jonathan. "Distortion, divine providence and genre in Nicetas Choniates's account of the collapse of Byzantium 1180–1204." *Journal of Medieval History* 26 (2000): 19–31.

Holzapfel, Theo. *Papst Innocenz III., Philipp II. August, Konig von Frankreich und die englisch-welfische Verbindung, 1198–1216.* Franfurt-am-Main, 1991. Europaische Hochschulschriften. Reihe III, Geschichte und ihre Hilfswissenschaften, Bd. 460.

Hucker, Bernd Ulrich. *Kaiser Otto IV.* Hannover, 1990.

Hurter, Friedrich. *Histoire du Pape Innocent III et de son siècle.* 2 vols. Trans. from the German and augmented by M. Jager and Th. Vial. Paris, 1840.

Ibanès, Jean. *La doctrine de l'église et les réalités économique au xiiie siècle: L'intérêt, les prix et la monnaie.* Paris, 1967.

Imkamp, Wilhelm. "Sermo ultimus, quem fecit Dominus Innocentius papa tercius in Lateranensi concilio generali." *Römische Quartalschrift fur christliche Altertumskunde und Kirkengeschichte* 70 (1975): 149–179.

———. "'Sicut Papa Verus'; Der Anfang der Primatialgewalt beim noch nicht zum Bischof Geweihten Elekten in Theorie und Praxis Papst Innocenz' III." *Apolinaris* 49 (1976): 106–132.

———. "'Virginitas quam ornavit humilitas'. Die Verehrung der Gottesmutter in den Sermones Papst Innocenz' III." *Lateranum,* n.s. 46 (1980): 344–378.

———. *Das Kirchenbild Innocenz' III.* (1198–1216). Stuttgart, 1983.

Ingoglia, Robert T. "'I have Neither Silver nor Gold': An Explanation of Medieval Papal Ritual." *Catholic Historical Review* 85 (1999): 531–540.

Jackson, W. T. H. *The Literature of the Middle Ages.* New York, 1960.

Jaffé, P. (ed.). *Regesta Pontificum Romanorum ab condita ecclesia ad annum post Christum natum MCXCVIII,* 2nd ed. by S. Loewenfeld, F. Kaltenbrunner, and P. Ewald under the direction of W. Wattenbach. 2 vols. Leipzig, 1885–1888.

Janssen, Wilhelm. *Die päpstlichen Legaten in Frankreich von Schisma Anaklets II. bis zum Tode Coelestins III. (1130–1198).* Cologne, 1961.

John XXIII, Pope. *Journal of a Soul.* Tr. Dorothy White. New York, 1965.

Jordan, William Chester. *The French Monarchy and the Jews: From Philip Augustus to the Last Capetians.* Philadelphia, 1989.

Kay, Richard. "Gerald of Wales and the Fourth Lateran Council." *Viator* 29 (1998): 79–93.

———. *The Council of Bourges 1225: A documentary history*. Forthcoming.

Kedar, Benjamin Z. *Crusade and Mission: European Approaches toward the Muslims*. Princeton, 1984.

Keen, Maurice. *Chivalry*. New Haven, 1984.

Kempf, Friederic. "Innocenz III. und der Thronstreit." *Archivum Historiae Pontificiae* 23 (1985): 63–91.

Kennan, Elizabeth. "Innocent III and the First Political Crusade: A Comment on the Limitations of Papal Power." *Traditio* 27 (1971): 230–249.

Kloczowski, Jerzy. "Innocent III et les pays chrétiens autour de la mer Baltique." In *Horizons marins. Itinéraires spirituels (V^e–XVIIIe siècles)*, ed. Henri Dubois et al. 2 vols. Paris, 1987. 1:163–170.

Kries, F. W. von. "Wolfger von Erla." In *Dictionary of the Middle Ages*, 12 (1989): 672–673.

Kuttner, Stephan. "Universal Pope or Servant of God's Servants. The Canonists, Papal Titles and Innocent III." *Revue de droit canonique* 31 (1981): 109–150. Repr. in Kuttner, *Studies in the History of Medieval Canon Law*. Hampshire, 1990.

Lackner, Christian. "Studien zur Verwaltung des Kirchenstaates unter Papst Innocenz III." *Römische Historische Mitteilungen* 29 (1987): 127–214.

Lambert, Malcom. *Medieval Heresy: Popular Movements from the Gregorian Reform to the Reformation*. 2nd ed. Oxford, 1992.

Lansing, Carol. *Power and Purity: Cathar Heresy in Medieval Europe*. New York, 1998.

Laufs, Manfred. *Politik und Recht bei Innocenz III. Kaiserprivilegien, Thronstreitregister und Egerer Goldbulle in der Reichs- und Rekuperationspolitik Papst Innocenz' III*. Cologne and Vienna, 1980.

Lawrence, C. H. *The Friars: the Impact of the Early Mendicant Movement on Western Society*. London, 1994.

Le Goff, Jacques. *Your Money or Your Life: Economy and Religion in the Middle Ages*. Trans. from French by Urzone, Inc. New York, 1988.

Lerner, Robert E. *The Feast of Saint Abraham: Medieval Millenarians and the Jews*. Philadelphia, 2001.

Linehan, Peter. *The Spanish Church and the Papacy in the Thirteenth Century*. Cambridge, 1971.

Linskill, Joseph. Ed. and trans. *The Poems of the Troubadour Raimbaut de Vaqueiras*. Hague, 1964.

Little, Lester K. *Religious Poverty and the Profit Economy in Medieval Europe*. Ithaca, 1978.

Loud, G. A. "Royal Control of the Church in The Twelfth-Century Kingdom of Sicily." *Studies in Church History* 18 (1982): 147–159.

Luchaire, Achille. *Innocent III*. 6 vols. Paris, 1905–1908. Some volumes appeared in later editions.

Maccarrone, Michele. *Vicarius Christi: storia del titolo papale*. Rome, 1952

———. "Riforme e innovazioni di Innocenzo III nella vita religiosa." In *Studi su Innocenzo III*. Padua, 1972. Pp. 223–337.

———. "Le costituzioni del IV concilio Lateranense sui religiosi," *Dizionario degli istituti di perfezione*, 5 (Rome, 1975): 474–495, repr. in *Nuovi studi su Innocenzo III*, pp. 1–45.

———. "Sacramentalità e indissolubilità del matrimonio nella dottrina di Innocenzo III." *Lateranum*, 44, n. ser. 6 (1978): 449–514. Repr. in Maccarrone, *Nuovi Studi su Innocenzo III*, pp. 47–110.

———. "I Papi e gli inizi della Cristianizzazione della Livonia." In *Gli inizi del cristianesimo in Livonia-Lettonia*. Vatican City, 1989, repr. in Maccarrone, *Nuovi Studi su Innocenzo III* pp. 369–416.

———. *Nuovi studi su Innocenzo III*. Ed. Roberto Lambertini. Rome, 1995.

Madden, Thomas F. "Venice and Constantinople in 1171 and 1172: Enrico Dandolo's Attitudes towards Byzantium." *Mediterranean Historical Review* 8 (1993): 166–185.

———. "Vows and Contracts in the Fourth Crusade: The Treaty of Zara and the Attack on Constantinople." *International History Review* 15 (1993): 441–468.

——. "Outside and Inside the Fourth Crusade." *International History Review* 17 (1995): 726–743.

Maffei, Domenico. *La Donazione di Costantino nei Giuristi Medievali.* Milan, 1964.

Maier, Christoph T. "Mass, the Eucharist and the Cross: Innocent III and the Relocation of the Crusade." In *Pope Innocent III and his World*, pp. 351–360.

Maleczek, Werner. *Papst und Kardinalskolleg von 1191 bis 1216.* Vienna, 1984.

——. *Petrus Capuanus.* Vienna, 1988.

Manselli, Raoul. "I vescovi italiani, gli ordini religiosi e I movimenti popolari religiosi nel secolo XIII." In *Vescovi e Diocesi in Italia nel Medioevo (sec. IX–XIII): Atti del II Convengno di Storia della Chiesa in Italia.* Padua, 1964.

Mansilla, Demetrio. "Inocencio III y los reinos hispanos." *Anthologica Annua* 2 (1954): 18–19.

Matossian, Mary Kilbourne. *Poisons of the Past: Molds, Epidemics, and History.* New Haven, 1989.

Mattingly, Garrett. *The Defeat of the Spanish Armada.* 2nd ed. London, 1983.

McCullough, David. *Truman.* New York, 1992.

McLaughlin, T. P. "The Teaching of the Canonists on Usury (XII, XIII, and XIV Centuries." *Mediaeval Studies* 1 (1939): 81–147; 2 (1940): 1–22.

Melloni, Alberto. *Innocenzo IV: La concezione e l'esperienza della cristianità come regimen unius personae.* Genoa, 1990.

Mollat, Michel. *The Poor in the Middle Ages: An Essay in Social History.* Trans. Arthur Goldhammer. New Haven, 1986.

Moore, John C. "Pope Innocent III and His Relations with the French Princes." Ph. D. diss., Johns Hopkins University, 1960.

——. "Count Baldwin IX of Flanders, Philip Augustus, and the Papal Power." *Speculum* 37 (1962): 79–89.

——. "Papal Justice in France Around the Time of Pope Innocent III." *Church History* 41 (1972): 295–306.

——. "Innocent III's *De Miseria Humanae Conditionis:* A *Speculum curiae?*" *Catholic Historical Review* 67 (1981): 553–564.

——. "Pope Innocent III, Sardinia, and the Papal State." *Speculum* 62 (1987): 81–101.

——. "Peter of Lucedio (Cistercian Patriarch of Antioch) and Pope Innocent III." *Römische Historische Mitteilungen* 29 (1987): 221–249.

——. "Lotario dei Conti di Segni (Pope Innocent III) in the 1180s," *Archivum Historiae Pontificiae*, 29 (1991): 255–258.

——. "The Sermons of Pope Innocent III." *Römische Historische Mitteilungen* 36 (1994): 81–142.

Moore, John C., ed. See *Pope Innocent III and his World.*

Morris, Colin. *The Papal Monarchy: The Western Church from 1050 to 1250.* Oxford, 1989.

Mundy, John H. "Urban Society and Culture: Toulouse and Its Region." In *Renaissance and Renewal in the Twelfth Century*, ed. Robert L. Benson and Giles Constable, pp. 229–247. Cambridge MA, 1982.

——. *The Repression of Catharism at Toulouse: The Royal Diploma of 1279.* Toronto, 1985.

——. *Society and Government at Toulouse in the Age of the Cathars.* Toronto, 1997.

Munz, Peter. *Frederick Barbarossa: A Study in Medieval Politics.* London, 1969.

Norwich, John Julius. *A History of Venice.* New York, 1982.

Nyberg, Tore S. "Skandinavien und die Christianisierung des südöstlichen Baltikums." In *La cristianizzazione della Lituania: atti del Colloquio internazionale di storia ecclesiastica in occasione del VI centenario della Lituania cristiana (1387–1987)*, Roma, 24–26 giugno 1987. Ed. Paulius Rabikauskas, S.J., pp. 235–261. Vatican, 1989.

O'Callaghan, Joseph F. *A History of Medieval Spain.* Ithaca, 1975.

——. "Innocent III and the Kingdoms of Castile and Leon." In *Pope Innocent III and His World*, pp. 317–336.

O'Neill, Ynez Violé. "Innocent III and the Evolution of Anatomy." *Medical History*, 20 (1976): 429–433.

Paravicini Bagliani, Agostino. *Il Trono di Pietro*. Rome, 1996.

Pennington, Kenneth. "Pope Innocent III's Views on Church and State: A Gloss to *Per Venerabilem*." *Law, Church, and Society: Essays in Honor of Stephan Kuttner*. Ed. K. Pennington and Robert Somerville, pp. 49–67. Philadelphia, 1977. Repr. in Pennington, *Popes, Canonists and Texts, 1150–1550*. Aldershot: 1993.

———. "The Making of a Decretal Collection. The Genesis of 'Compilatio tertia.'" In *Proceedings of the Fifth International Congress of Medieval Canon Law*. Vatican City, 1980. Pp. 68–92.

———. *Pope and Bishops: The Papal Monarchy in the Twelfth and Thirteenth Centuries*. Philadelphia, 1984.

Peters, Edward. "Lotario dei Conti di Segni becomes Pope Innocent III: The Man and the Pope," in *Pope Innocent III and His World*, pp. 3–24.

Pixton, Paul B. *The German Episcopacy and the Implementation of the Decrees of the Fourth Lateran Council, 1216–1245: Watchmen on the Tower*. Leiden, 1995.

Pope Innocent III and His World. Ed. John C. Moore. Aldershot, 1999.

Potthast, Augustus. *Regesta Pontificum Romanorum inde ab a. post Christum natum MCXCVIII ad al. MCCCIV*, vol. 1 (of 2). Berlin, 1874.

Powell, James M. *Anatomy of a Crusade: 1213–1221*. Philadelphia, 1986.

———. "Innocent III and Petrus Benevantanus: Reconstructing a Career at the Papal Curia." In *Pope Innocent III and His World*, pp. 51–62.

Queller, Donald E., Thomas K. Compton, and Donald A. Campbell. "The Fourth Crusade: The Neglected Majority." *Speculum* 49 (1974): 441–465.

Queller, Donald, and Thomas Madden. *The Fourth Crusade: The Conquest of Constantinople, 1201–1204*. 2nd ed. Philadelphia, 1997.

Raedts, Peter. "The Children's crusade of 1212." *Journal of Medieval History* 3 (1977): 279–323.

Reynolds, Susan. *Kingdoms and Communities in Western Europe, 900–1300*. 2nd ed. Oxford, 1997.

Richter, Michael. *Giraldus Cambrensis: The Growth of the Welsh Nation*. 2nd ed. Aberystwyth, 1976.

Riley-Smith, Jonathan. *The Crusades: A Short History*. New Haven and London, 1987.

Roberts, Phyllis Barzillay. *Studies in the Sermons of Stephen Langton*. Toronto, 1968.

Robinson, I. S. *The Papacy: 1073–1198: Continuity and Innovation*. Cambridge, 1990.

Rogers, R. *Latin Siege Warfare in the Twelfth Century*. Oxford, 1992.

Roscher, Helmut. *Papst Innocenz III. und die Kreuzzüge*. Göttingen, 1969.

Rousseau, Constance M. "Pope Innocent III and the Familial Relationships of Clergy and Religious." *Studies in Medieval and Renaissance History* 14 (1993): 105–148.

———. "The Spousal Relationship: Marital Society and Sexuality in the Letters of Pope Innocent III." *Mediaeval Studies* 56 (1994): 89–109.

———. "Innocent III, Defender of the Innocents and the Law: Children and Papal Policy (1198–1216)." *Archivum Historiae Pontificiae* 32 (1994): 31–42.

———. "A Papal Matchmaker: Principle and Pragmatism during Innocent III's Pontificate." *Journal of Medieval History* 24 (1998): 259–271.

Sayers, Jane. *Innocent III: Leader of Europe 1198–1216*. London, 1994.

Siberry, Elizabeth. *Criticism of Crusading: 1095–1274*. Oxford, 1985.

Smalley, Beryl. *The Study of the Bible in the Middle Ages*. Notre Dame, 1964.

Swanson, R. N. *Religion and Devotion in Europe, c. 1215–c. 1515*. Cambridge, 1995.

Sweeney, James Ross. "Innocent III, Hungary and the Bulgarian Coronation: A Study in Medieval Papal Diplomacy." *Church History* 42 (1973): 320–334.

———. "Innocent III, Canon Law, and Papal Judges Delegate in Hungary." In *Popes, Teachers, and Canon Law in the Middle Ages*. Ed. James Ross Sweeney and Stanley Chodorow. Ithaca, 1989. Pp. 26–52.

Taitz, Emily. *The Jews of Medieval France: The Community of Champagne.* Westport CN, 1994.

Taylor, Claire. "Innocent III, John of England and the Albigensians Crusade." In *Pope Innocent III and his World,* pp. 205–228.

Taylor, Maria L. "The Election of Innocent III." In Wood, *Church and Sovereignty,* pp. 97–112.

Thijssen, J. M. M. H. "Master Amalric and the Amalricians: Inquisitorial Procedure and the Suppression of Heresy at the University of Paris." *Speculum* 71 (1966): 43–65.

Thorndike, Lynn, ed. *University Records and Life in the Middle Ages.* New York, 1944.

Tierney, Brian. *Foundations of the Conciliar Theory: The Contribution of the Medieval Canonists from Gratian to the Great Schism.* Cambridge, 1955.

Tillmann, Helene. *Pope Innocent III.* Trans. Walter Sax. Amsterdam, 1980.

Turner, Ralph V. *King John.* London, 1994.

Ullmann, Walter. "Innocent III, Pope," *New Catholic Encyclopedia,* 7:521–524. New York, 1967.

Van Cleve, Thomas Curtis. *Markward of Anweiler and the Sicilian Regency.* Princeton, 1937.

———. *The Emperor Frederick II of Hohenstaufen: Immutator Mundi.* Oxford, 1972.

Waley, Daniel. *The Papal Sate in the Thirteenth Century.* London, 1961.

Walter, Christopher. "Papal Political Imagery in the Medieval Lateran Palace." *Cahiers archéologiques* 29 (1970): 155–176 and 21 (1971 [1972]): 109–136.

Warren, W. L. *King John.* Berkeley, 1978.

Webb, Diana M. "The Pope and the Cities: Anticlericalism and Heresy in Innocent's Italy." In Wood, *Church and Sovereignty,* pp. 135–152.

Wolff, Robert Lee. "The 'Second Bulgarian empire.' Its Origin and History to 1204." *Speculum* 24 (1949): 189.

———. "Politics in the Latin Patriarchate of Constantinople, 1204–1261." *Dumbarton Oaks Papers,* Number 8 (1954), pp. 225–303.

Wood, Diana, ed. *The Church and Sovereignty c. 590–1918: Essays in Honour of Michael Wilks. Studies in Church History* Subsidia Series, 9. Oxford, 1991.

Young, Charles R. *Hubert Walter, Lord of Canterbury and Lord of England.* Durham, NC, 1968.

Yunck, John A. *The Lineage of Lady Meed. The Development of Mediaeval Venality Satire.* Notre Dame, 1963.

Zacour, Norman P. "The Children's Crusade." In *A History of the Crusades,* ed. Kenneth M. Setton, 2:325–342. Madison, 1969.

INDEX

Abbreviations: abp = archbishop, bp = bishop

Aachen, 64, 135, 235
Abelard, 8
Abruzzi, 13
Acerra, 13
Acre, bp, 287
active and contemplative lives, 20–21, 89–90, 125, 154, 161–162, 264
Acton, Lord, 285
Ad abolendum, 149
Ad liberandam, 236, 250
Adela, rejected wife of duke of Bohemia, 52
Adolf, abp of Cologne, 65, 132, 135; deposed, 160
Agde, bp, 233
Agnes of Méran, mistress of Philip Augustus, 58–59, 61–63
agricultural revolution, 270–271
al-ʿĀdil, sultan of Damascus and Babylon, 208–209
Alatri, 184
Alban hills, 2
Alberic, prior of Spello, 38
Albert, count of Dagsburg and Metz, 261
Albert, St., bp of Vercelli, patriarch of Jerusalem, 186, 194, 196–197, 205, 208–209, 233
Albigensian Crusade, 153–154, 174–181, 200, 217, 222, 229, 268, 287. *See also* Raymond VI of Toulouse, Simon de Montfort
Albigensians. *See* Cathars
Alexander III, pope, 4, 7
Alexandria, 139, 140, 230, 241, 278
Alexius III, emperor of Constantinople, 47, 108, 113, 205
Alexius IV, emperor of Constantinople, 108–109, 115–116, 121–122, 131; death, 128–129. *See also* Fourth Crusade
Alexius V, emperor of Constantinople. *See* Mourtzouphlus
Alfonso II, king of Portugal, 201
Alfonso IX, king of León, 45, 70–72, 118

Alfonso VIII, king of Castile, 70–72, 118, 155, 197, 200, 203
allegorical view of life, 17
alliances, Welf-Angevin/English and Hohenstaufen-French, 66; Europe-wide of 1212, 216–217. *See also* Welf; Hohenstaufen
Almaric of Bène, 240
Almohads. *See* Muslims
Amaury, 222
Ambrose, St., 9
Amelia, 40
an-Nasir, caliph. *See* Miramamolin
Anagni, 2, 4, 85, 124, 183–184
Ancona, march, 13, 33–34, 38, 40, 66
Anders Sunesen, abp of Lund, 59, 173
Andrea, Alfred, xv
Andres, 8
Andrew of Hungary, duke and prince, 31, 45, 73–4; king of Hungary, 229. *See also* Hungary
Anjou, counts, 41, 56. *See also* Kings Henry II, Richard the Lion-Hearted, John
anti-Christ, 103, 254, 291
anti-popes, 4, 229
Antioch, 157; patriarch, 43, 194, 230, 263. *See also* Prince Bohemond; Peter, Cistercian abbot of Lucedio
Antivari, abp, 74
Apocalypse of St. John, 210
Apostolic See. *See* papacy
appeals to papacy, 37–38, 273–274
Apulia, 109, 155, 185, 188
Aquileia. *See* Wolfger (patriarch)
Aquitaine, dukes, 41, 56, 217. *See also* Kings Henry II, Richard the Lion-Hearted, John
Aragon, 41, 43. *See also* Pedro II, Marie (queen)
Aristotle, 8, 226
Arles, abp, 135
Armada, Spanish, 253
Armagh, abp, 43, 278
Armenia, Armenians, 132, 138. *See also* Leo II

Arnaud Amalric, abbot of Cîteaux, abp of Narbonne, 176, 178–181
Arras, 36; bp, 284
Asia Minor, 14, 41
Assisi, 40, 92, 228; bp, 177. *See also* Francis of Assisi, St.
Asti, bp, 264
Auch, abp, 149, 180, 212, 264
Auch, bp, 212
Augustine, St., 9
Augustinian Rule, 270
Austria, duke, 57, 186
authority, relationship between relationship between lay and clerical, 169, 176, 244–245, 248, 257–264, 268–269, 273
Auxerre, bp, 61, 151, 195, 199–200, 269
Avignon, 228

Babylon. *See* Cairo
Baldwin, count of Flanders, 57, 108, 119; use of forged document, 39; takes cross, 76, 103–104; Latin emperor of Constantinople, 130–134, 136, 140, 280; captured by Kalojan, 159
Balkans, 41, 73–75, 104, 112, 123
Baltic region. *See* crusaders, German; Livonia
baptism, forced, 273
Bar-le-Duc, count, 107
Basil (boy sent by Kalojan), 136
Basilica Nova, 1
Béarn, count, 230
Beauvais, bp, 61
Becket, Thomas. *See* Thomas Becket, St.
Benedict, friend of Innocent III, 16
Benedictine Rule, 270
Beowulf, 253
Berengar, abp of Narbonne, 149, 152, 166–167, 180
Berengaria, daughter of Sancho VI of Navarre and wife of King Richard of England, 57
Berenguela, daughter of Alfonso VIII of Castile, 45, 71–73
Berlin Conference (1884–1886), 262
Bernard, cardinal, 32
Bernard of Clairvaux, St., 180, 268, 285
Besançon, bp, 212
Bethlehem (boy sent by Kalojan), 136

Béziers, 178, 180; bishop, 264
Biaggio, abp of Torres, 117
Bible, interpretation, 9–10, 16–20, 253, 264, 268
Biographer, xvii, 30, 86, 91, 98, 100, 107, 129, 164, 253, 264, 265
bishop-elect, authority of, 30–31
Blanche of Navarre, countess of Champagne, 221–222, 278
Blois. *See* Louis of Blois
Boboni, family of Celestine III, 91, 110
Bohemia, duchy and duke, 41, 52
Bohemond, prince of Antioch, 194
Bologna, university, 3, 10, 11, 186, 228; bp, 151, 212; money-lenders, 96–97, 284; university, 186
Boniface, marquis of Montferrat, 107–109, 111, 115–116
Boniface VIII, pope, 244, 248
Bordeaux, council, 225
Bosnia, 74. *See also* Kulin
Boulogne, count, 178
Bourges, 225; abp, 43;
Bouvines, battle, 218–219, 227, 235
Bremen, 140
Brindisi, 113, 250
Brittany, 163–164, 222
Brixen, bishop-elect, 43
Bruges, 76, 216
Bruno, abp of Cologne, 182
Bulgaria, Bulgars, 41, 73, 132, 138. *See also* Kalojan
Burgundy, 78. *See also* Eudes
Byzantine empire, emperor. *See* Constantinople, emperor and empire
Byzantines. *See* Greek Christians

Cagliari, bp, 161
Cahors, 287
Cairo, 103, 208
Caithness, bp, 90
Calatrava, knights, 197
Calixtus II, pope, 229
Campagna, 2, 183
Canterbury, abp, 43; disputed election, 168, 170, 173, 191–195, 214, 269. *See also* Hubert Walter; Christ Church of Canturbury
capital punishment, 172, 277
Carcasonne, 178; bp, 180, 264
Carpentras, bp, 167
Cassino. *See* San Germano

Castile, 41. *See also* King Alfonso VIII
Cathars, Catharism, 147–148, 156, 164–166, 280. *See also* heresy
Catholic Poor. *See* Poor Catholics
Ceccano, city and count, 184, 282
Celestin V, pope, 256
Celestine III, pope, 1, 13, 15, 24, 32, 43, 58, 91; crusade against king of León, 67, 70
celibacy, 6, 193
Chair of St. Peter, feast, 30
Châlons-sur-Marne, bp, 61
Champagne, 78, 102, 206, 212, 221–222, 282. *See also* Counts Henry, Thibaut, Countess Blanche
Charlemagne, Roman emperor, 63–64
Chartres, bp, 61
Chaucer, 247, 276
Cheney, C.R., xv
Children's Crusade, 201–202
Christ Chuch of Canterbury, monks, 53–54. *See also* Canterbury (disputed election)
Christendom, 5–6, 24; principal regions and modern nations, 55. *See also* Innocent III (vision)
church and state. *See* authority, relationship between lay and clerical
Cistercian monks, Cîteaux, 149, 153–154, 164, 180, 211; general chapter, 48, 107, 162, 242. *See also* Arnaud Amalric
Cîteaux, 107. *See also* Arnaud Amalric, Cistercian monks
Cívita Castellana, 40
Clairvaux, 124
Clarice, mother of Innocent III, 3, 91
Clement, fictitious pope, 124
Clement III, pope, 11, 12
clergy: position between popes and princes, 53–55; reform, regulation, and income in canons of Lateran IV, 241–242, 246–248; control of property, 268–269. *See also* Innocent III
Clermont-Dessous, council, 225
Cluny, 228
Coimbra, bp, 196
coliseum, 228
Cologne: abp, 5, 64, 160, 183, 235, 264; city, 216. *See also* alliances; abps Adolf, Bruno, Siegfried, Liupold

colonization (Latin) of Constantinople, 140
Comminges, count, 230
Compiègne, 104
Compilatio Tertia, 186
Compostella, abp, 79, 197
Concordat of Worms, 229
concubinage, 76
confession, sacrament, and confessors, 248–250, 275, 279, 287
Conrad, castellan of Sorella, 183
Conrad, chancellor of Roman empire, b. of Hildesheim, 53, 55
Conrad of Montferrat, king of Jerusalem, 14
Conrad of Urslingen, 13, 33, 40, 114 n. 32
Constance, city and abp, 203–204, 216
Constance, queen of Sicily, 12, 13, 24, 35; death, 50; concessions to Innocent, 64–65
Constantine, Roman emperor, 34; Donation of, 229, 258
Constantinople, 41, 73, 108; captured, 122–132, 136, 157–158; Latin aristocrats and church income, 195; patriarch, 139, 220, 233, 241, 258 (*see also* Thomas Morosini); Greek emperor and empire, 104–5, 113, 121, 138 (*see also* Alexius III; Isaac II; Alexius IV, Mourtzouphlus [Alexius V]); Latin emperor and empire, 206, 217 (*see also* Baldwin, count of Flanders; Henry I). *See also* Fourth Crusade
contemplative life. *See* active and contemplative lives
Corfu, 121
counterfeiters of papal letters, seals, 38–39
Coutances, 192
Croatia, Croats, 41, 74
crusade, 24, 44–45, 201; call for, 14; impeded by civil war in Germany, 66. *See also* First Crusade; Third Crusade; Fourth Crusade; Albigensian Crusade; Children's Crusade; Fifth Crusade; Innocent III
crusaders: German, 33, 39; German in Baltic area, 41, 140; Latin, 73, 139, 157–159; Flemish and French, 103; Burgundian, 107.

crusaders' privileges, 46, 140, 144, 176–177, 184, 250, 259, 283–284. *See also* indulgences
Cumans, 113, 157
Cyprus, king of, 205, 229

Dalmatia, 42, 74, 92. *See also* Vukan
Dax, bp, 212
Decretum of Gratian, 186
democratic revolutions, 269, 277
Denmark, Danes, 41. *See also* Kings Knut VI; Waldemar
Dioclea. *See* Vukan
Dipold of Acera, 68, 183, 188, 190
Dipold of Schweinspeunt, 13
dispensations, 287
documents, importance of written, 82–83
Dominic, archpriest, 113
Dominic of Osma, St., 180, 280
Dominican Friars, 180, 272
Dover, 214
Dublin, 118, 192
Durand, knight Templar, 195
Durand of Huesca, 177, 280
Dvina River, 41

Easter Duty, 248
Écry-sur-Aisne, 76, 102
Egypt, 106, 227
Ely, bp, 191
emperor, Roman. *See* empire, medieval Roman; Constantine
empire, medieval Roman, 13, 14, 35, 63–70, 113, 188, 236, 258, 260. *See also* Charlemagne, Henry V, Lotarius II, Frederick I (Barbarossa), Henry VI, Philip of Swabia, Frederick II
England and English, 10, 14, 55, 161, 236, 253; under interdict, 191–193; kings' control of episcopal elections, 192; kings' power compared to barons', 213; becomes fief of papacy, 214–215, 227, 258; royal chancery, 82; invaded by Prince Louis, 251–252. *See also* Innocent III, Kings Henry II, Richard the Lion-Hearted, John
Enrico Dandolo, doge of Venice, 105, 110, 136
Erard of Brienne, 221–222
ergot poisoning, 151
Esterp, l', canons, 43

Estonia, 41, 236
Étampes, 118
Eu, count, 186
Eucharist, 19, 29, 147, 240, 285
Eudes, duke of Burgundy, 107, 144, 178, 226
Eugenius III, pope, 199
Europe. *See* Innocent III (vision)
evangelical poverty, 145

famine. *See* food shortages
Ferentino, 2, 96–97, 111, 117–118, 121, 162–163, 185, 228; bp, 184
Ferrand, count of Flanders, 218–219
Ferrara, 12, 166, 228
Fifth Crusade: summons and plans, 209–212, 236–237, 250–252, 254, 270; conclusion, 288
Fiore. *See* Joachim
First Crusade, 6, 201
Flanders, Flemish, 8, 109, 116, 169, 216, 218–219, 225. *See also* Baldwin and Ferrand (counts)
Florence, 228
Foligno, 40
food shortages: in Italy, 85–86; in northern Europe, 103
Foreville, Raymond, xv
Fossanova, abbey, 184
Four Kinds of Marriage, 16–19, 21–22
Fourth Crusade, 102–134, 206, 282; at Venice, 87, 109–111; occupation of Zara, 92, 95, 101, 112, 114–117, 179; possible routes to Holy Land, 104; contract between Franks and Venetians, 105–106, 109–110, 115; contract between crusaders and Alexius IV, 115–116, 122, 126; occupation of Constantinople, 124–134, 213; conspiracy theories, 109 n. 19
France, French, 7, 55; historic ties to papacy, 58, 73; under interdict, 60–61, 76, 103; kings, 14. *See also* Louis VII, Philip Augustus, Louis VIII, Albigensian Crusade
Francis of Assisi, St., 92, 147, 155, 177, 256, 266, 272, 280
Franciscan Friars and sisters, 155, 178, 266, 272
Frankfurt, 190
Franks (non-Venetian Latin crusaders), 139
Frascati, 2

Frederick I (Barbarossa), king of the Germans, emperor of the Romans, 5, 7, 12–15, 64, 84, 190

Frederick II, king of Sicily, king of the Germans, emperor of the Romans, 13, 35, 68, 148, 183–184, 190, 201, 213, 217, 267, 277; progress in Germany, 203–204, 216–219, 235, 254; elected king of Romans and crowned, 216, 227; oath (Golden Bull) of Eger to obey Innocent, 216, 227; election confirmed by Innocent at Lateran IV, 235–237

Fulk of Neuilly, 76, 103, 107, 219–220

Gallura, 160

Garnier, bp of Troyes, 102

Gavignano, 3

Genoa, 4, 104, 106, 108, 109, 190, 252

Gentiles. See infidels

Geoffrey de Villehardouin, marshall of Champagne, 102–107, 116

Gerald, abbot of Casamari, 118

Gerald of S. Adriano, cardinal deacon, 37

Gerald of Wales, archdeacon of Brecon, 77–79, 84–85, 92–101, 102, 115, 117, 118, 284; settlement with King John and Hubert Walter, 97–98

German princes, 63–66, 189, 200, 267; opposition to papal claims, 67, 70. See also Germany,

Germany, Germans, 5, 13, 55, 266–267; civil war, 66, 114, 154, 168, 182, 267; in Italy, 5, 13, 24, 39, 50, 66–68, 85, 183, 190, 267–268; kings, 64 (see also Frederick I, Henry VI, Philip of Swabia, Otto of Brunswick, Frederick II); historians, 260. See also alliances; crusades; German princes; Livonia

Ghent, 216

Gibraltar, 109, 197

Giotto, 272

Girard, cardinal, 38

Giuliano, 184

Gnesen, 196

Grandmont, 11, 14; prior, 223

Gratian, 186

Greek Christians and Christianity, 24, 41, 157, 217. See also Constantinople; schism

Gregorian reforms and reformers, 5, 6, 13, 51, 53, 64, 276

Gregory, cardinal of S. Maria in Portico, 48

Gregory, cardinal-deacon of S. Maria in Aquiro, 40

Gregory Pierleone, 129

Gregory (I) the Great, pope, St., 9, 255

Gregory VII, pope, 5. See also Gregorian reforms and reformers

Gregory VIII, pope, 11, 12, 14, 254

Gregory IX, pope. See Hugolino

Grendel, 253

Guala Bicchieri, cardinal, 183, 220, 230 n. 6, 251

Gubbio, 40

Guido, monk, 47, 71, 149

Gurk, bp, 264

Guy de Paray (Guido de Paredo), abbot of Cîteaux, cardinal bishop of Palestrina, abp of Rheims, 157, 178

Guy of Montpellier, 278

Hagenau, 108

Halberstadt, bp, 212

Henry, count of Kuik, 261

Henry, count palatine of the Rhine, 135

Henry, duke of Lotharingia and Brabant, 261

Henry I, Latin emperor of Constantinople (brother of Count Baldwin IX of Flanders), 159, 195, 229

Henry II, count of Champagne, king of Jerusalem, 14, 103

Henry II, king of England, duke of Aquitaine and Normandy, count of Anjou, 7, 56, 192

Henry V, king of the Germans, emperor of the Romans, 229

Henry VI, king of the Germans, emperor of the Romans, 12–15, 24, 33, 35, 57, 64–66, 185, 190

heresy and heretics, 54, 140, 145–154, 159, 206; in southern France, 47, 72, 135, 149; in northern France, 150; in Italy, 47–48, 161, 288; in Papal State, 150, 155–156, 169–172; worse than Saracens, 176–177; condemned at Lateran IV, 236–237, 239–241. See also Waldensians; Cathars; Albigensian Crusade

Hervé, count of Nevers, 144–145, 178, 222, 225
Hildebrand, count, 170
Hildesheim, bp, 212, 264
Hohenstaufen: interests, 13, 24, 32, 39, 63–69, 108, 113, 154, 188, 267; emperors, 41, 258. *See also* Frederick I; Henry VI; Philip of Swabia; Frederick II
Holy Land, 14, 15, 24, 31, 39, 157, 227; Christian principalities, 41, 209
Holy Roman Empire: *See* empire, medieval Roman
Holy Sepulcher, church, 122
Honorius III, pope, 266
Horace, 8, 117
Hospital of Santo Spirito, 278–279
Hospitalers, 46, 157, 186, 205
House of Representative, U.S. Congress, 275. *See also* List of Illustrations
Hubert Walter, abp of Canturbury, 53, 55, 87; ignorance, 94; death, 168: *See also* Gerald of Wales
Hugolino, cardinal (Pope Gregory IX), 81, 95, 173, 182, 272
Hum, 74
Humiliati, 146–147, 150–152, 280, 288
Hungary: kings and kingdom, 41, 104, 123; rebellion of Prince Andrew against the king, 51, 73; historic ties to papacy, 73. *See also* Prince Andrew, King Imre
Hurter, Friedrich, xiii

Iceland, 41
Île de la Cité, 8
Immaculate Conception, 281
Imre, king of Hungary, 31, 73–75, 111–113, 123–124, 149: *See also* Hungary
indulgences, 46, 103, 140, 153, 179, 287; regulated, 247
infidels and pagans, 134, 140, 156, 161, 254, 273, 285; anticipated conversion, 133–134, 254, 285. *See also* Muslims, Livonia
Ingeborg, disputed marriage to Philip Augustus, 31, 45, 47, 52, 58–63, 87, 118, 124, 153, 155, 168, 183, 198–200, 205, 220, 278; accepted by Philip Augustus, 227, 254
Innocent II, pope, 229

Innocent III, pope (Lotario dei Conti): attitudes, xiv; election, 1; family, 3; visit to Canterbury, 7–8, 170; ordination and consecration, 25–29; health, 50, 124, 187; stay at Subiaco, 87–90; death and epitaphs, 288–289; personal writings, 16–24, 275–276; motto, 48–49, 126, 132, 159, 187, 203, 208, 227, 254–255, 288; and Jeremiah's prophecy, 256–276; character and personal beliefs, 98–99, 277–287; and gifts, 98–100, 265–266, 281; protector of women and children, 205, 221–222, 278–279; charitable works, 86; and use of force, violence, 263–264, 267; understanding of papacy, 23, 34, 42, 127–128, 255–262, 276–277; hope for general council, 114, 131, 206; vision of history, of future of Christendom and world, 34, 126, 136–139, 169–172, 259–264, 271, 279–280; legislator for Christendom, 185–186, 242–243, 275; attitude toward recapturing Holy Land, 253–254, 262, 286; major issues of his pontificate, 44, 118, 155, 207; judgements of modern historian, 289–291; reform of clergy, 43, 164–167, 232–233, 252, 264–266, 270–271; reform of laity, 248–250, 270; reforms in the curia, 164, 265–266; canonization of saints, 272; policy regarding Italy, 34–35, 39, 135, 173, 258; policy regarding Spain, 73, 197, 271; policy regarding Sardinia, 117, 173; understanding of Roman empire, 63, 66, 69, 190, 266–267; guardian and feudal overlord of King Frederick of Sicily, 65, 68, 184; efforts to make peace between kings of England and France, 46, 57, 59–60, 103, 118, 153, 155, 218, 224–225; efforts against Markward of Anweiler, 66–67; interdict on England, 191–193, 215; attitude toward Jews, 142–143, 156, 286; understanding of Islam, 210; support for crusade and crusaders, 44–45, 183, 186, 187, 209, 274; papal taxes on self and others, 50, 177, 250, 257, 284; attitude toward beginning of Fourth Crusade, 107–110; regarding attack on Zara, 111–112, 116–121, 267–268; regarding crusaders' conquest of Constantinople, 125–126, 128–129, 130–134, 136–139, 157–158, 187–188, 203, 251, 267–268, 281. *See also* King John, Philip Augustus, Philip of Swabia, Otto of Brunswick, Raymond VI of Toulouse, Pedro of Aragon, Fourth Crusade, Albigensian Crusade, Children's Crusade, Fifth Crusade, heresy and heretics, schism and relations between Latin and Greek churches, interest on loans, Canterbury (disputed election), Milan, Cathars, Waldensians, Rome, Lateran Council IV, Robert of Courson; marriage

Innocent IV, pope, 244, 277

interest on loans, 143–144, 147; in canons of Lateran Councils, 241, 283–284; Innocent's attitude, 283–284. *See also* crusaders' privileges; usury

Ireland, 43, 160; becomes fief of papacy, 214–215, 227, 258

Isaac II, emperor of Constantinople, 108, 122

Islam, 24, 44. *See also* Innocent III; Muslims

Italian resistence to Germans, 13, 33

Italy, 3, 12–13, 15, 24. *See also* Innocent III

Ivrea, bp, 264. *See also* Peter, Cistercian abbot of Lucedio

Jacques de Vitry, 266, 287–288

Jerome, St., 9

Jerusalem, 6, 14, 106, 139, 140, 227, 228; kings and kingdom, 14, 33, 108, 205, 229 (*see also* Conrad of Montferrat, Henry II); undefended, 157; patriarch, 230, 241 (*see also* Albert, St.)

Jews, 54, 140, 156, 159, 161, 179, 273; position in Latin Christendom, 141–145, 280; in Spain, 72, 155, 261; in Rome, 185; anticipated conversion, 134, 169, 254, 285; in canons of Lateran IV, 241, 284, 286; and Pius XII, 258

Jiménez de Rada, abp of Toledo, 197, 233

Joachim, abbot of Fiore, 134, 137, 240, 254

Johanitsa Asen. *See* Kalojan

John, bishop of Limoges, 37

John Capoccio, 83–84, 129

John, cardinal-bishop of Albano, 78

John de Gray, bp of Norwich, 191

John, king of England, xiii, 56, 60, 135, 163, 188; loss of Normandy, 70, 132, 213; relations with Innocent III, 87, 118, 168, 181, 191–195, 199, 200, 212–215, 269; relations with Philip Augustus, 60, 63, 160, 163, 194, 213, 215–219; excommunicated, 194–195, 201; becomes vassal of Innocent, 214–215, 227, 254; supported against barons by Innocent III, 230, 236, 251. *See also* Innocent III; Canterbury (disputed election); Gerald of Wales; alliances

John of Bellesmains, bp of Poitiers, abp of Lyons, 124–125

John of Casamari, papal chaplain, 74, 113, 123; bishop of Perugia, 287

John of Matha, 272, 278

John of St. Paul, cardinal, 66–67, 177

John Pierleone, 83–84, 129

John XXIII, pope, 275

judgment of God, 51, 132, 187, 203, 253–255. *See also* trial (by ordeal, battle)

Kalojan (Johanitsa Asen), king of Vlachs and Bulgars, 113–114, 123–124, 126–128, 136, 157, 158–159

Knut VI, king of Denmark, brother of Ingeborg, 58

Kulin, ban of Bosnia, 74–75, 112, 123

La-Charité-sur-Loire, 151

Lago di Garda, 228

Lambeth, 54

Lando Collis de Medio, 86

Langres, 206; bp, 264

Languedoc, 47. *See also* Albigensian Crusade

Las Navas de Tolosa, battle, 73, 203, 205, 211, 223, 227, 254

Lateran Council I, 6

Lateran Council II, 6, 282–283

Lateran Council III, 6, 176–177, 207, 283

Lateran Council IV, 225, 228–252, 257, 282; Innocent's summons and those summoned, 206–208; preparation, 207–208, 211, 219–227, 254, 270; canons, 237–251; summary of Christian belief, 239–240, 275

Lateran. *See* St. John Lateran, basilica and palace

Latin language used in schools, 11

law, canon, xiii, 8, 10, 34, 44, 52, 79–80, 161, 185–186, 245, 284. *See also* papal decretals, Lateran IV

law, Roman, 10, 43, 150

lawyers in papal court, 37–38, 161

Le Puy, citizens and bp, 167

Leah. *See* active and contemplative lives

Leo Brancaleo, cardinal, 173, 182

Leo II, king of Armenia, 157, 196, 201, 204–205

Leo III, pope, 229

León, 41, 67, 70. *See also* Alfonso IX

Leonine residence, 30

Leopold, duke of Austria, 14

liberal arts, 8

liberty of the church, 51

Lido, 109–111

Liège (Lüttich), bp, 263

Limoges, 11, 37, 38, 224

Lincoln, 192

Line of Demarcation (1493), 262

Liupold, bp of Worms, 135–136

Liupold, candidate for archbishopric of Cologne, 182

Livonia, 41, 138, 140, 173, 217

Livonian Brothers of the Sword, 140, 217

logion, 28

Lombardy, 11, 14, 48

Lomberd, 90

London, bp, 191

Lotario dei Conti of Segni. *See* Innocent III

Lotarius II, king of the Germans, emperor of the Romans, 229

Louis, count of Blois, 76, 102–104

Louis VII, king of France, 7

Louis, Prince (VIII, king of France), 153; claim to English crown and invasion of England, 213, 215, 236, 251–252

Lucedio. *See* Peter (abbot)

Luchaire, Achille, xiii

Lucius III, pope, 11, 149

Lund. *See* Anders Sunesen

Luther, Martin, 247, 274

Lyons, 178, 228

Maccarrone, Michele, xv

Madden, Thomas, 106 n. 11

Magna Carta, 230

Maguelonne, provost, 135

Maidens' Fountain, 93

Mainz, city and abps, 5, 41, 152, 183, 216, 264

Manicheus and Manicheans, 164–165

Marie, countess of Champagne, 102

Marie, queen of Aragon, 205–206, 278

Marittima, 83, 183

Markward of Anweiler, duke of Ravenna and the Romagna and margrave of Ancona, 13, 33, 50, 76; Hohenstaufen champion in Italy, 66–68, 266, 284; death, 68, 90, 114 n. 32

marriage: as understood by Innocent, 16–19, 274; clerical regulation, 52, 245–246, 257; condemned by heretics, 163, 165

Marseilles, 109, 116, 201–202

Martha. *See* active and contemplative lives

Marxist revolutionaries, 5

mater et magistra, 23

matter of peace and faith, 179

Meaux, bp, 61

Melfi, bp, 264

mercenary soldiers, 176, 200

Messina, 4, 250

Metz, 150

Milan, 287–288; support for Otto of Brunswick, 190, 235; threatened by Innocent, 204; abp, 43, 264

Milo, papal legate, 178–179

Miramamolin (Caliph an-Nasir), 197, 203

Misery of the Human Condition, 16, 20, 21, 275–276

Mohammed, 210

money-lending. *See* interest on loans

Mongols, 41

Monreale, abp, 43

Mont Cenis pass, 106

Monte Aragon, abbey, 166

Monte Cassino, abbey and abbot, 183–184

Monte Porzio, 2
Montefiascone, 170
Monteveglio, 34
Montferrat, marquis. *See* Conrad;
  Boniface; William
Montpellier, 205, 273; council, 225
Morocco, king, 272
Morris, Colin, xiii
Moscow, patriarch, 258
Mourtzouphlus (Alexius V), emperor of
  Constantinople, 129, 130–131
Mühlhausen, 65
Münster, 154
Muret, battle, 217, 222
Muslims, 6, 14, 15, 55, 73, 106,
  121, 157, 159, 176, 181, 201–202,
  208, 241, 250–251, 261, 272, 278;
  in Italy, 183; position within
  Christendom, 280; lands, 40, 278;
  Almohads in Spain, 70–73, 169,
  181, 197–198, 200, 201, 203.
  See also Islam; al-ʿĀdil, sultan

Nantes, 163
Napoleon, 228, 267
Narbonne, abp, province, 72, 264.
  See also Berengar
Navarre, 41, 70. *See also* Sancho VI
  and VII
necessitas, 23
nepotism, 3, 287
Nevers, 150. *See also* Hervé (count)
Nicaea, 217
Nicholas de Romanis, cardinal bishop
  of Tusculum, 215
Nivelon, bp of Soissons, 61, 114, 159,
  282
Normandy, 41, 56, 155, 160, 222.
  See also Kings Henry II, Richard the
  Lion-Hearted, John
Norway, kings, 41, 51–52, 76
Norwich, 191
Notre Dame, cathedral, 8
Noyons, bp, 61
Nuremberg, bp, 264

oaths: rejected by heretics, 148, 280;
  dispensations by pope, 175, 260,
  261
occasione peccati, xiii
Octavian, cardinal bishop of Ostia, 25,
  61–62, 96, 107
Octavian, cardinal, cousin of Innocent
  III, 3

Oporto, bp, 195–196
Order of the Holy Spirit, 278
ordination ceremonies, 12
Orléans, bp, 61, 195, 199–200, 269
Orsini family, 91
Orte, 40
Orvieto, 255, 263, 287
Osma, bp, 180
Ostia, 25
Otto IV (of Brunswick), count of
  Poitou, king of the Germans,
  emperor of the Romans, 84, 108,
  124, 126, 132, 160, 168, 181–182,
  261, 267; elected king of Romans,
  65; relations with Innocent III, 66,
  69–70, 90, 135, 163, 183, 187–190,
  192, 194, 195, 200, 212–213;
  excommunicated, 189, 201;
  agreement with Philip of Swabia,
  182; oath of Speyer to obey
  Innocent, 187–188, 216; crowned
  emperor, 188, 194; excommunicated,
  189; rival to Frederick II, 204,
  215–216, 235–237; defeated at
  Bouvines, 218–219; opposed to
  Gerald of Wales, 96. *See also*
  Innocent III
Otto von Barkenstein, 114 n. 32
Ovid, 8

pagans. *See* infidels
Palatine hill, 1
Palencia, bp, 72
Palermo, abp, 68, 235, 264
Palestine, 33. *See also* Holy Land
Palestrina, 2, 96, 117
pallium, 20, 25
Pandulf, cardinal, 32
Pandulf de Subuxa, Roman senator,
  91, 129
Pandulf, papal subdeacon, 195, 214
papacy, 138; common view of, 15, 39;
  position in Italy, 13; ranking with
  other patriarchs, 241. *See also*
  Innocent III
papal archives, 228
papal chamberlain, 93
papal consistory: *See* procedure,
  judicial and legal
papal curia, 11, 14, 15, 23, 36, 39–40,
  161, 162–163, 183, 185, 200, 217,
  228, 250; expenses and alleged
  venality, 98–100; divisions within,
  126; response to capture of

Constantinople, 132. *See also* procedure, judicial and legal

papal decretals, xiii, xiv, 79–80, 149, 236, 241, 250, 277 n. 84; official collections, 186, 272, 274–275.

papal judges-delegate, 37, 185

papal legates, 11, 34, 38, 46, 136, 153–154

papal letters and registers, 36–37, 80, 82–83, 126, 159, 161, 206, 217, 222, 227, 228, 272; forgeries, 38–39. *See also* papal decretals

papal provisions and reservations, 100, 269, 287

papal seal, 31, 36; counterfeits, 38–39

papal travels, 40

Papal State, 39, 50, 64, 92, 160, 185, 187, 188, 216, 255, 271, 277; government, 40, 169–172, 254, 281. *See also* heresy and heretics

Paris, 3, 6–7, 10, 11, 62, 76; bp, 31, 59, 60–61, 156, 220; schools, scholars, university, 8, 20, 58, 77, 140, 185, 220, 226, 244; council (1213), 220–222, 225, 226, 249

Parma, 31

Pascal's wager, 281

Patarines. *See* Cathars

patriarchs, ranking of, 241

Patrimony, Papal. *See* Papal State

Paul, St., 15, 251

Pavia, 204

Pedro II, king of Aragon, 160, 203, 205, 223; makes Aragon a tributary of the papacy, 135, 258; killed, 217

Pelagius, cardinal, 217

Perche, count, 103

perfecti, 147

Perugia, 32, 37, 38, 40, 92, 228, 255, 287, 288

Peter Annibaldi, brother-in-law of Innocent III, 3, 129

Peter Beneventano, cardinal, 186, 225

Peter Capuano, cardinal of St. Maria in Vialata, of S. Marcello, 31, 46, 59, 84, 87, 103, 107, 111, 113–116, 251, 263; released crusaders from vows, 157–158

Peter Chalboini, Master, 38

Peter, Cistercian abbot of Lucedio, bp of Ivrea, patriarch of Antioch, 111, 194, 205

Peter de Sasso, cardinal, papal rector of Campagna and Marittima, 183

Peter Ismaele, abbot of S. Andrea al Celio, bishop of Sutri, 4

Peter of Castelnau, murdered, 175–176, 181, 186, 200, 263

Peter of Corbeil, bp of Cambrai, abp of Sens, 4, 155, 156, 178, 199

Peter of Vico, urban prefect of Rome, 33

Peter, St., 15, 23, 26, 27, 29, 176, 229

Peter the Chanter, 8 n. 21, 219–220

Peter the Hermit, 201

Peter Waldo. *See* Waldes

Petit Pont, 8

Petrarch, 275

Philip (II) Augustus, king of France, xiii, 7, 8, 14, 60, 108, 224, 226, 229; personality, 61–62; relations with King Richard, 57; relations with King John, 60, 63, 160, 194, 213, 215–219; relations with Innocent III, 57–58, 118, 176, 188–190, 195, 199–200, 236, 251, 261; preferences for Roman emperor, 69, 216; attitude toward Jews, 143–144; and Albigensian Crusade, 153–154, 175, 181. *See also* Innocent III; Ingeborg (queen); France; alliances

Philip, duke of Swabia, 13, 33, 108, 115, 124, 132, 154, 160, 163, 168, 170, 190, 205, 261; relations with Innocent III, 66, 69–70, 76, 135–136, 163, 173, 181–183, 200, 266–267; elected king of Germans, 65; suspected of murder, 92; agreement with Otto of Brunswick, 182; murdered, 186–187, 213. *See also* Innocent III; Hohenstaufen

Philip of Bari, brother of Gerald of Wales, 77–78

Piacenza, 31

Pisa, 11, 104, 110, 160, 173, 188, 190

Pius XII, pope, 258

plenitude of power (*plenitudo potestatis*), 23, 29, 257

Ploaghe, bp, 263

Poitou, 41, 65, 218

Poland, 31, 41, 196

Poor Catholics, 177

Portugal, 70, 262. *See also* Sancho I, Alfonso II

Powell, James, xv

prelates, position between popes and princes, 53–55

Prémontre, canons, 36
priests, sacramental power, 163–164.
  See also clergy
princes of Christendom, 40–41;
  Innocent's problems with, 51, 169
  197, 200–201; understanding of the
  papacy, 52–53, 57–58; their sins
  thought responsible for loss of
  Jerusalem, 44, 51, 59, 71, 254;
  attacks on clergy, 263; desire to use
  clerical property, 268–269
procedure, judicial and legal, 37–39,
  79–80, 242–244, 273–275
proctors in papal court, 37–38
Protestant Reformation, 269, 277
purgation (oath-taking), 244
Purim, 241

Rachel. See active and contemplative
  lives
Ragusa, abp, 112
Rainerius, monk, 44–45, 46, 47,
  71–72, 149
ransoming Christians from Muslims,
  272, 278
ratione peccati, xiii
Ravenna, 13, 33, 34, 40, 66
Raymond Roger, count of Foix,
  180–181, 230, 233–234
Raymond Roger, nephew of Raymond
  VI of Toulouse, 178–179
Raymond VI, count of Toulouse, 167,
  173–175, 179–181, 200–201, 205,
  212–213, 217, 225, 268; at Lateran
  Council IV, 229–230, 233–234, 237.
  See also Albigensian Crusade
Reginald, subprior of Christ Church,
  191
Regno, see Sicily (kingdom)
relics, 247, 251
Renaud, count of Boulogne, 218–219
Renaud de Montmirail, 102
Rheims, 220. See also William of
  Champagne; Guy de Paray
Richard, brother of Innocent III, 3,
  84, 86, 91, 124, 183; named count
  of Sora, 184
Richard the Lion-Hearted, king of
  England, duke of Aquitaine and
  Normandy, count of Anjou, 14, 41,
  56–57, 65, 135, 160, 192, 261;
  death, 67
Rieti, 39–40
Riga: bp, 217; abp, 236

Robert Courson, cardinal, papal legate
  in France, 198, 212, 219–226, 237,
  282, 287; death, 227
Rocca Priora, 2
Rodez, bp, 180, 264
Roland Bandinelli. See Alexander III
Romagna, 13, 66, 271
Romans, kings of, 64; see also
  Frederick Barbarossa, Henry VI,
  Philip of Swabia; Otto of Brunswick,
  Frederick II
Rome, 2, 3, 6, 8, 12, 15, 111,
  228–229; government and people,
  4–5, 11, 29, 33, 83–86, 91–92,
  95, 115, 129–130, 185, 193, 284;
  day of prayer and aftermath, 198,
  203. See also papacy, Lateran IV
Rouen: abp, 38, 178; council, 222,
  225

S. Andrea al Celio, Benedictine
  monastery, 4
Sabina, 83
sacraments: efficacy, 163–164; number,
  250
Sacred Mystery of the Altar, 9, 16, 19, 20,
  22–23
Sacred Scripture. See Bible
Saint Martial of Limoges, abbot, 224
Saladin, 14, 208
Salerno, abp, 13, 263, 266
Salvatierra, 197
Salzburg, abp, 264
San Germano (Cassino), 186;
  parliament, 184–185, 200, 236,
  254, 259, 281
Sancho I, king of Portugal, 70–71,
  195–196
Sancho VI, king of Navarre, 57
Sancho VII, king of Navarre, 70–71,
  76, 203
Sandwich, 78
Santa Anastasia, church, 198
Santa Croce, church, 198
Santa Maria in Trastevere, church,
  234
Santa Maria Maggiore, church, 198
Santi Apostoli, church, 198
Saracens. See Muslims
Sardinia, 117, 160, 161, 173, 263
Saxony, dukes, 41
Sayers, Jane, xiii
schism and relations between Latin
  and Greek churches, 73–74, 116,

126, 138–140, 157, 169, 183, 203, 206, 230, 241–242, 254, 271
Scotti, family, 3, 91, 110
secular, temporal rulers. *See* authority, relationship between lay and clerical
Séez, 192, bp, 118
Segni, 2, 3, 4, 7, 85, 200–201, 203, 227, 253
Segovia, bishop-elect, 197
Seine River, 8
Sens, 4, 150; synagogue, 143. *See also* Peter of Corbeil
Septizonium, monastery, 1, 24
Serbia, Serbs, 41, 74–75
servant of the servants of God, 31, 48, 255–256
share in the solicitude, 23, 29
Sicily, kingdom (the Regno), 12–13, 24, 35, 50, 64–68, 84, 173, 183, 188, 235, 250, 254, 268. *See also* Frederick II
Siegfried II von Eppstein, abp of Mainz, 182, 216, 236
Simon de Montfort, earl of Leicester, 102, 179, 181, 222, 224–225, 268, 287; awarded county of Toulouse at Lateran IV, 234. *See also* Albigensian Crusade
Simon, papal subdeacon, 74
simony, 265
Slesvik, bp, 160
Soffredus, cardinal of St. Praxed, 46, 84, 107, 122, 157–158
Soissons, 107. *See also* Nivelon
Song of Roland, 54, 267
Sora, city and count, 183–184, 186
Sorella, 183
Sorrento, bp, 212
Soviet regime, 258
Spain, Spanish, 55, 70–73, 118, 253, 261, 262; archbishops, 233; emperor of, 70; abbess hearing confessions, 279; Armada, 253
Spello, canons, 38
Speyer. *See* Otto of Brunswick
Spoleto, 13, 33, 38, 40, 188
St. Davids, status and disputed election. *See* Gerald of Wales
St. Denis (Dionysius), saint and monastery, 251
St. Dogmaelis, Cistercian abbey, 84
St. John Lateran, basilica and palace, 1, 2, 29, 30, 36, 93, 95, 163, 187,

198, 203. *See also* Lateran Council IV
St. Malo, 163
St. Omer, 78
St. Paul's outside the Walls, church, 91
St. Peter's, basilica, 3, 5, 11, 25, 29, 36, 91, 95, 130, 135, 174, 234; doors, 84
St. Pol, count, 103, 178
St. Scholastica, monastery, 87
St. Sergio and Bacco, church, 12
St. Severina, bp, 31, n. 13
St. Silvester, chapel, 2
St. Sophia, church and canons, 139
St. Vaast, monastery, 36
St. Victor, abbey and school, 8
Ste. Geneviève, abbey and school, 8
Stefan, Grand Zupan of Serbia, 74–75
Stephen Conti, cardinal and nephew of Innocent III, 3
Stephen Langton, cardinal priest of S. Crisgono, 168; consecrated abp of Canterbury, 173, 191; suspended, 230, 265. *See also* Canterbury (disputed election)
Stephen, papal chamberlain, 183
Subiaco, monastery, 87–90, 110
Sutri, 4
Sweden, kings, 41
Swerri Sigurdsson, king of Norway, 51–52, 76
swords, spiritual and temporal, 169, 176
synagogue in Sens, 143

Tartars, 41
taxes. *See* Innocent III; authority, relationship between lay and clerical
Te Deum, 1, 250
Templars, 46, 130, 157, 186, 195, 196, 205
Terra di Lavoro, 188
Thessalonica, abp, 159
Thibaut III, count of Champagne, 76, 102–104; death, 107, 221
Thibaut IV, count of Champagne, 221
Third Crusade, 14
Thomas Becket, St., abp of Canterbury, 6, 7, 8, 170, 173, 175–176, 192, 194, 246, 263
Thomas Morosini, patriarch of Constantinople, 139

Thomas of Marborough, 133, 161
Thorn, Linton S., xv
Tiber River, 234, 279
Tillmann, Helene, xv, 260
tithes, 144, 147, 241
Tivoli, 94
Todi, 40, 255, 287
Toledo, 15; abp, 72, 197
Torres, abp, 117, 160
Tortona, bp, 79
Toulouse: city, 136, 148, 149, 179, 283; bp, 264. *See also* Raymond VI
Tournai, canons, 36
tournaments, 43, 76, 102, 212, 251, 282–283
transubstantiation, 240, 285
Trasmondo, cousin of Innocent III, 160
Trasmondo, father of Innocent III, 3, 253
Trent, Council of, 275
Treves, bp, 154
trial: by jury, 244; by ordeal, battle, 244, 254, 275
Trier, abp, 43
Trinitarian Order, 272, 278
Tripoli, count, 157
Trnovo (Zagoro), 123, 128
Troyes, bp, 61, 102, 199
Truman, President Harry, 256
Turks, 157
Tuscan League, 32
Tuscany, 13, 32, 34, 40, 67, 266, 271
Tusculum, 2, 4, 5

Ullmann, Walter, xiv
Urban II, pope, 6
Urban III, pope, 11, 14
usury, 76, 151, 224, 225. *See also* interest on loans
utilitas, 23
Uzès, bp, 180–181

Van Cleve, Thomas Curtis, 188
Vatican, 5, 277. *See also* St. Peter's
Velletri, 90
Vence, bp, 264
Venice, Venetians, 87, 92, 104–107, 110–112, 115–116, 121, 139, 179, 261, 268; government, 105. *See also* Enrico Dondolo; Fourth Crusade
Venus, 21

Vergentis in senium, 241, 277 n. 84
Veroli, 4
Verona, 11, 109, 150, 151; council of clergy, 48
Vézelay, monastery, 36, 222
Via Casilina, 2, 6, 96, 97, 169, 170, 183
vicar of Christ, 29, 30, 256–257, 259, 291
Victor IV, anti-pope, 4
Vienne, bp, 180, 264
Villa d'Este, 94
Viterbo, 32, 150, 156, 191, 194, 255; defeat by Romans, 84; papal parliament, 169–173, 200, 236, 254, 259, 281
Viviers, bp, 264
Vlachia, Vlachs, 113, 132, 138; *see also* Kalojan
Vukan, ruler of Zeta, king of Dioclea and Dalmatia, 50, 74–75, 123–124

Waldemar, king of Denmark, 160
Waldensians, Waldensianism, 146–147, 164, 177, 280
Waldes, 146
Wales, 213. *See also* Gerald of Wales
Walter, Cistercian abbot of St. Dogmaelis, 84, 92
Walter of Brienne, 67–68, 84, 85, 90, 102, 106, 124, 155, 183, 284
Walter of Palear, chancellor of kingdom of Sicily, 68
Walter von der Vogelweide, 32 and n. 17, 216
Welf interests, 63–66, 154. *See also* Otto of Brunswick; alliances
William, bp of Paris, 220
William Capparone, 68
William IV, marquis of Montferrat, 236
William of Andres, 169–170, 185, 189
William of Champagne, abp of Rheims, 58, 61
William of Montpellier, 273
William Pallavicino, margrave, 31
William the Breton, 225–226
Winchester, 160
Wladyslaw, duke of Poland, 196
Wolfger, patriarch of Aquileia, 163, 182
Worcester, bp, 191
Worms, bp, 264

Würzburg, 53, 55, 264; bishop
    murdered, 92, 263

York, 192
Ypres, 216

Zamora, bp, 72
Zara (Zadar), 110–111. *See also*
    Fourth Crusade
Zeta (Duklja, Dioclea, Montenegro),
    74